ESSAYS ON LAW AND GOVERNMENT
THE CITIZEN AND THE STATE IN THE COURTS

HEAD OFFICE: 50 Waterloo Road NORTH RYDE NSW 2113
Tel: (02) 9936 6444 Fax: (02) 888 2287

For all sales inquiries please ring 1800 25 2314

NEW ZEALAND

Brooker's

Wellington, Auckland

SINGAPORE AND MALAYSIA

Thomson Information
(SE Asia)

CANADA

Carswell

Ontario

UNITED KINGDOM

Sweet & Maxwell Ltd
London

HONG KONG

Bloomsbury Books Ltd

USA

Wm W Gaunt & Sons, Inc
Holmes Beach, Florida

ESSAYS ON LAW AND GOVERNMENT

Volume 2

The Citizen and the State in the Courts

Edited by

P D FINN

*Judge of the Federal
Court of Australia*

LBC INFORMATION SERVICES

1996

Published in Sydney by

LBC Information Services
44-50 Waterloo Road, North Ryde, NSW

National Library of Australia
  Cataloguing-in-Publication entry

Essays on law and government: Volume 2, The citizen and the state in the
courts.

  Includes index.
  ISBN 0 455 21525 5.

  1. Justice, Administration of—Australia. 2. Courts—Australia.
  I. Finn, P. D. (Paul Desmond), 1946-.

347.9401

Designed and edited by Amanda Phillips

Typeset in Times Roman, 10 on 11 point and Garamond, by Mercier
    Typesetters Pty Ltd, Granville, NSW
  Printed by Ligare Pty Ltd, Riverwood, NSW

Preface

This, the second volume of this series of essays, moves to a more particular theme. It is that of the citizen-state relationship as that relationship is worked out in our courts. For this reason the volume does not limit itself to any one particular body of legal doctrine which regulates that relationship. Rather, it ranges widely across different bodies of law. Its object in this is to reveal more fully than would otherwise be the case, the manner in which the courts (with or without statutory impetus) mediate between the citizen and the state and the techniques and values relied upon in that process.

As with its predecessor, this collection of essays is the product of a small seminar held at the Australian National University in August 1995. Save for Sir Anthony Mason's welcome overview, the essays were commented upon at the seminar and revised thereafter for publication. It is necessary to acknowledge once more the willing contribution made to the series by essayists and participants alike. Equally, I note with gratitude the support of the Research School of Social Sciences, ANU, the Law Book Company Limited and of Chief Justice Michael Black of my own Court.

One additional matter requires mention in relation to this volume in particular. The law in the areas covered in the following pages is by no means static. Some number of quite significant decisions have been handed down by the High Court and by State and federal apellate courts during the period in which this volume was being prepared for publication. A consideration of these could not be included in the text of the following essays. I mention specifically the decisions in *Langer v Commonwealth* (1996) 70 ALJR 176; *McGinty v Western Australia* (1996) 70 ALJR 200 and *Minister for Immigration and Ethnic Affairs v Wu Shan Liang*, High Court of Australia, 27 May 1996.

PDF

Canberra
1996

Table of Contents

Essayists

Margaret Allars
Associate Professor of Law, University of Sydney

Enid Campbell
Professor of Law, Monash University

Paul Finn
Judge of the Federal Court of Australia

The Hon Mr Justice T M Gault
Judge of the Court of Appeal of New Zealand

John Griffiths
Barrister, New South Wales

Susan Kenny
Barrister, Victoria

The Hon Justice K E Lindgren
Judge of the Federal Court of Australia

Sir Anthony Mason
National Fellow, Australian National University

Keith Mason, QC
Solicitor-General for New South Wales

Mark Weinberg, QC
Barrister, Victoria

Leslie Zines
Emeritus Professor, Australian National University

Seminar Participants

The Rt Hon Sir Robin Cooke
President, Court of Appeal of New Zealand

The Hon Justice W M C Gummow
Justice of the High Court of Australia

The Hon Mr Justice F H Callaway
Judge of the Court of Appeal of Victoria

The Hon Mr Justice C Steytler
Judge of the Supreme Court of Western Australia

David Jackson, QC
Barrister, New South Wales

James Douglas, QC
Barrister, Queensland

Alan Robertson, SC
Barrister, New South Wales

Henry Burmester
Commonwealth Attorney-General's Department

Ian Taylor
Solicitor, Victoria

David Solomon
Journalist, Queensland

Professor Michael Taggart
Law School, University of Auckland

Professor Mark Aronson
Law School, University of Sydney

Dr John Uhr
Federalism Research Centre, Australian National University

Professor Marcia Neave
RSSS, Australian National University

Professor Dennis Pearce
Law Faculty, Australian National University

John McMillan
Law Faculty, Australian National University

Simon Bronitt
Law Faculty, Australian National University

Fiona Wheeler
RSSS, Australian National University

Table of Cases

Chapter 1

The Citizen and the State in the Courts

Enid Campbell

INTRODUCTION

Litigation between citizens and the state—between non-governmental and governmental parties—takes many forms. Some of it is initiated by governmental parties, for example, most criminal prosecutions, including for regulatory offences such as engaging in an activity which has been prohibited by statute except under licence. Some of it is initiated by non-governmental parties: by ordinary action for recovery of damages, debts or property; by suit for declarations or injunctions; or by an application for judicial review. Sometimes agencies of government may become involved in litigation between non-governmental parties, for example, when a party seeks production of documents in the possession of a government agency and the agency objects to production of the documents on the ground that disclosure of their contents would be contrary to the public interest.

The law which controls or affects the outcome of litigation between governmental and non-governmental parties may be common law (that is, judge-made law), statute law or, a combination of both. Sometimes that law is no different from that which would be applicable if the litigation were between non-governmental parties. However, sometimes that law is, or includes, law which applies peculiarly to agencies of government, or to proceedings by and against them. Bodies of law which apply peculiarly to agencies of government include constitutional law (in the broadest sense), the law applied by courts in proceedings for judicial review of administrative action, and the vast array of statutory laws which endow agents and officers of government with special powers, which accord them special privileges and immunities from liabilities, or which subject them to special duties and liabilities.

The laws which control and affect the outcomes of litigation between governmental and non-governmental parties express principles and policies regarding the legal relationships which the law-makers have determined should operate as between the two. Those laws also reflect understandings about the appropriate role of courts in adjudicating disputes in which the legality or validity of the acts of other agencies of government is called into question. Our understandings about the role of courts in this regard are largely ones which have been inherited from Great Britain.

1

JUDICIAL REVIEW OF THE LEGALITY AND VALIDITY OF GOVERNMENTAL ACTS

By the time Great Britain colonised Australia, it was well understood that under the common law of England certain activities were unlawful unless clearly authorised by statute, that is to say, an enactment of the King or Queen in Parliament. Such activities were unlawful in the sense that persons engaging in them (including public officers and the servants and agents of the Crown) were liable to be visited with judicial sanctions, civil or criminal.[1] It had also been accepted that the royal prerogatives rested on the common law and that, therefore, any controversy over the existence and ambit of the prerogatives was determinable by the courts.[2] Like authority had been asserted by the courts in relation to the powers, privileges and immunities of the Houses of Parliament and their members.[3]

Parliamentary supremacy was a political fact. Courts had recognised the paramountcy of parliamentary enactments over both incompatible common law and prior statute law. The validity of a duly enacted statute could not be called into question in a court of law. Courts were obliged to apply relevant statutes regardless of what they might think about their merits.[4]

The English doctrine of parliamentary supremacy proved to be a central element in the development by the courts of principles regarding their role as superintendents of the activities of all those agents of government whose powers and duties derived from statute. Statutes would frequently be the touchstone for determining whether an act was ultra vires, illegal or in breach of duty. Statutes would often be critical in determining whether a defendant was protected against common law liabilities. At the same time, statutes might be invoked by courts to justify their refusal to override decisions made in the exercise of discretionary powers which the Parliament had chosen to repose in bodies other than courts.

Neither in England nor in countries whose legal systems are derived from that of England has the doctrine of parliamentary supremacy been accepted without qualification. In the course of applying parliamentary enactments the courts have developed principles of statutory interpretation, among them certain assumptions or presumptions about parliamentary intentions. These assumptions or presumptions include some which signify that the courts will decline to recognise a statute as having achieved certain legal effects unless the statute, by express words or necessary implication, makes

1. Important cases in which the defendants were governmental parties included *Wilkes v Wood* (1765) 19 St Tr 1153; *Leach v Money* (1765) 19 St Tr 1001 and *Entick v Carrington* (1765) 2 Wils KB 275. See also A Rubinstein, *Jurisdiction and Illegality* (1965), Ch 6.
2. See eg *Willion v Berkley* (1561) 1 Plow 223; *Case of Monopolies* (1602) 11 Co Rep 84b; *Prohibitions del Roy* (1607) 12 Co Rep 63; *Case of Proclamations* (1611) 12 Co Rep 74. It is only within recent years that courts have begun to review the manner in which some of the prerogative powers have been exercised. See F Wheeler, "Judicial Review of Prerogative Power in Australia" (1992) 14 Syd LR 432; see also *R v Secretary of State for the Home Department; Ex parte Bentley* [1994] QB 340; cf *Burt v Governor-General* [1992] 3 NZLR 672 (prerogative of mercy).
3. See E Campbell, *Parliamentary Privilege in Australia* (1966), Introduction.
4. Statements in some judicial opinions that statutes which violated "fundamental law" would not be recognised as law were no more than dicta.

it clear that the legislators intended to achieve those legal effects. By assumptions or presumptions of this kind, courts have indicated their commitment to what they regard as important rights and freedoms of individuals.[5] In applying the presumption that a parliament does not intend to abrogate, or derogate from, fundamental rights and freedoms:

> "the judges seem to have in their minds an ideal constitution, comprising those fundamental rules of common law which seem essential to the liberties of the subject and the proper government of the country. These rules cannot be repealed but by direct and unequivocal enactment. In the absence of express words or necessary intendment, statutes will be applied subject to them. They do not override the statute, but are treated, as it were, as implied terms of the statute."[6]

Parliamentary supremacy has also proved not to be any great impediment to the development by courts (mainly in exercise of a supervisory jurisdiction) of what is now a substantial corpus of judge-made law which controls the exercise of statutory powers and functions by the administrative arms of government, according to general standards such as procedural fairness, legality, rationality and even "good administration".[7]

The English doctrine of parliamentary supremacy was part of the corpus of law received by the Australian colonies. However, it was never applied to the Australian legislatures in precisely the same way as it had been applied to the Imperial Parliament. From the beginning it was accepted that the validity of enactments of the colonial legislatures was susceptible to judicial review.[8] The authority of the colonial legislatures to legislate was derived from enactments of the supreme Imperial Parliament. Enactments of the colonial legislatures might be adjudged invalid on the ground that they exceeded the statutory charter of the colonial legislature or else were inconsistent with Imperial enactments applying in the colony by paramount force. Until the enactment of the *Colonial Laws Validity Act* 1865 (Imp) enactments of the colonial legislatures might also be adjudged invalid on the ground that they were repugnant to the fundamental laws of England.[9] Judicial review of colonial legislation would certainly have been familiar to the framers of the Australian Constitution, a constitution which was to be formally enacted by the supreme Imperial Parliament. The constitutional framework erected by the Australian Constitution nevertheless obliged the courts to consider a number of questions concerning their relationship with other branches of government which had not arisen under prior Australian constitutional arrangements. Most of these questions are ones which have arisen under Chapter III—The Judicature—of the Constitution.

5. See, for example, *Coco v The Queen* (1994) 179 CLR 427. See also essay by S Kenny in Ch 8, below.
6. D L Keir and F H Lawson, *Cases in Constitutional Law* (5th ed, 1967), p 11.
7. *Council of Civil Service Unions v Minister for the Civil Service* [1983] 2 AC 237 at 280-281 per Lord Diplock (*GCHQ* case). See also Sir Robin Cooke, "Empowerment and Accountability: The Quest for Administrative Justice" (1992) 18 CLB 1326.
8. See G Lindell, "The Duty to Exercise Judicial Review" in L Zines (ed), *Commentaries on the Australian Constitution* (1977), pp 169-173.
9. See E Campbell, "Colonial Legislation and the Laws of England" (1965) 2 Tas ULR 148; D B Swinfen, "The Genesis of the Colonial Laws Validity Act" [1967] *Juridical Review* 29; D B Swinfen, *Imperial Control of Colonial Legislation 1813-1865* (1970), Pt II.

THE SEPARATION OF JUDICIAL AND NON-JUDICIAL POWERS

As judicially interpreted, Chapter III of the Constitution makes the judicial powers of the Commonwealth exercisable only by the courts mentioned in s 71, they being the High Court of Australia, State courts and courts created by the federal Parliament. (The matters encompassed within the Commonwealth's judicial powers are listed in ss 75 and 76.) The judicial tenure provisions of s 72 of the Constitution are designed to secure the independence of members of the High Court and of other federal courts from the other branches of federal government. The tenure of judges of State courts is, however, governed by State laws only.

A federal statute which assigns any one or more of the judicial powers of the Commonwealth to a body other than a s 71 court is invalid. [10] It follows that the federal Parliament cannot itself exercise any of the judicial powers of the Commonwealth, though it has been acknowledged that s 49 of the Constitution authorises the Houses of the federal Parliament to exercise a limited adjudicatory function, namely that of determining whether parliamentary privileges have been infringed or whether someone is guilty of contempt of Parliament. [11] The High Court has also held that Chapter III may be infringed by federal legislation which interferes with the performance of the judicial functions of the Commonwealth. [12]

The Constitution has also been interpreted to mean that the federal Parliament cannot invest non-judicial powers in s 71 courts, save those which can be characterised as ancillary to the exercise of judicial power, for example, the legislative power involved in the making of rules governing court procedures. [13] Nevertheless, this constraint has been held not to preclude the enactment of federal legislation which invests judges of courts with non-judicial powers as *persona designata*. [14]

Judicial exegesis on Chapter III of the Constitution has involved both identification of characteristics of judicial power and consideration of the purpose of the separation of powers which the chapter ordains. Judicial power has generally been regarded as not extending to powers of a kind which entail exercise of open-ended discretions. [15] The Parliament has thus been precluded from using s 71 courts as agencies to administer many legislative schemes and to review many administrative decisions on their merits. The concept of judicial power has not, however, precluded supervisory judicial review of decisions made in the exercise of administrative discretions or the exercise by courts of discretionary powers as part of that supervisory jurisdiction.

10. The cases are reviewed in *Brandy v Human Rights and Equal Opportunity Commission* (1995) 69 ALJR 191.
11. *R v Richards; Ex parte Fitzpatrick and Browne* (1955) 92 CLR 157.
12. The case law is reviewed in G Winterton, "The Separation of Judicial Powers as an Implied Bill of Rights" in G Lindell (ed), *Future Directions in Australian Constitutional Law* (1994), p 185. See also essay by L Zines, Ch 5 below.
13. *R v Davison* (1954) 90 CLR 353 at 369.
14. *Hilton v Wells* (1985) 157 CLR 57.
15. See L Zines, *The High Court and the Constitution* (3rd ed, 1992), pp 170-174.

Chapter III, as judicially interpreted, has not stood in the way of establishment by federal statute of tribunals whose members are not accorded the security of tenure prescribed by s 72 of the Constitution and whose adjudicatory functions may appear, at first sight, to involve exercise of judicial power. Arrangements of this kind are, however, tolerated only if they leave scope for an ultimate adjudication by a s 71 court of issues of law.[16] What count as issues of law, and as errors of law, are matters upon which the courts have claimed to have the final voice.

Chapter III is not, at least in form, a chapter on individual rights. Nevertheless, it operates as a constraint on the powers exercisable by other branches of government and, at the same time, provides individuals with some guarantee that some independent judicial forum will be available to those (with the requisite standing to sue) who contest the validity or legality of governmental action. I say "some guarantee" because the judicial powers which Chapter III makes the exclusive preserve of s 71 courts do not cover all cases in which the validity or legality of governmental actions is contested. Judicial power, for the purposes of Chapter III, includes matters arising under the Constitution, or involving its interpretation (s 76(i)) and matters arising under enactments of the federal Parliament (s 76(ii)). But the judicial powers of the Commonwealth do not extend to a matter arising under State law except when the matter is one "between States, or between residents of different States, or between a State and a resident of another State" (s 75(iv)).

THE ENTRENCHED JURISDICTION OF THE HIGH COURT OF AUSTRALIA

Section 75 of the Australian Constitution gives to the High Court of Australia original jurisdiction in five matters, among them suits by and against the Commonwealth, or a person suing or being sued on behalf of the Commonwealth,[17] and matters "in which a writ of Mandamus or prohibition or an injunction is sought against an officer of the Commonwealth".[18] Since this jurisdiction is conferred by the Constitution, it cannot be removed or reduced by parliamentary enactment. So far as federal government is concerned, s 75 thus secures to the High Court a central role in adjudication of disputes, according to law, between non-governmental and Commonwealth government parties.

Judicial case law on s 75 is substantial but by no means exhaustive of the issues which may arise under the section. The High Court has held that, for the purposes of s 75(v), officers of the Commonwealth do not include corporations.[19] On the other hand the court has indicated that, for the

16. Ibid, pp 153-169.
17. s 75(iii).
18. s 75(v).
19. *Broken Hill Proprietary Co Ltd v National Companies and Securities Commission* (1986) 61 ALJR 124; *Businessworld Computers Pty Ltd v Australian Telecommunications Commission* (1988) 82 ALR 499; *Post Office Agents Association Ltd v Australian Postal Commission* (1988) 84 ALR 563.

purposes of s 75(iii), parties suing or being sued on behalf of the Commonwealth can include persons and corporate entities which are recognisable as agencies of the federal branch of government, notwithstanding that, for other legal purposes, they would not be recognised as coming within the shield of the Crown in right of the Commonwealth.[20] The definition of the court's original jurisdiction under s 75(v) does not, it has also been held, preclude award of associated remedies such as certiorari and declarations.[21]

Although the federal Parliament cannot derogate from the jurisdiction conferred by s 75(v), the High Court has accepted that the federal Parliament may exercise its legislative powers so as to limit the scope of judicial review. Section 60 of the *Conciliation and Arbitration Act* 1904 (now s 150 of the *Industrial Relations Act* 1988)[22] has been held effective to preclude judicial invalidation of an industrial award on the ground that the maker of the award failed to comply with statutory procedural requirements or exceeded the limits of power laid down by the instrument giving it authority, "provided . . . that its decision is a bona fide attempt to exercise its power, that it relates to the subject matter of the legislation, and that it is reasonably capable of reference to the power given to the body".[23] Section 60 of the *Conciliation and Arbitration Act* 1904, it has been said, "does not qualify the jurisdiction" of the High Court under s 75(v) of the Constitution. It does not define the jurisdiction of the court. Rather it "extends the limits of the award-making power [of the Conciliation and Arbitration Commission] and governs the effect of its exercise".[24] The section does not, however, preclude challenge of the validity of an award on constitutional grounds.[25]

20. *Inglis v Commonwealth Trading Bank of Australia* (1969) 119 CLR 334. For other cases see Administrative Review Council, *Government Business Enterprises and Commonwealth Administrative Law*, Report No 38 (1995), pp 28-30.
21. *R v Toohey; Ex parte Northern Land Council* (1981) 145 CLR 374.
22. Section 60 of the *Conciliation and Arbitration Act* 1904 provided:
    "(1) Subject to this Act, an award (including an award made on appeal)—
      (a) is final and conclusive;
      (b) shall not be challenged, appealed against, reviewed, quashed or called in question in any court; and
      (c) is not subject to prohibition, mandamus or injunction in any court on any account.
    (2) A determination or finding of the Commission upon a question as to the existence of an industrial dispute is, in all courts and for all purposes, conclusive and binding on all persons affected by that question.
    (3) An award shall not be called in question in any way on the ground that it was made by the Commission constituted otherwise than as provided by this Act."
    Section 150 of the *Industrial Relations Act* 1988 provides:
    "(1) Subject to this Act, an award (including an award made on appeal)—
      (a) is final and conclusive;
      (b) shall not be challenged, appealed against, reviewed, quashed or called in question in any court; and
      (c) is not subject to prohibition, mandamus or injunction in any court on any account."
23. *R v Hickman; Ex parte Fox* (1945) 70 CLR 598 at 615 per Dixon J.
24. *O'Toole v Charles David Pty Ltd* (1991) 171 CLR 232 at 250 per Mason CJ.
25. Ibid at 250-252 per Mason CJ, at 270 per Brennan J, at 288 per Deane, Gaudron and McHugh JJ, at 306 per Dawson J.

The position adopted by the High Court in relation to s 60 of the *Conciliation and Arbitration Act* 1904 may have been coloured by its appreciation of the desirability of judicial restraint in the exercise of the supervisory jurisdiction in relation to the industrial tribunals of the Commonwealth.[26] There is, however, no reason to suppose that the court would be prepared to treat provisions like s 60 which are contained in other federal legislation any differently. The court's interpretation of s 60 therefore affords a foothold for enactment of like statutory clauses the object of which is to restrict the grounds upon which the validity of decisions made under federal enactments may be challenged in proceedings brought under s 75(v) of the Constitution. If, for example, the federal Parliament, in exercise of its powers under s 51, validly confers a statutory power, and the exercise of that power would be subject to a duty (at common law) to accord procedural fairness, there can be no good reason why the Parliament could not (again in reliance on s 51) make it clear that the power in question is not attended by any duty to accord procedural fairness. Such a law would not detract from the High Court's entrenched jurisdiction. It would do no more than affect the law to be applied in the exercise of that jurisdiction.[27]

The High Court's interpretation of the effects of s 60 of the *Conciliation and Arbitration Act* 1904 should be contrasted with the approach of the House of Lords in *Anisminic v Foreign Compensation Commission*.[28] In *Anisminic* and subsequent cases,[29] the House of Lords has effectively denied the British Parliament authority to enact legislation to preclude judicial review of administrative decisions on the ground that they are ultra

26. In *Public Service Association of South Australia v Federated Clerks' Union of Australia, South Australian Branch* (1991) 173 CLR 132, Deane J made the following observations (at 147-148, footnotes omitted):

> "Industrial tribunals, when they are not themselves specialist courts of law, customarily include members who either are judges of a court or are possessed of legal training and experience comparable to that required of an appointee to judicial office. Their functions commonly extend to the making of awards or orders which lay down general standards of conduct which bind whole sections of the community in their future conduct and relations. The efficient discharge of such quasi-legislative functions may well require departure from traditional curial methods and procedures. Even where the resolution of a narrow actual dispute between individual parties is involved, the advantages of compulsory mediation or conciliation have been availed of by industrial tribunals to an extent unaccepted in most ordinary courts. In a context where prompt action—sometimes at a tribunal's own initiative—to prevent and resolve disputes is necessary in the public interest, there is much to be said for the view that such specialist industrial tribunals should be empowered to determine promptly and with finality the questions involved in the actual and potential industrial disputes which they are called upon to resolve. The delays and expense of proceedings in the ordinary courts of this country serve to reinforce such a policy and its rationale."

27. For a similar analysis in the context of ss 18 and 85 of Victoria's *Constitution Act* 1975—provisions which prescribe "manner and form" requirements for the enactment of laws which affect the jurisdiction of the Supreme Court—see *Collingwood City v Victoria (No 2)* [1994] VR 652. See also *Deputy Commissioner of Taxation v Richard Walter Pty Ltd* (1995) 69 ALJR 223.

28. [1969] 2 AC 147.

29. These are reviewed in *R v Lord President of the Privy Council; Ex parte Page* [1993] AC 682.

vires or in excess of jurisdiction.[30] The Lords have extended the concepts of ultra vires and excess of jurisdiction to encompass nearly all decisions which are tainted by error of law. It is, however, possible that, in practice, the result of applying the High Court's approach and the Lords' approach may not be markedly different. Both approaches allow reviewing courts considerable leeway for choice in determining whether the act or decision under review should be recognised as valid.

The High Court of Australia is not the only court invested with a supervisory jurisdiction in federal matters. Federal legislation enacted under s 77 of the Constitution invests federal supervisory jurisdiction in the Federal Court of Australia (*Administrative Decisions (Judicial Review) Act* 1977 and s 39B of the *Judiciary Act* 1903). State Supreme Courts and the Supreme Courts of the Australian Capital Territory and the Northern Territory are invested with federal supervisory jurisdiction under the *Jurisdiction of Courts (Cross-vesting) Act* 1987 (Cth). There can be little doubt that s 77 of the Constitution allows the federal Parliament to delimit the supervisory jurisdiction conferred on federal and State courts. The supervisory jurisdiction conferred by a federal Act may be defined in terms which deny the court jurisdiction to review the acts or decisions of specified federal bodies, or to review decisions made under specified statutes or statutory provisions. Federal legislation which confers and defines a supervisory jurisdiction may also restrict the grounds on which a court may review decisions, or decisions made under specified statutory provisions. Recent amendments to the *Migration Act* 1958 (Cth) have restricted the grounds on which the Federal Court may review many decisions made under that Act. Grounds which formerly could have been relied upon in an application for judicial review under the *Administrative Decisions (Judicial Review) Act* 1977 or s 39B of the *Judiciary Act* 1903 can now not be relied upon, in many cases, when the application for judicial review relates to a decision in purported exercise of powers conferred by the *Migration Act*.

These new restrictions on the judicial review function of the Federal Court have been cast in terms of its jurisdiction to review. They do not purport to alter the substantive law which controls the exercise of the relevant powers under the *Migration Act* 1958. Persons aggrieved by decisions made under the Act, on grounds not available on an application for review to the Federal Court, are not precluded from making an application for judicial review to the High Court, in the exercise of its original jurisdiction under s 75 of the Constitution, and, upon such an application, from relying on grounds which cannot be raised in proceedings before the Federal Court.

STATUTORY PROTECTIONS AGAINST LIABILITY

Statutes which seek to preclude or limit judicial review in the exercise of a supervisory jurisdiction are not, of course, the only statutes which may have a bearing on the outcomes of litigation in which the legality or validity of

30. See H W R Wade and C F Forsyth, *Administrative Law* (7th ed, 1994), p 737.

governmental action is in issue. There is now a considerable volume of statute law which has a bearing on the civil liabilities of governmental parties. This law presupposes, and builds upon, antecedent common law. Some of it removes protections against liabilities conferred by common law; some of it confers protections against liabilities which would not (or might not) be enjoyed under the common law.

Crown proceedings legislation[31] has, generally speaking, removed the protections against liability which were accorded to the Crown at common law, notably immunity from vicarious and direct liability in tort. The broad thrust of Crown proceedings legislation has been towards subjection of Crown parties to the same liability rules as would be applicable in proceedings between subject and subject. But some such legislation expressly or impliedly preserves common law which is protective of the Crown against liability, for example:

• immunity from vicarious liability for acts done in the exercise of independent discretions;[32]

• judicial immunities from suit;[33]

• immunity from mandatory injunctions;[34]

• immunity of Crown property from seizure and disposal in execution of judgments.[35]

Today there are many situations where the law according to which the civil liabilities of governmental parties is determined is no different from the law according to which the civil liabilities of non-governmental parties would be determined. Some aspects of the general law to do with civil liabilities can, however, have a particular bearing on cases involving governmental parties, for example, the law on the defence of statutory authority, principles regarding actions for damages for breach of statutory duty, and the rule according to which an employer is not vicariously liable

31. The current Australian legislation is as follows—Cth: *Judiciary Act* 1903; NSW: *Crown Proceedings Act* 1988; Qld: *Crown Proceedings Act* 1980; SA: *Crown Proceedings Act* 1992; Tas: *Crown Proceedings Act* 1993; Vic: *Crown Proceedings Act* 1958; WA: *Crown Suits Act* 1971; ACT: *Crown Proceedings Act* 1992; NT: *Crown Proceedings Act* 1993.
    This legislation and its antecedents are dealt with in Justice Finn's essay at Ch 2, below.
32. Contrast NSW *Law Reform (Vicarious Liability) Act* 1983 (as amended).
33. Vic: *Crown Proceedings Act* 1958, s 23(2). Some of the other Acts contain provisions which preserve limitations on Crown liability conferred by statute (see SA, s 6; ACT, s 6; NT, s 6). Provisions which immunise the Crown against liability for "judicial acts" have probably been enacted out of an abundance of caution. Judicial and quasi-judicial officers of government would, at common law, be persons exercising independent discretions and thus persons for whose wrongs no one is vicariously liable.
34. In South Australia (s 7), Tasmania (s 8), the ACT (s 8) and the Northern Territory (s 8) mandatory injunctions cannot be awarded against the Crown. Under the UK's *Crown Proceedings Act* 1947 no injunctions may be issued against the Crown. Injunctions may, however, be issued against Ministers: see *M v Home Office* [1994] 1 AC 377.
35. This immunity is expressly preserved in all the Australian legislation except Queensland's. But the abrogation of the immunity in Queensland is subject to qualifications and certain Crown properties are still subject to the immunity: s 11(2).
    In some jurisdictions the Crown Proceedings legislation provides a standing appropriation of moneys to satisfy the judgment debts of the Crown (eg SA, s 10; Tas, s 11; Vic, s 26; WA, s 10; ACT, s 13; NT, s 11).

for torts committed by employees in the purported exercise of independent discretions. Some special problems can arise when governmental parties are sued for negligence in the exercise of statutory discretions. These problems relate principally to the existence or nature of a duty of care.[36]

Although our legal system generally subjects governmental parties to the same liability rules as apply to non-governmental parties, it includes a number of principles which apply only to governmental parties or activities. Officials of government alone incur liability for the tort of misfeasance in a public office. Judicial and quasi-judicial immunities from suit are, for the most part, confined to agents of government. Statutes which confer powers on agencies and officers of government not infrequently contain clauses which are designed to protect those agencies and officers against liability, even when it can be shown that they have exceeded their statutory authority or have failed to perform their statutory duties.

Statutory provisions to protect governmental agents against civil liabilities take various forms. Some debar legal proceedings for loss or damage occasioned by specified acts and omissions[37] or else debar specified actions for particular acts.[38] Some give protection against liability to those who act in obedience to or in reliance on warrants or orders issued by others or as court processes.[39] Some give protection against liability for acts done in purported exercise of statutory powers or in purported performance of statutory duties, though in such cases the protection may be qualified by a requirement that what has been done has been done in good faith and with reasonable care.[40] Some give to members of tribunals and investigatory bodies (and participants in proceedings before those bodies) the same protections as are possessed by members of a named court of law (and participants in proceedings before the court).[41]

Statutory provisions which afford officials protection against civil liabilities presuppose common law according to which the officials could be held liable for acts in excess of their statutory authority. Such provisions will often presuppose also that no one could be held vicariously liable for illegal acts on the part of the officials concerned, inasmuch as they would be regarded as exercising an independent discretion. Some protective provisions also reflect an appreciation that officials may sometimes exceed their statutory authority by reason of honest mistakes of law or fact (or law and fact) and that imposition of civil liability to compensate for illegalities may lead to excessive caution on the part of officials in the performance of the functions assigned to them. Protective clauses thus often reflect a desire

36. See essay by M Allars in Ch 3, below.
37. See eg *Postal Services Act* 1975, s 104 (Cth). This Act was repealed by s 75 of Act No 63, 1989.
38. For example, *Freedom of Information Act* 1982 (Cth), s 91. This gives protection against actions for defamation, breach of confidence and infringement of copyright for the giving of access to documents, including in cases where the giving of access was authorised by certain officers "in the bona fide belief that the access was required to be given" under the Act.
39. For example, *Police Regulation Act* 1958 (Vic), s 124; *Mental Health Act* 1986 (Vic), s 122.
40. There are many variations on this formula.
41. See eg *Administrative Appeals Tribunal Act* 1975 (Cth), s 60.

that civil liabilities should not be imposed on officials without proof of inexcusable fault on their part. Similar considerations may inform the enactment of statutory clauses which accord members of a tribunal the same protections against civil liabilities as are accorded to members of a specified court.

Statute law may affect not merely the substantive law according to which the civil liabilities of officials is to be adjudged. Protection against such liabilities may also be afforded by statutory provisions which govern access to courts for the purpose of pursuing claims to civil redress. Statutory provisions in this category include provisions which preclude actions except by leave of a court,[42] provisions which require a plaintiff to have given notice of an intention to initiate action within a specified period of time,[43] and provisions to limit the time within which actions may be initiated—time running from accrual of the cause of action.[44] Statutory limitations on the time within which certain civil actions must be initiated are complemented by statutory provisions relating to the time within which applications for judicial review are to be initiated (subject to judicial discretions to extend the prescribed time).[45] Generally speaking, the standard time for initiation

42. For example, *Ombudsman Act* 1973 (Vic), s 29(2).
43. The purpose of such notice requirements seems to be to give the potential governmental defendant an opportunity to make amends, without need to establish its legal liability to make amends by court proceedings: *Attorney-General v Hackney Local Board* (1875) LR 20 Eq 626.
44. The rationale for shorter than usual periods of limitation for commencement of civil actions against public bodies was considered in *Grewer v Auckland Hospital Board* [1957] NZLR 951. The court there pointed out that those in charge of many governmental agencies cannot be expected to have personal knowledge of the circumstances of the mishaps which occur in the course of the conduct of the agency's activities:
      "The effects of the passage of time in respect of changes of personnel comprising staff and upon human recollections are such that unless a public authority has early opportunity of investigating allegations of negligence intended to be made against it and of briefing or recording evidence relevant thereto, it it likely to be prejudiced in dealing with the matters at a later date." (at 959)
   (That argument can be applied also to many large organisations in the private sector.)
      Nowadays the prescription of special limitation periods for actions against the Crown and public authorities is exceptional (S Simpson, "Limitation Periods—Public Authorities" [1977] ACL, DT 253). Special, short limitation periods have been prescribed by recent Australian legislation for commencement of actions to recover moneys paid to governmental agencies as taxes or other imposts. The relevant statutory provisions, and their rationale, are examined in the essay of Keith Mason QC in Ch 4, below.
45. Commonly, the statutory provisions on the time within which applications for judicial review must be commenced prescribe a period of one month, dating from notification of the decision which is subject to judicial review, or supply of written reasons for the decision, in response to requests for such reasons, under a statutory rights-to-reasons regime.
      The rationale for imposition of relatively short limitation periods for initiation of applications for judicial review by courts invested with a supervisory jurisdiction was described by Lord Diplock in *O'Reilly v Mackman* [1983] 2 AC 237 at 280-281 thus:
      "The public interest in good administration requires that public authorities and third parties should not be kept in suspense as to the legal validity of a decision the authority has reached in purported exercise of decision-making powers for any longer period than is absolutely necessary in fairness to the person affected by the decision."
   Discretions invested in courts, by statute, to extend statutory limitation periods for initiation of proceedings for judicial review have, as might be expected, attracted a considerable volume of judicial case law on principles which should be applied in the exercise of a judicial discretion of that character. A useful starting point for search of the Australian case law is *Hunter Valley Developments Pty Ltd v Cohen* (1984) 58 ALR 305.

of applications for judicial review is considerably shorter than the time for initiation of ordinary civil proceedings, and the standard time for initiation of certain civil proceedings against official parties is much shorter than that which would be applicable in comparable proceedings between non-governmental parties.

Courts of law have accepted that, subject to paramount constitutional constraints, parliaments possess a capacity to alter the common law which bears on the civil liabilities of agents of government. Nevertheless, the courts have tended to construe statutory protection clauses restrictively so as to preserve, as far as possible, the operation of antecedent common law.[46]

CONSTITUTIONAL CONSTRAINTS ON STATUTORY LIMITATIONS OF LIABILITY

How far the Australian Constitution restricts the powers of the Parliaments of the federation to extinguish or limit governmental liabilities is not entirely clear. In exercise of its legislative powers under s 51 of the Constitution, the federal Parliament may validate, retroactively, action which is not authorised by prior valid federal legislation.[47] Equally, the Parliament may legislate, retroactively, to debar actions for such unauthorised acts.[48] It may even enact legislation to limit rights to recover taxes paid under legislation which has been held to violate s 55 of the Constitution.[49] Section 61 in combination with s 51(xxxix) is another source of power to enact such legislation, though it is not as wide.[50] Section 78 would appear to authorise federal legislation to withdraw rights to proceed against the Commonwealth and States which have been conferred by prior legislation enacted under that section.[51]

The power under s 51 to validate conduct and to bar actions is qualified by s 51(xxxi). In *Georgiadis v Australian and Overseas Telecommunications Corp (AOTC)*[52] a majority of the High Court[53] held that, for the purposes

---

46. Judicial interpretations of statutory protection clauses are considered in M Aronson and H Whitmore, *Public Torts and Contracts* (1982), pp 162-173. The statutory protection clauses there considered are ones designed to protect agents of government against civil and, sometimes, criminal liabilities as well. The English Court of Appeal's decision in *Ex parte Waldron* [1986] 1 QB 824 indicates that protective clauses of that kind are not efficient to preclude judicial review in the exercise of a supervisory judicial jurisdiction, and the award of judicial remedies which are peculiar to that jurisdiction.
47. *Werrin v Commonwealth* (1938) 59 CLR 150.
48. Such legislation would be sustainable under one or more of the heads of legislative power conferred by s 61 of the Constitution.
49. *Mutual Pools and Staff Pty Ltd v Commonwealth* (1994) 68 ALJR 216.
50. Ibid at 243-244 per McHugh J.
51. Section 78 provides that "The Parliament may make laws conferring rights to proceed against the Commonwealth or a State in respect of matters within the limits of judicial power."
52. (1994) 68 ALJR 272.
53. Mason CJ, Brennan, Deane and Gaudron JJ; Dawson, Toohey and McHugh JJ dissenting.

of this paragraph, a federal law which extinguishes an accrued cause of action which arises under the general law (for example, an action for negligence) and which "results in a direct benefit or financial gain", is a law with respect to the acquisition of property and, accordingly, is invalid if it does not provide for just terms.

A more important constitutional restriction on legislative power to extinguish or limit governmental liabilities stems from the general principle that a parliament cannot do indirectly what it cannot do directly. This restriction affects the power of the Australian parliaments, State and federal, to enact legislation to bar actions or limit liabilities for acts done pursuant to unconstitutional statutes. State legislation to debar recovery of moneys paid or property seized under prior State legislation held to violate s 92 of the Constitution has been held invalid on the ground that it too violates s 92.[54] State legislation imposing a short time for commencement of actions to recover unconstitutional levies has also been held invalid.[55] If constitutional limitations on governmental powers are to be regarded as meaningful, there must surely be some restriction on the power of parliaments to enact legislation the effect of which is to deny appropriate remedy for the unconstitutional action. If State parliaments are denied power to impose duties of excise, there must surely be some constitutional prohibition against enactment of legislation to preclude recovery of moneys paid under a State statute which imposes a tax of that description.[56] If a federal statute which authorises the detention of persons is held to be invalid, there must surely be some constitutional prohibition against enactment of further federal legislation which precludes any action for damages for detention pursuant to the statute which authorised detention.

The Constitution does not, however, contain any provisions which clearly confer entrenched rights to civil remedies for unconstitutional action. In *New South Wales v Commonwealth*[57] a majority of the High Court[58] were of the view that s 75(iii) of the Constitution was effective to remove the Commonwealth's common law immunity from liability in tort. While this decision has never been expressly overruled, later opinions have generally preferred the view that s 75(iii) does no more than confer an original jurisdiction on the High Court: it does not prescribe law governing the substantive liabilities of the Commonwealth.[59] Enactment of legislation to remove or modify the common law immunities of the Commonwealth from suit was rather to be a function of the federal Parliament in exercise of its powers under s 78.

54. *Antill Ranger and Co Pty Ltd v Commissioner of Road Transport; Deacon v Grimshaw* (1955) 93 CLR 83; *Commissioner of Road Transport v Antill Ranger and Co Pty Ltd* (1956) 93 CLR 177.
55. *Barton v Commissioner for Motor Transport* (1957) 97 CLR 633.
56. See E Campbell, "Unconstitutionality and its Consequences" in G Lindell (ed), *Future Directions in Australian Constitutional Law* (1994), pp 118-120 and Keith Mason QC, Ch 4, below.
57. (1923) 32 CLR 200.
58. Knox CJ, Isaacs, Rich and Starke JJ; Higgins J dissenting.
59. *Werrin v Commonwealth* (1938) 59 CLR 150 at 167-168 per Dixon J; *Washington v Commonwealth* (1939) 39 SR (NSW) 133 at 140, 142 per Jordan CJ; *Suehle v Commonwealth* (1967) 116 CLR 353 at 419-420 per Windeyer J; *Maguire v Simpson* (1977) 139 CLR 362; *Commonwealth v Evans Deakin Industries Ltd* (1986) 161 CLR 254 at 263-264; *Breavington v Godleman* (1988) 169 CLR 41 at 68-69 per Mason CJ at 101-105, per Wilson and

Even if s 78 is construed as encompassing power to alter common law regarding rights to proceed against Crown parties in matters within federal jurisdiction—the matters itemised in ss 75 and 76—it may be, and has been, argued that legislation which has been enacted pursuant to the section to alter the antecedent common law may be overridden by subsequent legislation, including by legislation to restore the common law.[60]

The present Justices of the High Court have not been disposed to read s 78 as endowing the federal Parliament with an unlimited power to legislate in relation to governmental liabilities. McHugh J, in particular, has suggested that it does not enable the federal Parliament to enact legislation which protects the Commonwealth against the consequences of action which is beyond the constitutional powers of the Commonwealth. He has said that even, as he thinks is the case, s 75(iii):

"is not itself the source of the Commonwealth liability in tort and contract, it may well be that its inclusion in the Constitution enables an action to be brought against the Commonwealth in this court [the High Court] in respect of matters concerning, or not severable from, the scope of the Commonwealth's constitutional powers. In that event it would not be open to the federal Parliament to bar the right to proceed against the Commonwealth in respect of the scope of its constitutional powers."[61]

If s 75(iii) is not a source of liability in tort or contract, or indeed any other civil liability from which the Commonwealth would, at common law, be immune, and the Commonwealth's civil liabilities exist only by reason of federal statute law, it would seem to follow that those liabilities can be removed by statute, subject only to the restriction imposed by s 51(xxxi). However, legislation which purports to exclude civil liability for acts done in reliance on an unconstitutional statute can effectively validate those acts. Can such legislation be regarded as constitutional?

Consider this hypothetical case. A federal statute authorises a federal Minister to order the detention of persons. A detainee successfully challenges the validity of the statute. The High Court rules that the statute is not a law with respect to any of the matters on which the federal Parliament may legislate. Another statute is then enacted by the federal Parliament to preclude actions for damages by other detainees. It removes any right to proceed against the Commonwealth. It also protects from liability all officers of the Commonwealth who have acted pursuant to orders of the Minister. Standing alone the latter element of the statute

59. *Continued*
    Gaudron JJ at 117-118, per Brennan J at 139-140, per Deane J at 151-153; *Mutual Pools and Staff Pty Ltd v Commonwealth* (1994) 68 ALJR 216 at 246 per McHugh J; cf at 278 per Brennan J; *Georgiadis v AOTC* (1994) 68 ALJR 272 at 286 per McHugh J. See also Z Cowen and L Zines, *Federal Jurisdiction in Australia* (2nd ed, 1978), pp 35-38. Contrast the views of L Aitken in "The Liability of the Commonwealth under Section 75(iii) and Related Questions" (1992) 15 UNSWLJ 483 and "The Commonwealth's Entrenched Liability—Further Refinements" (1994) 68 ALJ 690.

60. *Georgiadis v AOTC* (1994) 68 ALJR 272, at 286 per McHugh J; cf at 278 per Brennan J. See also L Aitken, "The Commonwealth's Entrenched Liability—Further Refinements" (1994) 68 ALJ 690.

61. *Mutual Pools and Staff Pty Ltd v Commonwealth* (1994) 68 ALJR 216 at 246.

might, conceivably, be regarded as a law made under s 51(xxxix), in combination with s 61. But, read as a whole, the statute validates acts which, under the common law of the States and Territories, are unlawful and which the federal Parliament cannot, constitutionally, authorise. If this statute is adjudged unconstitutional, it can only be on the basis that it attempts to do indirectly what the federal Parliament cannot do directly. And, if the statute is unconstitutional, existing statutory rights to proceed against the Commonwealth (conferred by the *Judiciary Act* 1903) would not be affected. The personal liabilities of the tortfeasors under the applicable State and Territory laws would equally not be affected.

I doubt whether the hypothetical statute I have postulated would be one to which the technique of severance could be applied. However, what if two statutes had been enacted: one to withdraw rights to proceed against the Commonwealth, the other to protect officers of the Commonwealth against personal liability? There is much to be said in favour of legislation which protects officials against common law liabilities they may incur when they act pursuant to legislation the unconstitutionality of which has not been established, so long as the legislation preserves the vicarious liability of the government they serve, or else creates a suitable alternative compensation scheme. But, if the separate legislation to remove the rights to proceed against the Commonwealth is also upheld as a valid exercise of the power conferred by s 78 of the Constitution, the end result is that the federal Parliament will have achieved indirectly a result it cannot achieve directly.

The above discussion of the hypothetical federal legislation has not referred to the possible relevance of s 51(xxxi). For the purposes of argument we may assume that, at the time the federal legislation is enacted, numerous detainees or former detainees have accrued causes of action against the Commonwealth and its officials, arising under the general law. We may assume also that, for the purposes of s 51(xxxi), the legislative powers of the federal Parliament extend to laws with respect to the liabilities of the Commonwealth and its officials. Applying the test approved by the majority in *Georgiadis*,[62] one would have to conclude that the hypothetical legislation effects an acquisition of property. The terms of the acquisition cannot, however, be regarded as just, for the purposes of s 51(xxxi), unless the legislation provides legally enforceable rights to compensation for the proprietary rights which have been acquired. In our hypothetical case s 51(xxxi) may not stand in the way of extinction of the personal liabilities of the Commonwealth's agents, but it will probably serve to invalidate the attempted extinction of the Commonwealth's liabilities.

Although s 51(xxxi) inhibits the capacity of the federal Parliament to enact legislation to affect liabilities and remedies for acts done pursuant to unconstitutional statutes (State as well as federal), it has no bearing on the powers of the federal Parliament to enact laws which are determinative of when a cause of action arises, that is, what is, in law, efficient to create a chose in action. Section 51(xxxi) therefore has little or no relevance to the question of whether a clause in a federal statute which protects officials against civil liabilities may be a valid provision, severable from the rest of the statute which is adjudged to be ultra vires.

62.   (1994) 68 ALJR 272.

JUDICIAL REMEDIES FOR UNAUTHORISED GOVERNMENTAL ACTION—ARE THEY ADEQUATE?

Are the judicial remedies which are available when agents or agencies of government exceed their legal authority, or fail to perform their public duties, adequate? In particular, are they adequate to provide reparation to those who have been injured or have sustained loss by reason of an excess of authority or non-performance of a public duty? Some would say no.

The principal judicial remedies for excesses of governmental power and non-performance of public duties are those available on an application for judicial review: the prerogative writs of certiorari, mandamus and prohibition, or orders in the nature thereof, or declarations and injunctions. Invalid action, or non-performance of a public duty, does not, however, by itself attract any liability to pay damages or make restitution. A party who seeks remedies of those kinds must establish that the defendant agent or agency has committed a recognised civil wrong. Our legal system does not recognise any special category of compensable civil wrongs by governmental parties, apart from the tort of misfeasance in a public office.[63] For the most part our law on civil liabilities treats governmental parties as if they were private (that is, non-governmental) parties. It "takes no account of the fact that the administration is capable of inflicting damage in ways in which a private person cannot".[64]

Consider the following hypothetical case. A State statute makes it a criminal offence for a person to exercise or carry on the business of a private agent unless licensed. Authority to issue licences is vested in a registrar. The registrar is empowered to cancel a licence if he or she is of the opinion that there are grounds for believing that the holder of a licence has engaged in conduct as a private agent which is unfair, dishonest or discreditable. The registrar cancelled X's licence. On an application for judicial review, the Supreme Court held that the registrar's decision was invalid for these reasons:

(a) the registrar had denied X his right to procedural fairness;

(b) the registrar had misinterpreted the statutory provision on cancellation of licences and in consequence had taken irrelevant considerations into account; and

(c) there was no evidence of any probative value to justify the registrar's conclusion that X had engaged in conduct as a private agent which was unfair, dishonest or discreditable.

Assume that on receipt of notice of the registrar's decision to cancel his licence, X, acting on the advice of his solicitor, ceased to carry on the business of a private agent and did not resume that business until the Supreme Court had dealt with his application for judicial review.[65] X

---

63. The elements of misfeasance in a public office were considered by the High Court of Australia in *Northern Territory v Mengel* (1995) 129 ALR 1. This case is discussed in M Allars' paper in Ch 3, below.
64. JUSTICE-All Souls, *Administrative Justice: Some Necessary Reforms* (1988), p 352.
65. I here assume that the solicitor accepts the now common view that most administrative decisions should be treated as valid until their invalidity is established by a court of law:

might well think he had a just claim to be compensated for the pecuniary loss suffered by him as a result of his compliance with the registrar's decision, pending the outcome of the judicial proceedings. X might well be aggrieved when he learned from his solicitor that he had no enforceable legal right to be compensated for his loss, there being no basis for an action for damages for misfeasance in a public office, or an action for damages for breach of statutory duty, or an action for damages for negligence.[66] (X's solicitor may also have advised him that the registrar might also rely on a quasi-judicial immunity from liability.)

Should not X have a legal right to be compensated for his pecuniary loss, if not by the registrar then by the State? It is doubtful whether the courts would be prepared to extend the frontiers of civil liability to cover such a case if to do so would be to impose on the registrar (and only on that officer) a strict liability to pay damages—a liability which does not depend on proof of any fault. If there is to be any legal right to be compensated in a case such as X's, that right would probably need to be conferred by statute.

Some years ago the New Zealand Public and Administrative Law Reform Committee presented a report, entitled *Damages in Administrative Law*,[67] in which it considered several options for reform. One option was enactment of an Administrative Law Damages Act along the following general lines:

"Any person who, being a person who may exercise a statutory power:

(i) exercises that power with the intention of causing harm or loss to any other person, other than harm or loss resulting or that may result from a bona fide exercise of the power; or

(ii) exercises that power, knowing that the power exercised does not extend to authorising him to do the act or make the decision which he in fact does or makes; or

(iii) fails to exercise his power with the intention of causing harm or loss, other than harm or loss resulting or that may result from a bona fide refusal to exercise the power; or

(iv) exercises the power maliciously—

65. *Continued*
    see *F Hoffman-La Roche and Co v Secretary of State for Trade and Industry* [1975] AC 295 at 365-366 per Lord Diplock; *London and Clydesdale Estates Ltd v Aberdeen District Council* [1980] 1 WLR 182 at 189-190 per Lord Hailsham; *AJ Burr Ltd v Blenheim Borough Council* [1980] 2 NZLR 1 at 4 per Cooke J; *Wattmaster Alco Pty Ltd v Button* (1986) 70 ALR 330 at 335 per Sheppard and Wilcox JJ; *Martin v Ryan* [1990] 2 NZLR 209. Contrast the statement of the Judicial Committee of the Privy Council in *Dunlop v Woollahra Municipal Council* [1982] AC 158 at 172 that:
    "The effect of the failure [to comply with a duty to afford a fair hearing] is to render the exercise of the power void and the person complaining of the failure is in as good a position as a public authority to know that that is so. He can ignore the purported exercise of the power. It is incapable of affecting his legal rights."
66. I am assuming that a duty of care could arise in this situation.
67. Fourteenth Report (1980). For a commentary on the Report see G P Barton, "Damages in Administrative Law" in M Taggart (ed), *Judicial Review of Administrative Action in the 1980s* (1986), pp 145-151.

shall be liable in damages to any person suffering harm or loss thereby caused, to the same extent as if his act or decision were a tort independently of this section.''[68]

The committee indicated that this enactment "would no doubt have to be subject to the specific exemptions conferred by any other Act".[69] It did not, however, favour such an enactment because it "would . . . result in a very narrow liability", would probably do "no more than restate existing law . . ."[70] and "would leave untouched the . . . significant area of unlawful administrative decisions reached with or without negligence, but certainly in good faith and without any 'malice' (in all its possible connotations)".[71]

The committee also did not favour legislation which imposed "a broad new liability to pay damages for loss suffered in consequence of unlawful administrative acts or decisions".[72] One reason was that legislation of this kind "would fall to be applied by the courts to a bewildering variety of fact situations, so much so that . . . [the committee could not] be confident that the remedy would not create as much injustice to defendants as it remedied for plaintiffs".[73]

The option preferred by the committee was a statute-by-statute approach. It recommended:

"that whenever a new statute confers powers that, if exercised unlawfully will cause economic loss, consideration be given to the inclusion of a provision relating to compensation for losses flowing from any unlawful decision given by the donee(s) of the power".[74]

It suggested several guidelines to assist consideration of whether a statute should include such a provision.[75]

The later Report of the Committee of the JUSTICE-All Souls Review of Administrative Law in the United Kingdom—entitled *Administrative Justice: Some Necessary Reforms*[76]—recommended legislation along the following lines:

"Subject to such exceptions and immunities as may be specifically provided, compensation in accordance with the provisions of this Act shall be recoverable by any person who sustains loss as a result of either

(a) any act, decision, determination, instrument or order of a public body which materially affects him and which is for any reason wrongful or contrary to law; or

(b) unreasonable or excessive delay on the part of any public body in taking any action, reaching any decision or determination, making any order or carrying out any duty.''[77]

68. Ibid, p 26.
69. Ibid.
70. Ibid, p 33.
71. Ibid.
72. Ibid.
73. Ibid, p 31.
74. Ibid, p 31.
75. Ibid, pp 31-32.
76. (Oxford, 1988).
77. Para 11.83.

The report recognises that the terms "wrongful" and "public body" "would need to be carefully defined",[78] but the authors of the report seem to have envisaged that "wrongful" acts would include invalid acts.

Many problems attend enactment of legislation of the kind recommended by the JUSTICE-All Souls Committee. I shall attempt to identify some of them.

Problem 1

These days the causes which can render administrative action invalid are many and those who are responsible for invalid action are not necessarily guilty of any fault. A statutory compensation scheme of the kind envisaged would render the general law on civil liabilities, so far as it relates to public bodies, otiose. That law, to a large extent, limits liability to occasions on which primary actors are recognised to have been at fault.

Problem 2

The suggested legislation does not clearly indicate on whom the liability to compensate would fall, though one may infer that it would fall on the relevant public body. That body could be a body which, for the purposes of tort law, exercises an independent discretion and for whose acts no one is vicariously liable. To impose what is, effectively, a strict liability to compensate upon those immediately responsible for invalid action would be to impose on them a liability which many (perhaps most) of them could not discharge. It might also have a chilling effect on the efficient and effective discharge of their official functions.[79]

Problem 3

Even if the liability to compensate falls only on the Crown and statutory corporations, the number of potential claimants and the amounts of compensation payable may be very substantial and so substantial as to disrupt or distort budgetary arrangements.[80]

Problem 4

It is not indicated how compensation would be recoverable. Would it be recoverable only in proceedings for judicial review? Prompt recourse to

78. Ibid.
79. In *Northern Territory v Mengel* (1995) 124 ALR 1 at 27 Brennan J explained why he considered that liability for the tort of misfeasance in a public office should not extend to cases where the defendant officer simply failed to exercise reasonable care in ascertaining the extent of his/her powers. His Honour observed that:
    "If liability were imposed upon public officers who, though honestly assuming the availability of powers to perform their functions, were found to fall short of curial standards of reasonable care in ascertaining the existence of those powers, there would be a chilling effect on the performance of their functions by public officers. The avoidance of damage to persons who might be affected by the exercise of the authority or powers of the office rather than the advancing of the public interest would be the focus of concern."
80. A similar concern may affect judicial decisions on whether public authorities owe a duty of care: see J Stapleton, "Duty of Care: Peripheral Parties and Alternative Opportunities for Deterrence" (1995) 111 LQR 301 at 313-314.

judicial review may serve to limit the loss which individuals sustain in consequence of invalid acts. Statutory time limits for initiating application for judicial review are meant to encourage prompt recourse to courts to contest the validity of administrative acts.[81] A regime which allows for award of compensation to those who sustain loss by reason of invalid administrative action must surely not diminish incentives to seek judicial review within the prescribed time limits. A system under which awards of compensation can be made only on an application for judicial review does not, however, have regard to the fact that sometimes the party who applies for judicial review is not the only person or body affected by the action which is the subject of the application for review. The action challenged by the applicant may be an action affecting a class of persons.

Problem 5

If persons are accorded a statutory right to be compensated for losses sustained by them as a result of invalid administrative action, courts might be disposed to refine the criteria of invalidity. These criteria have, in modern times, been developed by courts exercising a supervisory jurisdiction more or less independently of the law to do with liabilities to make monetary recompense.

Problem 6

What are to be counted as compensable losses or injuries which are caused by invalid acts? If an application for a licence is invalidly refused, would the applicant have any claim to be compensated if it is shown that the applicant had no right to be granted a licence and that the licensing agency could, in the exercise of its discretion, have made a valid decision to refuse the application?[82] Would a claimant be entitled to compensation if it were shown that the licensing agency invalidly refused to issue a licence to which the claimant was entitled?

Problem 7

Should a liability to compensate be imposed in respect of losses occasioned by invalid decisions of bodies exercising judicial powers or whose members enjoy judicial immunities from suit? The JUSTICE-All Souls Committee considered that no "liability should be imposed on any person or body in connection with a decision taken by a court or tribunal exercising judicial powers."[83] The committee did not explain what should be regarded as judicial powers for this purpose.

A NEW PUBLIC LAW REMEDY

Neither the recommendation of the New Zealand Committee nor that of the JUSTICE-All Souls Committee has been implemented. The New Zealand

81. But judicial review proceedings are not necessarily dealt with speedily.
82. The JUSTICE-All Souls report (para 11.86) recognised that a discretionary power to refuse a licence would be relevant "in determining damages".
83. Para 11.89.

Court of Appeal has, however, in *Simpson v Attorney-General*[84]—*Baigent's* case—established a compensation scheme which could cover a number of official wrongs which, at common law, are non-compensable. A majority of the court (Cooke P, Casey, Hardie Boys and McKay JJ; Gault J dissenting) held that a court may, in its discretion, award monetary compensation for a breach of the civil and political rights and freedoms set out in Pt II of the *New Zealand Bill of Rights Act* 1990. Such an award is against the Crown and is a public law, rather than a private law, remedy.

The *New Zealand Bill of Rights Act* is an ordinary statute and can be overridden by later statutes. It is to be a guide in statutory interpretation. Section 6 provides that:

"Wherever an enactment can be given a meaning that is consistent with the rights and freedoms contained in this Bill of Rights, that meaning shall be preferred to any other meaning."

Section 4 limits the Act's effects. It provides that:

"No court shall, in relation to any enactment (whether passed or made before or after the commencement of this Bill of Rights)—

(a) Hold any provision of the enactment to be impliedly repealed or revoked, or to be in any way invalid or ineffective; or

(b) Decline to apply any provision of the enactment—

by reason only that the provision is inconsistent with any provision of this Bill of Rights."

Section 3 makes it clear that the Bill of Rights applies only to governmental acts, specifically acts done:

"(a) By the legislature, executive, or judicial branches of the government of New Zealand; or

(b) By any person or body in the performance of any public function, power, or duty conferred or imposed on that person or body by or pursuant to law."

The Act contains no remedies clause, though such a clause had been proposed in the White Paper *A Bill of Rights for New Zealand* (1985).[85] The omission of a remedies clause was deliberate. The Bill for the Act, the Prime Minister stated in his second reading speech, "creates no new legal remedies for courts to grant. The judges will continue to have the same legal remedies as they have now, irrespective of whether the Bill of Rights is an issue."[86]

---

84. [1994] 3 NZLR 667. See also the companion case of *Auckland Unemployed Workers' Rights Centre Inc v Attorney-General* [1994] 3 NZLR 720.
85. Clause 25 of the draft Bill appended to the White Paper would, if enacted, have allowed anyone whose rights or freedoms had been infringed or denied to "apply to a court of competent jurisdiction to obtain such remedy as the court considers appropriate and just in the circumstances". This proposed clause was noted by the Court of Appeal in *Baigent's* case.
86. 510 NZ Parl Deb 3450. The Court of Appeal made no reference to these observations.

The right alleged to have been violated in *Baigent's* case was that affirmed in s 21 of the Bill of Rights, namely "the right to be secure against unreasonable search or seizure, whether of the person, property, or correspondence or otherwise". Police officers, it was claimed, had conducted an unreasonable search of Mrs Baigent's house when they proceeded to search the house, notwithstanding that they had conceded that the address specified in the search warrant was wrong. The house they wished to search was another house. There was no contest over the validity of the warrant.

The plaintiffs in the case sought damages not only for infringement of the right affirmed in s 21 of the Bill of Rights, but also for negligence in the procurement of the search warrant, for trespass to land and goods, and abuse of process (or misfeasance in a public office). At first instance all claims in the statement of claim were struck out on the ground that the defendant police were protected against liability by various statutory provisions and that the Crown was protected by s 6(5) of the *Crown Proceedings Act* 1950. On appeal the Court of Appeal reinstated all claims save that for negligence. The statutory protection clauses did not, the court held, extend to acts done in bad faith, as were the acts here alleged by the plaintiffs. And in the opinion of the majority, s 6(5) of the *Crown Proceedings Act* 1950[87] afforded the Crown protection against vicarious liability only. It did not protect the Crown against direct liability for acts in breach of the Bill of Rights.

In support of their conclusion that compensation could, in appropriate cases, be awarded for violations of the declared rights and freedoms, the majority in *Baigent's* case referred to a number of decisions of courts in other jurisdictions.[88] The majority seem not to have attached any significance to the fact that the decisions related to compensation for breach of rights and freedoms which were constitutionally entrenched. They did however attach significance to the fundamental character of the declared rights and freedoms and the purposes of the Act as revealed in its long title, that being:

"An Act:

(a) To affirm, protect, and promote human rights and fundamental freedoms in New Zealand; and

(b) To affirm New Zealand's commitment to the International Covenant on Civil and Political Rights."

(Reference was made to Art 2(3) of the International Covenant which obliges the states which are party to the Covenant to ensure that persons whose rights under the Covenant are violated have an effective remedy.)

87. This provides that "No proceedings shall be against the Crown by virtue of this section in respect of anything done or omitted to be done by any person while discharging or purporting to discharge any responsibilities of a judicial nature vested in him, or any responsibilities which he has in connection with the execution of judicial process."

88. Reference was made to the leading case of *Maharaj v Attorney-General of Trinidad and Tobago (No 2)* [1979] AC 385, to Irish cases, to an Indian case, and cases under s 24 of the Canadian Charter of Rights and Freedoms: see, for example, the citations of Hardie Boys J at 700-702.

Essentially the majority's position was that the purposes of the Bill of Rights will be achieved only if there are effective judicial remedies for violations of the rights and freedoms it affirms, and that in some cases the only effective remedy may be an award of monetary compensation. The fact that the Act did not, in the opinion of the majority, include a remedies clause did not preclude the courts from making such awards.[89]

What the majority view means is that, notwithstanding the clear direction in s 4 of the Bill of Rights that the statute does not affect other enactments,[90] provisions in other statutes which confer protections against civil liabilities will not preclude award of compensation (payable by the Crown) for violations of the declared rights and freedoms. Indeed, the very presence of those statutory protection clauses might be the very reason why a court is moved to exercise its discretion to subject the Crown to a liability to pay compensation. Compensatory remedy may be adjudged the only or the most appropriate remedy.

What the New Zealand Court of Appeal has created is an entirely new discretionary remedy for governmental wrongdoing. That wrongdoing may not fall into any of the existing categories of legal wrongs. There is no suggestion that exercise of the discretion to award of this new remedy will be affected by whether there is any fault on the part of those responsible for violations of the declared rights and freedoms[91] or by the kinds of factors which, in the United States of America, are determinative of liability for what are known as constitutional torts.[92] There is now even potential for award of compensation for invalid administrative acts which, under private law, do not attract any liability to pay damages.

I return to the hypothetical case of the private agent whose licence was invalidly revoked.[93] It will be recalled that one of the reasons why the decision to revoke the licence was in that case adjudged invalid was that the licensee had been denied his right to procedural fairness. Were a case of this kind now to arise in New Zealand, might not the licensee seek compensation for violation of the right affirmed by s 27(1) of the Bill of Rights? That subsection provides that:

"Every person has the right to the observance of the principles of natural justice by any tribunal or other public authority which has the power to make a determination in respect of that person's rights, obligations, or interests protected or recognised by law."

According to the majority view in *Baigent's* case, a claim to compensation for violation of that right would not be affected by any common law or statutory immunities from suit enjoyed by the members of the tribunal or

---

89. It was noted that the Irish Constitution does not include a remedies clause.
90. See p 21 above.
91. Cooke P (at 678) thought that "the gravity of the breach" was a consideration a court could take into account in determining the level of compensation.
92. I have dealt briefly with the constitutional torts doctrine in "Liability to Compensate for Denial of a Right to a Fair Hearing" (1989) 15 Mon LR 383 at 427-429. See also G R Nichol, "Bivens, Chilinsky and Constitutional Damages Claims" (1989) 75 Va LR 1117; J C Jeffries Jr, "Compensation for Constitutional Torts: Reflections on the Significance of Fault" (1989) 88 Mich LR 82.
93. See p 16 above.

public authority. Nor would the claim be defeated by s 6(5) of the *Crown Proceedings Act* 1950.[94]

Some may applaud the New Zealand court's preparedness to create a new public law remedy; others may think that the court has exceeded acceptable limits of judicial creativity and has effectively circumvented the direction contained in s 4 of the Bill of Rights.[95] The New Zealand government decided not to appeal to New Zealand's ultimate court of appeal, the Judicial Committee of the Privy Council. The Minister for Justice has, however, asked the Law Commission to give attention to the issues raised by *Baigent's* case. These issues include the practical consequences of the Court of Appeal's decision and its impact on the many statutory provisions which confer immunities from liability on public officials or which limit their liabilities in respect of acts done in purported exercise of their public powers. No doubt the Commission will, in the course of its proceedings, examine the circumstances in which protective provisions may be justifiable.[96]

---

94. Set out in n 87, above.
95. For critical commentaries on the case see J Allan, "Speaking with the Tongues of Angels. The Bill of Rights, Simpson and the Court of Appeal" (1994) *Bill of Rights Bulletin* (Issue 1) 2; J Allan, "Was Sir Geoffrey Wrong? Seeing Through a Glass Darkly" (1995) *Bill of Rights Bulletin* (Issue 3) 43; J A Smillie, " 'Fundamental Rights', Parliamentary Supremacy and the New Zealand Court of Appeal" (1995) 111 LQR 209. For critique of Dr Allan's critique see R Harrison, "He That is Without Sophistry, Let Him Cast the First Epithet" (1995) *Bill of Rights Bulletin* (Issue 2) 22; R Harrison, "A Brief Response to a Rejoinder to a Reply by Dr James Allan. A Shortish Reply to a Lengthy Diatribe on *Baigent*" (1995) *Bill of Rights Bulletin* (Issue 3) 47. For other comments on the case see J Dawson, "Simpson Liability" (1994) *Bill of Rights Bulletin* (Issue 1) 8; S Anderson, "Simpson: A Short Plea to Rationalise Crown Immunity" (1994) *Bill of Rights Bulletin* (Issue 1) 10. I thank Professor Michael Taggart of the University of Auckland for drawing my attention to the articles in the *Bill of Rights Bulletin*.
96. See Sir Kenneth Keith, "Rights and Wrongs: The Theory and the Practice: The Bill of Rights: Some Thoughts on Remedies", Waitangi 1995, 25th Anniversary Seminar, 2 June 1995. (Sir Kenneth Keith chairs the Law Commission.)

Chapter 2

Claims Against the Government Legislation

Paul Finn

The small and unflattering portrait of WH Walsh in the *Australian Dictionary of Biography*[1] provides no hint that here was the author of a revolution in Australian law. Within a week of first entering Queensland's Legislative Assembly in 1865 as member for Maryborough, he set to framing a private member's Bill which, when enacted as the *Claims Against the Government Act* 1866, provided the dominant model in Australian Crown proceedings legislation to this day.[2]

Some of the blessings and pitfalls of that model reflect its provenance. Walsh was not a member of the government of the day: indeed, it opposed his measure strenuously. Neither was he a lawyer: he claimed little experience of the law. Yet the substance of the Bill enacted—"the language of it, the sentences of it"[3]—though vetted by the colony's Parliamentary Draftsman, he claimed as his own creature. Distinctive both in its expression and in its unconcern for legal forms and fawnings, it struck at a range of orthodoxies in the law. The extent to which Walsh intended all of this is open to question. What is not is the revolutionary potential of the type of legislation he authored—a potential still not fully realised though in some respects perhaps fortunately so. This chapter is as much about that abiding potential as it is about the present achievement.

By way of preface, it is important to note that the Australian innovation long predated legislation in the major common law jurisdictions abolishing or significantly curtailing Crown or "sovereign"[4] immunity from suit. In Britain this did not occur until 1947 and then in an incomplete way and in an inelegant piece of legislation.[5] In the United States sovereign immunity was qualifiedly abolished at federal level in 1946 in the *Federal Tort Claims Act* and thereafter progressively in the States. The common law Provinces

1. *Australian Dictionary of Biography* (MUP, Melbourne, 1976), Vol 6, p 348. A more benign view is to be found in C A Bernays, *Queensland Politics During Sixty Years* (Govt Printer, Brisbane, 1919), p 41.
2. It was copied in the *Claims Against the Colonial Government Act* 1876 (NSW), s 3 of which in turn influenced the language of the *Judiciary Act* 1903 (Cth), s 64. As will be noted below, while we still lack uniformity in *Crown Proceedings Acts* across the country, there is a convergence today in their scope and effect: see generally P W Hogg, *Liability of the Crown* (2nd ed, Law Book Co, Sydney, 1989).
3. *Queensland Parliamentary Debates* (1865), Vol 2, p 337 per Walsh MLA.
4. In the United States.
5. *Crown Proceedings Act* 1947 (UK).

of Canada were even more tardy, Manitoba and New Brunswick being the first to move in 1951, British Columbia the last in 1974.[6] And though New Zealand was to allow tort claims arising out of public works as early as 1881,[7] its major statutory incursion into Crown immunity came in 1910,[8] the same year, coincidentally, as the Union of South Africa passed its comprehensive abolition legislation,[9] which, in turn, was based on a *Cape of Good Hope Act* of 1888.[10] The impression should not, however, be created that the movement in Australia was uniformly enlightened. While the Commonwealth was relatively quick to move in this matter after federation,[11] Victoria continued to stand apart. It did not abolish the Crown's immunity in tort until 1955.[12]

A BRIEF HISTORICAL SKETCH[13]

This is not the place to describe in any detail the privileges and immunities enjoyed by the Crown in legal proceedings in the Australian colonies around the time of the initial grants of responsible government in the mid-19th century. Suffice it to say that the two of greatest moment to the colonists were:

(i) the rule that the Queen could not be sued in her own courts without her consent—hence the need for royal assent in proceedings by way of petition of right;[14] and

(ii) the immunity of the Crown in any event from liability in tort, an immunity probably manufactured by English courts in the 19th century as an expression of their sense of the medieval maxim "the King can do no wrong".[15]

It is not open to doubt that it was the first rather than the second of these that was the inspiration for Walsh's Bill. Under the legislation inherited from New South Wales on separation in 1859, any claim made against the Queensland government required the assent of the Governor in Council

6. See C H H McNairn, *Governmental and Intergovernmental Immunity in Australia and Canada* (ANU Press, Canberra, 1978), p 46ff. It is, however, noteworthy that federal withdrawal of the immunity began to occur as early as 1887 and in a way which mirrored New Zealand legislation of 1881: see n 7, below.

7. *Crown Suits Act* 1881 (NZ), s 37.

8. *Crown Suits Amendment Act* 1910 (NZ), s 3. For a discussion of the New Zealand History see Editorial, "The Crown Proceedings Act, 1950" (1952) 28 NZLJ 17 and P A Joseph, *Constitutional and Administrative Law in New Zealand* (Law Book Co, Sydney, 1993), p 533 ff.

9. See *Crown Liabilities Act*, No 1 of 1910 (SAf).

10. See Act No 37 of 1888 which was passed at judicial suggestion to impose liability in tort: see *Minister of Finance v Barbeton Municipal Council* [1914] AD 335 at 342ff.

11. Passing first the *Claims Against the Commonwealth Act* 1902 as a temporary measure and then, more comprehensively, the *Judiciary Act* 1903, Pt IX.

12. As to the effects of this inaction, see for example W Harrison Moore, "A Century of Victorian Law" (1934) 16 J Comp Leg & Int Law, 3rd Series, 175 at 189.

13. The colonial dimension of this history is considered in some detail in P D Finn, *Law and Government in Colonial Australia* (OUP, Melbourne, 1987), Ch 6.

14. On which see generally G S Robertson, *Civil Proceedings By and Against the Crown* (Stevens, London, 1908), Bk III.

15. Compare Hogg, op cit, p 6.

(hence the ministry of the day) before it could proceed in the courts. [16] With the disposition of the Crown lands being in the forefront of contemporary public controversy, [17] for the government to retain the capacity to control its exposure to liability through the assent procedure was wholly unacceptable to Walsh and to the Bill's supporters: when its own interests or actions were called in question a government could not be relied upon as of course to do justice. Significantly, the immediate target of the Bill was not any perceived deficiency in the types of claim that could then be made against the government [18]—though by the time of the Bill's second passage through the Queensland Parliament (it failed to receive royal assent in London at the first attempt) the assumption even of its critics was that it exposed the government to liability in tort. [19]

The premise of Walsh's Bill inhered in the system of responsible government itself. Its burden was seen as having everything to do with the responsibility a colonial government should bear for its own and its officers' actions—and as having nothing to do with the Queen herself: there was "no question of infringing the dignity of the Crown". [20] Later generations of lawyers may have found this a difficult dichotomy [21] but, with such premises, the Bill could espouse a markedly egalitarian philosophy. The government was to be deprived of "an immunity which no private individual in the community possessed". [22] It was, in effect, to be relegated to the status of an ordinary litigant in the courts of the colony. The logic of this was given uncompromising expression in provisions which encapsulate a distinctively Australian conception of the citizen-State relationship in the common law world at least for the purposes of civil litigation. [23]

The core of the 1866 Act was provisions:

(i) enabling a person with any claim (unrestricted) against the government to proceed as of right against a nominal defendant who was to represent the government in the matter; [24] and

16. See 20 Vict No 15 (1857, NSW).
17. The parliamentary debates on the Bill made governmental exposure under land claims the essence of opposition to the proposal and resulted in the Bill being denied retrospective effect in relation to Crown lands.
18. Both the preamble to 20 Vict No 15 and the reference in s 1 to "any claim" may seem to suggest that claims beyond those allowable under petition of right procedures and, in particular, claims in tort were contemplated: see for example the views of Barwick CJ in *Maguire v Simpson* (1977) 139 CLR 362 at 371. This probably is an anachronistic reading of the Act. The preamble, relevantly, is an almost verbatim copy of an earlier South Australian statute (No 6 of 1853) which was quite different in its effect; on the reference to "any claim" see Finn, op cit, p 143.
19. *Queensland Parliamentary Debates* (1866), Vol 3, p 150 per Bramston MLC.
20. *Queensland Parliamentary Debates* (1865), Vol 2, p 341 per Lilley MLA.
21. See below.
22. *Queensland Parliamentary Debates* (1865), Vol 2, p 345 per Douglas MLA.
23. It must be conceded at once that not all Australian jurisdictions have been prepared to give full effect to the consequences of that conception, for example, in their provisions governing remedies available against and the enforcement of judgments against the Crown: compare for example *Crown Proceedings Act* 1980 (Qld), ss 10 and 11 and *Crown Proceedings Act* 1992 (SA), ss 7 and 10.
24. The Act initially required that a claim be certified by a Supreme Court judge as disclosing a prima facie case before the nominal defendant procedure was activated. This requirement was repealed in 1874.

(ii) requiring that in that claim "the proceedings and rights of parties therein shall as nearly as possible be the same and judgment and costs shall follow on either side as in an ordinary case between subject and subject."[25]

The refreshing hand of the non-lawyer is at work here.[26] This is perhaps the difficulty. Could language, should language, which is capable of having an iconoclastic effect on the preferred position of the Crown in our legal system, be given its apparently plain and natural meaning?

A South African decision given under legislation of similar purport (though different in its precise wording) points up the fundamental question. At issue was whether the South African *Crown Liabilities Act*, 1910 had the effect of making the Crown bound by a statute, notwithstanding the common law rules on when statutes bind the Crown. As de Villiers CJ put the matter:

"The argument is that the Act [of 1910] makes justiciable by the court any claim against the Crown which, had it been against a private person, would have been enforceable by action *with the implication that all prerogatives and rights have therefore gone by the board*."[27]

And the judicial response? It was merely a counter assertion:

"This argument in one stroke does away with all the prerogatives of the Crown, which is its own conclusive refutation . . . The Act gives a right of action against the Crown and to that extent the prerogative of the Crown must be taken to have been abrogated by the Act. *All other prerogatives and rights of the Crown remain*."[28]

I will return to this matter below. It goes to the heart of Claims legislation.

Beyond the core provisions noted above, the *Walsh Act* was uncompromising in prosecuting its philosophy. The common law orthodoxy was that the Queen's courts would not make coercive orders against the Queen.[29] But, given this Act's premise,[30] it would allow "every species of relief whether by way of specific performance or restitution of rights or recovery of lands or chattels or payments of money or damages or otherwise."[31] Contemporary Australian legislation (unlike that of Britain, Canada and New Zealand) retains this robust view, though in the 1990s that of South Australia, Tasmania, ACT and the Northern Territory has faltered, curiously, when it comes to the award of mandatory injunctions against the Crown.[32]

---

25. *Claims Against the Government Act* 1866 (Qld), s 5.
26. While it is the case that both the "as of right"/nominal defendant and the "as nearly as possible" provisions incorporate language and ideas to be found in prior New South Wales (20 Vict No 15), Victorian (Act No 49 of 1858) and South Australian (Act No 6 of 1853) legislation, their combination and effect are both distinctive and original in the *Walsh Act*.
27. *South African Railways & Harbours v Smith's Coasters (Prop) Ltd* [1931] AD 113 at 123, (emphasis added).
28. Ibid at 123-124 (emphasis added).
29. See Hogg, op cit, p 22.
30. See the text accompanying n 20, above.
31. *Claims Against the Government Act* 1866 (Qld), s 7.
32. *Crown Proceedings Act* 1992, (SA) s 7(1); *Crown Proceedings Act* 1993 (Tas), s 8(2); *Crown Proceedings Act* 1992 (ACT), s 8(2); *Crown Proceedings Act* 1993 (NT), s 8(2).

Perhaps the most stunning provision of the *Walsh Act* was that which allowed for the execution of unsatisfied judgments against government property.[33] There is a story in this which reveals something of Imperial legal attitudes to the legislation. When Walsh's original Bill was passed in 1865 it was undiscriminating in the government property against which it would allow execution. Reserved by the Governor for royal assent, this was refused on the advice of the Imperial Law Officers who feared the execution provisions might expose Imperial property to the risk of seizure. This difficulty was attended to when the legislation was re-enacted in 1866: property held etc for Imperial purposes was exempted from the execution provision. And there was this additional afterthought: as noted in the second reading of the amended Bill in the Legislative Council:

> "It had also been thought advisable to except the Colonial Parliamentary buildings, court-houses and prisons; for it might be very awkward to have the bailiff taking possession of the President's or the Speaker's chair, or the Judges' benches."[34]

As if to accentuate this gulf between the Imperial and the local, between the Queen and the colonial government, when New South Wales enacted legislation in 1875 similar to Queensland's abortive 1865 Act, it likewise was refused royal assent because of a similar vice in its execution provisions. But objection also was taken to the language of the Act. It referred to claims against the "Crown". This, it was suggested by the Secretary of State for the Colonies, should be amended to claims against the "Colonial Government".[35] If the premise for Walsh's 1866 Act in Queensland be thought an odd one, it was one shared in high places in London![36]

Today the Queensland Act alone[37] retains an execution provision, with New South Wales (the only other jurisdiction to copy this particular measure) abandoning it in its latest *Crown Proceedings Act*.[38] Though the legislation of all jurisdictions makes provision for the satisfaction of judgments, it is not altogether surprising that the Walsh approach, at least in this respect, has not commended itself to other Australian legislatures. It, perhaps more than anything else, can be seen as the symbol of a distrust of governments which Parliaments would not wish to foster.

Now, briefly, to bring Claims legislation down to modern times. Queensland, then New South Wales and the Commonwealth (in its *Judiciary Act* 1903) were Australia's trail-blazers in comprehensive legislation. Though the Acts in the two States have been updated and re-enacted, all three in their essentials retain the core provisions of Walsh's Act.

33. *Claims Against the Government Act* 1866 (Qld), s 8.
34. *Queensland Parliamentary Debates* (1866), Vol 3, p 149 per Wood MLC.
35. *Sydney Morning Herald*, 25 February 1876, p 3 per Sir William Manning.
36. See also Finn, op cit, p 148. The dichotomy between Crown (or Governor) and government was regularly drawn even in legislation in the first two to three decades after responsible government.
37. *Crown Proceedings Act* 1980 (Qld), s 11.
38. See *Crown Proceedings Act* 1988 (NSW), s 7.

In the other colonies, then States, progress to legislation of equivalent effect has been more halting. The predominant colonial concern, as with the *Walsh Act*, was that whatever the types of claim that could be made against the government, they should be able to be made as of right and not by the grace and favour of the Executive.[39] Nonetheless, by federation all colonies, with the exception of Victoria and South Australia,[40] had removed wholly or significantly Crown immunity from suit in tort.[41] Today all statutes, Commonwealth, State and Territorial (again Victoria excepted), have put the substantive rights and liabilities of the government—now uniformly referred to as the "Crown"[42]—in civil proceedings on the same or, as nearly as possible on the same, footing as are the liabilities and rights of the individual person.[43] Victoria for its part has legislated somewhat more limitedly, particularising in its *Crown Proceedings Act* 1958 the circumstances in which liability in contract and tort will be imposed on the Crown, but in these circumstances it also applies the "as nearly as possible" formula.[44]

Quite apart from according Walsh his due, one of the purposes of this brief historical sketch is to illustrate that, whatever contrary view may have been entertained in other common law jurisdictions,[45] the Australian colonists by the turn of the century regarded immunity from suit as a proper object of abolition. For this reason, when the issue of immunity came squarely before our Constitution's framers at the Melbourne Convention in 1898,[46] the substantial question they were to decide was not whether the Commonwealth or a State should enjoy immunity from suit in matters of federal jurisdiction but how best to confront immunity—in the Constitution itself or through legislation passed under the Constitution.[47] Their answer is contained in the Constitution, s 78.

The Australian attitude had its own and very obvious explanation. The raw conditions of the colonies, the patterns of settlement and investment, and the imperatives of development impelled governments into activities which were without counterpart in Britain or which in that country were

39. See Act No 6 of 1853 (SA); Act No 49 of 1858 and Act No 241 of 1865 (Vict); *Crown Redress Act* 1859 (Tas); but compare Ordinance 31 Vict No 7 (WA)—a copy of 20 Vict No 15 (NSW).
40. For the history and changing interpretation of the SA legislation see *De Bruyn v South Australia* (1990) 54 SASR 231 and the cases referred to therein by Legoe J.
41. *Crown Redress Act* 1891 (Tas); *Crown Suits Act* 1898 (WA) which, as in NZ, tied tort liability to "public works". While Act No 6 of 1853 (SA) referred to a "pecuniary claim" contemporary understanding was that this did not extend to tort claims: see Quick and Garran, *Annotated Constitution of the Australian Commonwealth* (Angus & Robertson, Sydney, 1901), p 806; pace Hogg, op cit, p 81.
42. For the reasons for the change see below.
43. See *Judiciary Act* 1903 (Cth), Pt IX; *Crown Proceedings Act* 1988 (NSW), s 5; *Crown Proceedings Act* 1992 (SA), s 5; *Crown Suits Act* 1947 (WA) s 5; *Crown Proceedings Act* 1993 (Tas) s 5; *Crown Proceedings Act* 1993 (NT), s s 5; *Crown Proceedings Act* 1992 (ACT), s 5.
44. See ss 22 and 25.
45. By 1921 even the British were restive, with Lord Chancellor Birkenhead constituting a committee to propose amendments to the law: see (1952) 28 NZLJ 17 at 18.
46. The subject had received consideration in earlier iterations of the Constitution: see Quick and Garran, op cit, p 804.
47. See *Convention Debates*, Melbourne 1898, Vol 5, 1653 et seq.

conducted by local government, private enterprise or private and charitable organisations. Such was a regular refrain in reports, writings and judicial decision across the second half of the 19th century. Practical necessity created a very distinctive citizen-government relationship, if only because of the scale of governmental activity and of its corresponding capacity to help and to harm. Not surprising, then, is the distinction drawn between the "government" with whom the citizen dealt locally, and the Queen who resided in a distant country. Not surprising is the recognition that "the great variety of transactions which the Colonial government undertakes and carries on" rendered immunity doctrines "in a large degree inapplicable to the state of things existing here".[48] And beyond this was the note of egalitarianism:

> "Why, because you have the longer purse, and a greater power of fighting your opponent, should you be exempt from action if you do wrong as a state, when the humblest citizen is not exempt from any responsibility for any injury done by him to his fellows."[49]

I emphasise what I here describe as the "Australian attitude" because later in this chapter I will question why still a strange deference persists in our treatment of the Crown in the law.

Before closing this historical sketch, comment should be made on the reception given by the judiciary to, particularly, the New South Wales Act of 1876.[50] It has had enduring effects.

1. If it was the intent both of the proponents of the Queensland Act and of the Imperial authorities to take the Crown out of the Act, the judges for their part were very much minded to put the Crown back in. Baulking at the term "the government", they were to conclude that litigation under the legislation was "still an action against the Crown".[51] Unobjectionable in itself, this conclusion had an effect which the separation of "Crown" and "government" seemingly avoided: it brought back into more direct consideration such privileges and immunities of the Crown as might be affected by the legislation. Despite the strong indication given by the Privy Council in *Farnell v Bowman*[52] that effect should be given to the "plain words" of the legislation, they have been, and continue to be, construed under the shadow of the prerogatives on which they entrench.

2. The ameliorative purposes of the legislation were conceded sparingly by the courts. The New South Wales Supreme Court, for example, divided sharply on the issue whether the Act of 1876 allowed tort claims. It took the Privy Council in *Farnell's* case to put this issue to rest and in the affirmative. However, the judiciary's posture was an obstructive one for the citizen-litigant. It was more than 20 years before they would make an order for discovery against a nominal defendant.[53] Only in 1908 was it admitted

---

48. *Bowman v Farnell* (1886) 7 LR (NSW) 1 at 13-14 per Faucett J.
49. *Convention Debates*, Melbourne, 1898, Vol 5, 1662 per Sir John Downer.
50. That it was a copy of Queensland's Act has long since been forgotten. The Queensland Act in any event provided little that found its way into the law reports.
51. *Bowman v Farnell* (1886) 7 NSWR (L) 1 at 13 per Faucett J.
52. (1887) 12 App Cas 643 at 648, 650.
53. *Morissey v Young* (1896) 17 NSWR (Eq) 157.

that an injunction could be granted in proceedings under the Act—and this despite the unfettered language in which the Act's remedy section was cast. When it came to the persons or bodies for whose acts the government could be held liable, a narrow conservatism triumphed: liability would only ensue if those acts occurred in the discharge of functions authorised by the government, performed on its behalf, or subject to its control. The by-product of this was that if a tort was committed in the purported exercise of a power or duty imposed directly on a Crown servant, the government would not be liable for that tort.[54] This led to the courts drawing a mystical distinction between "servants of Her Majesty", for whom the government was not liable, and "ordinary servants of the Crown", for whom it was.[55] I will return later to this, the notorious "independent discretion" rule. Suffice it to say here it paid no regard at all to how government characteristically was structured and functions allocated under local legislation.

3. The judges were, with some notable exceptions, to assert that a benevolent interpretation of the Act would forebode dire though unspecified consequences. In an early High Court decision, for example, Barton J raised the spectre of "the whole fabric of the State" being brought to "confusion and disaster"[56] if the maxim respondeat superior was not adhered to faithfully! More measuredly though, was the appreciation that not all of the activities of government were ones upon which it was necessarily appropriate to impose liabilities, particularly in tort. One could not after all treat the government in all circumstances as if it were just another subject. Significantly, in the first case squarely to face this issue in 1901—*Gibson v Young*,[57] where a negligence action was brought for an injury sustained in a prison—the Full Court of New South Wales did not seek to manoeuvre the government out of liability through the "as nearly as possible" provision. Rather, it denied liability on grounds of public interest and public policy. This raises another dimension to the question about how we should approach the interpretation and application of Claims legislation today.

THE SCOPE AND DILEMMAS OF MODERN CLAIMS LEGISLATION

Save for Victoria[58] and, notwithstanding the apparent limitation of the *Judiciary Act* 1903 (Cth), ss 56-58 to claims in contract or tort,[59] the types of civil proceeding that can be initiated against the Crown are

---

54. See for example *Enever v The King* (1906) 3 CLR 969.
55. *Delacauw v Fosbery* (1896) 13 WN (NSW) 49.
56. *Enever v The King* (1906) 3 CLR 969.
57. (1900) 21 LR (NSW) 7.
58. See *Crown Proceedings Act* 1958, s 22.
59. Notwithstanding the seeming acceptance in *Breavington v Godleman* (1988) 169 CLR 41 that those sections were so limited, the correct view in the writer's opinion, given the history and evolution of Claims legislation, is that the reference in this section to

unrestricted.[60] And, Western Australia apart,[61] the statutes of all jurisdictions provide, both in civil proceedings against the Crown and (excepting New South Wales)[62] in civil proceedings by the Crown, either that the rights of the parties shall as nearly as possible be the same as in a proceeding between subject and subject[63] or, and this in legislation of this decade, that "the same substantive law is to be applied in such proceedings as in the case of proceedings between subjects".[64] Save in one important respect noted later,[65] these alternatives would seem to be similar in their effect.

Their egalitarian purpose is obvious enough. They invite, first, a disregard of the Crown's status as one of the parties. And, secondly, in the law to be applied—that as between subject and subject—they appear to discountenance any operative effect being given to such public purposes and responsibilities as the Crown may have in the matter in question. Predictably, the courts have not been prepared for all purposes to concede that the wording of the legislation has either of these effects: the Crown cannot always be treated merely as a subject with its rights being determined as if a subject. Herein, as will be seen, lies the central dilemma of Claims legislation: if the Crown is not always to be treated "similarly", when and why is it to be treated differently and how can that difference in treatment be eked out of the language of the legislation? This dilemma, as will be seen, is exacerbated by the presence in our law of a body of doctrines which in various ways privilege the Crown in legal proceedings but without regard being had at all to the existence, let alone to the language, of Claims legislation.

59. *Continued*
    "contract and tort" should not be taken as words of limitation: compare *Commissioner for Railways (Queensland) v Peters* (1991) 24 NSWLR 407 per Priestley JA. Their purpose is to indicate that in allowing claims as of right, those claims were not limited to those which previously under a petition of right could be brought by act of grace of the Crown: tort claims fell outside the petition. In other words the reference to tort here was to indicate that the section was not merely a procedural one. In any event the significance of s 56 etc at least for the purpose of the types of claim allowable against the Commonwealth, etc seems negligible given present attitudes to the scope of the *Judiciary Act* 1903, s 64: see *Commonwealth v Evans Deakin Industries Ltd* (1986) 161 CLR 254, esp at 263-264.

60. See *Judiciary Act* 1903 (Cth), s 2 "suit" and s 64; *Crown Proceedings Act* 1988 (NSW), ss 3 and 5; *Crown Proceedings Act* 1980 (Qld), ss 7 and 8; *Crown Proceedings Act* 1992 (SA), ss 4 and 5; *Crown Suits Act* 1947 (WA), s 5; *Crown Proceedings Act* 1993 (Tas), ss 4 and 5; *Crown Proceedings Act* 1993 (NT), ss 4 and 5; *Crown Proceedings Act* 1992 (ACT), ss 3 and 5.

61. The WA statute is silent on this matter.

62. See *Crown Proceedings Act* 1988 (NSW), s 5.

63. *Judiciary Act* 1903 (Cth), s 64; *Crown Proceedings Act* 1988 (NSW), s 5(2); *Crown Proceedings Act* 1980 (Qld), s 9(2); *Crown Proceedings Act* 1958 (Vic), s 25. There are slight differences in language between the above which have no operative effect for present purposes.

64. *Crown Proceedings Act* 1992 (SA), s 5(1); *Crown Proceedings Act* 1993 (Tas), s 5(1); *Crown Proceedings Act* 1993 (NT), s 5(1); *Crown Proceedings Act* 1992 (ACT), s 5(1). This newer formulation is possibly a legislative response to the suggestion of Barwick CJ in *Maguire v Simpson* (1977) 139 CLR 362 at 372 that "more direct language" than that contained in the *Walsh Act* model could be used to convey that the legislation was intended to apply to substantive as well as to procedural rights.

65. See below.

Little purpose would be served in attempting to find the answers to the dilemma posed above merely in the analyses courts have made of this type of legislation—and for ease in exposition reference hereafter will be limited to the *Judiciary Act* 1903 (Cth), s 64. Widely divergent views have, for example, been expressed in the High Court about the meaning of s 64.[66] They range from the blunt view of Kitto J that the law is to be applied as if "the Commonwealth . . . were a subject instead of being the Crown",[67] through the Dixonian view that, if s 64 identifies the law to be applied, it does not "say how and with what effect the principles of that law do apply in substance",[68] to the suggestion flowing from observations in *Commonwealth v Evans Deakin Industries Ltd*[69] that the "as nearly as possible" formula itself may justify distinctive treatment of the Crown in some circumstances.

It clearly is the case that we need to arrive at some principled view of the scope of s 64 and of the deviations from similarity of treatment which are consistent with its purposes. But, in doing this, we equally need to address that body of doctrines which have had no regard to s 64. Justices of the High Court in particular seem increasingly to be mindful of this. So, in *Maguire v Simpson*[70] for example, Gibbs J posed (without answering) the question of whether s 64 undercut the *Auckland Harbour Board* rule,[71] which allows the Crown the unqualified right to recover money paid from consolidated revenue without legislative authority while, in the same case, both Mason and Jacobs JJ suggested that s 64 was relevant to the issue of priority of Crown debts in *Commonwealth v Cigamatic Pty Ltd*[72] though no mention there was made of it. More recently, in *Northern Territory v Mengel*,[73] five justices suggested that "it may well be contrary to [s 64 and its equivalents] to assign liability to governments and their officers on a basis not applicable to private individuals".

Case law on civil proceedings involving the Crown can, for present purposes, be divided into three broad groupings. The first and, for the most part, least contentious, is that in which no relevant distinction is drawn between the Crown and a subject in the law applied in the proceedings and this because in the circumstances and for the purposes of that law the Crown appropriately can be treated as if a subject. An example of this is *Commonwealth v Verwayen*[74] where liability turned on the application to a representation made by the Commonwealth of the general law of estoppel and of waiver. This, for convenience, will be called the "similar treatment" category.

The second grouping does acknowledge that the parties cannot and should not for all purposes be treated in the matter as if the Crown were

66. For a relatively recent judicial survey see *Maguire v Simpson* (1977) 139 CLR 362 at 393-395 per Stephen J.
67. *Asiatic Steam Navigation Co Ltd v Commonwealth* (1956) 96 CLR 397 at 427.
68. *South Australia v Commonwealth* (1962) 108 CLR 130 at 140.
69. (1986) 161 CLR 254 at 264-265.
70. (1977) 139 CLR 362.
71. *Auckland Harbour Board v The King* [1924] AC 318.
72. (1962) 108 CLR 372.
73. (1995) 129 ALR 1.
74. (1990) 170 CLR 394.

merely a subject. The reasons for this may be various, as will be seen. But, importantly, the effect of acknowledging difference is not to exempt the Crown from the operation of the general law applicable between subject and subject (for example the law of negligence) but rather is to accommodate the reasons for the difference in the manner of application of the law itself. Illustrative of this are the adaptations made to the law of negligence as applied to the statutory discretions of public officers and authorities[75] and the now decidedly thin "presumption" against finding that the Crown, its servant, or agent is a trustee of property vested in it in the absence of clear words to this effect.[76] This second grouping will be referred to as the "differential treatment" category.

The third grouping is of that body of doctrines which do not purport at all to apply the law as between subject and subject but rather apply rules distinctive to government and governmental agencies. The now slowly unravelling rules on when statutes bind the Crown,[77] and the *Auckland Harbour Board* rule referred to above are illustrative of this. Because they diverge so sharply from the law as between subject and subject, doctrines in this, the "exceptional treatment", category are quite problematic.

Similar treatment

In much the greater part of litigation by and against the Crown the law applied, be it common law[78] or statute,[79] is simply that applied as between ordinary subjects. Given the requisition of s 64 and its equivalents this is unsurprising. Characteristically the fact situations one encounters in this category are of two types. The first is where the relevant Crown activity giving rise to the claim has a direct or near analogue in the activities of private individuals (for example, the conduct of a factory) with that analogue itself buttressing the imperative of similar treatment.[80] The second type is where:

(i) the relevant activity, though distinctively governmental (for example requisitioning ships in wartime)[81] can, for the purposes of the claim, be brought within the requirements of the general law appropriate to that claim,[82] and

75. Compare *Sutherland Shire Council v Heyman* (1985) 157 CLR 424.
76. See *Registrar of the Accident Compensation Tribunal v Federal Commissioner of Taxation* (1993) 117 ALR 27.
77. See for example, *Bropho v Western Australia* (1990) 171 CLR 1.
78. See for example, *Commonwealth v Verwayen* (1990) 170 CLR 394 (estoppel); *Mason v New South Wales* (1959) 102 CLR 108 (duress—money had and received); *Groves v Commonwealth* (1982) 150 CLR 113; and on contract see generally D Rose, "The Government and Contract", in P D Finn, *Essays on Contract* (Law Book Co, Sydney, 1987).
79. See for example, *Asiatic Steam Navigation Co Ltd v Commonwealth* (1956) 96 CLR 397; *Strods v Commonwealth* [1982] 2 NSWLR 182; *Commonwealth v Evans Deakin Industries Ltd* (1986) 161 CLR 254.
80. Compare *Strods v Commonwealth* [1982] 2 NSWLR 182.
81. Compare *Limerick Steamship Co Ltd v Commonwealth* (1924) 24 SR (NSW) 214. The distinction drawn by Pincus JA in *Metway Bank Qld v Queensland* (unreported, CA Qld, 20 May 1993) between "commercial" and "purely governmental functions" is, with respect, untenable.
82. For example, trespass or negligence.

(ii) the character and purpose of that activity provides no significant reason in public policy requiring other than equal treatment.[83]

Illustrative of the latter of the above types is the decision in *Groves v Commonwealth* where, in holding a negligence action could be brought by a member of the armed forces for injury sustained while on duty in peacetime as a result of the actions of another member, four of the justices could "see no policy considerations which require that this court . . . should deprive this serviceman of the rights of common law which protect all other members of the community".[84]

In two respects, however, applying similar treatment to the Crown has been distinctly and, I would suggest, unjustly disadvantageous to the subject. The first of these has involved the insistence that, cases of duress colori officii[85] apart, the private law of duress is to be applied to claims for the recovery of money exacted by the State.[86] This has been despite the recognition that the application of "the law relating to the recovery by one subject from another of moneys paid" in consequence of an unjustifiable demand seemed distinctly inappropriate where the demand is backed by the de facto weight and authority of government.[87] But, if treating similarly here has resulted in treating the subject unfairly in fact, that unfairness has fortuitously been undone in large measure by unrelated developments in the common law which facilitate the recovery of money paid under mistake.[88]

Secondly, and more importantly, the subject has been severely disadvantaged by the manner in which the Crown was to be held liable for the actions of its servants and agents. The law applied was the private law of vicarious liability[89]—an understandable approach it might be thought, given the terms of s 64 and its equivalents, but one which has had particularly unfortunate consequences. Whatever the scope of vicarious liability (and this has varied with changes in its informing theory) it was from the outset taken as excluding liability for acts, etc performed by a Crown servant in the exercise of an independent duty or discretion cast upon that servant by statute or by the common law. The supposed justification for this exemption—sustained by a long line of High Court authority[90]—was that in exercising such a duty or discretion the servant is acting independently: "the Crown is not acting through him".[91]

---

83. Compare *Limerick Steamship Co Ltd v Commonwealth* (1924) 24 SR (NSW) 214.
84. (1982) 150 CLR 113 at 133.
85. On which see *Bell Bros Pty Ltd v Shire of Serpentine-Jarrahdale* (1969) 121 CLR 137.
86. It needs to be emphasised that reliance upon English case law and *not* attention to s 64 and its equivalents has produced this result.
87. See *Mason v New South Wales* (1959) 102 CLR 108, esp at 116-117 per Dixon CJ.
88. See *Commissioner of State Revenue v Royal Insurance Australia Ltd* (1994) 126 ALR 1 and *David Securities Pty Ltd v Commonwealth Bank of Australia* (1992) 175 CLR 353.
89. See generally Aronson and Whitmore, op cit, p 22 ff; Hogg, op cit, p 86 ff; Finn, op cit, p 150 ff.
90. Beginning with *Enever v The King* (1906) 3 CLR 969. Many of the cases are usefully collected in the decision of Yeldham J in *Oriental Foods (Wholesalers) Co Pty Ltd v Commonwealth* (1983) 50 ALR 452.
91. *Attorney-General (NSW) v Perpetual Trustee Co (Ltd)* (1952) 85 CLR 237 at 249 per Dixon J.

The vices in this conclusion are, it is respectfully suggested, many. First, it was only from around the middle of the last century that one could begin reasonably to speak of office holders under the Crown being in some instances in a position similar to employees. And these, for the most part, were the holders of minor positions. In any event, the great majority of public officers of any significance were, usually by statute, made the direct repositories of duties and discretions. From the early colonial period in this country it was the common practice to statutorily allocate functions directly to officials, not for reasons of constitutional principle, but rather for reasons of convenience, precedent and pragmatism. It is to this writer not at all obvious why it should be assumed that Crown liability should turn on the quite arbitrary fashion in which functions were—and are—allocated by statute. [92]

Secondly, while it may be said that the "as nearly as possible" requirement itself ordains use of the law of vicarious liability, this fails to take adequate account, it is suggested, of one important consideration. It is precisely in those cases where officials exercise independent functions that they act as the Executive State. They will of course be personally liable for such wrongs as they commit in or under colour of office. But considered from the subject's standpoint this surely is the quintessential case of where the Crown (and the public purse) should provide redress: an injury has been occasioned by a person acting in or under colour of public office and while exercising the actual or apparent authority conferred by the State. How the State internally organises its relationships and its distributions of power between the Crown and officers of the Crown should, it is suggested, be a matter of indifference to the subject at least for present purposes. [93] As will be seen in the section following, considerations of public policy can justify departures from similar treatment and in ways which disadvantage the Crown. Here, where the core issue is the nature of the relationship of the Crown *not* with its officials but with its subjects—a citizen-State matter—there is, I would venture, reason enough to contemplate a departure from applying the law as between subject and subject.

There is no merit in the independent discretion rule. It has been abolished by statute in most jurisdictions of major common law countries. [94] Perhaps the High Court may be induced to reconsider this matter—and overrule a significant number of its own decisions. [95]

---

92. In *Enever v The King* (1906) 3 CLR 969 at 979 Griffith CJ was prepared to assume such a legislative intent in Crown Proceedings legislation. Debate on the *Walsh Act*, especially in its references to liability for the acts of Land Boards and Commissioners of Crown Lands would seem to suggest a contrary view in colonial Queensland: see *Queensland Parliamentary Debates* (1865), Vol 2.
93. There seems to be some recognition of this—acharacteristic it must be admitted—in *Zachariassen v Commonwealth* (1917) 24 CLR 166 at 180.
94. See Hogg, op cit, pp 95-96 and the references therein.
95. A by-product of the rule's rejection would be the elimination of the need to invoke the "de facto authority" requirement for ultra vires actions in order to bring liability home to the Crown: see *James v Commonwealth* (1939) 62 CLR 339 at 359-360. The requirement has seemingly been endorsed recently by the High Court in *Northern Territory v Mengel* (1995) 69 ALJR 527.

Differential treatment

In *South Australia v Commonwealth*[96] Sir Owen Dixon commented:

"it is one thing to find legislative authority for applying the law as between subject and subject to a cause concerning the rights and obligations of governments; *it is another thing to say how and with what effect the principles of that law do apply in substance.* For the subject matters of private and public law are necessarily different."[97]

Though made in the context of a suit between governments, this observation has equal salience to suits between Crown and subject.

In the slow evolution of the common law it has long been recognised that there can be occasions on which the unmodified application of a rule or doctrine to particular activities or states of affair might itself produce quite untoward and unwanted effects. Historically, this commonly (but by no means exclusively) occurred where public service and public utility functions were being provided and the question arose whether the authority or body discharging the function should be subjected to the unrestricted application of the ordinary law of nuisance, negligence or breach of statutory duty. Should a local authority, for example, be held liable in nuisance for non performance of its general duty to repair a highway, or in negligence for failure to exercise care in relation to known dangers arising from non-repair?[98] Should a public utility be liable for breach of statutory duty in not providing the service required by statute?[99] And so on.

What invited attention in such cases was not the particular status of the defendant (Crown, local authority or company) but the public character of, and the public purposes served by, the public interests affected by, the activity in question. Did these suggest a need for modification of the ordinary law as it applied to the activity in question? Would, for example, unmodified liability have untoward economic consequences for the ratepayers or taxpayers who ultimately fund the body responsible for the activity—one of the original justifications for the non-feasance rule applied to highway authorities? Would it imperil the provision of the very service in question either for economic reasons[100] or because of a "chill factor"?[101] What, in short, was being asked for was an evaluation of whether the public policy furthered by a rule or doctrine was not offset in some way by a countervailing public policy which justified, in the circumstances, some modification (not necessarily favourable) to the usual application of that rule or doctrine.

There is a considerable number of instances where this can—and does—occur in litigation involving the Crown. In s 64-type cases, for example, it

96. (1962) 108 CLR 130.
97. Ibid at 140, emphasis added.
98. Compare the body of law that has built upon the decision of *Russell v Men of Devon* (1788) 2 TR 667, for example, *Gorringe v Transport Commission* (Tas) (1950) 80 CLR 357.
99. See *Atkinson v Newcastle and Gateshead Waterworks Co* (1877) 2 Ex D 441 and P D Finn, "A Road Not Taken: The Boyce Plaintiff and Lord Cairns Act" (1983) 57 ALJ 493, esp at 495 ff.
100. See Finn, n 99 at 496-497.
101. Compare *Gibson v Young* (1900) 21 LR (NSW) 7.

was conceded relatively early that, though discovery could be ordered against the Crown, it in turn could raise a "State papers" (now public interest) privilege. [102] A more recent and telling illustration is found in the judgment of Mason J in *Commonwealth v John Fairfax & Sons Ltd*[103] when considering the application of the action for breach of confidence to the unauthorised disclosure of governmental information:

> "The equitable principle has been fashioned to protect the personal, private and proprietary interests of the citizen, not to protect the very different interests of the executive government. It acts, or is supposed to act, not according to standards of private interest, but in the public interest. This is not to say that equity will not protect information in the hands of the government, but it is to say that when equity protects government information it will look at the matter through different spectacles . . . Unless disclosure is likely to injure the public interest, it will not be protected." [104]

There is no trace of "similar treatment" here—and, for the quality of our democracy, fortunately so. Other instances of this process of modification can be seen, for example, in the manner in which the law of negligence is applied to the exercise of the discretions of public authorities (including the Crown)[105] or to injury to services personnel occasioned by their own number; [106] in the now weakening presumption against finding an intention in the Crown to constitute itself a trustee of property vested in it; [107] in the emergence of the planning-operational distinction in the application of the law of promissory estoppel to the representations of government; [108] and, at least in the opinion of some commentators, in the subtle modifications made to contract law where the issue is one of government's intent to create legal relations. [109]

102. See for example *Morissey v Young* (1896) 17 NSWR (Eq) 157; *Marconi's Wireless Telegraph Co Ltd v Commonwealth (No 2)* (1913) 16 CLR 178. While this can be rationalised with s 64 through the device of saying that that privilege can also be raised by the subject this, it is suggested, is an anachronistic explanation of what occurred.
103. (1980) 147 CLR 39; see also *Esso Australia Resources Ltd v Plowman* (1995) 69 ALJR 404.
104. *John Fairfax & Sons Ltd* at 51-52.
105. See generally *Sutherland Shire Council v Heyman* (1985) 157 CLR 424; see also *L v Commonwealth* (1976) 10 ALR 269.
106. Compare *Groves v Commonwealth* (1982) 150 CLR 113 and *Shaw Savill & Albion Co Ltd v Commonwealth* (1940) 66 CLR 344.
107. See, for example, the case law which has built on *Kinloch v Secretary of State for India* (1887) 7 App Cas 619. These are collected in *Aboriginal Development Commission v Treka Aboriginal Arts and Crafts Ltd* [1984] 3 NSWLR 502. See also *New South Wales v Commonwealth (No 3)* (1932) 46 CLR 246, seemingly a claim under the *Judiciary Act* 1903, in which no consideration whatever is given to whether the "law as between subject and subject" should be applied. For the presumption now under strain see *Registrar of the Accident Compensation Tribunal v Federal Commissioner of Taxation* (1993) 117 ALR 27.
108. See *Minister for Immigration, Local Government and Ethnic Affairs v Kurtovic* (1990) 92 ALR 93. Case law on the application of estoppel to the powers and duties of public bodies is today a subject of some controversy because of changes in equitable estoppel: see P D Finn and K J Smith, "The Citizen, the Government and 'Reasonable Expectations' " (1992) 66 ALJ 139, at 146-147.
109. For a treatment of this matter see D Rose, "The Government and Contract", in Finn, *Essays on Contract* (Law Book Co Sydney), pp 238-239; compare Aronson and Whitmore, op cit, pp 204-205.

The matter to be noted in all of this is that, though subject to modification for reasons of public policy, the law applied to the Crown— negligence, contract, estoppel or whatever—is the same substantive law as is applied between subject and subject. It is this, I venture, which is the burden of the Dixon J quotation heading this section. And what it suggests about the "as nearly as possible" formula is that it here means "as near to similar treatment as is appropriate, given the demands of countervailing public policies".[110] This in turn implies that either as the substantive law itself evolves or as public policies change, the need for or the extent of differential treatment in a given instance will itself require re-evaluation. Examples where this has occurred or is occurring are:

(a) the changing application of the law of negligence to the conduct of prisons over this century;[111] and

(b) the reappraisal that is beginning to occur in the light of recent High Court decisions, as to the appropriate application of the law of estoppel to the representations of government and its officers.[112]

Over time differential treatment can give way to similar treatment.

Exceptional treatment

While it can be said of the previous two categories that the substantive law applied, even where modified in some way, is the ordinary law applicable to suits between subject and subject, such is not the case here. What we have is a range of common law rules:

(i) which for the most part apply exclusively to claims involving the Crown;[113]

(ii) which are without counterpart in subject and subject litigation; and

(iii) which, because of the manner of their application, produce results quite different from those which would ensue if the law as between subject and subject were applied.

A very obvious example of this is the rule of statutory construction that the Crown will only be bound by statutes which themselves bind it expressly or by necessary implication—a rule, admittedly, undergoing some relaxation today.[114] This rule is the emblem of a problem. Save where *Acts Interpretation Acts* have themselves dealt with the matter,[115] why is it not

---

110. This view it must be acknowledged sits uneasily beside the more generally espoused modern view of s 64; see for example, *DTR Securities Pty Ltd v Deputy Commissioner of Taxation* (1987) 72 ALR 513 at 525-526 per McHugh JA; reversed on other grounds (1988) 78 ALR 641.

111. Compare *Gibson v Young* (1900) 21 LR (NSW) 7 and *L v Commonwealth* (1976) 10 ALR 269.

112. For a brief treatment of this see P D Finn and K J Smith, op cit, pp 146-147.

113. Some, for example, the "fetter rule" which is later noted in the text applies equally to public authorities.

114. See *Bropho v Western Australia* (1990) 171 CLR 1; see also *Jacobsen v Rogers* (unreported, HC, 17 February 1995).

115. See *Acts Interpretation Act* 1954 (Qld), s 3; *Acts Interpretation Act* 1915 (SA), s 20; *Interpretation Act* 1967 (ACT), s 7(1).

the effect of s 64 and its equivalents that all statutes bind the Crown for *s 64's purposes*, unless this is excluded expressly or by necessary implication by a particular statute and for its purposes? [116] Why, despite s 64, do we still adhere to a rule of construction of exactly opposite effect?

Rules about which like questions can be asked include:

(i) the *Auckland Harbour Board* rule [117] which, as earlier noted, allows the recovery as of right of moneys paid out of consolidated revenue without legislative authority and despite such defences (for example estoppel or change of position) as the defendant would have in an action to recover money brought by a private plaintiff; [118]

(ii) the immunity of the Crown from the writ of mandamus; [119]

(iii) the priority given Crown debts over other debts of equal degree; [120]

(iv) the doctrine which invalidates contractual "fetters" on discretions given to be exercised as and when the public interest so requires. [121]

With the possible exception of the *Auckland Harbour Board* rule, it is, in the writer's view, difficult to find a principled justification for any of these (including the immunity from statutes rule) which on balance would warrant total disregard of s 64 and its equivalents. As noted earlier, the judges themselves are becoming sensitive to this. [122]

The *Auckland Harbour Board* rule doubtless buttresses a fundamental principle of our constitutional system: the power to appropriate belongs to Parliament. [123] Given that Claims legislation was designed initially to facilitate claims *against* the Crown, and that the coalescence of suits against and by the Crown in common legislative provisions such as s 64 seems more a matter of legislative streamlining, it may be open to serious doubt whether our legislatures should be taken to have intended the removal of the main

116. As noted in the "Historical Sketch" above, this question when posed to the Supreme Court of South Africa elicited no effective answer save its denial: *South African Railways & Harbours v Smith Coasters (Prop) Ltd* [1931] AD 113, esp at 123-124; see also *Downs v Williams* (1971) 126 CLR 61.
117. *Auckland Harbour Board v The King* [1924] AC 318 at 326-332.
118. See Hogg, op cit, p 185; on the unavailability of defences see *Commonwealth v Burns* [1971] VR 825; *Attorney-General v Gray* [1977] 1 NSWLR 406.
119. See generally, Aronson and Franklin, *Review of Administrative Action* (Law Book Co, Sydney, 1987), pp 492-503. This immunity is less severe in those Australian jurisdictions which allow mandatory injunctions to be awarded under their Crown Proceedings legislation—a remedy denied in the Acts of SA, Tas, NT and ACT.
120. See *Commonwealth v Cigamatic Pty Ltd* (1962) 108 CLR 372; *The Laws of Australia*, 19.3, para 57. Legislation has reversed this privilege in the spheres of bankruptcy and company liquidation.
121. One supposed manifestation of this is the doctrine of "executive necessity": see *Rederiactiebolaget "Amphitrite" v The King* [1921] 3 KB 500. A like rule is that which applies more generally to public bodies in relation to their statutory powers: see Hogg, op cit, p 170 ff. A counterpart rule in private law relating to fiduciary powers does not invalidate a fetter. It merely makes damages—and not direct enforcement—the only available remedy for its breach: see Finn, *Fiduciary Obligations* (Law Book Co, Sydney, 1977), Ch 7.
122. See for example *Maguire v Simpson* (1977) 139 CLR 362 at 387-388 per Gibbs J; at 402 per Mason J; at 403-404 per Jacobs J; *Northern Territory v Mengel* (1995) 69 ALJR 527.
123. Compare *South Australia v Commonwealth* (1962) 108 CLR 130 at 140.

safeguard of that constitutional principle in a statutory provision so generally worded. Such judicial opinion as we have on the matter (admittedly slight) inclines against giving s 64 such overriding effect.[124] The aspect of the rule which, in the writer's view, is unpalatable and which may lead still to an embrace of s 64 when the issue is fully agitated,[125] is the denial to the subject of the defences of estoppel and change of position.[126] There are obvious grounds for objecting to rules which make the individual subject the insurer of the regularity of government action.

For its part the rule of statutory construction preferring the Crown seems explicable today only on the grounds of an early but sustained antipathy to the language and ameliorative purposes of s 64.[127] And, in the writer's view, the only justification for its being allowed to continue to survive despite a marked windchange in judicial attitude to s 64[128] is similar to that referred to in *Bropho v Western Australia*[129] statutes have long been drafted on the basis of that rule of construction. As will be seen later in this chapter, however, the failure to apply s 64 directly to Commonwealth statutes has produced an apparent anomaly when it performs its "federal" role of picking up State statutes and applying them to the Commonwealth[130] or to another State.[131]

The Crown debt-priority rule, for its part, is of no particular consequence today because of the legislative reversals it has suffered.[132] The "no mandamus" rule should have quietly passed from view in this country with the availability of the private law remedy of mandatory injunction under Crown Proceedings legislation.[133] What now is regrettable is that in the four new *Crown Proceedings Acts* passed in the 1990s—those of South Australia, Tasmania, the Northern Territory and the Australian Capital Territory—this remedy is expressly denied to the subject. Finally, the "no fetter" rule. It raises the s 64 issue in sharp form in that there is a parallel rule in the law applied as between subjects which is quite different in its effect. A "fetter" in the private sector will not be enforced directly, but

---

124. See for example *Commonwealth v Crothall Hospital Services (Aust) Ltd* (1981) 36 ALR 567 at 580 per Ellicott J; *Commonwealth v Burns* [1971] VR 825 at 830 per Newton J. The observations in *Trimboli v Secretary, Department of Social Security* (1989) 86 ALR 64 at 68 on s 64 and the rule are directed to a different issue.

125. Now with the decision in *David Securities Pty Ltd v Commonwealth Bank of Australia* (1992) 175 CLR 353, the private law rule for recovery of money is moving closer to *Auckland Harbour*.

126. *Attorney-General v Gray* [1977] 1 NSWLR 406.

127. See *Downs v Williams* (1971) 126 CLR 61. The issue has been raised in South Africa and was dismissed out of hand but with no convincing reasons given: *South African Railways & Harbours v Smith's Coasters (Prop) Ltd* [1931] AD 113.

128. Recent case law has embraced the approach of Kitto J in *Asiatic Steam Navigation Co Ltd v Commonwealth* (1956) 96 CLR 397 at 427—an approach spurned in cases such as *Downs v Williams* (1971) 126 CLR 61.

129. (1990) 171 CLR 1.

130. See for example *Commonwealth v Evans Deakin Industries Ltd* (1986) 161 CLR 254.

131. See for example *Commissioner for Railways (Queensland) v Peters* (1991) 24 NSWLR 407.

132. See *Crown Debts (Priority) Act* 1980; *Bankruptcy Act* 1966, s 8; Corporations Law (Cth), s 556.

133. It is noteworthy that South African courts seem to have been quick to appreciate the scope for mandatory orders under that country's equivalent legislation: *Minister for Finance v Barbeton Municipal Council* [1914] AD 335.

unlike in the public sector, it will not be treated as a void contractual obligation. Its breach in consequence will sound in damages.[134] Considered in the light of s 64 the public sector rule could well be brought into closer or complete harmony with the private sector counterpart.[135] And this brings one to the heart of the matter.

Despite what has been said above, there well may be found a continuing place in our law for some or all of the rules noted, be this in their present or in some modified form. But if this is to be the case we should openly acknowledge and justify the departure being made from s 64 and its equivalents. That process may warrant differential treatment on "as nearly as possible" grounds—at least in the jurisdictions where that formula is used.[136] The underlying point, though, is that whatever the rationales for these rules in their present form, these must be weighed in the balance against the requisition of s 64. To the extent that they are found wanting in this, the rules should be abandoned or modified.

A STATUTE FOR A FEDERATION

Because of their bearing on the discussion to follow it is appropriate to note at the outset the terms of s 78 of the Constitution and of ss 56 and 64 of the *Judiciary Act* 1903 (Cth), s 56 being quoted here in its original form.[137]

"78. Proceedings against Commonwealth or State.—The Parliament may make laws conferring rights to proceed against the Commonwealth or a State in respect of matters within the limits of the judicial power.[138]

56. Any person making any claim against the Commonwealth, whether in contract or in tort, may in respect of the claim bring a suit against the Commonwealth in the High Court or in the Supreme Court of the State in which the claim arose.

64. In any suit to which the Commonwealth or a State is a party, the rights of parties shall as nearly as possible be the same, and judgment may be given and costs awarded on either side, as in a suit between subject and subject."

In the hard passage of the Judiciary Bill 1903, the provisions of Pt IX— "Suits by and Against the Commonwealth and the States"—attracted little debate.[139] This lack of parliamentary consideration both of the intent of

134. See PD Finn, *Fiduciary Obligations*, Ch 7.
135. Compare *Ansett Transport Industries (Operations) Pty Ltd v Commonwealth* (1977) 139 CLR 54 at 76 per Mason J.
136. How it could be justified in the four jurisdictions which use "the same substantive law" formula is more difficult to see.
137. Later amendment has no bearing on the issues to be considered in the text.
138. Quick and Garran, op cit, pp 806-807 suggest that the phrases "within the limits of the judicial power" were left in the text by an oversight. See also *Final Report of the Constitutional Commission* (AGPS, Canberra, 1988), Vol 1, p 421 ff.
139. The Part itself was a composite of a late series of amendments to the Bill (now the existing ss 56-60) and of provisions transferred from the parallel High Court Procedure Bill (now the existing ss 61-67): see *Parliamentary Debates*, Vol 14, 1537, 1717 (Cth). This provenance may help explain the uneasy fit of ss 56 and 64.

some of Pt IX's provisions and of their relationship to the Constitution has been matched over the century by some diversity in judicial opinion as to the burden particularly of ss 56 and 64 and as to the constitutional validity of s 64 in its outer reaches. Does the liability of the Commonwealth to suit, for example, proceed from the Constitution, s 75(iii) or from the *Judiciary Act*?[140] Is it from s 56 or s 64, or from the combination of the two that the right to proceed against the Commonwealth is established?[141] And relatedly are the words "whether in contract or in tort" words of limitation on the scope of the section[142] or are they rather designed merely to emphasise that the claims now allowable *as of right* against the Commonwealth are not limited to those which in the absence of legislation could be brought within the scope of the petition of right?[143] Is the reference to "a State" in s 64 beyond the legislative competence of the Commonwealth Parliament insofar as it purports to "affect the substantive rights of the States in proceedings in the exercise of federal jurisdiction"?[144]

This chapter is not the place to consider these questions in detail. For the most part they have been well rehearsed elsewhere.[145] Suffice it to say here the present orthodoxies[146] seem to be that the right to proceed against the Crown derives from the *Judiciary Act*; that s 64 alone seems capable of sustaining any type of suit by or against the Commonwealth or, within federal jurisdiction, a State; and that to the extent that s 64 refers to "a State" it is unconstitutional insofar as it applies to proceedings *by* a State[147] and is arguably so in proceedings against a State to the extent that it affects the substantive rights of a State.[148]

140. See *Georgiadis v Australian and Overseas Telecommunications Corp* (1994) 119 ALR 629 at 650-651 per McHugh J and the authorities referred to therein.
141. See *Maguire v Simpson* (1977) 139 CLR 362.
142. As seems to have been assumed in *Breavington v Godleman* (1988) 169 CLR 41.
143. See *Commissioner for Railways (Queensland) v Peters* (1991) 24 NSWLR 407 per Priestley JA; see also *South African Railways and Harbours v Edwards* [1930] AD 3 (SAf).
144. *Commonwealth v Evans Deakin Industries Ltd* (1986) 161 CLR 254 at 263; and see *Commissioner for Railways (Queensland) v Peters* (1991) 24 NSWLR 407.
145. See the cases referred to above; L R Zines, *The High Court and the Constitution* (Butterworths, Sydney, 3rd ed, 1992), p 316 ff; Cowen and Zines, *Federal Jurisdiction in Australia* (Oxford, Melbourne, 2nd ed, 1978), p 32 ff.
146. See nn 140, 141, above.
147. Constitution, s 78 refers only to proceedings *against* the State.
148. A contrary conclusion was arrived at in *Commissioner for Railways (Queensland) v Peters* (1991) 24 NSWLR 407. The argument in favour of validity would, in the writer's opinion, have the following foundation:

   (i) Before Crown Proceedings legislation the bar to a subject's proceeding as of right against the Crown in matters falling within the petition of right was procedural, the substantive law in petition cases being essentially the law applied as between subject and subject.

   (ii) In claims beyond the petition, at least in relation to wrongs, the bar itself was substantive and this because the King could do no wrong.

   (iii) In the case of (ii) it would be insufficient simply to remove the bar to proceeding (as in (i)) unless at the same time it was indicated what was to be the applicable law by which the liability of the Crown was to be judged—it could have been a completely new body of law or as in s 64, the general law.

   (iv) Selecting the appropriate body of law for at least (iii) above was necessary if the subject was to have a substantive right to proceed against a State under the Constitution s 78.

The balance of this chapter is concerned solely with what unquestionably is the centrepiece of Pt IX—s 64. It is, perhaps, superfluous to say that though its language is that of the *Walsh Act* of 1866 that language is being put to purposes which the member for Maryborough could never have envisaged.

Section 64

The scheme of the *Judiciary Act* 1903 is, subject to the Constitution and to any relevant laws of the Commonwealth, to make the laws for the time being[149] of each State or Territory binding on all courts exercising federal jurisdiction in that State or Territory.[150] Section 64, in turn, operates on those laws, be they procedural or substantive. Its general effect, as noted by Kitto J in *Asiatic Steam Navigation Co Ltd v Commonwealth* is that:

"[it] must be interpreted as taking up and enacting, as the law to be applied in every suit to which the Commonwealth or a State is a party, the whole body of the law, statutory or not, by which the rights of the parties would be governed if the Commonwealth or State were a subject instead of being the Crown. The portion of that law which is taken by s 64 from statutes, whether Imperial, Commonwealth or State, is then to be applied in such suits by the independent force of that section; and if, in its original setting any provision of that law was so expressed as not to apply to the Crown, s 64 nevertheless explicitly makes it applicable, as completely as possible, to the determination of the rights of the Commonwealth or State against its opponents and of their rights against the Commonwealth or State."[151]

The apparent oddity in this of the Commonwealth being bound by State statutes which do not bind the Crown in that State, is returned to below. What needs here to be emphasised is that, while broad in its application and operation, s 64 is itself subject to now reasonably well settled qualifications and limitations.

First, notwithstanding the law the section "picks up", the "as nearly as possible" formula may nonetheless warrant differential treatment being given the Commonwealth (or State in a matter of federal jurisdiction). Sufficient has been said of this earlier in this chapter.

Secondly, though "s 64 plays a pivotal role in the federal legal system, it . . . enjoys no special authority among statutes of the Commonwealth. It is neither a constitutional provision nor an entrenched law."[152] In consequence, a later and inconsistent Commonwealth Act will exclude its application or operation to the extent of that inconsistency.[153] Characteristically, such inconsistency arises where a State law which otherwise would be picked up and applied to the Commonwealth by virtue of s 64, would be invalidated by the operation of s 109 of the Constitution

149. The operation of the section in this respect is said to be "ambulatory": see *Maguire v Simpson* (1977) 139 CLR 362 at 388 per Gibbs J.
150. *Judiciary Act* 1903, ss 79 and 80.
151. (1956) 96 CLR 397 at 427.
152. *Deputy Commissioner of Taxation v Moorebank Pty Ltd* (1988) 165 CLR 55 at 62-63.
153. Ibid.

for inconsistency with a law of the Commonwealth if that State law was applied directly to the matter in question.[154] Thus we have a number of recent decisions in which it has been held that particular provisions in Commonwealth bankruptcy and taxation statutes have precluded the use of s 64 to pick up State legislation where the Commonwealth provisions "have left no room" for that State law.[155]

Thirdly, despite the language of Kitto J, the application of s 64 to Commonwealth legislation is affected by the survival of the rule of construction that the Commonwealth Crown is not bound by a Commonwealth statute unless by express words or by necessary implication.[156] Sufficient has been said of that rule earlier in this chapter. What needs to be noted here is the oddity produced when one contrasts this with the amenability of the Commonwealth, via s 64, to State statutes which do not bind the Crown of that State because of that same rule of construction. The present orthodoxy is that the statute law of a State or Territory applies to the Commonwealth as if the Commonwealth were a subject. In consequence "it is an irrelevant consideration that the [State] Crown is excluded from the operation of the State law".[157] In other words, s 64 can expose the Commonwealth to liability under a State statute in respect of an activity in that State where the State itself is not so exposed because it is not bound by that statute as a matter of construction. This result may seem even more unusual when one bears in mind that if the Commonwealth had legislative competence to do so and passed a similar Act, it equally would *not* be bound by it.

At first blush this may seem to suggest we have a distinct problem with s 64. And we know that the *Walsh Act* formula it uses was not evolved with a federation in mind. But the present vice in the section's operation on State statutes lies first and foremost in the rule of statutory construction which so often exempts a State Crown from the effects of that State's laws. If the presumption contained in the rule of construction was reversed—if the consequential onus was placed directly on a State or, for that matter, the Commonwealth, to exclude itself expressly from the operation of a particular statute it passes[158]—the s 64 "anomaly" would then be confined to cases where a State statute positively excludes the State from that statute's operation. The elimination of that anomaly may well be thought an appropriate matter for legislative action.[159] But this, I would

154. See *Dao v Australian Postal Commission* (1987) 162 CLR 317.
155. See *Re Pollack; Ex parte Deputy Commissioner of Taxation* (1991) 103 ALR 133 and the cases referred to therein.
156. Compare *Downs v Williams* (1971) 126 CLR 61.
157. *Maguire v Simpson* (1977) 139 CLR 362 at 402 per Mason J; see also *Strods v Commonwealth* [1982] 2 NSWLR 182.
158. There are strong accountability reasons justifying such an approach: compare the reasoning in *Coco v The Queen* (1994) 120 ALR 415 at 419.
159. It is difficult to see how interpretation of s 64 could produce the desired result unless (a) the fact that a State positively excluded the State Crown from a statute be said, as a matter of public policy, to be sufficient to justify exemption under the "as nearly as possible" formula; or (b) given that if the Commonwealth had passed a like Act it also would have been exempt, s 64 should not be presumed to give any State Act an operation different from that it would have if a law of the Commonwealth. The latter, in essence, is the converse of the reasoning in *Deputy Commissioner of Taxation v Moorebank Pty Ltd* (1988) 165 CLR 55.

emphasise, should only be done if at the same time the rule of construction favouring the Crown was itself reversed. To legislate without this would merely perpetuate in the most comprehensive way the anomaly and the injustice of the rule of construction.

A CONSTITUTIONAL CURIOSITY

Were it not for s 51 (xxxi) of the Constitution, it would probably be unnecessary to advert to an issue which today should be of antiquarian interest only. It can be put in these terms. Given that the "right to proceed against the Commonwealth"[160] is one conferred by statute (that is, by the *Judiciary Act* 1903, ss 56 and 64), should the claims that can in consequence be made against the Commonwealth be themselves regarded as the creatures of that Act, even if in form they are claims under the general law in any given instance?

In *Georgiadis v Australian Overseas Telecommunications Corporation*[161] a majority of the High Court, with little[162] or no[163] explanation, answered this question in the negative. A claim against the Commonwealth in tort, for example, is a claim in respect of a cause of action arising under the general law. That cause of action is not a creature of the *Judiciary Act*. This would seem to suggest that the *Judiciary Act's* provisions should probably be regarded as conferring "rights to proceed" only, with the general law for its part providing such causes of action as are able to be brought against the Commonwealth. But is this not, with respect, a somewhat too easy explanation of the effects of ss 56 and 64?

Those provisions serve several purposes. First, they clearly allow claims to be made as of right against the Commonwealth in those cases where, under older petition of rights procedures, claims only could be made by the grace and favour of the Crown. To this extent the sections properly can be said, in terms of the Constitution s 78, to be procedural in the sense of conferring "*rights* to proceed against the Commonwealth". Secondly, and this is the innovative consequence of the *Walsh Act*, the sections equally allow claims as of right in circumstances where no claim at all previously could be brought. This was because there was no substantive law applicable to the Crown which could be enforced in a court even if the Crown itself waived such procedural bar as there was to its being sued in its own courts. To a 19th century English judge this was the true explanation of the Crown's immunity from suit in tort.[164]

It is of course well accepted that the sections allow claims in tort against the Commonwealth. But to have this effect they had to do more than confer a bare right to proceed. They needed by one means or another to make

160. Constitution, s 78.
161. (1994) 119 ALR 629.
162. Ibid at 639 per Brennan J.
163. Ibid at 634 per Mason CJ and Deane and Gaudron JJ.
164. See G S Robertson, *Civil Proceedings By and Against the Crown* (Stevens & Sons, London, 1908), p 350 ff.

actionable conduct etc which previously gave rise to no liability in the Crown. This was achieved, not by altering the substantive law itself, but by altering the status of the Crown for the purposes of the substantive law. The Crown, in essence, was "privatised". That was one of the burdens of the "as nearly as possible" formula. The end result is, it is suggested, that if a claim against the Commonwealth in tort can be said to arise under the general law, it does so because and only because the *Judiciary Act* creates a basis on which tort law can be made applicable at all to the Commonwealth. [165]

The *Judiciary Act* provisions, then, have several effects. They remove such procedural bars as there to suits against the Crown. But equally they create causes of action against the Commonwealth under the general law where such did not previously exist. This conclusion, in the writer's view, does not affect the correctness of the majority's holding in *Georgiadis* in relation to the application of s 51(xxxi) to the legislative extinguishment of vested causes of action against the Commonwealth. [166] It does suggest, though, that the issue is a more complex one than the High Court's judgment would imply.

---

165. This is not so in contrast with contract claims precisely because the bar to suit there was merely procedural. Waive that bar and there was a substantive law available to resolve the claim.
166. The dissent of McHugh J in that case—(1994) 119 ALR at 650-651—while correct, it is respectfully submitted, in identifying that ss 56 and 64 have a pivotal role in creating a tort liability, do not in the writer's view give full effect to what the sections confer on the subject (ie a substantive cause of action under the general law) in order to confer a "right to proceed". To modify the right to proceed, in consequence, involves the modification of more than a procedural right of the subject.

Chapter 3

Tort and Equity Claims Against the State

Margaret Allars*

1. INTRODUCTION

The equality proposition

The proposition that the law should apply to government in the same way that it applies to the governed has immediate appeal. It accords with common conceptions of the rule of law as requiring equality in the application of the law, including the subjection of those who govern to the law.[1] This "equality proposition" was articulated by Dicey when he argued that private individuals should be able to bring government officials to account in ordinary courts of law.[2] Claims against the Crown statutes appear to require that the equality proposition be applied by the courts, at least "as nearly as possible".[3] However, the substantive principles of tort and equity do not always apply to government without qualification. Equality in the application of the law to government and governed is therefore no more than a proposition. Where the operation of the ordinary principles is qualified, the equality proposition is offended. Commentators who endorse the equality proposition argue that such qualifications in the law of tort and equity should be removed.[4] I shall argue that the equality proposition cannot be accepted without qualification. The rationale and scope of the qualifications nevertheless are in urgent need of review.

Government power exceeds the power of individuals to a vast degree. The Executive's power to make rules applying to all members of the public, whether in the form of delegated legislation or policy, involves the exercise of strong discretion.[5] The Executive's power to apply the rules includes a less well understood discretionary component. By comparison, individuals have a personal capacity to make rules or apply them in only limited senses,

* Associate Professor, Faculty of Law, The University of Sydney.
1. J Raz, *The Authority of Law* (Clarendon Press, Oxford, 1979), pp 214-219.
2. A V Dicey, *Introduction to the Study of the Constitution* (1885, 10th ed, 1959), pp 187-188.
3. *Judiciary Act* 1901 (Cth), ss 56, 64.
4. P Finn and K J Smith, "The Citizen, the Government and 'Reasonable Expectations' " (1992) 66 ALJ 139.
5. "Strong discretion" is exercised where the decision-maker is free to choose standards on the basis of moral or political values, without restrictions set by any authority. On the other hand "weak discretion as judgment" is exercised where the decision maker is bound by standards which cannot be mechanically applied but which require judgments of

mainly through the law of contract.[6] The extensive and discretionary nature of its power provides government with innumerable opportunities to inflict damage upon individuals, in a way which is not commensurate with the power of individuals to inflict damage on each other or on government.

The power imbalance between government and governed is frequently relied upon in support of the equality proposition. It is also relied upon as justification for departures from the equality proposition, for example in arguments that the law should require government to meet higher standards than individuals, such as duties to ensure that human rights of individuals are respected, or to operate as a model employer or model commercial dealer. What is neglected is that governmental power, although in a composite sense immense, is, in another sense, more limited than the power of ordinary individuals. Particular governmental powers are conferred and limited by statute or by the common law definition of the subject-matter of a prerogative power. The common law principles of administrative law reinforce the statutory confinement and structuring of discretionary power and generally imply a common law duty to act in a procedurally fair manner in exercising power. By contrast, the capacity of individuals to enter contracts or to engage in conduct which may prove to be tortious is not limited by statute and administrative law in the way that governmental power is. Private individuals are not subject to common law principles of administrative law proscribing excess and abuse of power and requiring compliance with procedural fairness.

The power imbalance therefore must be understood not just from a private law perspective, but also from a public law perspective which appreciates both the extent and the limitation of governmental power. A public law perspective requires that qualifications be made to the equality proposition in the law of tort and equity in order that administrative law principles be preserved. The rationale for those qualifications, and their scope, require careful justification.

The qualifications

Statutes authorise administrators to engage in conduct which would otherwise be tortious. At this obvious and fundamental level, the equality

5. *Continued*
   degree. These expressions, used by Ronald Dworkin in *Taking Rights Seriously* (Duckworth, London, 1977), pp 31-34, 68-71, have prompted criticism that weak discretion collapses into strong discretion because of the interpretative activity which occurs in the course of all communication. See K Greenawalt, "Discretion and Judicial Decision: The Elusive Quest for the Fetters that Bind Judges" (1975) 75 Col L Rev 359 at 366; D J Galligan, *Discretionary Powers: A Legal Study of Official Discretion* (Clarendon Press, Oxford, 1986), pp 14-20. The argument which follows in this paper regarding the collapse of the policy/operational distinction mirrors and can be partially explained, by the collapse of the distinction between strong and weak discretion. See M Allars, *Introduction to Australian Administrative Law* (Butterworths, Sydney, 1990), p 13.
6. Rule-making power is exercised by individuals only in the limited sense of making rules governing their relationship with a limited number of other individuals under the law of contract. Rule application is engaged in again only in the limited sense that claims may be made on the basis of rules. Determination of the lawfulness and legitimacy of those claims rests with the executive and judicial branches of government.

proposition is undermined at the outset by reason of the very conferral of power, much of it discretionary, on administrators. However, all administrative power is confined in scope and structured in its manner of exercise, normally by statute and always by the common law. An administrative decision which is unlawful, because it is ultra vires or procedurally unfair, exposes an administrator to liability in tort. Liability of course depends upon successfully establishing all the elements of the tort. The equality proposition is also infringed by a statute which protects an administrator from private law liability for actions which have been shown to be unlawful. A glaring example is the enactment of a statute specifically to confer immunity from liability to a particular class of plaintiffs who have already established in judicial review proceedings that the public authority acted unlawfully.[7] Such statutory restriction of government liability requires a response at a constitutional level, protecting human rights to compensation for wrongful government action.[8]

The equality proposition makes its strongest claim in relation to the law of negligence. Here it is argued that government should be liable for loss caused to individuals by reason of careless or incompetent exercise of power, whether the conduct be ultra vires or intra vires. If the conduct is ultra vires, the statute provides no protection against application of the ordinary principles of the law of negligence.[9] An early view was that statutory power impliedly must be exercised without negligence, so that a negligent exercise of power is ultra vires. The better view is that negligence arises on account of a common law duty of care in accordance with the ordinary principles of negligence.[10] Whilst the equality proposition has been asserted in relation to intra vires exercises of power, it has also been qualified by the policy/operational distinction, introduced by Lord Wilberforce in *Anns v Merton London Borough Council*.[11] No duty of care arises in respect of "policy or planning" decisions, as distinct from

---

7. In *Lim v Minister for Immigration, Local Government and Ethnic Affairs* (1992) 176 CLR 1 the High Court held that the detention of a group of boat people, classified under the *Migration Act* 1958 (Cth) as "designated persons" was for a period of time unlawful. These asylum seekers brought actions seeking damages for the tort of false imprisonment. Amendments were then made to the *Migration Act* limiting the compensation which a designated person may be awarded in an action against the Commonwealth in respect of unlawful detention to one dollar a day: *Migration Amendment Act* (No 4) 1992 (Cth). Following the High Court decision in *Georgiadis v Australian and Overseas Telecommunications Corp* (1994) 179 CLR 297, the actions were amended to challenge the constitutional validity of the new provision as an infringement of the requirement in the commonwealth Constitution s 51(xxxi) that acquisition of property by the Commonwealth be on just terms. See *Ly Sok Pheng v Minister for Immigration and Ethnic Affiars* (High Court proceedings No S 199 of 1992), which is still pending. The *Migration Legislation Amendment Act (No 6)* 1995 (Cth) was then enacted, with the object of giving retrospective lawfulness to the detention, removing retrospectively any constitutional invalidity and replacing the provision for restricted damages with a provision retrospectively extinguishing the basis for the claim. For discussion, see *Migration Legislation Amendment Bill (No 2) 1994* Report by the Senate Standing Committee on Legal and Constitutional Affairs (August 1994).

8. See *International Covenant on Civil and Political Rights*, Arts 2.3, 9.5.

9. *Northern Territory v Mengel* (1995) 129 ALR 1 at 27 per Brennan J.

10. *Shire of Sutherland v Heyman* (1984) 157 CLR 424 at 458 per Mason J, at 484 per Brennan J; *Northern Territory v Mengel* (1995) 129 ALR 1 at 27 per Brennan J.

11. [1978] AC 728.

"operational" decisions of government. The rationale and justification for the scope of this qualification will be examined in relation to negligence and negligent misstatement in Parts 2 and 3, below, respectively.

The equality proposition has also been argued to require that administrators have a duty of care to ensure they do not act in excess or abuse of power. It is a matter of controversy as to whether there exists such an "administrative tort", arising because the action was ultra vires, rather than because the action involved a lack of care in avoiding foreseeable harm. In reality, since no private individual can be liable in this category of negligence, the equality proposition would be infringed by its existence. On the other hand, the administrative tort, at least superficially, offers a common law response to the imbalance of power between government and individuals. The arguments for and against an administrative tort are examined in Part 4, below. These arguments for infringement of the equality proposition are usefully compared with those relating to another tort which is available against government, but not individuals. This is misfeasance in public office, which is examined in Part 5, below. Breach of statutory duty, a tort available against government and private individuals, but more frequently government, will not be examined. The principle in *Beaudesert Shire Council v Smith*,[12] in terms of its formulation, has applied equally to private individuals and public authorities. In its operation it offended the equality proposition in that a critical element of the tort—"unlawful, intentional and positive acts"—tended to be established more readily in the case of a public authority, whose power is limited by statute and the common law principles of administrative law. Since the principle was recently overruled by the High Court in *Northern Territory v Mengel*,[13] it will not be considered further.

This essay also examines the position of government in the equity context, confining attention to the doctrine of equitable estoppel. The principle that estoppel cannot be raised against government in judicial review operates as a qualification to the equality proposition. Attempts to confine the principle have promoted the equality proposition, but have raised new questions, such as whether the policy/operational distinction developed in private law can be translated to the context of estoppel in public law. Moreover, it is problematic whether the principles relating to estoppel ought to apply without qualification in private law actions brought against government. These questions are examined in Part 6, below.

2. NEGLIGENCE

General principles or incrementalism?

The equality proposition is regularly asserted in negligence cases, in the form of the principle that it is well-established that the ordinary principles

---

12. (1966) 120 CLR 145. In *Beaudesert* the High Court held that "independently of trespass, negligence or nuisance but by an action for damages upon the case a person who suffers harm or loss as the inevitable consequence of the unlawful, intentional and positive acts of another is entitled to recover damages from that other."
13. (1995) 129 ALR 1.

of negligence apply to public authorities.[14] However, in the same cases the courts affirm restrictions upon the scope for finding a duty of care of public authorities—restrictions which do not apply where the defendant is a private individual.

Whether a duty of care arises under the law of negligence turns upon whether there exists a relationship of proximity between the parties with respect to the class of act or omission alleged to be tortious and the relevant kind of damage.[15] Where the injury is physical, the law tends to be more settled, and reasonable foreseeability of such injury normally suffices to establish the relationship of proximity. In the field of economic loss, the principles are still developing. In these novel factual situations, the High Court regards the relationship of proximity as a conceptual framework within which necessary factual components in the relationship may be articulated for each situation, together with policy considerations limiting the scope of liability.[16] Commonly reliance on the wrongdoer or an assumption of responsibility by the wrongdoer will be a central necessary factual component.[17] A common policy consideration is that liability should not be imposed by the courts "in an indeterminate amount for an indeterminate time to an indeterminate class".[18] This is a consideration which applies irrespective of whether the defendant is government or a private individual. An alternative approach of Brennan J acknowledges that liability is a matter of "incremental" development of the common law by the exercise of judicial discretion in hard cases where new categories of the duty of care are discovered.[19] Proximity is recognised to be a conceptual umbrella of little practical assistance, rather than a principle which provides guidance to government and individuals in assessing liability in these novel factual situations.

The two approaches share an abandonment of the idea that there is one general principle or test which indicates for all factual situations whether a duty of care exists.[20] It is curious then that the courts have continued to

14. *Shire of Sutherland v Heyman* (1984) 157 CLR 424 at 436, 445 per Gibbs CJ and Wilson J, at 457-458 per Mason J.
15. *Bryan v Maloney* (1995) 128 ALR 163 at 165.
16. Ibid at 165-166 per Mason CJ, Deane and Gaudron JJ; at 193, 197-199 per Toohey J.
17. *Shire of Sutherland v Heyman* (1984) 157 CLR 424 at 508; *Bryan v Maloney* (1995) 128 ALR 163 at 166.
18. *Ultramares Corp v Touche* (1931) 174 NE 441 at 444 per Cardozo J, quoted in *Bryan v Maloney* (1995) 128 ALR 163 at 166, 169. See also *L Shaddock & Assoc Pty Ltd v City of Parramatta* (1980) 150 CLR 225 at 231 per Gibbs CJ; *San Sebastian Pty Ltd v Minister Administering the Environmental Planning and Assessment Act 1979* (1986) 162 CLR 340 at 353-354 per Gibbs CJ, Mason, Wilson and Dawson JJ; at 367 per Brennan J. A second common policy consideration is that in a competitive world damaging another person economically may be done legitimately in the pursuit of personal advantage: *Bryan v Maloney* (1995) 128 ALR 163 at 166.
19. *Council of the Shire of Sutherland v Heyman* (1984) 157 CLR 424 at per Brennan J; *San Sebastian Pty Ltd* (1986) 162 CLR 340 at 367-369 per Brennan J; *Bryan v Maloney* (1995) 128 ALR 163 at 191-192 per Brennan J. In *Murphy v Brentwood District Council* [1991] 1 AC 398 the House of Lords adopted Brennan J's incrementalist approach in preference to general principles (the two-stage test formulated by Lord Wilberforce in *Anns*) for ascertaining a duty of care.
20. However, there is force in the argument of Brennan J that the "amorphous notion of proximity" with its inclusion of policy considerations, is a return to the two-stage test of Lord Wilberforce in *Anns*, which the High Court rejected in *Heyman*: see *Bryan v Maloney* (1995) 128 ALR 163 at 192-193.

articulate a general policy consideration which restricts the liability of government, apparently in all categories of negligence. This policy consideration offends the equality proposition. It is the policy/operational distinction.

Origins of the policy/operational distinction

The policy/operational distinction has its origins in the judgment of Lord Wilberforce in *Anns v Merton London Borough Council.*[21] Lord Wilberforce (with whom four other Lords agreed) formulated a two-stage test of the existence and scope of a duty of care in the law of negligence. The two-stage test was intended to provide one general test of negligence which would account for existing categories of negligence and for novel factual situations where it was argued that a duty of care arose. First, there must exist a sufficient relationship of proximity or neighbourhood between the wrongdoer and plaintiff "such that in the reasonable contemplation of the former, carelessness on his part may be likely to cause damage to the latter—in which case a prima facie duty of care arises". A second stage arises in some factual situations on account of public policy. The court should consider "whether there are any considerations which ought to negative, or to reduce or limit the scope of the duty or the class of person to whom it is owed or the damages to which a breach of it may give rise". In Lord Wilberforce's view, a council is in a relationship of proximity with owners and occupiers of houses which later are found to have structural defects not detected by council inspectors. However, a consideration which might negative or limit the scope of the duty, at the second stage of the test, is the council's status as a public body with statutory powers and duties defined within the realm of public law. Lord Wilberforce held that at the second stage of the test the restriction upon government liability rests upon a distinction between "policy" and "operational" decisions. "Policy" decisions are those which may require an administrator "to strike a balance between the claims of efficiency and thrift",[22] such as a decision of a council regarding the number of inspectors to be appointed. "Operational" decisions are decisions made to execute policy decisions, such as the actual performance of an inspection. A common law duty of care will be more easily imposed upon "operational" decisions than upon policy or "planning" decisions.

21. [1978] AC 728. Although *Anns* is conventionally accepted as commencing point for the policy/operational distinction in Anglo-Australian law, the distinction was adopted in 1976 by Ward J, following textwriters and *East Suffolk Rivers Catchment Board v Kent* [1941] AC 74, in holding prison authorities in breach of a duty of care towards unsentenced prisoners: *L v Commonwealth* (1976) 10 ALR 269 at 276.

22. Ibid at 754, quoting from the judgment of du Parcq LJ in *Kent v East Suffolk Rivers Catchment Board* [1940] 1 KB 319 at 338. Lord Wilberforce also relied upon some of the reasoning in *Dutton v Bognor Regis Urban District Council* [1972] 1 QB 373 and *Ayr Harbour Trustees v Oswald* (1883) 8 App Cas 623 at 639. The distinction had been explicitly drawn in Canadian cases not cited by Lord Wilberforce. See especially *Welbridge Holdings Ltd v Metropolitan Corp of Greater Winnipeg* (1970) 12 DLR (3d) 124.

There is a suggestion in the speech of Lord Wilberforce in *Anns* that there may be scope for establishing breach of a duty of care where there is a discretionary element, whether the decision falls into the policy or operational area, if it is shown that the administrator acted ultra vires.[23] The council in *Anns* would have been liable for failure to inspect, if this reflected implementation of an ultra vires policy not to make any inspections. This suggestion, narrowing the application of the policy/operational distinction to intra vires decisions, emphasises the importance of statute in justifying departure from the equality proposition. An administrative decision made in excess or abuse of power is governed by the ordinary principles of negligence, for here it is inappropriate to protect the administrator from interference by the courts—the administrator had no authority to make the policy choices which have resulted in loss.

Lord Wilberforce acknowledged in *Anns* that the distinction between policy and operational areas was "one of degree", since many operational powers and duties have elements of discretion in them.[24] The question is whether the distinction is nevertheless a "convenient" one, as Lord Wilberforce claimed. The idea that administrative decision-making can be classified into a sphere of policy-making at senior levels of the Executive and a sphere of administration, or mechanical implementation of policy by their subordinate officers, has been long criticised in public administration theory. Peter Wilenski has described the distinction as a myth which is continually resurrected because it provides a convenient basis for legitimising administrative decisions.[25] Administrative decision-making is not a mechanical application of pre-existing rules, but involves the exercise of discretion at every level of the executive hierarchy:

> "belief in the policy-administration dichotomy which, no matter how often it is destroyed in the academic literature, remains as the dominant paradigm for practitioners of public administration almost everywhere and nowhere more so than in Australian public services. Basically the dichotomy refers to the view that policy-making and administration are separate activities, the first being a political activity based on value choices and undertaken by elected office-bearers and the second being a neutral instrumental activity based on professional expertise and carried out by appointed officials . . . What academics insist upon and practitioners resist—is that each act of 'administration' defines and refines 'policy' and itself is a 'policy-making' activity. It requires the exercise of value judgments."[26]

23. "But this duty, heavily operational though it may be, is still a duty arising under the statute. There may a discretionary element in its exercise—discretionary as to the time and manner of inspection, and the techniques to be used. A plaintiff complaining of negligence must prove, the burden being on him, that action taken was not within the limits of a discretion bona fide exercised, before he can begin to rely upon a common law duty of care. But if he can do this, he should, in principle, be able to sue": *Anns* [1978] AC 728 at 755. See also at 757-758, 760.
24. At 754.
25. P Wilenski, *Public Power and Public Administration* (Hale & Ironmonger, Sydney, 1986), pp 51-54; R Stewart, "The Reformation of American Administrative Law" (1975) 88 Harv Law Rev 1667 at 1675-1681; R Baldwin and R Hawkins, "Discretionary Justice: Davis Reconsidered" (1984) PL 570.
26. Wilenski, op cit, pp 51-52.

If Wilenski and other theorists are correct in their analysis of administrative decision-making, there is serious doubt as to whether the policy/administration distinction can claim to draw a convenient or even a rough line between two types of administrative decision-making. Whilst a small number of decisions may be exclusively of a policy nature, a discretionary policy-making function permeates the administrative process. The presence of policy-making or the exercise of strong discretion may fail to identify those areas which Lord Wilberforce sought to privilege from the duty of care. However, since *Anns*, courts have explained the rationale of the policy/operational distinction, providing an opportunity to consider whether such a qualification to the equality proposition is certain and justified.

Heyman's case and the policy/operational distinction

The leading Australian authority on government liability in negligence is *Shire of Sutherland v Heyman*,[27] a case concerned with the liability of a local council where a building purchased by the plaintiff was found to have structural defects. Although, on the facts of *Heyman* the council was not liable, the decision affirms that public authorities may be liable for negligent failure to act when under a duty to do so, or for negligence in the exercise of a power where the plaintiff has relied upon the authority.[28]

Mason, Brennan and Deane JJ rejected the notion that there are general principles for determining whether a duty of care arises, as in Lord Wilberforce's two-stage test, and emphasised the importance of reliance in establishing a duty of care.[29] The approach of Mason and Deane JJ to future development of principles governing the duty of care differed from the approach of Brennan J at a theoretical level, and that difference has persisted.[30] It does not affect the argument which follows regarding the continued adherence to the policy/operational distinction as a policy consideration restricting the liability of government.

In *Heyman*, Gibbs CJ, Mason, Wilson and Deane JJ endorsed the policy/operational distinction.[31] Gibbs CJ (with whom Wilson J agreed) described the distinction as "a logical and convenient one".[32] Mason J appreciated the usefulness of the policy/operational distinction in excluding the courts from interfering in policy decisions of the Executive branch regarding the allocation of resources where questions of "efficiency and thrift" play a part.[33] However, Mason J was troubled as to how the courts should approach operational decisions which contain elements of discretion:

27. (1984) 157 CLR 424.
28. See text accompanying nn 50-57, 118-119, below.
29. Gibbs CJ (with whom Wilson J agreed) attempted to explain and apply Lord Wilberforce's test.
30. See the description of the two approaches in the text accompanying nn 15-20, a difference still evident in *Bryan v Maloney* (1995) 128 ALR 163.
31. (1984) 157 CLR 424 at 438-439, 442, 468, 471, 500.
32. Ibid at 442.
33. Ibid at 468.

"It is possible that a duty of care may exist in relation to discretionary considerations which stand outside the policy category in the division between policy factors on the one hand and operational factors on the other. This classification has evolved in the judicial interpretation of the 'discretionary function' exception in the United States *Federal Tort Claims Act*."[34]

Mason J implicitly recognised that the presence or absence of discretion does not provide a necessary and sufficient test for distinguishing the policy area from the operational area. He provided a rationale for the distinction by reference to the nature of the discretion, amplifying Lord Wilberforce's reference to noninterference in matters of efficiency and thrift:

"The distinction between the policy and operational factors is not easy to formulate, but the dividing line between them will be observed if we recognise that a public authority is under no duty of care in relation to decisions which involve or are dictated by financial, economic, social or political factors or constraints. Thus budgetary allocations and the constraints which they entail in terms of allocation of resources cannot be made the subject of a duty of care. But it may be otherwise when the courts are called upon to apply a standard of care to action or inaction that is merely the product of administrative direction, expert or professional opinion, technical standards or general standards of reasonableness."[35]

This passage conveys the impression that the policy/operational distinction has been expressed too broadly, and requires reformulation to reflect its rationale more accurately. The types of administrative decisions which the distinction is intended to privilege from the duty of care are discretionary decisions concerning allocation of scarce resources and similar types of decisions involving social or political factors.[36] Although the rationale is specifically noninterference by courts in governmental resource allocation, this description has the strong flavour of the test of justiciability of nonstatutory powers in public law. At general law this is a "political questions" test which excludes from judicial review a decision which is a complex mix of political factors, particularly if made at the highest level of the Executive branch and related to national security or international relations.[37] A more explicit linking of the policy/operational distinction of private law with the public law concept of justiciability was made three years later, in the Privy Council decision *Rowling v Takaro Properties Ltd*, which is considered below.[38]

34. Ibid at 469.
35. Ibid.
36. P P Craig, "Negligence in the Exercise of a Statutory Power" (1978) LQR 428 at 456.
37. *Minister for Arts, Heritage and the Environment v Peko-Wallsend Ltd* (1987) 75 ALR 218. The allocation of quotas of a scarce resource to a class of recipients is regarded as an instance of a "polycentric" decision which is typically unsuitable for review by an adjudicative tribunal, such as the Administrative Appeals Tribunal, although some of its jurisdiction does fall into this category. See Administrative Review Council, *Eleventh Annual Report 1986-87* (AGPS, Canberra, 1987), Ch 9.
38. [1988] 1 AC 473. See discussion text accompanying nn 68-74, below.

In *Heyman*, Mason J proceeded to consider whether there was proximity giving rise to a duty of care. Presumably this was done on the basis of an assessment by Mason J that the council inspector's decision about the soundness of the particular house's frame was an operational one which involved an element of discretion in the formation of expert opinion. The issue of whether foundations were to be inspected in relation to every building application was a policy or planning matter, in relation to which no duty of care arose.

One possible interpretation of the approach of Mason J is that the policy/operational distinction is an initial hurdle to be overcome by a plaintiff who sues a public authority in negligence, before the reliance test is applied. As a precondition to the court's proceeding to consider whether there was a relationship of proximity or whether incremental development of the law should include a new category of factual situation as generating a duty of care, the distinction would operate like a justiciability test in public law.

In *Heyman*, Deane J expressed the rationale for the policy/operational distinction as "a matter of assumed legislative intent".[39] There must be an express or implied intent in the relevant legislation that the administrator is to enjoy immunity from liability to private individuals. Such a legislative intent can normally be implied "where what is involved are actions taken in the exercise of policy-making powers and functions of a quasi-legislative character".[40] Since *Heyman* concerned powers of a routine or operational nature, the requisite legislative intent to exclude liability could not be implied:

> "No such legislative intent can be assumed however in a case, such as the present, where the relevant powers and functions are of a routine administrative or 'operational' nature. In such a case, the mere fact that a public body or instrumentality is exercising statutory powers and functions does not mean that it enjoys immunity from liability to private individuals under the ordinary law beyond the extent that there can be actually discerned in the relevant legislation an express or implied intent that the private rights of individuals be displaced or subordinated. Nor does it mean that the existence of the statutory powers or functions, the assumption of responsibility which may be involved in their exercise, or any reliance which may be placed upon a presumption that they have been or are being properly exercised is to be ignored or discounted in determining whether there existed in the relationship between public body or instrumentality and private citizen a degree of proximity which was adequate to give rise to a duty of care under the principles of common law negligence."[41]

On this analysis, interpretation of the statute is contingent upon how the power was exercised. A statutory power may be exercised at a broad level, by setting policy regarding the extent and procedure for building inspections. The same power is also exercised in a more practical fashion

---

39. (1984) 157 CLR 424 at 500.
40. Ibid.
41. Ibid at 500-501.

by the inspectors themselves, probably as delegates, in actual building inspections. According to Deane J, legislative intent with regard to liability in negligence differs according to whether the power is exercised at the first order or at the second order. This "legislative intent" analysis fails to avoid the problem of the blurred nature of the policy/operational distinction. Certainly Deane J emphasised that the fact that the powers exercised have a statutory source need not detract from the fact that a person had placed reliance upon the public authority so as to create a sufficient degree of proximity to give rise to a duty of care. However, Deane J was clearly concerned, as was Mason J, to exclude from liability in negligence government decisions of a "policy" or "quasi-legislative nature", irrespective of any reliance placed upon their proper exercise.

Brennan J did not expressly deal with the policy/operational distinction. Having embraced an incrementalist approach to development of novel categories of negligence, Brennan J regarded the fate of the second stage of Lord Wilberforce's test as follows:

> "The proper role of the 'second stage', as I attempted to explain in *Jaensch v Coffey* (1984) 155 CLR at 576, embraces no more than 'those further elements [in addition to the neighbour principle] which are appropriate to the particular category of negligence and which confine the duty of care within narrower limits than those which would be defined by an unqualified application of the neighbour principle."[42]

Brennan J did not endorse a general policy consideration restricting government liability in all categories of negligence. It is likely that he regarded the policy/operational distinction as unhelpful, like Lord Wilberforce's two-stage test or the concept of proximity. Rather, he recognised the possibility of particular principles limiting liability in a manner appropriate to the particular category of negligence. Having concluded that there was no statutory or common law basis for finding a relationship of proximity in *Heyman* itself, Brennan J concluded the council had no duty of care. There was no need for him to proceed to consider how such a duty may need to be restricted. If he had done, the policy or principle identified would have been particular to the factual situation of the duty owed by a council to a building owner with regard to compliance with statutory requirements.

Breach of duty of care where ultra vires exercise of discretion

In *Heyman*, Gibbs CJ (Wilson J agreeing) accepted the proposition of Lord Wilberforce[43] that administrators may be in breach of a duty of care in relation to discretionary decisions, whether in the policy or operational area, if the decision is an excess or abuse of power. Gibbs CJ regarded the inspection as an operational decision with an element of discretion. Having accepted, as Lord Wilberforce did, that where an inspection is made the

42. Ibid at 481.
43. See text accompanying n 23, above.

action or omission is "heavily operational",[44] the plaintiff has the burden of proving that the action was taken in excess of the discretion bona fide exercised:[45]

> "If the performance of their duties or the exercise of their powers involves the exercise of a discretion, an act will not be negligent if it was done in good faith in the exercise of, and within the limits of the discretion."[46]

This appears to have been critical to Gibbs CJ's conclusion that the inspector did not act negligently in inspecting only the frame of the house. It was important in the present case that "there was no evidence that [the inspector] acted other than in the bona fide exercise of his discretion in inspecting the frame only".[47]

On the other hand, Mason J in *Heyman* said that despite Lord Wilberforce's view in *Anns* regarding the policy and discretion area, "there is no compelling reason for confining such a duty of care to situations in which a public authority or its officers are acting in excess of power or authority."[48] The scope for arguing that a duty of care arises in relation to intra vires policy decisions, or intra vires operational decisions with a discretionary element, remains unclear. There is a core area of policy-making which Mason J, despite his difference with Lord Wilberforce, would regard as immune from any liability in negligence.[49] All that is common ground in *Heyman* is that a duty of care arises in relation to ultra vires actions in the policy and discretionary area. Possibly these dicta of Lord Wilberforce, Gibbs CJ and Mason J are of some relevance to the issue of whether there exists an administrative tort, a question examined in Part 4, below.

Reliance and government liability

Since the component of reliance developed by Mason, Brennan and Deane JJ in *Heyman* is an important factor in establishing proximity in actions for damages for economic loss, the relationship of reliance with the policy/operational distinction needs to be understood.[50]

Mason J held that reliance may be either general or specific. General reliance by the public is rarely the source of a duty of care. However, Mason J provided three examples of general reliance, drawn from United States authorities, which he would apparently have been prepared to follow

44. (1984) 157 CLR 424 at 439.
45. Ibid at 439, quoting from Lord Wilberforce in *Anns* [1978] AC 728 at 755.
46. Ibid at 442.
47. Ibid at 448.
48. Ibid at 458. The other members of the High Court did not deal with this aspect of Lord Wilberforce's judgment.
49. See text accompanying nn 33-37, above.
50. Gibbs CJ held that the fact that a statutory power or duty confers no private right upon any individual member of the public, but is enacted for the benefit of the public generally, does not indicate that no duty of care is owed at common law: *Heyman* (1984) 157 CLR 424 at 436. Rather than directly considering whether a duty of care may be implied from a statute, Gibbs CJ slid into consideration of a particular type of nonfeasance: see nn 118-119, below.

in similar situations. In these cases government liability arose in situations of general reliance by the public on government responsibility for air traffic controllers, the inspection and certification of civil aircraft, and the fighting of fire in a building by a fire authority.[51] Mason J regarded as a more complex question whether the inspection of motor vehicles for registration purposes generates such a general reliance. What the three examples have in common is:

> "Reliance or dependence in this general sense is in general the product of the grant (and exercise) of powers designed to prevent or minimise a risk of personal injury or disability, recognised by the legislature as being of such magnitude or complexity that individuals cannot, or may not, take adequate steps for their own protection. This situation generates on one side (the individual) a general expectation that the power will be exercised and on the other side (the authority) a realisation that there is a general reliance or dependence on its exercise of power."[52]

Mason J concluded in *Heyman* that the building owners had not advanced a case of general reliance and would encounter great difficulty in establishing such a case where the statutory scheme includes provision for a certificate of compliance, and permits inquiries to be made regarding inspections or use of one's own expert.[53]

Mason J held that more commonly a duty of care arises on account of reliance in the specific circumstances of the plaintiff on account of the contributing conduct of the public authority, usually of a positive character:[54]

> "There are situations in which a public authority, not otherwise under a relevant duty, may place itself in such a position that others rely on it to take care for their safety so that the authority comes under a duty of care calling for positive action."[55]

In *Heyman* Mason J found no evidence of specific reliance.[56] Although Brennan and Deane JJ did not expressly adopt the language of general or specific reliance, their approach was the same as that of Mason J.[57]

After Heyman's case

The upshot of *Heyman* was that while the High Court rejected the two-stage test of Lord Wilberforce, Gibbs CJ, Mason, Wilson and Deane JJ

51. At 462-464.
52. Ibid at 464.
53. Ibid at 470-471.
54. Ibid at 460, 463-464.
55. Ibid at 461.
56. Reliance would have been shown by the owners having obtained a certificate pursuant to the *Local Government Act* 1919 (NSW), s 317A of compliance with legislative requirements, or having made inquiries of the council. However, there was no evidence of their reliance on the council's having satisfied itself of the stability of the foundations: (1984) 157 CLR 424 at 470.
57. At 486, 508. Brennan J added that any "special element restricting a cause of action for negligence occasioning damage of that kind is satisfied": at 486.

retained the policy/operational distinction. This is a rather curious position. A rejection of the idea that there is a general test which determines whether a duty of care arises in new factual situations would seem to compel a rejection of a general principle for restricting government liability in those new situations. [58] In the aftermath of *Heyman* the role of the policy/operational distinction has remained uncertain in relation to negligence generally, and negligence of highway authorities and occupiers.

General negligence

In *Skuse v Commonwealth* [59] the Full Federal Court held that the Commonwealth had no general duty of care arising from its administration of the system of justice to care for the safety of people in courthouses under its control. Lockhart J (with whom Northrop J agreed) held that the courts should not permit, through private law actions for damages in negligence against the Commonwealth, interference in the area of the Commonwealth's responsibility for security of courts, and judges' control of activities within their courts:

> "These are delicate matters requiring care and respect on the part of all concerned. They demonstrate that the preservation of public safety within court houses is closely associated with matters of policy which involve the various arms of government and which do not fit happily with the general law of negligence resting, as it does, upon the standards of the reasonable man." [60]

Whilst there was no reference to the policy/operational distinction, the argument for excluding courts from scrutinising high level policy decisions concerning resource allocation matched the rationale provided by Lord Wilberforce and by Mason J.

58. A similar position emerged in the United Kingdom. In *Murphy v Brentwood District Council* [1991] 1 AC 398 the House of Lords accepted the reasoning of Brennan and Deane JJ in *Heyman* as compelling and concluded that *Anns* was wrongly decided and that *Dutton v Bognor Regis Urban District Council* [1972] 1 QB 373 should be overruled. The House of Lords rejected the two-stage test of Lord Wilberforce and adopted Brennan J's incrementalist approach to arguments for a duty of care in novel factual situations. However, the House of Lords did not spell out the implications of its decision for the policy/operational distinction.
59. (1985) 62 ALR 108.
60. Ibid at 118. Nevertheless, Lockhart J considered whether a duty of care of the Commonwealth arose in the particular factual situation where an assailant who had previously made threats of violence with regard to other people on account of his experiences with justice and the law, shot a barrister inside the Alice Springs courthouse. Lockhart J concluded that there was no duty of care. Cf *Wodrow v Commonwealth* (1993) 45 FCR 52 where the Full Federal Court did not mention the policy/operational distinction in concluding that no duty of care was owed to a public servant who suffered a stress reaction when he was directed to recall a report which he had distributed without approval and in breach of his instructions. The ordinary principles relating to liability in negligence with regard to psychiatric damage applied to the public authority which employed him. There was a relationship of proximity between the officer who issued the memorandum giving the direction, with its threat of disciplinary action, but the psychiatric damage was not foreseeable and there were no special circumstances indicating this employee should be treated differently.

The concept of general reliance of Mason J in *Heyman* was accepted by McHugh JA in the New South Wales Court of Appeal decision in *Parramatta City Council v Lutz*.[61] In this case a council breached its duty of care to a plaintiff houseowner to exercise its statutory powers to order the demolition of a derelict house next door, from which a fire spread to the plaintiff's property. McHugh JA was prepared to extend the concept of general reliance to a subject which may not be perceived to be a hazard, but which, in terms of the statutory power, was a "building in . . . a dilapidated or unsightly condition". The policy/operational distinction was not considered.

The policy/operational distinction was considered in *McCauley v Hamilton Island Enterprises Pty Ltd*,[62] a case concerning injuries suffered when a helicopter attempted to land on a pontoon. Part IX of the Air Navigation Regulations provided for the licensing of aerodromes and prohibited the use of unlicensed places for taking off or landing of aircraft.[63] The Commonwealth sought to have struck out part of the statement of claim alleging negligence due to nonfeasance—the Commonwealth's failure to take action to stop the use of the unlicensed pontoon as an aerodrome. Beaumont J dismissed the strike-out motion, holding the plaintiff had an arguable case that the Commonwealth owed him a common law duty "to try to forestall and prevent a peril".[64]

Applying Mason J's definition and examples of general reliance in *Heyman*,[65] Beaumont J was inclined to regard the case before him as sufficiently similar to the examples to be a case of general reliance. General reliance upon the responsibility of the Commonwealth, by implication from the Air Navigation Regulations, satisfied the test of proximity giving rise to a duty of care, and was not restricted by the policy/operational distinction.

Had Beaumont J applied the policy/operational distinction, the failure to monitor would have appeared to be a policy decision, or an operational decision with a large policy element. Discretionary resource allocation would clearly be a prominent aspect of governmental decisions to permit helicopters to use a pontoon as an aerodrome and to monitor breaches of the regulations. How then was the reliance component to be reconciled with the policy/operational distinction? Beaumont J said:

> "Moreover, a real question arises here whether a duty of care should
> be excluded merely on 'policy' or 'discretionary' grounds. It is at least
> doubtful whether that exception could have any application here."[66]

61. (1988) 12 NSWLR 293 at 330-331. Kirby P did not explicitly accept Mason J's notion of general reliance, and may only have applied the reliance principle common to the judgments of Mason, Brennan and Deane JJ. Mahoney JA based his judgment on negligent misstatement rather than general negligence.
62. (1987) 75 ALR 257.
63. Ibid at 263.
64. *Hargrave v Goldman* (1963) 110 CLR 40 at 66 per Windeyer J, and subsequent authorities, cited in *McCauley* (1987) 75 ALR 257 at 262.
65. See text accompanying nn 51-52, above.
66. *McCauley* (1987) 75 ALR 257 at 263.

Beaumont J regarded the High Court decision in *Heyman* as having altered the impact of the policy/operational distinction.[67] This is the converse of the position which I suggested might be inferred from the judgment of Mason J in *Heyman*—that the policy/operational distinction is a preliminary hurdle whose non-fulfilment will indicate the court will not proceed to consider whether reliance establishes proximity.

Doubts about the viability of the policy/operational distinction were fully articulated in the Privy Council decision of *Rowling v Takaro Properties Ltd*.[68] *Takaro* differs from other cases considered so far because it raised the issue of whether government is liable in negligence on a basis which cannot apply to a private individual: for breach of a duty of care not to exercise statutory power unlawfully. On account of policy considerations particular to this category of negligence, called administrative tort, the Privy Council was inclined to hold there was no duty of care.[69]

In *Takaro* a developer whose tourist resort project had fallen into financial difficulties arranged a rescue attempt, in which shares were to be issued to a Japanese company. When the New Zealand Minister of Finance, pursuant to a statutory power, refused to give consent to the share issue, the rescue attempt failed and the developer sought damages for economic loss. It was argued that the Minister had abused his power by taking into account the irrelevant consideration that if the development did not proceed the land would revert to indigenous ownership. In the event, on the findings of fact, the Privy Council held that no error of law was made and there was no breach of a duty of care if one did exist.

The present discussion is confined to the approach taken by the Privy Council to the role of the policy/operational distinction. Whilst the judge at first instance regarded the Minister's decision as "the antithesis of policy or discretion",[70] Lord Keith, delivering the judgment of the Privy Council, held the decision was capable of being characterised as of a policy nature and cast doubt on the usefulness of the policy/operational distinction:

> "[Their Lordships] incline to the opinion, expressed in the literature, that this distinction [the policy/operational distinction] does not provide a touchstone of liability, but rather is expressive of the need to exclude altogether those cases in which the decision under attack is of such a kind that a question whether it has been made negligently is unsuitable for judicial resolution, of which notable examples are discretionary decisions on the allocation of scarce resources or the

67. Beaumont J referred ((1987) 75 ALR 257 at 263) to *Sasin v Commonwealth* (1984) 52 ALR 299, which was decided prior to the High Court's decision, and which applied the New South Wales Court of Appeal decision in *Heyman*. In *Sasin* Hodgson J dismissed a claim in negligence against the Commonwealth for approving a seat belt reel in an aircraft, on the ground that this approval was a policy rather than an operational decision. Beaumont J implied that that case may have been decided differently had the High Court decision been available.
68. [1988] 1 AC 473.
69. See text accompanying nn 121-123, below.
70. [1986] 1 NZLR 22 at 35.

distribution of risks: see especially the discussion in *Craig on Administrative Law* (1983), pp 534-538. If this is right, classification of the relevant decision as a policy or planning decision in this sense may exclude liability; but a conclusion that it does not fall within that category does not, in their Lordships' opinion, mean that a duty of care will necessarily exist."[71]

Despite having formed the view that the Minister's decision fell into the policy area, Lord Keith held there was the potential for establishing a duty of care because the allegation of negligence was not "of itself of such a character as to render the case unsuitable for judicial decision".[72] Whilst Lord Wilberforce in *Anns* and Mason J in *Heyman* had acknowledged that a duty of care may arise in relation to discretionary decisions in the operational area, Lord Keith in *Takaro* held that a duty of care may arise in relation to some discretionary decisions falling into the policy area. Lord Keith explicitly linked the rationale and scope of the policy/operational distinction in private law with the rationale and scope of the concept of justiciability in public law.[73] The description of the test of justiciability is, however, very loose. Some decisions allocating resources are justiciable, and distribution of risk has not featured as an explicit factor in the test of justiciability. According to *Takaro* then, a duty of care may be owed in respect of policy decisions or operational decisions with discretionary components, which do not fall foul of this loose justiciability concept. Of course proximity must be established and account taken of any other policy considerations relevant to that category of negligence.[74]

Despite the doubts expressed in *McCauley* and *Takaro*, in *Alec Finlayson Pty Ltd v Armidale City Council*,[75] Burchett J regarded the policy/operational distinction as still applicable. A developer brought a negligence action against the Armidale City Council in respect of its decision to rezone the site of a timber treatment works as residential, and its decision to approve a development application for subdivision of the site for residential purposes. The sole issue was whether the council had a duty of care to the developer who had purchased the site without having any reason to suspect that it was contaminated. The Council's city health surveyor had for many years been involved in investigating complaints of creosote and arsenic contamination on and nearby the site. Burchett J held that no duty of care arose with respect to the decision to rezone the land,

71. [1988] 1 AC 473 at 501.
72. Ibid.
73. This link is evoked by the expression "unsuited for judicial resolution" and was advocated by Craig in *Administrative Law* (Sweet & Maxwell, London, 1983), pp 534-538, which was cited by Lord Keith.
74. In a more recent attempt to argue for an administrative tort in the United Kingdom, *Lonrho Plc v Tebbit* [1992] 4 All ER 280, the defendant Secretary of State sought to strike out a claim that he had negligently failed to release a company from an undertaking as soon as it ceased to be in the public interest to maintain it. The Court of Appeal regarded the policy/operational distinction as still in place. However the court accepted the criticism of the distinction made by Lord Keith in *Takaro* and regarded this as providing further support for an incrementalist approach to novel categories of negligence: *Tebbit* at 287.
75. (1994) 123 ALR 155.

because this decision fell into the policy area. The court should not interfere with the council's policy decision regarding the amount of resources devoted to investigation of the suitability of the land for the proposed zoning.[76] However, the approval of the development application fell within the operational area. Here, a duty of care could be established on account of specific reliance. The council's approval of the development application was a positive act which created a danger. A duty of care of the council arose to take reasonable care to avoid threatened injury. However, a duty of care could also be established on the basis of general reliance. The council had a statutory duty to take into account risks in determining development applications.[77]

According to Burchett J, the rationale of general reliance lies in the *control* which a public authority exercises in circumstances where it is in a superior position to investigate and assess a hidden hazard in comparison to ordinary individuals who, on account of the complexity of modern life, have to rely on the due performance of the functions of the public authority.[78] An ordinary individual, even a developer, cannot be expected to take responsibility for obtaining chemical analyses of land which is zoned residential.

Burchett J added to the three examples provided by Mason J in *Heyman*, the example in *Parramatta City Council v Lutz* and the example in *McCauley*, a sixth category of general reliance in the context of government control over hazards of chemical contamination of land. However, with respect to the zoning decision, the policy/operational distinction precluded a duty of care and the argument for general reliance was not considered. *Alec Finlayson* suggests that the policy/operational distinction is a precondition to be satisfied before a court proceeds to consider whether there is general or specific reliance and other policy considerations relevant to the particular category of negligence. If it were otherwise, in similar fashion to Beaumont J in *McCauley*, Burchett J would have concluded that the decision to rezone the land was also subject to a duty of care on account of the general reliance individuals place upon the council.

McCauley and *Alec Finlayson* expose a tension between the policy/operational distinction and the component of general reliance in the concept of proximity. Why did the zoning decision, but not the development application decision, fall into the policy area? Was the zoning decision a policy decision in terms of the approach of Mason J in *Heyman* and Lord Keith in *Takaro*? A zoning decision has nothing to do with allocation of resources or (normally) distribution of risks and does not seem to be non-justiciable for any other reason. By finding the council had a duty of care with respect to the operational decision to grant the development application, the court in any event indirectly interfered with the policy decision about zoning the land. In *Alec Finlayson* it was pointless to privilege the zoning decision and not the development application decision.

76. Ibid at 182.
77. Pursuant to the *Environmental Planning and Assessment Act* 1979 (NSW), s 90: ibid at 187.
78. Ibid at 188.

A case of general reliance can potentially be argued by any resident who suffers loss as a result of a rezoning decision, particularly if it is relatively site-specific. The general reliance cases will tend to challenge the policy/operational distinction. An exercise of power intended to prevent or minimise risk or personal injury or disability is a typical case for arguing general reliance, but also is a typical case for failing the policy/operational distinction understood according to the *Takaro* rationale, because it is concerned with risk distribution. The concepts of technical complexity of the subject matter of decision, the public authority's control over hazards, and the taking of a positive step by the public authority are all present.

Highway authorities

Principles relating to negligence of highway authorities have developed from old authorities, without reference to the policy/operational distinction. It is well established that highway authorities have no duty of care in respect of nonfeasance, but only in respect of misfeasance.[79] This rule applies to the Commonwealth in its capacity as a highway authority. The rule was affirmed following *Heyman* in *McDonagh v Commonwealth*,[80] where the Full Federal Court held that failure to do any maintenance work on a highway is not actionable. However, in this case the Commonwealth owed a duty of care and was found negligent, because it had maintained the smooth surface of the road without providing warnings that the edges of the surface were soft and liable to collapse under heavy vehicles. This was a narrow decision. Neaves J dissented on the ground that to hold there was a duty of care would be to impose upon the Commonwealth a duty to ensure that the Mount Franklin Road was maintained to a sufficient standard to permit vehicles weighing 18 tonnes to travel safely upon it.

Superficially, the nonfeasance/misfeasance rule regarding highway authorities reinforces the policy/operational distinction because it achieves the same end: noninterference by courts in government decisions regarding allocation of resources for road building or maintenance. However, the dissenting judgment of Neaves J highlights the fact that permitting liability for misfeasance at the operational level also may involve judicial interference in resource allocation.

Occupiers

In the category of negligence of occupiers, ordinary principles of negligence tend to be applied to government with occasional reference to the policy/operational distinction.[81] The equality proposition has not been

---

79. *Buckle v Bayswater Road Board* (1936) 57 CLR 259; *Gorringe v Transport Commission (Tas)* (1950) 80 CLR 357; *McDonagh v Commonwealth* (1985) 73 ALR 148 at 151, 158.
80. (1985) 73 ALR 148.
81. See *Glasheen v Municipality of Waverley* (1990) Aust Torts Reports 81-016; *Wilmot v South Australia* (1992) 59 SASR 156 at 185-188 (where no planning or policy area could be identified).

accepted in this arena without dissent. There is a view that the liability of public authorities as occupiers ought to be limited, but the basis for the restriction is unclear.

Glasheen v Municipality of Waverley[82] was an action for damages by a girl who sustained injuries making her a quadriplegic, when hit by a surfboard rider at Bondi Beach. She had been swimming in the surf area marked by flags for swimmers, where surfboard riding was prohibited. Shortly before the school vacation the council had reduced the number of beach inspectors from three to two. At the time the injury occurred one inspector was at lunch and the other had walked to the other end of the beach. Sharpe J categorised the decision about the number of inspectors as falling into the policy area. However, Sharpe J held that in the light of the policy reducing the number of beach inspectors to two, the duty of care of the sole inspector on duty during the lunch hour was increased. There was a breach of the duty of care because at that time of day the inspector should have remained near the flagged area in order to carry out his prime responsibility of ensuring the safety of swimmers in that area.[83]

Glasheen illustrates how policy-making and its application are interconnected and how each involves the exercise of discretion. The inspector's failure to keep watch fell into the operational area, parallel with the actual performance of inspections of building work categorised as operational in *Anns* and *Heyman*. The discretionary element of the beach inspector's operational decisions which became important was the decision whether or not to walk away from the flagged area during the lunch hour. Sharpe J held that this discretion was constrained by the council's policy decision to reduce the number of inspectors to two and its exercise was subject to a duty of care. The court indirectly interfered in the policy regarding allocation of resources to beach inspection services by imposing a higher duty of care where only one inspector was on duty. Raising the standard of care compensated for the reduction in the resources made available.

In *Nagle v Rottnest Island Authority*,[84] a majority of the High Court held that the Rottnest Island Authority's predecessor brought itself into a relationship of proximity with members of the public who were encouraged to visit Rottnest Island and to swim there, with respect to any foreseeable risks of injury to which they might be exposed. A breach of duty occurred through failure to erect signs warning that a ledge was unsafe for diving on account of submerged rocks. Whilst Mason CJ, Deane, Dawson and Gaudron JJ in a joint judgment accepted without discussion that the duty of care of a public authority as occupier of land does not differ from the duty of a private occupier of land, Brennan J dissented on the basis that there is a need to differentiate. According to Brennan J, in a situation where

82. (1990) Aust Torts Reports 81-016.
83. The component of reliance required by *Heyman* to establish a duty of care is not spelt out in the judgment. However, it was implicit in the facts that the plaintiff relied on the safety of the flagged area—in the invitation to swimmers to use the flagged area and warnings to surfboard riders not to do so.
84. (1992) 177 CLR 423.

a public authority has control and management of premises on which the public enter, whether the authority has a duty to warn depends on whether such a duty was owed to the public at large. An important factual component is whether the danger of diving at the particular spot was apparent and could be avoided by the exercise of ordinary care. Brennan J concluded that in this case the danger of diving in the particular place was obvious and the duty of care did not require that the possibility of carelessness in diving be forestalled by a warning sign. Brennan J observed that the position would be different if a public authority gave an assurance to the public that there were no dangers on its premises or that any dangers were obvious even to those who do not exercise reasonable care, so that members of the public were induced to rely upon the assurance. Then, applying the reliance principle in *Heyman*, the public authority would have a duty of care which called for positive action. [85]

Nagle provides no assistance with regard to the application of the policy/operational distinction. Whilst the distinction was applied in *Glasheen*, it did not prevent indirect interference with resource allocation. The fact that the distinction played no role in *Nagle* in resolving the question of a duty of care, or how such a duty is to be limited, casts serious doubt on its acceptance as a general policy consideration where negligence actions are brought against government.

3. NEGLIGENT MISSTATEMENT

The equality proposition asserted

The principles governing negligent misstatement evolved after *Hedley Byrne & Co Ltd v Heller & Partners Ltd*[86] relatively independently from the case-law which included *Anns*, because the loss was economic. Well before *Heyman* made reliance an important component in establishing a duty of care in the general negligence cases, the courts insisted upon strict reliance on a misstatement in order to establish negligent misstatement. The equality proposition was explicitly embraced until 1986. The qualification to the equality proposition which then emerged in this private law context was not the policy/operational distinction, but a fundamental principle of public law.

The principles relating to government liability for negligent misstatement were established in *L Shaddock & Associates Pty Ltd v City of Parramatta*.[87] The High Court held that the principles applying to a private individual who carries on a business of supplying information also apply to a public authority which, in the course of its public functions, follows the practice of supplying information which is available to it more readily than to other persons, whether or not the authority has a statutory

85. Ibid at 440-441.
86. [1964] AC 465.
87. (1981) 150 CLR 225.

duty to do so.[88] When information or advice is sought on a serious matter, in such circumstances that the authority realises, or ought to realise, that the inquirer intends to act upon it, a duty of care arises in relation to the provision of the information or advice.[89] In *Shaddock* a local authority was liable for economic loss resulting from reliance by purchasers upon a certificate which was issued by the council under s 342AS of the *Local Government Act* 1919 (NSW) and which did not mention existing road-widening proposals. The council had no legal duty to provide this particular category of information, but it had a practice of so doing.

Shaddock represents a strong assertion of the equality proposition. There is no reference in *Shaddock* to the policy/operational distinction of *Anns* as a restriction upon government liability for negligent misstatement. The High Court saw no reason in principle why the law relating to negligent misstatement should be qualified in relation to representations made by public authorities.[90] Mason J addressed and rebutted the arguments against extension of the duty of care to public authorities.[91] It had been suggested to the court that imposition of a duty of care would unduly hamper local authorities in the discharge of their public functions. But, on the assumption that these authorities already endeavoured to provide accurate information, the standard of care would not be altered by a common law liability, which could always be insured against. Further, it was inconceivable that authorities would discontinue the practice of providing information which was of vital importance to intending purchasers and which the authority alone possessed. In a practical sense, authorities were obliged to provide this information and, if a fee were charged or an attempt made to exclude liability, that was a different matter.

Shaddock was concerned with a statement of fact with respect to a particular property.[92] In subsequent cases applying *Shaddock*, public authorities have been found liable where individuals have relied on representations specifically made to them.[93] Failure to establish that the requisite representation has been made is often an initial stumbling block, with the result that there is no occasion for the court to proceed to consider a policy consideration which qualifies the duty of care in relation to government.[94] If the applicability of the policy/operational distinction in

88. Ibid at 235 per Gibbs CJ.
89. The conditions for generation of the duty of care as formulated by Mason J: ibid at 252-253.
90. Ibid at 235 per Gibbs CJ, at 241 per Stephen J, at 252 per Mason J.
91. Ibid at 252.
92. See also *South Australia v Johnson* (1982) 42 ALR 161, where the State conceded that if there was a negligent misrepresentation it had a duty of care within the *Hedley Byrne* principle to a farmer who took a perpetual lease of land on Kangaroo Island. The court found that a misstatement was made, and proceeded to assess damages. The case therefore does not assist in the question whether the policy/operational distinction has a role in relation to negligent misstatement.
93. For example, *Mid Density Development Pty Ltd v Rockdale Muncipal Council* (1992) 39 FCR 579 (certificate issued under the *Environmental Planning and Assessment Act* 1979 (NSW), s 149 stating there was no risk of flooding of land).
94. For example, *Bienke v Minister for Primary Industries and Energy* (1994) 125 ALR 151 at 186.

this category of negligence were to be put to the test, in the light of in 1978 and *Heyman* in 1985, a case would need to arise where an action was brought in respect of a representation distinctively about policy, in particular a policy involving future allocation of resources. The issue was tested in 1986 in *San Sebastian Pty Ltd v Minister Administering the Environmental Planning and Assessment Act 1979.*[95]

A qualification emerges

In *San Sebastian*, developers bought property in Woolloomooloo, relying upon a publicly released scheme for redevelopment of the suburb as a residential area. When the State Planning Authority and Sydney City Council later abandoned the scheme, the developers sought damages for economic loss. In a joint judgment Gibbs CJ, Mason, Wilson and Dawson JJ took the opportunity to draw the authorities on negligent misstatement under the umbrella of the concept of proximity, which operates as a general limitation upon the test of reasonable foreseeability.[96] The principle of reliance plays an important part in establishing proximity, whether in relation to negligent misstatements or negligent acts. To establish negligent misstatement, a plaintiff must show:

(i) that the alleged representation was made; and

(ii) that the public authority made the representation with the intention of inducing members of the class of developers to act in reliance on it.[97]

The developers failed because they had not established (i)—that any representation was made that the scheme would proceed, in particular that transportation plans were feasible. It was not therefore necessary for the court to consider (ii).

Whilst treating the category of negligent misstatement as an instance of general liability in negligence, the High Court in *San Sebastian* did not expressly adopt the policy/operational distinction which was endorsed in *Heyman*.[98] However, in finding that the published scheme was a flexible policy which contained no representation that it would be adhered to in the future, the joint judgment in *San Sebastian* applied, without citing authority, a fundamental principle of administrative law. This, the no-fettering principle, provides that a public authority cannot fetter the future exercise of its statutory discretion by adopting a policy:[99]

"being creatures of an administrative and political process, proposals of this kind are subject to alteration, variation and revocation. The

95. (1986) 162 CLR 340.
96. Ibid at 355.
97. Ibid at 358.
98. In the New South Wales Court of Appeal only Hutley JA held no duty of care arose on account of the policy/operational distinction in *Anns*.
99. Central authorities on the no-fettering principle are *Ansett Transport Industries (Operations) Pty Ltd v Commonwealth* (1977) 139 CLR 54 at 73-77, 113-114; *Re Findlay* [1985] AC 318; *Peninsula Anglican Boys School v Ryan* (1985) 69 ALR 555 at 570; *Attorney-General (NSW) v Quin* (1989) 170 CLR 1 at 17-18.

implementation of a development plan inevitably generates planning and political pressures for changes at the instance of administrators, commercial interests, property owners, residents and other interest groups. Moreover, unless a development plan is given some entrenched or statutory status by relevant planning legislation it does not fetter the exercise by the responsible authority of its statutory discretions to approve or refuse development applications."[100]

Brennan J held in a separate judgment that there was no representation that the scheme was feasible, no inducement of the developers to rely upon such a representation, and no reasonable reliance by the developers. Brennan J regarded the no-fettering principle as important in precluding a finding of reasonable reliance by the developers:

"When persons chart their conduct in the expectation that a public authority will exercise in accordance with a policy a discretionary power which it is bound to exercise in the public interest, they have no justification for complaint if the public authority, without fraud or breach of contract, alters its policy and disappoints the expectations which the policy engendered, even if the reason for alteration is that the policy was carelessly prepared. . . .

In practice . . . it is understood that a public authority is free to alter a policy unless the policy is given binding effect by statute or by contract (where that is possible)."[101]

The policy concern of the court in *San Sebastian* was clear.[102] If a public authority feels constrained to adhere to a planning scheme upon which developers claim to have relied, for fear of a damages claim, its duty to exercise its discretion in the future in the public interest will be hindered. The common law duty of care owed to the developer would conflict with the common law duty implied by the no-fettering principle.[103] For this reason Brennan J suggested that "the remedy for carelessness in the preparation or adoption of such a policy must be found in the public arena not in private litigation."[104] The "public arena" is presumably the political process of accountability of a local council to its electorate for the soundness of its administration. Although that process will provide little comfort to developers who are not local residents, it is unlikely that Brennan J meant to refer to public law litigation. The availability of relief in public law would founder for the same reason: no estoppel could be raised against a planning authority which made a representation by publishing such a scheme.[105]

San Sebastian claimed to recognise negligent misstatement as an instance of general liability in negligence, yet bypassed the policy/operational distinction which had been approved in *Heyman* as the policy consideration

100. *San Sebastian* (1986) 162 CLR 340 at 359.
101. Ibid at 374.
102. Ibid at 374 per Brennan J.
103. Ibid.
104. Ibid.
105. If the policy/operational distinction confines the no-fettering principle in public law, the answer may well be the same because the scheme fell into the policy rather than the operational area. See text accompanying nn 175-180, below.

normally arising where government liability is in issue. The no-fettering principle had hitherto been confined to judicial review cases, particularly those where it is argued that an estoppel is raised against government. Perhaps the High Court silently declined to extend the policy/operational distinction to this category of negligence, preferring a public law principle whose authority was beyond question and whose rationale was clear.

The implications of *San Sebastian* for restriction of government liability for negligent misstatement remain uncertain. In *Unilan Holdings Pty Ltd v Kerin*,[106] the Minister for Primary Industries and Energy resiled from a "cast-iron guarantee" given in a speech to wool brokers that the government would not permit a further downward movement in the floor price of wool. When the wool marketing scheme was suspended eight months later by legislation, with a consequent slump in the price of wool, the plaintiffs sought damages for economic loss, having been induced to retain wool stockpiles in reliance on the speech. Hill J dismissed a strike-out motion by the Minister, in which it was argued that restrictions apply to government liability for negligent misstatement. Hill J did not refer to the policy/operational distinction. The Commonwealth relied on *San Sebastian*. Whilst accepting the authority of the no-fettering principle, Hill J paid regard to a dictum of Mason CJ in *Attorney-General (NSW) v Quin*.[107] This dictum suggests that, despite the no-fettering principle, an estoppel may be raised against the Executive where this would serve a public interest in preventing injustice to an individual.[108] Hill J rejected the submission that *San Sebastian* is authority for the "broad brush principle" that conduct of a public authority will be construed differently from conduct of private individuals for the purpose of determining whether a representation was made.

It is true that the joint judgment in *San Sebastian* does not treat the no fettering principle as a blanket bar to finding a representation in a government policy statement for the purposes of negligent misstatement. The case is capable of being confined as authority only on the issue whether for the purposes of negligent misstatement representations are made by a local council in a local development scheme. However, the no-fettering principle was clearly regarded in the joint judgment as a powerful factor in precluding an inference by the court that any representation was made:

"in the absence of indications to the contrary, it will not readily be inferred that a plan intended to serve as a guide to future development contains an assurance that it will be continuously and inflexibly applied in the future. Rather it is an expression of present intention and future expectation which would in ordinary circumstances deter developers and businessmen from relying on it as a solid and unchangeable foundation for development approvals. Instead, they make their own assessment and rely on their advisers and consultations, recognising that the function of the public documents is to provide a general and

106. (1992) 107 ALR 709.
107. (1989) 170 CLR 1 at 18.
108. *Unilan* (1992) 107 ALR 709 at 716. The authority is discussed in text accompanying nn 183-192, below.

flexible planning framework within which developers and businessmen are expected to make their own judgments." [109]

Alternatively, adopting the approach of Brennan J in *San Sebastian*, the no-fettering principle precludes any conclusion that the wool brokers relied on the "cast-iron guarantee".

However, the result in *Unilan Holdings* was that the strike-out motion was refused. Although confining the scope of the no-fettering principle as a qualification to government liability, Hill J recognised that government liability in the particular factual situation may be qualified by the policy consideration that resolution of the issue would require disclosure to the court of Cabinet communications.

Conclusion

It is surprising that the policy/operational distinction was not considered in *San Sebastian*, for it would have pointed to the desired result, that the court should not interfere in the council's policy decision. In *Unilan* the policy/operational distinction would at first glance have provided the Commonwealth with a strong argument that the action should be struck out. However, attention having been focused on the no-fettering principle as the basis for restricting government liability, Burchett J relied on a dictum which confines the no-fettering principle by reference to a balancing of public interests, but which is uncertain in its operation. [110] Yet the cases differ in their tenor. The policy in *San Sebastian* could be described as "pure policy" like a set of draft recommendations for reform of some area of public administration. The scheme was published in pursuit of a process of public consultation, without the implication of immediate steps for its implementation. By contrast, the policy in *Unilan* was capable of immediate practical implementation within a scheme which was in operation. A promise of immediate implementation was part of the representation. Within the category of negligent misstatement, any qualification to the equality proposition ought to capture this difference.

The introduction of the no-fettering principle in *San Sebastian* forges a strong link between private law qualifications to the equality proposition and public law restrictions upon the scope for finding government action unlawful. However, the no-fettering principle also provides a much broader basis for limiting tort liability, privileging policy-making without attempting to distinguish this activity from adjudicative decision-making, as the policy/operational distinction seeks to do. The ultimate question is whether the equality proposition in private law actions ought to be qualified by a public law principle firmly based in the doctrine of separation of powers. Whilst there is no doubt as to the authoritativeness of the no-fettering principle in judicial review actions, the discussion in Part 6, below, unfortunately suggests that this public law principle, like the policy/operational distinction, itself suffers from uncertainty in its scope.

109. *San Sebastian* (1986) 162 CLR 340 at 360.
110. See text accompanying nn 189-192, below.

4. ADMINISTRATIVE TORT

There is no firm authority that government is liable in a private law action for the administrative tort of negligently acting ultra vires or in denial of procedural fairness. Yet there are dicta which suggest that there is the potential for development of this new category of negligence. And there is a long-standing debate as to the desirability of an administrative tort. In public law there is a debate, although the law is settled, as to whether damages should be a remedy available in judicial review. [111] The argument in these debates is interdependent. [112] If an administrative tort develops, inadequacy of the tortious bases for obtaining damages against government fades away as an argument for the availability of damages in judicial review. If damages in judicial review are the appropriate mechanism for compensating individuals who suffer loss by reason of unlawful government action, the argument for an administrative tort as a separate category of negligence is undermined.

Common to both debates is a departure from the equality proposition. An administrative tort would provide a new category of liability in private law, applying to government but not to private individuals. Relief in the form of damages in judicial review would provide a public law avenue for obtaining compensation against government where no similar avenue of redress exists against private individuals. Justification for either departure from the equality proposition is sought in the imbalance of power between government and governed.

Public law: inadequate relief?

Damages in judicial review actions

Damages has never been an available form of relief in judicial review at general law, [113] nor pursuant to the *Administrative Decisions (Judicial*

---

111. New Zealand Public and Administrative Law Reform Committee, *Damages in Administrative Law*, 14th Report (Wellington 1980); *Administrative Justice: Some Necessary Reforms*, Report of the JUSTICE—All Souls Review of Administrative Law in the United Kingdom (Clarendon Press, Oxford, 1988), Ch 11; Sir Harry Woolf, *Protection of the Public—A New Challenge* (Stevens & Sons, London, 1990), pp 56-62; G P Barton, "Damages in Administrative Law" in M Taggart (ed), *Judicial Review of Administrative Action in the 1980s: Problems and Prospects* (Oxford University Press, Auckland, 1986).

112. For commentary which pays regard to both debates, see P P Craig, "Compensation in Public Law" (1980) 96 LQR 413; J McBride, "Damages as a Remedy for Unlawful Administrative Action" (1979) 38 CLJ 323; D Baker, "Maladministration and the Law of Torts" (1986) 10 Adel L Rev 207.

113. See D Baker, "Maladministration and the Law of Torts", op cit. Apparently contrary to this principle is the majority decision of the New South Wales Court of Appeal in *Macksville & District Hospital v Mayze* (1987) 10 NSWLR 708 that a trial judge in a judicial review action properly directed that damages be inquired into by the master. Kirby P dissented in relation to this order, holding that the direction was inappropriate because no cause of action in damages had been argued.

Review) Act 1977 (Cth) (*ADJR Act*).[114] However, an order of review under the *ADJR Act* declaring administrative action unlawful may assist in establishing one element in a tort action in a State or Territory court for damages say, for false imprisonment.[115] An application for judicial review may be joined with a claim for damages on tortious bases. Provided the factual matrix surrounding the damages claims is inseverable from the *ADJR Act* action, the Federal Court has accrued jurisdiction to hear both matters, even where the *ADJR Act* action ultimately does not succeed.[116] The Federal Court may also entertain a tort claim in its cross-vested jurisdiction.[117]

However, it is true that for many types of unlawful administrative action compensation is not available under a head of tortious liability. An obvious example is economic loss caused by revocation of a licence necessary to conduct a business. Although the revocation decision may be set aside in judicial review, the loss in the intervening period is not recoverable. Provided the tort of misfeasance in public office is available only where a strict intentional element is satisfied, examples could be multiplied, drawing upon a range of cases of ultra vires or procedurally unfair administrative action.

Private law

Dicta and arguments

There is authority that a duty of care arises at the earliest point of possible exercise of a statutory power, such that an administrator who fails to give proper consideration to exercising a power in the policy area may be liable in negligence.[118] However, the more persuasive view likely to attract support in the future is that the appropriate avenue of redress for such failure lies in public law rather than private law.[119]

114. *Park Oh Ho v Minister for Immigration and Ethnic Affairs* (1988) 81 ALR 288 at 298 (per Sweeney J), at 310 (per Morling J who dissented on the issue of the unlawfulness of the detention), at 317 (per Foster J); rev'd on other grounds *Park Oh Ho v Minister for Immigration and Ethnic Affairs* (1989) 167 CLR 637 at 645. See also *Conyngham v Minister for Immigration and Ethnic Affairs* (1986) 68 ALR 441; *Pearce v Button* (1986) 8 FCR 408; *O'Neil v Wratten* (1986) 65 ALR 451.
115. *Park Oh Ho* (1989) 167 CLR 637 at 645.
116. *Philip Morris Inc v Adam P Brown Male Fashions Pty Ltd* (1981) 148 CLR 457. In *Park Oh Ho v Minister for Immigration and Ethnic Affairs* (1988) 81 ALR 288 at 310, 318; *Kumar v Minister for Immigration, Local Government and Ethnic Affairs* (1991) 100 ALR 439 at 445 (invoking *ADJR Act* jurisdiction and the accrued jurisdiction to hear an action for damages for false arrest and imprisonment).
117. See *Chan Yee Kin v Minister for Immigration, Local Government and Ethnic Affairs* (1991) 103 ALR 499 at 504-505 (invoking the *ADJR Act* jurisdiction and claiming damages on several tortious bases, including administrative tort, none of which was established).
118. In *Heyman* (1984) 157 CLR 424 at 445 Gibbs CJ (Wilson J agreeing) agreed with Lord Wilberforce in *Anns* [1978] AC 728 at 755 that a failure to give proper consideration to exercise of a power in the policy area (a council's decision whether to exercise the power of inspection or not) may give rise to liability in negligence. On the evidence in *Heyman*, no failure of this nature was established.
119. Mason J in *Heyman* declined to follow *Anns* on this issue, holding there is a public duty at common law to give consideration as to whether a power should be exercised, enforceable by mandamus in judicial review: at 465.

Dicta suggesting a potential for development of an administrative tort commence with *Dunlop v Woollahra Municipal Council*,[120] where damages were sought for negligence of a council in passing resolutions which were ultra vires and procedurally unfair. Lord Diplock, delivering the judgment of the Privy Council, did not reject the argument that the council had a duty to seek legal advice as to whether the resolution would be within power.

The Privy Council decision in *Takaro*, already considered in relation to the policy/operational distinction, was an action for damages for administrative tort. In *Takaro* the Privy Council differed from the New Zealand Court of Appeal on the issue of whether the Minister's refusal of consent was ultra vires, concluding that the reversion factor was not an irrelevant consideration. It had been found as a fact that the Minister believed at all times that he acted within his powers in taking the reversion factor into account. There was no reason for him to seek legal advice regarding the extent of his power any more in this case than in many other of the wide range of cases which came before him. Because it was clear that there was no breach of any duty it was not necessary for Lord Keith to reach a final decision as to whether a duty of care arises on account of an excess of power.

Although not a concluded decision on the issue of the existence of an administrative tort, *Takaro* suggests that no such tort exists on account of the "relevant circumstances", or policy considerations, to be taken into account in determining whether a duty of care is owed.[121] These were four factors which "militate[d] against imposition of liability".[122] First, because an invalid administrative decision can always be set aside in judicial review, the only effect of the invalid decision is delay. Second, only rarely will a breach of the duty be established. Anyone is capable of misconstruing a statute, including judges. Even if the error is a serious one, that does not mean it involves "negligence". Third, there is a "danger of overkill". Local authorities may respond to the duty of care by setting standards which are unnecessarily onerous. Other administrators may go to extreme lengths to obtain legal advice, even run a test case, before exercising their powers, thereby delaying decision-making.[123] Fourth, it is difficult to identify any case where a Minister would be under a duty of care to seek legal advice. There are so many occasions when discretionary statutory power is exercised it could equally be argued that advice should be obtained in respect of every one.

Takaro influenced Einfeld J in *Chan Yee Kin v Minister for Immigration, Local Government and Ethnic Affairs*[124] to decline an invitation to introduce this "new tort". Einfeld J rejected the proposition that "a genuine good faith decision of an administrator, which is held on administrative law principles or in the exercise of a supervisory jurisdiction to be legally erroneous, can attract a liability in tort for damages".[125]

120. [1982] AC 158.
121. [1988] 1 AC 473 at 501.
122. Ibid.
123. Ibid at 502.
124. (1991) 103 ALR 499.
125. Ibid at 511.

Einfeld J accepted the reasoning of Lord Keith in *Takaro* that, in addition to the financial implications for government of successful actions based on such a new head of liability, the desire to protect decision-makers from successful actions would result in delays and expense in itself.[126]

Takaro did not close the door to the development of an administrative tort in Australia or the United Kingdom.[127] In *Bienke v Minister for Primary Industry and Energy*[128] Gummow J left open the question of whether a duty of care may arise where power of an administrative nature is exercised ultra vires.[129] A fishing operator argued that a plan of management for the Northern Prawn Fishery was made ultra vires and damages should be awarded for the administrative tort of "negligently invalid government activity". The argument for administrative tort failed at the outset because the management plan was not shown to be invalid. However, Gummow J held that if an "administrative tort" existed, it did not arise with regard to the making of delegated legislation, and the management plan was delegated legislation. A dictum of Dixon J in *James v Commonwealth*,[130] together with Canadian, United States and United Kingdom cases, provided consistent authority that government cannot be liable in tort for an exercise of legislative power. Of particular importance was *Bourgoin SA v Ministry of Agriculture, Fisheries and Food*,[131] where the English Court of Appeal held that the making of ultra vires delegated legislation did not give rise to a claim for damages. To this Gummow J added the policy consideration of the sheer difficulty of applying the concepts of proximity and reliance to an exercise of delegated law-making power, which normally affects broad classes of individuals in the same way.[132]

Takaro and *Bienke* demonstrate that the policy/operational distinction is but one of the host of policy considerations relevant to administrative tort. The distinction played a muted role in the examination of the authorities in *Bienke*. Gummow J referred to a leading Canadian authority, cited by the respondent Minister, in which the policy/operational distinction indicated a local authority owed no duty of care in exercising legislative or quasi-legislative power.[133] However, Gummow J did not explicitly justify his decision by reference to the distinction, and hence had no occasion to consider whether it was problematic, as Lord Keith did in *Takaro*. Had the distinction been regarded as the central policy consideration, support for Gummow J's conclusion would have been found in the judgment of Deane J in *Heyman*, where the policy/operational distinction was said to

126. Ibid at 501.
127. For a later decision in the United Kingdom see *Lonrho Plc v Tebbit* [1992] 4 All ER 280 where the Court of Appeal held that it was arguable that the Secretary assumed a private law duty to release a company from an undertaking when it was no longer needed in the public interest and that the Secretary owed a duty of care in private law as a result of misconstruction of his statutory power.
128. (1994) 125 ALR 151. Affirmed by the Full Federal Court in *Bienke v Minister for Primary Industries and Energy* (1996) 135 ALR 128.
129. Ibid at 171.
130. (1939) 62 CLR 339 at 372.
131. [1986] 1 QB 716.
132. *Bienke* (1994) 125 ALR 151 at 172.
133. *Welbridge Holdings Ltd v Metropolitan Corp of Greater Winnipeg* [1971] SCR 957.

preclude liability for the exercise of functions of a "policy-making" and "quasi-legislative character".[134]

With regard to administrative tort, application of the policy/operational distinction will produce different results in accordance with which rationale for the distinction is adopted. If the rationale of the distinction is to preclude the courts from interference in governmental resource allocation decisions, that rationale was easily satisfied in *Bienke*. The making of delegated legislation is an activity which is a distinctive exercise of strong discretion. At a theoretical level such decision-making could only be described as the making rather than the application of rules. In this the making of delegated legislation differs from the making of policy which, as analysed by Wilenski, permeates the entire administrative process.[135] *Bienke* was an easy case. Through a private law action the court was invited to interfere with a plan which effected a restructuring of the northern prawn industry by settling a formula for the allocation of the scarce resource of units of fishing capacity. The plan clearly fell into the "policy" area understood by reference to the resource allocation rationale.

If the rationale of the policy/operational distinction is a loose concept of justiciability, as suggested in *Takaro*, then the issue of its application in *Bienke* is problematic. At first glance it appears sensible to exclude from private law liability administrative action which cannot be shown in a public law action to be ultra vires because it is non-justiciable. However, there is no uniform test of justiciability in Australia. The tests at the federal level, under the *ADJR Act* and at general law, differ. The test at general law is in a state of some uncertainty. The exercise of delegated law-making power at the federal level is not justiciable under the *ADJR Act*, but is justiciable at general law.[136] Thus, in *Bienke* the making of the delegated legislation was justiciable under the *Judiciary Act* 1903 (Cth), s 39B and the Federal Court's associated jurisdiction under the *Federal Court of Australia Act* 1976 (Cth), s 32. Although the argument that the plan was ultra vires did not succeed in *Bienke*, there are cases where the courts have interfered on the ground of *Wednesbury* unreasonableness and declared delegated legislation invalid, including fishery management plans.[137] There are also cases of interference with first order resource allocation policy both at general law[138] and under the *ADJR Act*.[139]

134. See text accompanying n 40, above. The Full Federal Court in *Bienke* (1996) 135 ALR 128 examined the origins of the distinction without expressing disapproval of its operation in modern Australian cases.
135. See discussion at text accompanying nn 25-26, above. See also D Cohen and J C Smith, "Entitlement and the Body Politic: Rethinking Negligence in Public Law" (1986) 64 *Canadian Bar Review* 1 at 26-27, 49-57 for a position which criticises the policy/operational distinction but then seems to reinstate it using the different terminology of entitlement/distribution.
136. See Allars, op cit, n 5, p 92.
137. *Minister for Primary Industries and Energy v Austral Fisheries Pty Ltd* (1993) 112 ALR 211.
138. *R v Criminal Injuries Compensation Board; Ex parte Lain* [1967] QB 864.
139. *Perder Investments Pty Ltd v Lightowler* (1990) 101 ALR 151. In Queensland, decisions made under non-statutory schemes involving funds that are provided out of amounts appropriated by Parliament are justiciable under the *Judicial Review Act* 1991 (Qld), s 4. But these are second order resource allocation decisions. See *Macedab Pty Ltd v Director-General, Department of the Premier, Economic and Trade Development* (unreported, CA SC Qld, Macrossan CJ, Davies and Pincus JJA, 9 June 1995).

A policy/operational distinction whose rationale depends upon the public law concept of justiciability may not protect resource allocation decisions from a claimed duty of care. *Bienke* invoked both the public law and private law jurisdiction of the Federal Court. In the public law challenge to the validity of the plan, it was clear that the issue was justiciable. A policy/operational distinction whose rationale depended on the concept of justiciability could hardly then be relied upon in the private law claim to exclude a duty of care.

Mengel's case

The High Court decision in *Northern Territory v Mengel*[140] provides intriguing dicta, but no firm indication as to whether the policy considerations outlined in *Takaro* will be persuasive when liability for administrative tort is directly in issue in the future. Stock inspectors imposed restrictions on the movement of the plaintiffs' breeder cattle until they were cleared of brucellosis infection, thereby causing economic loss to the plaintiffs. Because of their incorrect assumption that the plaintiffs' stations were subject to "approved programmes" regarding the eradication of brucellosis, the inspectors acted in excess of their statutory power to impose such restrictions. The court held per curiam that since the trial judge had rejected negligence and the respondents had not pursued this point in the Court of Appeal of the Northern Territory, they could not succeed upon this ground in the High Court. In a joint judgment Mason CJ, Brennan, Dawson, Toohey, Gaudron and McHugh JJ held that to establish negligence the respondents had to prove that the inspectors should have known that their actions were unauthorised. To prove that, the Mengels had to establish that the inspectors knew there was no approved programme for the stations in September 1988. No positive finding had been made by the trial judge that there was no approved programme. It followed that the plaintiffs could not establish negligence.[141]

The joint judgment contemplates that an action in negligence might lie against the inspectors if they knew they acted ultra vires. This is reinforced by the approach in the joint judgment to the elements required to establish misfeasance in public office. Knowledge of an officer that her or his actions, calculated in the ordinary course to cause harm, are invalid is insufficient to establish misfeasance in public office. An intentional element, which is considered later, makes misfeasance in public office a counterpart to the intentional torts of private individuals. Misfeasance in public office should not be extended to cover acts the officer knows are in excess of power. The reason is as follows:

> "If it were the case that governments and public officers were not liable in negligence, or that they were not subject to the same general principles that apply to individuals, there would be something to be said for extending misfeasance in public office to cover acts which a

140. (1995) 129 ALR 1.
141. Ibid at 20. Contrary to the majority, Deane J thought that a positive finding that there was no approved programme was implicit in the judgment of the trial judge. On this basis, negligence being arguable, albeit with difficulty, Deane J would have extended to the Mengels the opportunity of appying for an order which would allow them to apply to the Court of Appeal to reformulate their case as an action in negligence: ibid at 39-40.

public officer ought to know are beyond his or her power and which involve a foreseeable risk of harm. But in this country governments and public officers are liable in negligence according to the same general principles that apply to individuals. And, in that context, the argument that misfeasance in public office should be reformulated to cover the case of a public officer who ought to know of his or her lack of power can be disposed of shortly. So far as unintended harm is concerned, the proposed reformulation suffers the same defect in relation to the law of negligence as does the principle in *Beaudesert*, namely, it serves no useful purpose if there is a duty of care to avoid the risk in question and is anomalous if there is not." [142]

The first sentence in this passage implies that an action in negligence lies in respect of an invalid administrative act which the decision-maker knew was beyond power, where the risk of harm was foreseeable. That is, it suggests that the reasoning in *Takaro* is to be rejected in Australia. The next sentence repeats the familiar equality proposition—that there is parity between private individuals and government with regard to application of the principles of negligence. In terms of the substantive law, this claim is false, as is demonstrated by the retention of the policy/operational distinction in *Heyman* and the intrusion of the no-fettering principle into negligent misstatement in *San Sebastian*. The last sentence leaves the reader unsure as to whether the suggestion in the first sentence is to be taken seriously. For the last sentence declines to commit to one view or the other—is there a duty of care of administrators to avoid foreseeable risks of harm caused by acts or omissions which are invalid and known by the administrator to be invalid? The joint judgment does not tell us. All we are told is that if there is such a tortious liability, it should be covered by the law of negligence, not by misfeasance in public office.

Yet, in the light of the joint judgment's rejection of the *Beaudesert* principle, it is difficult to conclude that support can be drawn from this passage for an administrative tort. Brennan J was more forthright, explicitly rejecting the idea of an administrative tort:

"Where a public officer takes action that causes loss to a plaintiff—in the present case by giving directions—and the sole irregularity consists of an error as to the extent of the power available to support the action, liability depends upon the officer's having one of the states of mind that is an element in the tort of misfeasance in public office. That element defines the legal balance between the officer's duty to ascertain the functions of the office which it is his or her duty to perform and the freedom of the individual from unauthorised interference with interests which the law protects. The balance that is struck is not to be undermined by applying a different standard of liability—namely, liability in negligence—where a plaintiff's loss is purely economic and the loss is attributable solely to a public officer's failure to appreciate the absence of power required to authorise the act or omission which caused the loss: cf *Takaro Properties Ltd v Rowling* [1986] 1 NZLR 22 esp at 68; but see *Rowling v Takaro Properties Ltd* [1988] AC 473 at 511-512." [143]

142. *Mengel* (1995) 129 ALR 1 at 19.
143. Ibid at 28.

Summarising the arguments

It is a difficult question whether there should exist an administrative tort. However, there are some powerful arguments against such a development.

First, as Gummow J pointed out in *Bienke*, administrative tort shifts the loss suffered by a private individual as a result of unlawful administrative action onto the community as taxpayers.[144] Some commentators regard this as an argument against an administrative tort, whilst others regard it as an argument for an administrative tort. The House of Lords changed its position with regard to liability of local councils for negligent inspection of defective buildings on account of its realisation that the assumption that "[t]heir shoulders are broad enough to bear the loss" may be false.[145] It is a legitimate policy consideration that imposition of tort liability upon public authorities spreads the burden of loss upon taxpayers. On the other hand, whilst negligence actions usually may be pursued against the builders of defective buildings, no such alternative defendant is available to the individual who suffers loss as a result of administrative error.

Second, an administrative tort would have a "chilling effect", not only upon administration[146] but also upon the evolution of the principles of administrative law. Judges would be likely to exercise extreme caution in interpreting administrative law principles and applying them, mindful of the possible economic ramifications of their decisions.

Third, a policy consideration raised in *Bienke* was that because delegated legislation affects many members of the community the concepts of proximity and reliance are difficult to apply. This argument can be raised with regard to policy-making as well. Here the power imbalance between a delegated law-maker or policy-maker and members of the community is claimed as an argument against, rather than in favour of, government liability. Yet where rules are applied to individuals unlawfully or unfairly, the power imbalance argument is regarded as having force. A distinction between policy and its application emerges as a determinant of whether the power imbalance supports assertion of the equality proposition by the imposition of tort liability. The unsatisfactory policy/operational distinction could emerge as a qualification to liability even though no liability can arise for private individuals.

Fourth, the extension of a duty of care to encompass an administrative tort would undercut the tort of misfeasance in public office, which requires intentional, malicious or knowing conduct.[147] This argument has force. Administrative tort offends the equality proposition more deeply than does misfeasance in public office because it does not insist upon this intentional element. Misfeasance in public office will be considered in Part 5, below.

144. Ibid at 172. The Full Federal Court agreed with Gummow J's conclusion without referring to *Mengel* or discussing the policy arguments: *Bienke* (1996) 135 ALR 128 at 149-154.
145. The words are Lord Denning's, in *Dutton v Bognor Regis Urban District Council* [1972] 1 QB 372 at 416, and the change of position occurred in *Murphy v Brentwood District Council* [1991] 1 AC 398. For discussion, see T Weir, "Governmental Liability" (1989) PL 40.
146. See the sixth argument below and the approach of Brennan J to misfeasance in public office in *Mengel*, examined in text accompanying nn 157-162, below, especially n 161.
147. *Bienke* (1994) 125 ALR 151 at 173.

A fifth question, raised in *Bienke*, is whether the "waiver" of immunity effected by the *Judiciary Act* 1903 (Cth) can be extended to new categories of tort liability.[148] This argument will not be examined here.

The sixth argument combines the second, third and fourth considerations outlined by Lord Keith in *Takaro*, regarding the ease with which an error of law may be made and the "danger of overkill". Administrative tort allows that an administrator who acts carefully and reasonably in reaching an incorrect interpretation of statutory power may be held negligent. Lack of care is assessed by reference to whether legal advice was sought regarding the scope of power or the appropriate hearing procedure. The argument for an administrative tort becomes a formalist one, assuming that there is always one correct answer to an interpretative issue and an idealistic one, in expecting that public sector legal officers will uniformly seize upon that correct answer. *Dunlop* shows that legal advice may be sought but be incorrect. The legal advice given to the council that its resolution would not be ultra vires proved to be wrong, but the legal issue was a difficult one. The Privy Council held that the fact that the council received incorrect legal advice could not amount to a breach of duty on its part.[149] Is it sufficient then to seek legal advice and proceed? At which point, by which officers and in respect of which aspects of the administrative process should legal advice be sought? Should the legal adviser be independent of the public authority? Suppose an administrator deliberately frames a request for advice or chooses the adviser so as to obtain advice in support of a course of action, which to a reasonable person without legal training appears unlawful and which is ultimately held unlawful by an appellate court. Should this administrator be in a better position than an administrator who, in an honest, humane and diligent effort to interpret the scope of her or his power without advice, nevertheless errs in law?

The prospect that liability of government in negligence should depend upon whether legal advice was sought with regard to the lawfulness of proposed action is inefficient and unpalatable. The clogging of the administrative process which occurs when each step is referred to a department's legal branch for clearance for fear of a massive damages claim cannot be underestimated. Administrative tort would not only cause delay in administration, as pointed out in *Takaro*. It would also ensure a legalistic and adversarial tone in administration, undermining the possibility of government responsive to members of the community.

5. MISFEASANCE IN PUBLIC OFFICE

As a private law action for damages in respect of unlawful administrative action, misfeasance in public office offers scope for redressing the absence of the remedy of damages in public law and the absence of clear authority

148. Ibid.
149. The view of the Privy Council with regard to the denial of procedural fairness which occurred when the council made its second resolution is unclear. The Privy Council held this could not amount to a breach of a duty of care, since "the person affected is in as good a position as the public authority to know" that the resolution is void and therefore incapable of affecting her or his legal rights: [1982] AC 158 at 172.

in support of an administrative tort.[150] Misfeasance in public office occurs where a public officer does an act which to her or his knowledge amounts to an abuse of office and thereby causes damage to another person. The ambit of this tort has been uncertain, with some cases suggesting a wide liability of government for damages wherever an officer acts in excess of power, even if he or she is unaware of the unlawfulness and does not act maliciously.[151] This view has frequently been doubted or rejected[152] and was finally expressly rejected by the High Court in *Northern Territory v Mengel*.[153]

As a tort particular to government, misfeasance in public office offends the equality proposition. However, this can arguably be justified by viewing misfeasance in public office as a counterpart to the intentional torts, such as trespass and assault, which tend to be established only against private individuals. This approach explains the decision of Mason CJ, Dawson, Toohey, Gaudron and McHugh JJ in *Mengel* that to establish misfeasance in public office there must be an intentional element in addition to knowledge of the officer that the act which results in damage is an excess of power.[154]

How is the intentional element to be satisfied? The joint judgment in *Mengel* considers and appears to reject foreseeable risk of harm as adequate to satisfy the intentional element. This would amount to saying that a public officer is liable for misfeasance because he or she has a duty not to exceed power if there is a risk of foreseeable harm.[155] If that were the test, misfeasance in public office would be no different from administrative tort. Foreseeability is to be rejected, since the tort of misfeasance in public office should not be extended to acts for which liability could be covered by the ordinary principles of negligence. Although open to different interpretations, the joint judgment ultimately appears to hold that the intentional element is satisfied by acts which are calculated in the ordinary course to cause harm, or which are done with reckless indifference to the harm that is likely to ensue.[156]

According to Brennan and Deane JJ, misfeasance in public office occurs where a public officer engages in conduct in purported exercise of a power otherwise than in an honest attempt to perform the functions of her or his office. The intentional element is satisfied by malice in the sense of intention to inflict injury with actual knowledge that there is no power to

150. For discussion of the absence of the remedy of damages in public law, see text accompanying nn 113-117, above.
151. *Brasyer v Maclean* (1875) LR 6 PC 396; *Wood v Blair and Helmsley Rural District Council* (1957) 2 Brit J Admin Law 243; *McGillivray v Kimber* (1915) 26 DLR 164. See J McBride, "Damages as a Remedy for Unlawful Administrative Action" (1979) 38 CLJ 323.
152. *Farrington v Thomson* [1959] VR 286 at 293; *Tampion v Anderson* [1973] VR 715 at 720; *Pemberton v Attorney-General* [1978] Tas SR 1 at 25-31; *Little v Law Institute of Victoria* [1990] VR 257 at 269-270.
153. (1995) 129 ALR 1.
154. Ibid at 18.
155. Ibid at 19.
156. Ibid at 18-19.

engage in that conduct and that the conduct would injure the plaintiff.[157] The intentional element is also satisfied by reckless indifference or deliberate blindness as to whether the power exists and as to the injury it is calculated to produce.[158] Misfeasance in public office was not established in this case because the inspectors were acting in good faith and there was no finding that they knew they had no power to impose the restrictions or that they were recklessly indifferent to the availability of that power.

The question arises of the extent to which misfeasance in public office differs from the administrative tort clearly rejected by Brennan J in *Mengel* and indirectly referred to in the joint judgment.[159] Brennan J rejected the argument that it is sufficient for the administrator to have "constructive knowledge" of absence of power together with foreseeability of the harm suffered by the plaintiff.[160] Whilst foreseeability is relevant to establish a duty of care in the law of negligence, it is not relevant to misfeasance in public office. Brennan J rejected this on the basis of the *Takaro* policy consideration:

> "If liability were imposed upon public officers who, though honestly assuming the availability of powers to perform their functions, were found to fall short of curial standards of reasonable care in ascertaining the existence of those powers, there would be a chilling effect on the performance of their functions by public officers. The avoidance of damage to persons who might be affected by the exercise of the authority or powers of the office rather than the advancing of the public interest would be the focus of concern."[161]

Brennan J thus insisted upon misfeasance in public office as the appropriate tort action where loss is caused by an error regarding the extent of the power available to support the action.[162] This ensures that liability depends upon establishing the officer's malice, knowledge or reckless indifference as to the existence of power.

Can misfeasance in public office offer a remedy as effective as the proposed administrative tort? On the basis of *Mengel*, how difficult will it be to establish the intentional element of misfeasance in public office?[163] Malice, it is hoped, rarely occurs and will be extremely difficult to prove. Excess and abuse of power is readily proved in public law. But establishing actual knowledge or reckless indifference of a public officer that her or his conduct was done in excess of power and was calculated in the ordinary

157. Ibid at 26-27, 37.
158. Ibid.
159. Ibid at 19. See text accompanying nn 140-143, above.
160. Ibid at 27.
161. Ibid.
162. However, Brennan J (at 28) appeared to be prepared to make a qualification to permit an action in negligence where there are additional factors such as express representation of authority or known reliance on authority. This would establish a case of specific reliance, as explained by Deane J in *Heyman*. See text accompanying nn 54-57, above.
163. See the reference by Gummow J in *Bienke v Minister for Primary Industry and Energy* (1994) 125 ALR 151 at 173 to the deficiency of administrative tort in departure from the "traditional concern of the common law with abuse of power by public officers which is intentional, malicious or at least knowing".

course to cause harm, is a more difficult task.[164] The role of legal advice in establishing actual knowledge may raise a series of questions similar to those raised in relation to administrative tort in Part 4, above.

6. EQUITY: RAISING AN ESTOPPEL AGAINST GOVERNMENT

The Southend-on-Sea principle

In public law, the equality proposition is radically qualified by a well-established principle modifying the application of the principles of equitable estoppel to government decisions. This, the *Southend-on-Sea* principle, provides that an estoppel may not be raised to prevent the performance of a statutory duty or to hinder the exercise of a statutory discretion.[165] This is one aspect of the more general no-fettering principle: that government should not be shackled in exercising its power to make decisions in the public interest in the future.[166]

It is noncontentious so far as legal principle is concerned that estoppel may not operate so as to excuse performance of a statutory duty or to permit an ultra vires act.[167] This qualification of the equality proposition is justified by the fact that, unlike the personal capacity of individuals, the power of administrators is limited, confined and often also structured by the empowering statute. The ultra vires doctrine is fundamental and no principle of estoppel can excuse an administrator from performing statutory duties or permit the administrator to act ultra vires. However, the power imbalance between a public authority with resources to provide accurate advice for its own purposes and to its clients, prompts arguments

---

164. For attempts in Australia to establish misfeasance in public office, preceding *Mengel*, which failed because malice or knowledge were not established, see *Dunlop v Woollahra Municipal Council* [1982] AC 158 at 172; *Chan Yee Kin v Minister for Immigration, Local Government and Ethnic Affairs* (1991) 103 ALR 499 at 509-510; *Austen v Civil Aviation Authority* (1994) 50 FCR 272 at 280.

165. *Southend-on-Sea Corp v Hodgson (Wickford) Ltd* [1962] 1 QB 416.

166. See authorities cited in n 99, above.

167. *Formosa v Secretary, Department of Social Security* (1988) 81 ALR 687; *Minister for Immigration, Local Government and Ethnic Affairs v Kurtovic* (1990) 92 ALR 93; *Chand v Minister for Immigration, Local Government and Ethnic Affairs* (1992) 30 ALD 777 at 780; *Brewer v Minister for Immigration, Local Government and Ethnic Affairs* (1993) 46 FCR 84; *Minister for Immigration and Ethnic Affairs v Polat* (1995) 37 ALD 394 at 398-401.

Although the basic principle is uncontentious, sometimes its application raises a difficult legal issue of whether noncompliance with a statutory procedure renders administrative action ultra vires. For example, in *Wells v Minister of Housing and Local Government* [1967] 1 WLR 1000 an estoppel could be raised against an authority on the basis of its practice of waiving a statutory procedural requirement, because noncompliance with the procedure would not, upon a proper construction of the statute, render the decision ultra vires. See *Kurtovic* (1990) 92 ALR 93 at 112-113. In addition a public authority cannot on the basis of a fiction as to facts which occurred in the past, give itself scope for the exercise of a statutory discretion which would otherwise not be available: *Glass v Defence Force Retirement and Death Benefits Authority* (1992) 38 FCR 534; *Roberts v Repatriation Commission* (1992) 39 FCR 420 at 425-426.

for confinement of the qualification, particularly where wrong advice results in a migrant's loss of opportunity to obtain resident status or where economic loss is caused to property owners.

As a result, there has emerged a fragmented group of cases which seek to confine the scope of this qualification, by relying upon other private law principles which are arguably applicable to administrators and which further support the raising of an estoppel. Thus, the law of agency is invoked to support the raising of an estoppel where an officer has apparent or ostensible authority to make a representation which is actually ultra vires.[168] The "indoor management" rule applicable to companies is invoked in a similar fashion in support of raising an estoppel against a public authority where it may be presumed that the regular internal procedures for conferral of authority would have been observed.[169] The authority of these private law arguments for confinement of the qualification is uncertain.[170]

Even more difficult, however, are cases where the estoppel would only confine or structure the future exercise of an administrator's discretion and the ultra vires doctrine is not challenged. Here, there are indications that new public law principles are evolving to confine the *Southend-on-Sea* principle.

Like damages, estoppel holds the promise of a more powerful form of relief than those familiar in public law. The minimum equity necessary to avoid detriment to the representee may be to hold the public authority to the representation, or at least to pay compensation for the detriment flowing from reliance upon the representation.[171] The normal relief in judicial review of setting aside a decision or declaring the rights of the parties appears inferior by comparison. A good example is provided by *Minister for Immigration, Local Government and Ethnic Affairs v Kurtovic*.[172] Had the deportee succeeded on the ground of estoppel he could have claimed it was unconscionable for the Minister to resile from the promise that if he committed no further offences he would not be deported. However, having succeeded only on the ground of procedural fairness, he obtained only an order setting aside the deportation decision. On determining the matter again according to law, affording a fair hearing, the Minister would be free to conclude again that he should be deported.

The policy/operational distinction in public law

Kurtovic's case

The most recent thorough examination of estoppel in the public law context is found in *Minister for Immigration, Local Government and*

---

168. *Western Fish Products Ltd v Penwith District Council* [1981] 2 All ER 204; *Kurtovic* (1990) 92 ALR 93 at 112, 114.
169. *Lever Finance Ltd v Westminster (City) London Borough Council* [1971] 1 QB 222 at 231; *Randwick Municipal Council v Derria Pty Ltd* (1979) 49 LGRA 95 at 104; *Kurtovic* at 113.
170. See *Kurtovic* at 114.
171. The minimum equity is considered further at text accompanying nn 197, 208, below.
172. (1990) 92 ALR 93.

Ethnic Affairs v Kurtovic,[173] a case concerned with an exercise of a statutory criminal deportation power. On review, the Administrative Appeals Tribunal recommended that the deportation order made against Kurtovic be revoked. The Minister adopted the recommendation and revoked the order. In a letter to Kurtovic advising of that decision, a departmental officer stated, "You are warned that any further conviction which renders you liable to deportation will lead to the question of your deportation being reconsidered by the Minister." A year later the successor Minister issued a deportation order against Kurtovic.

The Full Federal Court held that the power to deport could be exercised from time to time and hence the Minister was not functus officio. Further, the Minister was not estopped from exercising his discretion again to deport Kurtovic. The court affirmed the *Southend-on-Sea* principle. The argument for an estoppel failed at the outset for want of a sufficiently clear and unambiguous representation that Kurtovic would be free to remain in Australia if he gave no further cause to be deported. Neaves and Gummow JJ also held that detrimental reliance upon the representation is a requirement to raise an estoppel in the public law context, and this had not been established by Kurtovic.

Gummow J explained the rationale of the *Southend-on-Sea* principle by reference to the ultra vires doctrine.[174] The principle ensures that the administrator acts in accordance with the empowering statute and does not misconceive her or his power by being held to the representation. Gummow J also considered in detail the authorities which draw upon private law principles in order to confine the *Southend-on-Sea* principle.[175] Re-affirming the equality proposition in relation to private law actions, Gummow J said:

> "But what has been said above as to the role of estoppel in public law requires some qualifications in a particular class of case (of which it should be said at the outset of this section of these reasons, the present case is not one). In the exercise of powers derived from statute, a public authority may enter contracts or transfer property and will, in general, be subject to the ordinary private law rules dealing with contract, tort and property."[176]

However, Gummow J then recognised the qualification in private law to the equality proposition, expressed in the policy/operational distinction in *Anns*. Gummow J adopted the policy/operational distinction as a new confining component of the *Southend-on-Sea* principle in public law.[177] The more operational a statutory power or duty is, the easier it is for the doctrine of equitable estoppel to apply to its exercise.

Since the policy/operational distinction confines the application of the *Southend-on-Sea* principle to policy decisions, it promotes the equality proposition. The scope for raising an estoppel against a public authority is

173. Ibid.
174. *Attorney-General (NSW) v Quin* (1990) 170 CLR 1 at 17.
175. *Kurtovic* (1990) 92 ALR 93 at 113-114. See text accompanying nn 168-170, above.
176. Ibid at 115.
177. Ibid at 116.

broadened. Administrative decisions of an adjudicative nature involving representations made to individuals may give rise to estoppels. As in private law, the real difficulty will be establishing that the requisite representation was made and detrimental reliance on it.

Kurtovic raises the question whether the *Southend-on-Sea* principle, as a qualification to the equality proposition, should be weakened and, if so, whether the policy/operational distinction is the most appropriate mechanism for permitting estoppel to run more widely in public law.

Gummow J acknowledged, as did Lord Wilberforce in *Anns*, [178] that difficult borderline cases will arise in applying the policy/operational distinction. Whether applied in the public or private law context, the distinction remains subject to the criticism of Wilenski that it assumes an administration/policy dichotomy which does not exist even in a crude form. Putting this to one side, and assuming that the distinction offers a workable albeit rough mechanism for delineating the scope for raising an estoppel against government, is it an appropriate criterion?

Later cases

Since *Kurtovic*, the future of the policy/operational distinction as a confinement of the *Southend-on-Sea* principle has not been settled.

In *Li Fang v Minister for Immigration, Local Government and Ethnic Affairs (No 2)*, [179] Hill J accepted and applied the policy/operational distinction. [180] A Chinese citizen who had been issued with a visa on the nomination of her husband found when she arrived in Australia that her husband had withdrawn his sponsorship because he had formed a relationship with another person. The issue was whether the Minister was estopped from cancelling the visa because it was known to the Department at the time of its issue that the husband regarded the marriage as finished. Hill J found that no question of policy could be involved in a decision to cancel a visa. Detrimental reliance on the visa was shown by the applicant's travel, and relinquishment of her rights as a Chinese citizen to work and obtain food. However, the applicant failed to establish the necessary representation. The issue of a visa does not carry a representation that it will not be cancelled if a mistake is made in its original issue or if new facts arise.

Australian Securities Commission v Marlborough Gold Mines Ltd[181] illustrates the force of the Wilenski analysis. The Australian Securities Commission issued a policy statement that the Corporations Law permitted conversion from a limited company to a no liability company. The policy was based upon inadequate legal advice which failed to take account of a

---

178. See text accompanying n 24, above.
179. (1991) 25 ALD 455.
180. Curiously, Hill J also said (at 456) that the affirmation of the *Southend-on-Sea* principle in *Attorney-General (NSW) v Quin* (1990) 170 CLR 1 was enough to dispose of the submission on estoppel, without proceeding to consider the elements of representation and detrimental reliance. This leaves open the possibility that Hill J did not regard Gummow J's adoption of the policy/operational distinction as a confinement of the scope of the *Southend-on-Sea* principle.
181. (1993) 177 CLR 485.

recent Full Federal Court decision indicating that the weight of authority on this difficult question lay against the permissibility of such a conversion. The ASC represented to a company that it neither consented to nor objected to its application for conversion. Having become aware of the Full Federal Court decision, the ASC changed its policy, informed the company that it would oppose the approval of the conversion, proceeded to oppose at the hearing and appealed the decision made in favour of the company.

The High Court rejected a submission that the ASC was estopped from resiling from its policy. First, the ASC had not committed itself prior to the hearing to a position of not opposing the application, this being reinforced by the fact that the policy statement drew attention to the conflict of legal authority on the issue of conversion. Second, the ASC had an obligation in the performance of its general responsibilities under the Corporations Law to assist the court by presenting argument if it deemed this necessary or desirable. Third, once the ASC became aware of the Full Federal Court case, it was appropriate that it should change its policy and that it should oppose the application. In stating this finding, the court cited authority for the *Southend-on-Sea* principle, but did not elaborate further or refer to the policy/operational distinction.[182] Fourth, the High Court held it would not be unconscionable for the ASC to depart from the position it had previously taken with the company and it would have been unreasonable for the company to expect the ASC to adhere to its previous position once it became aware of the case.

The policy/operational distinction would not have provided guidance in *Marlborough*. The policy was changed in the course of its application in a particular case, just in the way that Wilenski has described. It is little wonder that the High Court veered away from an explicit discussion of the *Southend-on-Sea* principle. This would have required the court to articulate the limits of the principle in a case which did not fall clearly into private law or public law. This was not a judicial review action but an application for approval by a court of a scheme of arrangement under the Corporations Law. The flavour was private law, but the regulatory role of the ASC in such applications placed the action within the broader ambit of public law. The possible fettering of the discretion of the ASC to make policy in the nature of legal interpretations was squarely in issue.

Balancing public interests

A basis other than the policy/operational distinction for confinement of the *Southend-on-Sea* principle was suggested by Mason CJ in *Attorney-General (NSW) v Quin*.[183] As a case centrally concerned with the framing of a declaration granted in judicial review, the context was an unusual one for consideration of the *Southend-on-Sea* principle. Five former stipendiary magistrates were not re-appointed as magistrates when Courts of Petty Sessions in New South Wales were abolished and replaced by Local Courts.

---

182. The court cited (at 506, n 58) *Maritime Electric Co v General Dairies Ltd* [1937] AC 610, a case which forms the basis for the *Southend-on-Sea* principle.
183. (1990) 170 CLR 1.

The government policy regarding recommendations for reappointment under the *Local Courts Act* 1982 (NSW) was that former stipendiary magistrates would be appointed as magistrates of the Local Courts unless they were unfit for judicial office. Adverse allegations that they were not fit for office were received from other sources and taken into account, without being put to the magistrates. The New South Wales Court of Appeal made declarations that the decision of the Attorney-General (NSW) not to recommend the magistrates' appointment was made in denial of procedural fairness and void. [184] In the special circumstances of the case the former magistrates had a legitimate expectation which entitled them to procedural fairness, in this case an opportunity to respond to the adverse allegations. In 1987 the Attorney-General introduced a new policy on appointment of magistrates, requiring a process of advertisement, interview and merit selection procedure. One magistrate later sought a declaration that his case for appointment should be considered in accordance with the earlier policy, rather than in competition with new applicants on a merits basis under the new policy.

In a majority decision, the High Court declined to make a declaration in the form sought by the magistrate. The ratio of *Quin* was that the Executive should be free to apply the new policy to Quin, irrespective of the history of his case, including the declaration obtained by Quin in the New South Wales Court of Appeal.

The position of the dissenting judges, Deane and Toohey JJ, with regard to the *Southend-on-Sea* principle is not made explicit. Toohey J appeared to hold that the declaration sought would simply not affect the new policy because it:

> "does not strike at the power of the Executive. It does not seek to carry the area of judicial review beyond existing or permissible limits; it does not ask to have evaluated the fairness of the new policy." [185]

The main thrust of the majority judgments is the rejection of the notion that when an individual has a legitimate expectation, procedural fairness entitles her or him to substantive protection. Whilst Brennan J emphasised that this would involve an impermissible intrusion upon the merits of administrative decisions, Mason CJ and Dawson J linked their reasoning with the no-fettering principle. Dawson J held that procedural fairness cannot dictate the policy which a Minister must adopt nor preclude the Minister from adopting and giving effect to a change in policy. [186]

Mason CJ was the only judge in the majority to make explicit reference to the *Southend-on-Sea* principle, affirming the principle, although there was no direct argument that an estoppel was raised. Applying the principle, any representation made in the old policy could not preclude the Executive from adopting a new policy, or acting in accordance with the new policy. [187] It would therefore be inappropriate for the court to frame a declaration which operated as a fetter on the formation of new policy.

184. *Macrae v Attorney-General (NSW)* (1987) 9 NSWLR 268.
185. *Quin* (1990) 170 CLR 1 at 66.
186. Ibid at 60.
187. Ibid at 17.

However, Mason CJ formulated a basis for confining the *Southend-on-Sea* principle. An estoppel can be raised against the executive where:

"holding the Executive to its representation does not significantly hinder the exercise of the relevant discretion in the public interest. And, as the public interest necessarily comprehends an element of justice to the individual, one cannot exclude the possibility that the courts might in some situations grant relief on the basis that a refusal to hold the Executive to a representation by means of estoppel will occasion greater harm to the public interest by causing grave injustice to the individual who acted on the representation than any detriment to that interest that will arise from holding the Executive to its representation and thus narrowing the exercise of the discretion: see the observations of Lord Denning MR in *Laker Airways v Department of Trade* [1977] QB 643 at 707; but see also the criticism of this approach by Gummow J in *Kurtovic* (1990) 92 ALR 93 at 121-122."[188]

So confined, the *Southend-on-Sea* principle nevertheless precluded a declaration in the form sought by Quin. Mason CJ concluded that any injustice to Quin was outweighed by the public interest in maintenance of a general doctrine of separation of powers where the executive branch has sole control over the function of making appointments to the judicial branch.

There is a doubt about the place of the balancing of public interests test in the constellation of principles surrounding the legal effect of representations made by public authorities. The passage in the judgment of Lord Denning in *Laker Airways Ltd v Department of Trade*[189] applied by Mason CJ in *Quin* drew upon a line of decisions of Lord Denning where abuse of power and unfairness (both understood in a very broad sense) indicated that a public authority should not be permitted to resile from its representation. According to Lord Denning, the *Southend-on-Sea* principle is confined by a test involving judicial balancing of the injustice to the individual against countervailing benefit to the public. Mason CJ's dictum drew Lord Denning's balancing test into the mainstream of the Australian debate as to how far the *Southend-on-Sea* principle should bow to the equality proposition. Mason CJ's dictum recasts the test as the balancing of two public interests rather than the balancing of a private interest against a public interest. The avoidance of injustice to individuals is defined as a public interest. The rationale for this confinement of the *Southend-on-Sea* principle is that since the principle is intended to ensure government acts in the public interest, it must give way when the public interest is no longer served.

However, in the passage Mason CJ cited from *Kurtovic*,[190] Gummow J categorised this line of cases as an argument for a novel ground of review, called substantive unfairness, rather than as an argument for confinement of the *Southend-on-Sea* principle. Gummow J rejected substantive unfairness as a separate ground of review, whilst not disagreeing with

188. Ibid at 18.
189. [1977] QB 643.
190. (1990) 92 ALR 93 at 121-122.

another line of case law which expands the scope of procedural fairness in relation to representations made by government.[191] If substantive unfairness was a disguised argument for confinement of *Southend-on-Sea* then, according to Gummow J, it was to be rejected, for two reasons. First, balancing public and private interests is a matter of the merits, and is for the administrator not for the court. Second, if a representation is ultra vires, it is ineffective and cannot found an estoppel.

Mason CJ's dictum has later been interpreted as intended to apply only to statutory discretions and as not intended to qualify the *Southend-on-Sea* principle so far as it precludes the raising of an estoppel on the basis of ultra vires conduct or which would involve action inconsistent with the statute.[192] This leaves for further consideration the first reason of Gummow J, which goes to the heart of the rationale of the no-fettering principle—the doctrine of separation of powers.

The clear message of *Kurtovic* and *Quin* is a judicial discomfort with the *Southend-on-Sea* principle, different solutions being presented for confining that principle. Both Gummow J and Mason CJ sought to preserve the separation of powers protected by *Southend-on-Sea* but to leave the door open to do individual justice. Had Mason CJ applied the policy/operational distinction in *Quin*, the declaration would have been refused on the basis that the proposal to deal with Quin under the new policy would have been categorised as falling into the policy rather than the operational area. But a declaration that Quin's application should be dealt with under the old policy would not affect the application of the new policy to new applicants for the position of magistrate. The only issue was whether the old or the new policy should apply to Quin. It is arguable that this was an operational decision. Or was there really a third policy, perhaps unwritten, about how Quin was to be dealt with? Perhaps there was simply a need for a difficult decision to be made in which there was a complex interaction of the old and new policies together with the history of the matter? Had Gummow J applied the balancing of public interests test in *Kurtovic*, it is likely the public interest would have lain in non-interference with the new Minister's decision to deport.

Power to conduct private law litigation

It is difficult to assess the implications of *Commonwealth v Verwayen*[193] for estoppel in the public law context. Like *Quin* this case was unusual. The representation from which government resiled concerned the conduct of litigation itself, rather than a representation made in exercise of statutory power which itself was an issue in the litigation. In 1984 a member of the Royal Australian Navy sued the Commonwealth for damages for negligence in respect of injuries he received when *HMAS Voyager* collided with *HMAS Melbourne* in combat exercises near Jervis Bay in 1964. The injured delayed in commencing their actions on account of dicta in a High Court decision

191. *Attorney-General (Hong Kong) v Ng Yuen Shiu* [1983] 2 AC 629.
192. *Roberts v Repatriation Commission* (1992) 39 FCR 420 at 425.
193. (1990) 170 CLR 394.

to the effect that for reasons of public policy a member of the armed forces cannot recover damages for the negligence of another member of the armed forces in the course of duty. [194] Those dicta were disapproved by the High Court only in 1982. [195] The Commonwealth had a policy of not contesting liability in claims by survivors of the collision and not pleading a defence that the actions were barred under the *Limitation of Actions Act* 1958 (Vic). The plaintiff's solicitors had obtained written assurances from the Commonwealth that it would not plead the limitation defence. However, in December 1985 the Commonwealth altered the policy. The Commonwealth obtained leave from the court to amend its defence to plead the limitation defence and to assert that it owed no duty of care to the plaintiff because the *Voyager* was engaged in combat exercises.

By a majority of four to three, the High Court held that the Commonwealth could not rely upon the defences. Of the majority judges only Deane and Dawson JJ based their judgments upon estoppel. Toohey and Gaudron JJ based their judgments for the plaintiffs on the ground that the Commonwealth had waived its right to rely upon the defences.

Deane and Dawson JJ held that the elements of estoppel were satisfied. There was a pre-existing relationship between the Commonwealth and plaintiff: the relationship between an admitted wrongdoer and wronged or, at least, the relationship between defendant and plaintiff in the negligence action. The plaintiff relied on the assumption that the defences would not be pleaded, and the plaintiff proceeded with the action, without taking steps to settle or withdraw, expending time and money and subjecting himself to stress, anxiety and inconvenience. It would be unconscionable for the Commonwealth to resile from the induced assumption that the defences would not be pleaded.

Since *Verwayen* was a negligence action against government, the policy/operational distinction potentially had a role to play in restricting the scope of the duty of care. None of the judges adverted to the policy/operational distinction. At first glance this is understandable. To the point where it sought to amend the pleadings, the Commonwealth had admitted that it owed a duty of care, and on five occasions had joined with the plaintiff in applications for expedited hearings on the only issue arising, the question of injury or damage. Even if the policy/operational distinction were ultimately raised as a policy consideration restricting the Commonwealth's duty of care, it seems beyond argument that the tortious actions which resulted in the collision fell into the operational rather than the policy area.

As a private law action, *Verwayen* has no direct bearing upon the issue of the scope of the *Southend-on-Sea* principle in public law. Yet it is arguable that the rationale for restricting the scope of estoppel in judicial review should also apply when it is argued that estoppel is raised in tort actions against government. Here too the future exercise of statutory discretion in the public interest may be hindered. For the purposes of estoppel, in *Verwayen* the Commonwealth was treated no differently from

194. *Parker v Commonwealth* (1965) 112 CLR 295 at 301-302.
195. *Groves v Commonwealth* (1982) 150 CLR 113 at 118-119, 133-134, 136, 137.

a private sector defendant. The *Southend-on-Sea* principle was not even argued. Briefly referring to the claims against the Crown legislation, Gaudron J said that it was not argued that anything required the action to be determined on a basis different from that applicable in proceedings between individuals.[196] Mason CJ also said that no argument was based on the fact that government was the defendant. Only Mason CJ made a specific reference to the idea that it might have been argued that the principles of estoppel are qualified in private law actions against government:

> "the fact that the Commonwealth is the party against whom an estoppel is pleaded is not in this case a point of distinction. It was not argued that any special rule of estoppel applies to assumptions induced by government, either so as to expand or so as to contract the field of operation of the doctrine."[197]

Mason CJ dissented in *Verwayen* on the ground that holding the Commonwealth to its assurance would be a disproportionate response, and because of the absence of evidence of the detriment caused to the plaintiff by reliance upon the assurance. Had the *Southend-on-Sea* principle been argued, perhaps it may have persuaded some of the majority judges that the estoppel ought not to be raised.

Those who argue for the equality proposition would have no difficulty with the judgments of Deane and Dawson JJ in *Verwayen*. Yet this was a private law approach to a case which turned on the impact of a change in the government policy of not pleading the defences. The administrative conduct to be examined differed according to whether the issue was tort liability or the estoppel point. Tort liability focused on the acts or omissions which caused the collision. Estoppel focused upon the assurances that the defences would not be pleaded and the subsequent decision to plead the defences. The change of position, held to be unconscionable in the light of the plaintiff's reliance, is explained by a change in policy. By holding the Commonwealth estopped from resiling from its assurances, Deane and Dawson JJ precluded the Commonwealth from changing its policy to one where it would attempt to defeat the negligence claims.

There is force in the position taken by Mason CJ that holding the Commonwealth to the promise was a disproportionate response. The fundamental purpose of estoppel is to afford protection against the detriment which would flow from the Commonwealth's change of position. In *Verwayen* the High Court fettered the Executive's discretion to alter policy, without this relief being challenged as not only disproportionate but also an invasion of the *Southend-on-Sea* principle. By contrast, in the judicial review case of *Quin*, decided just a few months prior to *Verwayen*, the High Court declined to grant relief in a form which would have fettered the NSW government's discretion to change its policy regarding the selection procedure for appointment of magistrates.

Applying the analysis of Gummow J in *Kurtovic*, did the decision to change the policy fall within the operational rather than the policy area of

---

196. *Judiciary Act* 1903 (Cth), s 64. See *Verwayen* (1990) 170 CLR 394 at 486.
197. *Verwayen* (1990) 170 CLR 394 at 417.

administrative decision-making? Focusing on the individual case before the court, one might say that an operational decision had been made to plead the defences in that case, and this was simply an application of a new policy made at a first order level concerning the pleading of the defences in all the *Voyager* cases. Indeed, in *Kurtovic*, decided prior to the High Court decision in *Verwayen*, Gummow J expressed the view that the decision of the Full Court of the Victorian Supreme Court, which was ultimately upheld by the High Court, was correct because the decision estopped was an operational one.[198] However, in so doing Gummow J referred to the fact that the Commonwealth's promise not to plead the defences was not an exercise of statutory discretion. The implication here, and elsewhere in Gummow J's judgment, is that the *Southend-on-Sea* principle does not apply to the exercise of non-statutory power.[199] The formulation of the *Southend-on-Sea* principle in the cases has been in terms of statutory duties and powers. However in *Laker Airways*, Lord Denning assumed that *Southend-on-Sea* potentially applied to an exercise of prerogative power.[200] Whilst the courts have sought to confine *Southend-on-Sea*, its confinement to statutory powers, like any other confinement, requires justification, particularly now that some prerogative powers are justiciable at general law.

Supposing that the prerogative nature of the Commonwealth's power to conduct litigation made no difference, the decision to resile from the promise not to plead the limitation defence can also be argued to fall within the policy area. Assurances were made by the Commonwealth both as to the policy and its application to all the *Voyager* claimants. The conduct which was argued to be unconscionable was the simultaneous change of policy and application of the new policy to every member of the class of people affected by the policy—those members of the Royal Australian Navy who were involved in the collision and who were now seeking damages from the Commonwealth. It was fortuitous that Verwayen was the plaintiff who ran the test case arguing that an estoppel prevented the Commonwealth from resiling from a promise made to all the plaintiffs. Neither the Commonwealth's conduct nor the issue of the raising of an estoppel in the litigation was concerned with just one individual case.

The argument that this was a policy decision is more compelling. Mason CJ described the giving of the assurances as "a deliberate policy decision made by government at ministerial level at least".[201] The withdrawal of those assurances must also have been a high-level policy decision. This is how Lord Wilberforce envisaged the distinction would operate. The counterpart in *Anns*, would have been the policy decision of a council as to salary resources spent in appointment of sufficient inspectors to conduct thorough inspections of new buildings. The rationale identified by Deane J in *Heyman*, of precluding interference by the courts in resource

198. (1990) 92 ALR 93 at 116.
199. Ibid at 114, 116. See (at 114) the explanation for *Robertson v Minister of Pensions* [1949] 1 KB 227. The Full Federal Court adopted this explanation in *Roberts v Repatriation Commission* (1992) 39 FCR 420 at 425.
200. [1977] QB 643 at 707.
201. *Verwayen* (1990) 170 CLR 394 at 417.

allocation by government, is also satisfied. The resources of legal representatives of the Commonwealth were directed by the policy decision to pleading the defences. The objective was to minimise expenditure on satisfying the claims of the *Voyager* plaintiffs. If this were not a policy decision for the purposes of the distinction in negligence actions, what would be? Here policy-making and policy application could not be differentiated.

The integration of policy and its application also affects the analysis of *Metropolitan Transit Authority v Waverley Transit Pty Ltd*.[202] In that case the Supreme Court of Victoria held that an estoppel was raised against a regulatory agency which changed its policy relating to the award of bus service contracts, with the purpose of triggering a restructuring of the public transport system. The private law approach was so complete that the equitable principles set out in *Waltons Stores (Interstate) Ltd v Maher*[203] were applied without any reference to the *Southend-on-Sea* principle. This is all the more surprising in that *Waverley* was a judicial review action rather than a private law action like *Verwayen*. *Waverley* was probably decided per incuriam.

In *Kurtovic* Gummow J suggested that, had the *Southend-on-Sea* principle, confined by the policy/operational distinction, been applied in *Waverley*, the court's decision would have been different. The agency's exercise of the statutory power to renew contracts would have been categorised as falling into the policy area and no estoppel should have been raised.[204] However, it can also be argued upon close consideration of the facts of *Waverley* that the same power to renew contracts was first exercised at the policy level and then at the operational level. The policy decision was to introduce an open tender system and through it to attempt to undermine the solidarity of the Bus Proprietors' Association and precipitate a restructuring of the bus transport industry, to ensure its competitiveness and cost-efficiency. The operational decision was the agency's acceptance of a tender by an outside operator with no route experience, in preference to the tender at a lower price made by the plaintiff, an established operator.

The policy/operational distinction does not explain why the exercise of a power to enter contracts should in every instance be a policy decision. If it is a matter of degree, there is a much higher policy component in an initial decision to approach the renewal of all contracts in order to achieve a certain objective than there is in the decision whether or not to renew a particular contract in the light of that earlier decision. However, *Waverley*, like many other cases, illustrates just how narrow the choice between the policy and operational areas may be. Unless the agency had refused to renew the plaintiff's contract by awarding it to the other tenderer, its policy would have failed utterly. In one central decision the adoption and execution of a policy may be intimately connected.

To return to *Verwayen*, the argument here too is that neither a bright nor even a rough distinction could be drawn between policy and its application.

---

202. *Waverley Transit Pty Ltd v Metropolitan Transit Authority* (1988) 16 ALD 253; aff'd on appeal *Metropolitan Transit Authority v Waverley Transit Pty Ltd* [1991] 1 VR 181.
203. (1988) 164 CLR 387.
204. (1990) 92 ALR 93 at 117.

This is not to say that the decision in *Verwayen* involved an estoppel upon a Commonwealth policy of pleading the defences in other *Voyager* cases so that the Commonwealth could never resist a submission that it was estopped from applying the new policy. Following the High Court decision in *Verwayen*, as other actions for damages by *Voyager* survivors came on for hearing, the Commonwealth still sought to raise the defences. Given the need to establish the elements of estoppel, in particular, detrimental reliance, each case rests on its own facts. In the circumstances of another *Voyager* survivor, Clark, the elements of equitable estoppel were established, in particular detriment of a psychological nature.[205] The conduct of the Commonwealth in seeking to resile from its representation that it would not plead the defences was unconscionable and the minimum equity required to do justice between the parties was to hold the Commonwealth to those representations. However, at first instance in *Clark v Commonwealth*,[206] Coldrey J rejected an argument that by its conduct in relation to the *Verwayen* litigation the Commonwealth was estopped from raising these defences in all the other actions. Both parties had used the expression "test case" to describe the *Verwayen* litigation, but it was not clear that the Commonwealth had agreed to be bound by the outcome of the High Court decision in that case in relation to all the other litigation.[207]

Verwayen emphasises that the *Southend-on-Sea* principle will have little role to play when an estoppel is argued in a private law action against government. Here the equality proposition has much more force than in a judicial review action such as *Kurtovic* or *Quin*. However, this difference in promotion of the equality proposition needs to be justified. And the difference in protection of the doctrine of separation of powers, through the no-fettering principle, requires justification. Should it make a difference that the issue arises in a private law rather than a public law action?

The public law no-fettering principle may have a place in private law actions via the notion that only the minimum equity should be done to do justice between the parties. Where government is concerned, equity will rarely go so far as to enforce a promise in order to prevent the unconscionable conduct if to do so would be to fetter the future exercise of discretion in the public interest. In *Verwayen* Mason CJ drew a distinction between detriment in a broad sense and a narrow sense. Detriment in a broad sense results from the denial of the correctness of the assumption upon which the person relies.[208] This would have been the

---

205. *Commonwealth v Clark* [1994] 2 VR 333.
206. (1992) 26 ALD 496.
207. In dismissing the Commonwealth's appeal, the Full Court of the Supreme Court of Victoria found that Clark had a stronger case than Verwayen since he had commenced his action in reliance upon the Commonwealth's policy and evidence of detriment had been called at the trial. Ormiston J expressed some doubt as to the operation of the doctrine of precedent in relation to the High Court's decision in *Verwayen* and said that it would be "a very harsh conclusion" in the case of another *Voyager* survivor with experiences similar to those of Verwayen, not to hold the Commonwealth to the policy: *Commonwealth v Clark* [1994] 2 VR 333 at 385. These observations were made in a context where the Full Court had difficulty in discerning a clearly binding ratio in the High Court's decision in *Verwayen*.
208. *Verwayen* (1990) 170 CLR 394 at 415.

detriment of not proceeding immediately to assessment of damages. In a narrow sense there is the detriment the person suffers as a result of reliance upon the correctness of the assumption. This is the added stress of pursuing a legal action which is hopeless because the defences are ultimately pleaded. Detriment in the broad sense must exist in order to establish the resilement from the promise which is an element necessary to establish estoppel. But equity only protects against detriment in the narrow sense.

7. CONCLUSION

The policy/operational distinction, transported from private law to public law, was not truly a private law concept but a rough attempt under the rubric of the policy considerations relevant to particular categories of negligence to make a concession to public law principles. The distinction recognised a legitimate claim to qualification of the equality proposition. Yet private law would not accept the no-fettering principle fully. The policy/operational distinction offered a mechanism for weakening the principle in a private law context. The distinction's early rationale of non-interference with resource allocation, incipient in *Anns* and expanded by Mason J in *Heyman*, had some affinity with judicial reluctance about detailed enforcement of statutory duties. A later rationale, stemming from *Takaro*, was borrowed from the public law concept of justiciability but did not truly match that concept as it operated in public law. In addition, since *Heyman*, the general reliance component of proximity threatened the policy/operational distinction by placing a greater responsibility upon government in the discretionary regulation of hazardous or technically complex matters. In another category of negligence, negligent misstatement, where the policy/operational distinction might have been expected to restrict liability of government, it was displaced by a straightforward reliance upon the public law no-fettering principle. The operation of the public law principle in *San Sebastian* was undisguised and unconfined.

As private law struggled to rid itself of a coyness which forbade admission that public law principles intrude into private law, public law borrowed the policy/operational distinction as a welcome mechanism for confining the *Southend-on-Sea* principle. The policy/operational distinction could confine *Southend-on-Sea*, leave more scope for raising an estoppel against government in a judicial review action and hence for the equality proposition to operate.

Although it could provide a common principle for answering these issues in private law and public law, the policy/operational distinction was problematic. Its rationale had been linked loosely with non-interference in government resource allocation and the concept of justiciability, without sustained justification by reference to clear principles of public law. Moreover, the myth of a dichotomy between policy and administration could not be converted into a reality. That policy-making permeates the administrative decision-making process and may occur in the very process of policy application, is well illustrated by the cases on estoppel and government.

Private law now has to consider the future of the policy/operational distinction as a general policy consideration qualifying government liability in negligence. As an alternative means for qualifying government liability, the no-fettering principle offers a more drastic infringement of the equality proposition. Public law has to consider whether the policy/operational distinction or the balancing of public interests test provides an appropriate means for confining the *Southend-on-Sea* principle in order to tilt the balance a little more in favour of the equality proposition. In each context attention will turn to the rationale for the no-fettering principle. Fully explored and justified, that rationale may be found in the ultra vires doctrine, or in the notion of a political obligation of the executive branch to act in the public interest, and at a deeper level in the doctrine of separation of powers.

Chapter 4

Money Claims by and Against the State

Keith Mason

(A) PRINCIPLES

Constitutional principles have always informed the State's capacity to recover money and its exposure to money claims. Most money claims by the State involve levies imposed by Parliament on unwilling citizens which are collected by the Executive to be spent by the three branches of government. Collection regimes necessarily reflect the tensions of constitutional accountability inherent in this mix. When disputes arose in former times, the Crown's immunity from being impleaded reflected the historical notion that the judicial system was an emanation of the monarch, and the contentious view that the State would recognise and remedy injustices touching the interest of those at its helm. Justice Paul Finn's chapter demonstrates why these tender flowers did not take root in Australian soil. He also argues that changing perceptions of the State's legal accountability have influenced particular legal rules concerning money claims by and against the State. This is undoubtedly true, as is the need to recognise that the State's position cannot always be equated with that of the citizen.

Recognition of the State as a juristic person and the notion of equality before the law should mean that an increasingly firm onus rests on those who would deprive the State of the same rights and obligations as those of a citizen who enters into a corresponding obligation. This basal principle has been accepted in Australian law.[1]

Most monetary transactions involving the State lend themselves to analysis according to the private law principles of contract and restitution (formerly quasi-contract). Old remedies exclusive to the Crown, such as the writ of extent, have passed into legal history. The general impact of the trend noticed in the previous paragraph has been to reduce the privileges and immunities of the State as a contracting party, so that they are now confined to those appropriate to the proper exercise of public functions.

---

1. See, eg *New South Wales v Bardolph* (1934) 52 CLR 455; *Commonwealth v Evans Deakin Industries Ltd* (1986) 161 CLR 254 at 265; *Western Australia v Bropho* (1990) 171 CLR 1; *Northern Territory v Mengel* (1995) 69 ALJR 527.

Nowadays monetary obligations imposed by legislation are frequently recoverable as a "debt".[2] Nevertheless, it is hardly surprising that the State has sought to enhance its position by the enactment of special enforcement regimes with beneficial privative clauses and priority in insolvency, or the imposition of short limitation periods for challenge or recovery of overpayment.

In the realm of restitution, public law principles also shape and limit the right to recover money by and against the State. The Revenue's right to restitution of ultra vires disbursements is peculiar for its harshness compared with private rights based on mistake or failure of consideration, this harshness due largely to the fact that (ironically) what is vindicated is Parliament's hard-fought control of public expenditure over the Executive. On the debit side, involving restitution *to* the citizen of imposts demanded without authority, the State's exposure to more ready restitution than that touching citizens generally is coloured by the goal of ensuring that the State and its organs should be exemplary in subjection to the rule of law.[3]

Latterly, the private law restitutionary principle that a person should be stripped of an unjust enrichment earned at another's expense has offered itself as a theoretical underpinning of the legal rules at play in these exclusively governmental areas. This has changed some of the substantive rules. Thus, the unjust enrichment principle was the impetus for the withdrawal of the protection of the old rule precluding recovery from the State of payments made under mistake of law. Indeed, the law/fact dichotomy started to break down in relation to payments to the State before it was abolished entirely in *David Securities Pty Ltd v Commonwealth Bank of Australia*.[4] More recently, the House of Lords applied the unjust enrichment principle in *Woolwich Equitable Building Society v Inland Revenue Commissioners*,[5] when fashioning a new right of recovery against the Revenue flowing from the mere payment of an impost in response to an invalid demand. Exactly how sometimes incongruent public and private law principles work themselves out in that area will be a principal focus of this chapter. The converse right, where the Revenue recovers an ultra vires disbursement, predates judicial recognition of the unjust enrichment principle, deriving from Viscount Haldane's statement in *Auckland Harbour Board v The King*.[6] However, it will be seen that restitutionary principles are now pressing at the edges of this harsh remedy.

The State may be the victim or beneficiary of mistake, deception, improper pressure or other events which give rise to rights of restitution upon orthodox principles. This is illustrated by the list of leading cases in the law of restitution which happen to involve claims by or against the State

2. As to distinction between debt and mere breach of contract, see *Young v Queensland Trustees Ltd* (1956) 99 CLR 560 at 567-568; *Hungerfords v Walker* (1984) 171 CLR 125 at 139, 159.
3. As to this aspect of the rule of law, see Keith Mason, "The Rule of Law" in Finn, *Essays on Law and Government* (1995), pp 127-128.
4. (1992) 175 CLR 353. As to the qualified withdrawal from the State of the immunity of the old rule about the irrecoverability of moneys paid under mistake of law, see pp 120-121, below.
5. [1993] AC 70.
6. [1924] AC 318.

or emanations of the State: *David Securities Pty Ltd v Commonwealth Bank of Australia*[7] (mistake); *Smith v William Charlick Ltd*[8] (improper pressure); *Commonwealth v McCormack*[9] (restitution of moneys paid under reversed judgments); *Sabemo Pty Ltd v North Sydney Municipal Council*[10] (restitution of moneys paid under contracts that fail to materialise); *Reading v Attorney-General*[11] (restitution for wrongs). The recent decision in *Commissioner of Revenue v Royal Insurance Australia Ltd*[12] involved restitution of moneys paid to the Revenue on three bases, each of which entailed the application of general legal principles. Different parts of Royal Insurance's successful claim involved money paid under mistake, money paid provisionally and on an assumption that did not eventuate, and money paid pursuant to a statutory obligation that was retrospectively repealed. Another example of "ordinary" restitution against the State involves the category of duress *colore officii*, which is but a special application of the general principles of restitution of payments procured by improper pressure.

Before examining in detail the unique (or prerogative) rights and obligations of the State as regards restitution of money it is appropriate to consider:

(1) the nature of public moneys, and

(2) the capacity of the Constitution to shape remedies which touch upon the protection of constitutional principles.

(B) THE NATURE AND CONTROL OF PUBLIC MONEYS

The history of the constitutional principle that the raising of public revenue is under the control of Parliament is traced by McHugh J in *Northern Suburbs General Cemetery Reserve Trust v Commonwealth*.[13] The principle is asserted in the *Petition of Rights*,[14] and the *Bill of Rights*[15] and it is reflected in the federal and State Constitutions.

Subject to any appropriation affected by the Constitution itself, ss 81 and 83 (and their State counterparts), give effect to the constitutional principle "that no money can be taken out of the consolidated Fund into which the revenues of the State have been paid, excepting under a distinct authorisation from Parliament itself".[16] It has been stated categorically that "parliamentary authority is required for the expenditure of *any* moneys by the Crown."[17]

7. (1992) 175 CLR 353.
8. (1923) 34 CLR 38.
9. (1984) 155 CLR 273.
10. [1977] 2 NSWLR 880.
11. [1951] AC 507.
12. (1994) 182 CLR 51.
13. (1993) 176 CLR 555 at 597-599.
14. 1627, s 8.
15. 1689, s 1.
16. *Auckland Harbour Board v The King* [1924] AC 318 at 126, cited in *Brown v West* (1990) 169 CLR 195 at 205.
17. *Northern Suburbs General Cemetery Reserve Trust v Commonwealth* (1993) 176 CLR 555 at 572 per Mason CJ, Deane, Toohey and Gaudron JJ. See also per Brennan J at 580-581 and McHugh J at 597-599.

Moneys are appropriated from the Consolidated Fund by standing (or special) and annual appropriations. Several provisions in the Constitution itself amount to appropriations.[18] An appropriation may be implied, as with the provisions found in some, but not all States, for judgment debts against the Crown to be paid outright.[19] An appropriation is not a withdrawal of money from the Consolidated Fund, but authority to the Treasurer to make specified disbursements.[20]

Parliamentary control of expenditure developed through the establishment of the Consolidated Fund and the accounting and auditing procedures now found in the *Audit Act* 1901 (Cth) and its State counterparts.[21] The Commonwealth and the States have uniformly adopted the approach of assigning all taxes and charges to a single Consolidated Fund.[22] Not content with political and legal remedies designed to foster accountability, Parliaments have in recent years expanded the role and independence of the Auditor-General to act as a watchdog to ensure that the Executive spends in accordance with its statutory mandates. *New South Wales v Bardolph*[23] establishes that Parliament's monopoly on appropriations that are not directly effected by the Constitution itself does not touch the Executive's capacity to enter a binding contract which will be enforceable to judgment, even if (in some jurisdictions) appropriation is a prerequisite to payment. However, the principles relating to parliamentary control of the raising and expenditure of money have had a fundamental impact upon the development of the State's unique restitutionary rights and obligations. Before addressing them, I need to deal briefly with the impact of the Constitution upon the law of remedies.

(C) THE IMPACT OF THE CONSTITUTION UPON REMEDIES

Claims by and against the State to recover money may involve disbursements or imposts that are ultra vires statute or the Constitution itself. The Revenue's right to restitution of disbursements under the *Auckland Harbour Board* principle only arises where there has been an ultra vires payment.[24] The converse right, under the *Woolwich* principle or its antecedents, also involves ultra vires imposts, although it may also extend to payments in response to assessments vitiated by error or misinterpretation.

Ultra vires has a special sting when it involves money, because it strikes at Parliament's hard won control of the fisc. The Constitution itself may invalidate the levying or the appropriation or disbursement of money. For

18. *Northern Suburbs* at 581 per Brennan J.
19. See P Hogg, *Liability of the Crown* (2nd ed, 1989), pp 48-50.
20. *New South Wales v Commonwealth* (1908) 7 CLR 179 at 190.
21. See *Northern Suburbs* at 573, 579.
22. Ibid at 575, 579-580.
23. (1934) 52 CLR 455.
24. See esp *Commonwealth v Hamilton* [1992] 2 Qd R 257 at 263. See further pp 109-111, below.

example, a State tax may be an excise, or a State grant a bounty, in either case contravening s 90. A taxing Act may have been passed in breach of s 55 or its State counterparts, or involve other constitutional infractions such as breach of s 92. It will be seen that s 83 (and the historical principles it embodies) strikes down any disbursement of moneys from the Treasury except under appropriation made "by law", which means by the direct operation of the Constitution or by statute.

The first (and, for some, the last) instinct is to view constitutional ultra vires with particular disfavour and to regard its reversal as axiomatic. It will be seen, however, that constitutional and private law principles tug in opposite directions, and that the State's entitlement to restitution or its obligation to give it is neither axiomatic nor unconditional. The rule of law is not a self-executing principle, and the choice of remedies designed to promote it must take account of countervailing policies. Recipients of ultra vires disbursements have interests in the security of their receipts. The "unlawfulness" of an impost may come about through a change of the law as interpreted by the courts, despite earlier reliance on now reversed precedent. There may be a need to have regard to the potential disruption of the Treasury (and the programmes it provides in the public interest) of unrestricted restitution, sometimes in favour of those who have already benefited from those programmes. The law of restitution seeks to prevent or reverse unjust enrichment, not to merely transfer it from the defendant's to the plaintiff's pocket.

Ultimately, these tensions are worked out through the law of remedies, that body of largely judge-made law which translates legal rights into court orders, and in the process moulds and modifies the rights themselves. In some areas, statute has intervened to restrict the availability of remedies, for example by enacting limitation, change of position and passing-on defences.

However, a prior question is whether the Constitution, which may invalidate the tax or disbursement, does not implicitly create its own right of recovery. The question is critical because it affects the capacity of legislatures to tamper with recovery remedies. The general answer is that the Constitution is not self-executing. Rather, it assumes the prior existence of the common law and, by a related notion, allows legislative tinkering with it. For example, when State road transport licence fees were struck down in *Hughes and Vale Pty Ltd v New South Wales*[25] for breach of s 92, recovery rights depended upon claims being brought within the general principles relating to duress, albeit flexibly applied.[26] The States were permitted to enact prospective limitation provisions with shorter than usual limits, but attempts to deem pending claims to be barred on this ground were struck down as themselves inimical to s 92.[27] The precise limits of judicial deference to the legislature in this area will be addressed later. But, for the moment it is sufficient to note that s 92 did not itself carry an implied right of restitution of an impost levied in breach of its mandate.

25. (1954) 93 CLR 1.
26. *Mason v New South Wales* (1959) 102 CLR 108. See further p 124, below.
27. See below, pp 128-129.

An analogous issue was recently debated in *Northern Territory v Mengel*.[28] The High Court overturned the Court of Appeal of the Northern Territory[29] which had discovered new remedies in damages, independent of traditional torts, which were based (by Priestley J) upon a particular reading of *James v Commonwealth*,[30] and (by Angel J, Thomas J concurring) upon the principles of the rule of law. Cattle inspectors had, in good faith, exercised powers to direct that cattle suspected of being diseased should not be moved, and this had caused loss to the owners who complied. However, the statutory power to give such directions was not available because the owners (unknown to the inspectors) had not previously consented to enter the particular property into the legislative scheme for brucellosis testing. The High Court rejected the Court of Appeal's attempt to craft new damages remedies directly from constitutional principles. As Dixon J had pointed out in *James v Commonwealth*, (constitutional) ultra vires might strike down the justification for State action, but exposure to damages in that situation would depend on something more than unauthorised conduct. When s 92 of the Constitution invalidated a legislative scheme pursuant to which Mr James' goods had been seized, the plaintiff's cause of action for damages was found in ordinary tort law and not in the Constitution itself. It was unjustified interference with his property rights that led to damages, not the mere infringement of the Constitution.[31]

However, the law is not entirely consistent. In other fields, judges have been prepared to fashion new monetary remedies directly consequent upon constitutional infraction. Despite statements in the *Nationwide News Pty Ltd v Wills*[32] and the *Political Advertising* case,[33] suggesting that the constitutional implication of freedom of political communication affects the exercise of *public* power, notably that exercised by Parliament, *Theophanous v Herald & Weekly Times Ltd*[34] saw the free speech implication moulding the common law and statutory obligations of citizens in their private dealings, at least so far as they touched communication in the protected field. This most radical aspect of *Theophanous* is scarcely touched upon in the majority judgments. It involves a huge issue with which other constitutional courts have grappled, including the Supreme Courts of the United States and Canada.[35]

---

28. (1995) 69 ALJR 527.
29. (1994) 95 NTR 8.
30. (1939) 62 CLR 339.
31. *James v Commonwealth* (1939) 62 CLR 339 at 361-362; *Antill Ranger & Co Pty Ltd v Commissioner of Motor Transport* (1955) 93 CLR 83 at 99; *Mengel* (1995) 69 ALJR 527 at 542-544.
32. (1992) 177 CLR 1 at 52, 75-76, 94.
33. *Australian Capital Television Pty Ltd v Commonwealth* (1992) 177 CLR 106 at 143-144, 182, 217-218.
34. (1994) 182 CLR 104.
35. Cf *Shelley v Kraemer* 334 US 1 (1948); *Lugar v Edmondson Oil Co* 457 US 922, 936-937 (1982); *Tulsa Professional Collection Services Inc v Pope* 485 US 478, 485 (1988); *RWDSU v Dolphin Delivery* (1986) 33 DLR (4th) 174. See generally A S Butler, "Constitutional Rights in Private Litigation: A Critique and Comparative Analysis" (1993) 22 Anglo-American LR 1.

In the present context, it is sufficient to point to *Woolwich Equitable Building Society v Inland Revenue Commissioners*[36] as an example of a constitutional principle directly reaching into the common law and creating a new remedy. It is true that this field was fertile, because *Woolwich* can be explained as a development of the private law principles of unjust enrichment. But the necessary "unjust element" in *Woolwich* was ultra vires (admittedly touching the fisc). If this does not generate an automatic right to damages,[37] on what principle does the constitution (with a big or little "c") generate its own restitutionary remedy? And, if the *Auckland Harbour Board* principle derives from s 83 of the Constitution, whether for or against the recipient of the ultra vires payment, does this place any impediment upon legislative tinkering? I shall address these questions as I deal with the "common law" restitutionary rights and duties of the State.

(D) RESTITUTION TO THE REVENUE OF ULTRA VIRES DISBURSEMENTS

The high constitutional principle that Parliament alone may authorise the disbursement of money from the consolidated fund is declared in s 83 of the Commonwealth Constitution and reflected in corresponding provisions in each State.[38] The High Court has repeatedly affirmed it in recent years.[39] Parliamentary control is maintained through an *Appropriation Act*, which serves a twofold purpose: "Not only does it authorise the Crown to withdraw moneys from the Treasury, it restricts the expenditure to the particular purpose."[40]

The principle of parliamentary control of public money gives rise to a general restitutionary remedy exclusively available to the Crown.

The principle in Auckland Harbour Board v The King

In the leading case, *Auckland Harbour Board v The King*,[41] the New Zealand Minister of Railways had agreed with the Harbour Board that the Board should be paid £7,500 in consideration for granting a lease over part of its property to a third party. The agreement was sanctioned by an Act which was held to authorise the payment only on condition that the Board entered into the lease. The agreement was duly made, and the Board stood ready to grant the lease at the request of the Minister. That request was never made and the lease was not granted. Nevertheless the money was paid

36. [1993] AC 70. I shall discuss below whether this decision would be followed in Australia.
37. See *Northern Territory v Mengel* (1995) 69 ALJR 527 and cf also the reference there (at 538) to the requirements of the tort of breach of statutory duty.
38. See P J Hanks, *Constitutional Law in Australia* (1991), pp 148-149.
39. *Victoria v Commonwealth* (1975) 134 CLR 338 at 354, 386, 392, 410-411; *Davis v Commonwealth* (1988) 166 CLR 79 at 93, 115; *Brown v West* (1990) 169 CLR 195; *Northern Suburbs General Cemetery Reserve Trust v Commonwealth* (1993) 176 CLR 555.
40. *Brown v West* (1990) 169 CLR 195 at 208 per the court, quoting Mason J in *Victoria v Commonwealth* (1975) 134 CLR 338 at 392. The requirement of stating a purpose is questioned by McHugh J in *Northern Suburbs* at 600-602.
41. [1924] AC 318.

to the Board. Because no mistake was involved, the money was not recoverable under general restitutionary principles. The government eventually "resumed" the land in issue, thereby vesting title in the Crown and rendering it impossible for the Board to grant the lease as requested. On advice that the payment was illegal, £7,500 was set off against other money owing to the Board.

The Board's action to recover the sum that the Crown had set off failed before the Privy Council. Viscount Haldane said:

> "The payment was . . . an illegal one, which no merely executive ratification, even with the concurrence of the Controller and Auditor General, could divest of its illegal character. For it has been a principle of the British Constitution now for more than two centuries, a principle which their Lordships understand to have been inherited in the Constitution of New Zealand with the same stringency, that no money can be taken out of the consolidated Fund into which the revenues of the State have been paid, excepting under a distinct authorisation from Parliament itself. The days are long gone by in which the Crown, or its servants, apart from Parliament, could give such an authorisation or ratify an improper payment. Any payment out of the consolidated fund made without parliamentary authority is simply illegal and ultra vires, and may be recovered by the government if it can, as here, be traced."[42]

"Tracing" in this context does not refer to the proprietary remedy, but to tracing the identity of the recipient of the money.[43]

In *Maguire v Simpson*,[44] Gibbs J described *Auckland Harbour Board* as establishing that "any payment made out of the consolidated funds without parliamentary authority is illegal and ultra vires, and may be recovered by the Government if it can be traced." In *Commonwealth v Crothall Hospital Services (Aust) Ltd*,[45] Ellicott J speaking with the concurrence of Blackburn and Deane JJ summarised the *Auckland Harbour Board* line of cases as holding that:

> "where moneys are paid out of Consolidated Revenue without authority they may be recovered in an action by the government. This could occur if a condition on which money was appropriated by statute had not been met at the time it was paid out or if money was paid out by mistake even though not recoverable under ordinary principles. The basis of the action is that there has been a payment out of the revenue fund without authority."

This principle has been repeatedly endorsed and applied in Australia.[46]

---

42. At 326-327.
43. *Commonwealth v Burns* [1971] VR 825 at 828. Contra *Woolwich Equitable Building Soc v Inland Revenue Commissioners* [1993] AC 70 at 177. Cf Law Commission (UK), *Restitution: Mistakes of Law and Ultra Vires Public Authority Receipts and Payments*, Law Com No 227, 1994, § 17.12.
44. (1977) 139 CLR 362 at 388.
45. (1981) 54 FLR 439 at 45, 36 ALR 567 at 580.
46. See *Australian Railways Union v Victorian Railways Commissioners* (1930) 44 CLR 319 at 389; *New South Wales v Bardolph* (1934) 52 CLR 455 at 471, 522; *Sandvik Australia Pty Ltd v Commonwealth* (1989) 89 ALR 213; *Brown v West* (1990) 169 CLR 195 at 205.

A leading case is *Attorney-General v Gray*,[47] a decision of the New South Wales Court of Appeal. Money was paid to a public servant in excess of the salary authorised by statute for the position he in fact held. The *Public Service Act* 1902 (NSW) provided in effect that the salary payable to employees such as the defendant was the salary determined from time to time by the Public Service Board. The excess was held recoverable, without the need to prove that the payment had been made under any mistake,[48] and despite the fact that a defence by way of estoppel would have lain in relation to a mistake-based claim.

Attorney-General v Gray[49] demonstrates that the absence of parliamentary authority extends beyond absence of a relevant appropriation. It applies to any disbursement that is ultra vires, whatever the reason. In *Attorney-General v Gray* the defendant had argued that, because the *Appropriation Act* made provision for a sum which was adequate to permit the payments actually made, there was Parliamentary authority for the payment. This argument was rejected because the *Public Service Act* stated by implication that the only salary properly payable to the defendant was that determined by the Public Service Board as appropriate to his particular grading. To similar effect is the decision of Zeeman J in *Commonwealth v Ware*,[50] where a widow's pension paid to an unqualified person was recovered. If the purported authority for a disbursement from Consolidated Revenue is an ultra vires statute, the money paid is recoverable according to these principles.[51]

To the extent that a payment from the Revenue is unauthorised it is recoverable. In *Attorney-General v Gray*[52] there was a contract of employment pursuant to which the defendant performed services. But since he was paid more than was due according to statute, the excess was recoverable. According to Hutley JA:

> "As payment of part of the moneys was properly authorised by statute, I can see no difficulty in part being recoverable. The excess payment does not make the services rendered by the respondent illegal, and he is entitled to retain that which he is entitled to receive for them."[53]

If, however, any payment related to a contract to sell goods or render services, the mere fact that the statute authorising the sale or performance of services was invalid would not bring the case within the *Auckland Harbour Board* principle. The delivery of goods or services provided under the admittedly ultra vires contract would itself give rise to a restitutionary claim for a reasonable price or value.[54] But such a claim would be based on general principle, not the constitutional principle expounded in

---

47. [1977] 1 NSWLR 406.
48. See also *R v Toronto Terminals Railway Co* [1948] Ex C R 563.
49. [1977] 1 NSWLR 406.
50. Unreported, SC Tas, 2 July 1992. See also *Formosa v Secretary, Department of Social Security* (1988) 46 FCR 117 at 125; 81 ALR 687 at 696.
51. *Breckenridge Speedway Ltd v The Queen* (1970) 9 DLR (3d) 142.
52. [1977] 1 NSWLR 406.
53. At 410-411. See also per Glass JA at 413-414.
54. *Re K L Tractors Ltd* (1961) 106 CLR 318 at 335. See also Oliver P Field, *The Effect of an Unconstitutional Statute* (1935), p 15.

Auckland Harbour Board. The difference is critical to the extent that general defences, such as estoppel and change of position, are no answer to an *Auckland Harbour Board* claim.

The *Auckland Harbour Board* principle is confined to ultra vires payments. In all cases where recovery has been allowed, the recipient of the payment out of consolidated funds failed to satisfy the statutory requirement which constituted the sole authority to make the payment in question. In *Auckland Harbour Board v The King*,[55] the statutory authority for payment was conditional upon the happening of an event that never took place. In *Commonwealth v Burns*,[56] the statutory qualification for payment of the pension is not precisely set out in the report of the case; but it is clear enough that the title of the defendant's father to receive it ceased at his death, and with it the authority to pay it to her on his behalf. In *Attorney-General v Gray*,[57] the defendant did not possess the qualifications entitling him to payment at the rate appropriate under the relevant statutory provisions for teachers in a higher classification to which he did not belong. As McPherson ACJ put it in *Commonwealth v Hamilton*:

> "Before the principle of the *Auckland Harbour* case can be invoked it is necessary to identify the precise terms of the statutory authority to pay, and to ask whether the terms of that authority were exceeded. It applies only when it can be seen that no such authority exists, as where its operation is made to depend on the fulfilment of a statutory condition that is not satisfied; or on the absence in the recipient of a particular statutory characteristic or qualification that would entitle him to payment; or on some other defect in the source of authority to pay. It is in events like those that money paid out of consolidated funds under parliamentary control will be recoverable according to this principle. As was recognised by Viscount Haldane . . .,[58] and also by Gibbs CJ in *Maguire v Simpson*,[59] the rule is an application of the ultra vires doctrine, which means that the payment must be shown to have been made without or contrary to or in excess of the statutory authority to make it."[60]

In *Commonwealth v Hamilton* unemployment benefits had been paid to a person who fraudulently misrepresented his position. This was a basis for recovery, but not according to the *Auckland Harbour Board* principle. The facts as (mis)represented had given the Secretary of the Department of Social Security authority to pay the benefits. Accordingly, that payment was not ultra vires. The requirement of showing that the disbursement was ultra vires means that money paid in accordance with the exercise of a statutory discretion cannot be recovered by virtue of the *Auckland Harbour Board* principle.[61]

55. [1924] AC 318.
56. [1971] VR 825.
57. [1977] 1 NSWLR 406.
58. See the passage quoted above on p 108.
59. (1977) 139 CLR 362 at 388.
60. [1992] 2 Qd R 257 at 263.
61. See *Trimboli v Secretary, Department of Social Security* (1989) 86 ALR 64, where the statute authorised the compromise pursuant to which the payment was made.

It has been said that not every breach of procedural laws or regulations relating to payments of public moneys will suffice, at least where the payments are in accordance with a contractual obligation.[62]

Since the State has a general power to enter into contracts, even though the satisfaction thereof may depend upon parliamentary appropriation,[63] the *Auckland Harbour Board* principle does not apply in relation to valid contracts to the extent that they provide for payments thereunder. Those contracts may be enforced in the courts, although the statute law of the various Australian jurisdictions differs as to whether a money judgment is capable of execution in the absence of appropriation. If money is due under a contract and paid by the State it cannot be recovered otherwise than in accordance with the ordinary principles of the law of contract and restitution. In other words, the State cannot simply choose to ignore the executed contract and claim under the *Auckland Harbour Board* principle.[64] For example, in *Commonwealth v Crothall Hospital Services (Aust) Ltd*,[65] claims for payment were made upon the Commonwealth that were calculated otherwise than according to the written contract between the parties. By that contract, which provided for price variations, the claimant had agreed to perform services for, and at a price to be paid by, the Commonwealth. The respondent's claims for payment were held, on the facts, to be offers to vary the contract which were accepted by the Commonwealth's unqualified payments. Mistake in payment was not alleged: rather the claims that were acknowledged and met were accepted as the result of a conscious decision to do so by the officers concerned. The *Auckland Harbour Board* principle was held inapplicable because the Commonwealth's payments were unqualified, and constituted not only performance, but acceptance of offers to vary the original contract. In *Attorney-General v Gray*,[66] the defendant argued that the excess payments he had received were covered by this contract principle insofar as there was a contract of employment between him and the Crown. However, that contract did not, the New South Wales Court of Appeal held, impact upon the statutory restraint upon pay officers requiring them to pay no more than the salary determined by the Public Service Board as appropriate for the position in fact held by the defendant.

Limited defences available

The law of restitution has generally recognised defences of consideration received, estoppel and change of position.[67] However, the impact of constitutional principles in the present field has seen the rejection of those defences.

---

62. *Commonwealth v Crothall Hospital Services (Aust) Ltd* (1981) 54 FLR 439 at 454-455, 36 ALR 567 at 581-582 per Ellicott J; Blackburn & Deane JJ concurring.
63. *New South Wales v Bardolph* (1934) 52 CLR 455.
64. See *New South Wales v Bardolph* (1934) 52 CLR 455 at 471-472 per Evatt J.
65. (1981) 54 FLR 439; 36 ALR 567.
66. [1977] 1 NSWLR 406.
67. See generally Keith Mason and J W Carter, *Restitution Law in Australia* (1995) (hereafter *Mason and Carter*), Pt VII.

While payment will be irrecoverable, to the extent that it is in accordance with a contractual obligation, it does not follow that the mere fact that the payee gave valuable consideration in exchange will constitute a defence in a true ultra vires situation.[68] The failure to perform the condition pursuant to which the appropriated moneys were payable in *Auckland Harbour Board* (namely, the grant of a lease) meant that they were recoverable even though the Board had taken steps towards being able to do so.[69] In *Commonwealth v Burns*,[70] Newton J qualified his statement of the applicable principle by reserving the position of moneys paid "without any consideration". It is, however, doubtful if this qualification has any application outside the situation of a payment to the extent that it was due pursuant to a contract.

If the payment is unauthorised, a representation to the contrary cannot ground any defence based on estoppel. A representation of a state of affairs that is contrary to law cannot ground an estoppel.[71] This contrasts with the private law principle that a misrepresentation about legality attracts a right to rescind.[72] There are signs of a willingness to reconsider this approach in some situations,[73] but the high constitutional function of the *Auckland Harbour Board* principle makes it unlikely and, I believe, inappropriate that a misrepresentation by a Crown employee or agent could ground an estoppel. In *Attorney-General v Gray*,[74] the moneys disbursed without lawful authority were recoverable even though a defence based on estoppel would have been available had the plaintiff's case been based simply on mistake. As Hutley JA explained it:

> "no officer can certify so as to affect the State, otherwise than in accordance with parliamentary authority . . . Public moneys disbursed contrary to statute can be recovered, despite representations by those who disbursed them."[75]

This conclusion about estoppel is supported by other Australian authorities.[76] Arguments based on estoppel in similar circumstances have also been rejected in the United States and Canada.[77]

68. Contrast the general position regarding the defence of consideration received, discussed in *Mason and Carter*, ibid, Ch 25.
69. See also *Attorney-General v Gray* [1977] 1 NSWLR 406 at 413-414.
70. [1971] VR 825 at 827, citing *Re K L Tractors Ltd* (1961) 106 CLR 318 at 334, 335.
71. *Minister for Immigration & Ethnic Affairs v Kurtovic* (1990) 21 FCR 193; *Attorney-General (NSW) v Quin* (1990) 170 CLR 1; *Roberts v Repatriation Commission* (1992) 111 ALR 436.
72. See *David Securities Pty Ltd v Commonwealth Bank of Australia* (1992) 175 CLR 353 at 385.
73. See, eg *Attorney-General v Quin* (NSW) (1990) 170 CLR 1 at 18. Cf also P Finn and K J Smith, "The Citizen, the Government and 'Reasonable Expectations' " (1992) 66 ALJ 139 at 147, who cite the *Judiciary Act* 1903, s 64. Of course, the capacity to rely on s 64 may itself be affected if the *Auckland Harbour Board* principle were itself directly referable to s 83 of the Constitution in the federal context. See above, pp 104-107, for a discussion of this broader issue.
74. [1977] 1 NSWLR 406.
75. Ibid at 409, 410.
76. *Commonwealth v Thompson* (1962) 1 CCR (Vic) 37; *Commonwealth v Burns* [1971] VR 825; *Formosa v Secretary, Department of Social Security* (1988) 46 FCR 117 at 125, 81 ALR 687 at 696. See also *Commonwealth v Hamilton* [1992] 2 Qd R 257.
77. *United States v Wurts* 303 US 414 (1938); *Office of Personnel Management v Richmond* 496 US 414 (1990); *Corpus Juris Secundum*, "United States", para 134; *Breckenridge Speedway Ltd v The Queen* (1970) 9 DLR (3d) 142.

The change of position defence should be precluded for similar reasons. Since this defence requires that it be shown that the defendant acted to her or his detriment on the faith of the receipt,[78] it is difficult to see how reliance could properly be placed upon the faith of a payment prohibited by law.[79]

As already indicated,[80] these principles allow the recovery of pension or other welfare benefits paid to recipients who were not entitled to receive them. However, in this field one frequently encounters a statutory right of recovery, subject in some cases to proof of fault by the recipient and to a right of appeal, with (more significantly) a statutory discretion to refuse the State relief in some cases, having regard to hardship or other personal circumstances of the wrongful recipient.[81] Where the discretion not to pursue recovery is exercised in accordance with such provisions, either by the initial repository of the discretion, or on appeal by the Administrative Appeals Tribunal, then nothing in *Auckland Harbour Board* requires the repayment of the moneys that were wrongfully paid.[82] However, the mere fact that a statutory right of recovery may be in some respects wider and in other respects narrower than that conferred at common law under the *Auckland Harbour Board* principle does not in itself exclude the latter principle.[83]

To the extent that the rule is designed to enhance the authority of Parliament, the usefulness of depriving the citizen of any defence in the form of "consideration received", estoppel or change of position may be questionable. The main justification for imposing liability on a citizen is that the money received was paid out by a public servant in excess of authority. Yet the rule visits the consequences of the act upon the person who in many cases will be the victim, and not the perpetrator of the error. Because of this, calls have been made to mitigate the harshness of the *Auckland Harbour Board* principle, at least to the extent of allowing the citizen to raise usual restitutionary defences such as change of position and estoppel.[84] One criticism that in the past has been levied against the principle is that it does not acknowledge a reciprocal claim by the subject against the Crown: this of course may no longer be the case in the light of

78. *David Securities Pty Ltd v Commonwealth Bank of Australia* (1992) 175 CLR 353 at 385.

79. *Commonwealth v Burns* [1971] VR 825 at 830.

80. See p 109.

81. See, eg *Social Security Act* 1991 (Cth), Ch 5 (and the former s 140 of the *Social Security Act* 1947 (Cth)); *Customs Act* 1901 (Cth), s 165; *Director-General of Social Services v Hales* (1983) 78 FLR 373; *Re Keuker* (1984) 5 ALD 626; *Re Pappis* (1984) 1 AAR 315; *Secretary, Department of Social Security v Alvaro* (1994) 50 FCR 213.

82. *Director-General of Social Services v Hales* (1983) 78 FLR 373; *Walker v Secretary, Department of Social Security* (1995) 129 ALR 198.

83. *Commonwealth v Burns* [1971] VR 825 at 829.

84. Law Reform Commission of British Columbia, *Report on the Recovery of Unauthorised Disbursements of Public Funds*, 1980, LRC 48. The recommendation was adopted in that Province: see *Financial Arbitration Act*, SBC, 1981 c15 s 67. For a contrary view, see P Hogg, *Liability of the Crown* (2nd ed, 1989), pp 185-186. The Law Commission (UK) recommended against altering the principle, but did so on the highly debatable assumption that the standard restitutionary defence of change of position already applies: *Restitution: Mistakes of Law and Ultra Vires Public Authority Receipts and Payments*, Law Com No 227, 1994, § 17.20. But see pp 111-113, above.

Woolwich Equitable Building Society v Inland Revenue Commissioners.[85] To date calls for legislative reform of the appropriately stern rule based on *Auckland Harbour Board* appear to have fallen on deaf ears outside British Columbia.

(E) RESTITUTION AGAINST THE REVENUE

Introduction

A layperson would be surprised to learn that where the Revenue claims money pursuant to an assessment that was unauthorised or was issued under a statute that is unconstitutional, the taxpayer who pays and then discovers the money was not due cannot automatically recover the money back. The plaintiff has to demonstrate mistake (until recently, mistake of fact), that species of improper pressure relating to public officials called duress *colore officii*, a contract or understanding to repay, or a statutory right to reimbursement. That at least was the law in England until 1992. It is probably still the law in Australia, although the High Court would in my opinion be likely to follow the House of Lords in *Woolwich Equitable Building Society v Inland Revenue Commissioners*[86] in overturning it, at least in situations where the invalidity of the Revenue's demand did not come about by a change in the law. Special defences may be available to prevent fiscal chaos. Statute may of course confer a special right of recovery, and (subject to certain constitutional limits) abrogate any common law right to restitution.

Woolwich Equitable Building Society v Inland Revenue Commissioners involved an ultra vires regulation made under a valid law, where the validity of the regulation was promptly challenged and had not been the subject of earlier inconsistent judicial decision. Federations with controlled constitutions, like Australia, are likely to throw up problems of a completely different order.

Where the taxing Act is held invalid, an initial question is whether the plaintiff's restitutionary right can be located in the Constitution itself. A related question is whether breach of a constitution can give rise to rights as between citizen and citizen. I have already discussed the general issues here involved.[87] The traditional view, in Australian law, has been that the constitutional invalidity of a statute removes the statutory "defence" but does not itself establish a cause of action. In the discussion which follows, I shall assume that this approach continues, and that it applies to money claims derived from invalidity, even constitutional invalidity. The issue has important consequences, because if the traditional view changed this may affect the capacity of legislatures to enact laws blocking or modifying restitutionary claims.

The call to fashion a special right of recovery in the field of invalid taxes came from academic lawyers who took as their starting point the

85. [1993] AC 70.
86. Ibid.
87. See pp 104-107, above.

constitutional principle embodied in Declaration 4 of the *Bill of Rights* 1689 (Imp)[88] which provides that:

> "levying money for or to the use of the Crown, by pretence of prerogative, without grant of Parliament for longer time or in other manner than the same is or shall be granted is illegal."

At first the call was qualified,[89] but latterly uncompromising.[90]

The principle that Parliament alone may levy taxes[91] arguably provides a constitutional springboard for an independent right of recovery. So too does the need for the Crown, above all, to respect the rule of law in its letter and spirit. A third justification is more pragmatic: a government that expects its citizens to submit readily (if not cheerfully) to its revenue demands may find it easier to achieve that aim if it can assure the citizen that the money will be promptly returned (with interest) should the demand be shown to be unjustified.[92] A fourth strand of reasoning points to the apparent unfairness of the Revenue's position as defendant when contrasted with that as plaintiff. Under the principle in *Auckland Harbour Board v The King*[93] that has already been discussed, if the State pays money out of Consolidated Revenue without authority, it is *ipso facto* recoverable from the payee. The comparison with the position of the citizen under the "old law" was, as Lord Goff observed in *Woolwich Equitable Building Society v Inland Revenue Commissioners*,[94] "most unattractive". Fifth, there is a recognition that any demand for payment of a tax is implicitly backed by the coercive powers of the state which, if resisted, may lead to fines or penal interest, or damage to reputation in a society where "tax dodging" is no longer as socially acceptable as it once was. Sixth, the old law contained an intolerable irony that is exposed by Professor Birks. In licensing cases the logic of the duress principle means that the greater the invalidity the lower the chance of restitution:

> "If the whole scheme is ultra vires, fees paid for licences cannot be recovered in the absence of some collateral duress . . . The withholding of the licence itself is not duress for the citizen can have no entitlement to a nullity. If, however, the power to issue licences is itself valid and

88. 1 William & Mary sess 2 c2. It is in force throughout Australia: see, eg *Imperial Acts Application Act* 1969 (NSW), s 6.
89. See C Pannam, "The Recovery of Unconstitutional Taxes in Australia and the United States" (1964) 42 Texas LR 779; P Birks, "Restitution from Public Authorities" (1980) 33 CLP 191; J D McCamus, "Restitutionary Recovery of Moneys Paid to a Public Authority Under a Mistake of Law: Ignoratia Juris in the Supreme Court of Canada" (1983) 17 U Brit Col LR 233; R D Collins, "Restitution from Government Officers" (1984) 29 McGill LJ 407.
90. See W R Cornish, " 'Colour of Office': Restitutionary Redress Against Public Authority" (1987) Jo Malaysian and Comp Law 41; P Hogg, *Liability of the Crown* (2nd ed, 1989), pp 181-186; P Birks, "Restitution from the Executive: A Tercentenary Footnote to the Bill of Rights" in Finn, *Essays on Restitution*; G Jones, *Restitution in Public and Private Law* (1991), pp 42-43.
91. See also p 103, above.
92. Cf the rationale behind restitution for judgments that are reversed: see *Mason and Carter*, op cit, Ch 7.
93. [1924] AC 318.
94. [1993] AC 70 at 177. See also *Commissioner of State Revenue (Vic) v Royal Insurance Australia Ltd* (1994) 182 CLR 51 at 68 per Mason CJ.

only the demand for fees is ultra vires the fees can be recovered. For here . . . he is entitled to have the licence without charge and its withholding is itself duress."[95]

Nevertheless, respect for the rule of law does not provide an automatic answer as to what remedy is appropriate. The criminal law chooses to punish only those whose infraction is proved beyond reasonable doubt and (usually) shown to be wilful. Some duties are of "imperfect obligation", others are enforced only by an award of damages, in lieu of specific relief. Unlawfully obtained evidence is not per se inadmissible.

In the realm of public law, a retroactive declaration of voidness does not necessarily follow judicial determination of unauthorised conduct.[96] And doctrines such as the de facto officers doctrine, and the principles protecting those who act bona fide under what turns out to be an invalid warrant from personal liability, all emphasise the remedial choices that are open.[97] It is not axiomatic that vindication of Parliament's role in this area requires more than a declaration of invalidity that operates in futuro.[98]

As a general proposition, restitution is not available to a person who pays what is due anyway.[99] The fact that the plaintiff was mistaken[100] or subject to improper pressure[101] will not overcome the law's abhorrence of circuity of actions, which precludes giving a restitutionary right where the defendant would have a valid cross-claim to get the money back again. Do these principles apply in favour of the Revenue when, at the time when payment was made to it, "the law" regarded the payment as due? This question raises acute constitutional issues. First, as to whether the judicial function properly includes the right to limit the retroactive impact of a decision by the practice of prospective overruling. Second, as to the meaning of invalidity in a constitutional context.[102]

The abandonment of the myth of the declaratory theory of judicial law-making means that both theory and reality may recognise that "the law" may change when an authoritative judicial statement to that effect is made.[103] It follows that it may be simplistic in some situations to say that the Revenue had no right to receive taxes later declared to be unauthorised. And if it is accepted that the Revenue had a "right" to demand and receive the money when paid, a policy of automatic recovery might be questioned from the standpoint of a restitution theory that sets its face against recovery

95. P Birks, "Restitution from Public Authorities" (1980) 33 CLP 191 at 196-197.
96. See, eg *Parkes Rural Distributions Pty Ltd v Glasson* (1986) 7 NSWLR 332.
97. However, the application of those principles may vary if *constitutional* invalidity strikes: see *Ryder v United States* 132 L Ed 2d 136 (1995).
98. *Regional Municipality of Peel v Canada* (1992) 98 DLR(4th) 140 at 143-144.
99. See generally D Friedmann, "Valid, Voidable, Qualified, and Non-existing Obligations: An Alternative Perspective on the Law of Restitution" in Andrew Burrows (ed), *Essays on the Law of Restitution* (1991), Ch 10.
100. *David Securities Pty Ltd v Commonwealth Bank of Australia* (1992) 175 CLR 353 at 392.
101. See *Mason and Carter*, op cit, § 520.
102. These two issues and their present impact are developed at more length in *Mason and Carter*, ibid, § 2013.
103. But see *Harper v Virginia Department of Taxation* 125 L Ed 2d 74 (1993) for a vigorous judicial debate about this proposition.

of benefits in fulfilment of a valid obligation owed to the recipient. Governments, like citizens, may chart a course in reliance upon judicial decisions upholding the validity of a particular exaction or the constitutionality of the statute under which it was imposed. Judicial recognition of this may lead to refusal to overrule earlier decisions.[104] But, if overruling occurs, does it follow that it is unjust for the Revenue to retain what was due and collected under the "earlier" law? It is arguable that the Revenue should not be subjected to a restitutionary obligation to disgorge taxes received at a time when "the law", especially constitutional law as declared by the highest court, required them to be paid. Alternatively, reliance may in extreme cases establish the ingredients of a change of position defence.[105]

In *Air Canada v British Columbia*,[106] La Forest J (with whom Lamer and l'Heureux Dube JJ agreed) advanced more pragmatic reasons against the *Woolwich* principle. The practical consequence of allowing restitution is that where a large number of taxpayers have paid unlawful exactions, the State will be obliged to repay the money and then reimpose taxes to recover the moneys paid out. The burden of repayment will ultimately fall on the community. The expenditure of the invalid exactions will have benefited or will benefit the community, including the persons who have paid the exactions. A taxpayer may ultimately pay the same amount of tax, through re-imposed taxes, as it would be paid if it had not obtained a refund.[107] As La Forest J pointed out in *Air Canada*, the reimposition of invalid taxes is inefficient, and, until the tax is reimposed, the government's ability to manage its revenues is likely to be severely disrupted as it repays large amounts to claimants.[108]

Those who argue from pragmatic grounds that too much restitution may cause fiscal chaos are not bereft of principle. Leslie Green has categorised the philosophical approaches to the justification of the authority of States in terms of coordination, contract, consent and community.[109] Whatever theory is favoured, they all have in common a belief in the value of social cooperation. Government may effectively solve many coordination problems that it is not legally entitled to solve. From this premise, some writers have concluded that a government can be morally justified in exercising authority in some areas despite such exercise of power being unlawful.[110]

The difficulty is that judges could only accept the full consequences of this philosophical approach at the cost of denying their own function. But the argument, which I have developed very inadequately, does justify the

---

104. See, eg *Evda Nominees Pty Ltd v Victoria* (1984) 154 CLR 311; *Philip Morris Ltd v Commissioner of Business Franchises (Vic)* (1989) 167 CLR 399.
105. If it is available in this context. See pp 133-134, below.
106. (1989) 59 DLR (4th) 161 at 194.
107. See, generally B C Wells, "Restitution from the Crown: Private Rights and Public Interest" (1994) 16 Adel LR 191 at 212.
108. See also *Mercury Machine Importing Corp v City of New York* 154 NE 2d 400 (1957) (NYCA) at 426-427.
109. L Green, *The Authority of the State* (1988), pp 92-94.
110. See the review by Brian Fitzgerald, "Ultra Vires as an Unjust Factor in the Law of Unjust Enrichment" (1993) 2 Griffith LR 1 esp at 24-32.

conclusion that the unjust factor relied upon by Lord Goff, Professor Birks and others is certainly not self-evident. Lord Goff's reasoning has been criticised for failure to identify clearly the "unjust factor" involved.[111] In consequence, the restitutionary remedy is not axiomatic, nor should it be unyielding in its impact.

Having drawn attention to these competing policy factors, it will be seen below that I consider that the *balance* of justice favours restitution, but of a qualified and controlled nature. If the social disruption of a particular situation involving a right to restitution is too great, Parliament can usually[112] legislate to overcome its impact.

The law pre-Woolwich

The general law relating to restitution of payments made conditionally, or under mistake, or as the result of improper pressure is capable of providing redress against the Revenue in many cases. Until recently, writers and courts outside the United States have treated restitutionary principles relating to claims between citizen and citizen as equally applicable to the Executive and other public authorities. The 18th and 19th century case law is inconsistent, but the broad consensus of 20th century cases requires the citizen who claims repayment of taxes or other imposts demanded without authority to show something more than the mere invalidity of the Revenue's initial demand. But there are strands of recognition of constitutionally-based arguments favouring the taxpayer. Some of these are of merely historical interest.[113] Until very recently, most claims were rejected by characterising the payment as having been made under mistake of law. Such a mistake is now, of course, a ground of recovery,[114] but one that will not be available to the person who paid without consciously adverting to the validity of the Revenue's demand or who paid assuming its validity or irrespective of validity.[115] Where recovery has been granted in the past, it has been on the basis of mistake of fact, improper pressure (duress), an agreement or understanding implied from the circumstances of payment, or statute.

While some earlier cases suggested the "*Woolwich* principle",[116] later precedent turned its back upon it. The leading modern English case, before *Woolwich Equitable*, was *William Whiteley Ltd v The King*,[117] where a claimant failed to recover payments which turned out not to be legally due. The claimant employed staff to prepare and serve meals to its employees.

111. See E McKendrick, "Restitution of Unlawfully Demanded Tax" [1993] LMCLQ 88; B Fitzgerald, "Ultra Vires as an Unjust Factor in the Law of Unjust Enrichment" (1993) 2 Griffith LR 1. Cf *Northern Territory v Mengel* (1995) 69 ALJR 527.
112. But not invariably; see below, pp 128-130.
113. See, eg *Campbell v Hall* (1774) 1 Cowp 204; 98 ER 1045; *Attorney-General v Wilts United Dairies Ltd* (1921) 37 TLR 884 at 887.
114. *David Securities Pty Ltd v Commonwealth Bank of Australia* (1992) 175 CLR 353.
115. At 373-374, 402-403.
116. Notably *Steele v Williams* (1853) 8 Ex 625; 155 ER 1502; *Hooper v Exeter Corp* (1887) 56 LJ QB 457 and *Melbourne Tramway & Omnibus Co Ltd v Melbourne City Council* (1903) 28 VLR 647.
117. (1909) 101 LT 741.

The revenue authorities maintained that these persons were "male servants" in respect of whom licence duties were payable under the *Revenue Act* 1869 (UK). Although this was disputed, payments were made under protest for a number of years. After the Revenue's position was challenged successfully in separate proceedings,[118] the claimant sought repayment of the sums paid in the past years. Walton J rejected the claim on the ground that the payments had not been made in discharge of a demand illegally made under colour of office or any other form of duress vitiating the "voluntary" nature of the payment. The claimant knew all the relevant facts and could have resisted payment at any time. The case appears to have turned on the application of two principles: the irrecoverability of payments made under mistake of law; and a finding that the company had paid with intent to close the transaction. Until recently, at least, it was usually cited for the former proposition, and the applicability thereof in favour of the Revenue. It may now be "distinguishable" on the basis of the latter finding.[119]

Under this approach recovery was generally denied unless there was a demand *colore officii*,[120] or some other form of illegitimate pressure, amounting in law to duress,[121] or a mistake of fact, or some agreement or understanding to refund in the event of excessive payment or illegality of the impost being established.[122] Proof of the unlawfulness of the official demand was, standing alone, considered insufficient to base recovery at common law.[123] Nor did payment under protest or after a threat of legal action in itself establish improper pressure.[124]

Whether this approach involved a misunderstanding of the true ratio of *Mason v New South Wales*[125] or whether that decision would be followed

118. *Whiteley v Burns* [1908] 1 KB 705.
119. See, eg *Woolwich Equitable Building Soc v Inland Revenue Commissioners* [1993] AC 70 at 100 (Glidewell LJ), 204 (Lord Slynn of Hadley).
120. See *Sargood Brothers v Commonwealth* (1910) 11 CLR 258 esp at 301-302; *Mason v New South Wales* (1959) 102 CLR 108 at 140; *Bell Bros Pty Ltd v Shire of Serpentine-Jarrahdale* (1969) 121 CLR 137 at 145.
121. *Maskell v Horner* [1915] 3 KB 106; *McClintock v Commonwealth* (1947) 75 CLR 1 at 40-41.
122. *Queensland Trustees Ltd v Fowles* (1910) 12 CLR 111; *Precision Pools Pty Ltd v Commissioner of Taxation* (1992) 37 FCR 554. See also *Sebel Products Ltd v Custom and Excise Commissioners* [1949] Ch 409, a decision that was doubted on its facts and firmly distinguished in *Woolwich Equitable*. In *Commissioner of State Revenue (Vic) v Royal Insurance Australia Ltd* (1994) 182 CLR 51 sums paid on an understanding that they would be later adjusted gave rise to a restitutionary obligation to repay when the exact sum became known.
123. *National Pari-Mutual Assoc v The King* (1930) 47 TLR 110; *Twyford v Manchester Corp* [1946] Ch 236; *Glasgow Corp v Lord Advocate* [1959] SC 203. In *Blackpool and Fleetwood Tramroad Co v Bispham with Norbreck UDC* [1910] 1 KB 592 it was stated that sums paid to a public authority pursuant to an unlawful rating demand could be set off against sums owed by the payer to the same authority, although they might be irrecoverable if an action were brought for repayment. This distinction was, however, doubted by Lord Bridge in *R v Tower Hamlets LBC; Ex parte Chetnik Developments Ltd* [1988] AC 858 at 877.
124. See, eg *Air India v Commonwealth* [1977] 1 NSWLR 449. There is no reason to think that any different principle applied if the taxing statute was valid, but the particular levy was unauthorised: see *Jax Tyres Pty Ltd v Commissioner of Taxation* (1986) 5 NSWLR 329 at 333.
125. (1959) 102 CLR 108. See discussion at p 124, below.

today will be considered further in the context of my discussion of the *Woolwich* principle.

The reasoning in many of the earlier cases is affected by now discredited statements denying a general right of recovery of moneys paid under mistake of law. Now that mistake of law may ground recovery,[126] retention of the "old law" has the added anomaly that the taxpayer who mistakes liability or the constitutional validity of the impost may recover, whereas the taxpayer who pays protesting liability or validity may not.[127] I shall suggest below that these concerns should find proper reflection in a broader range of defences available to governments faced with restitutionary claims to recover imposts.

Sometimes existing rules were stretched in the opposite direction, to facilitate recovery from the government. This tended to undermine the rules themselves. Once the Revenue was accountable to the courts for acting shabbily by keeping money paid under a mistake of law,[128] it became difficult to explain why the citizen should be in any better position. The integrity of the old rule precluding recovery of moneys paid under mistake of law could not and did not long survive "exceptions" of so great a size and so slender a principled justification.

Restitution based on mistake of law should not be available (and is definitely not available in claims against the State to recover taxes in the Australian Capital Territory, New South Wales and Western Australia)[129] where the law at the time of payment required it to be made. A subsequent change in that law does not establish the payer's mistake, or otherwise make the payee's receipt necessarily unjust.[130]

Will Australian law adopt the Woolwich principle?

A growing appreciation that government is in a superior position to the citizen, and different from the private defendant to a restitutionary claim, led initially to tampering with ordinary restitutionary principles where a taxpayer's claim from a public authority was involved. For example, duress was seen by some judges to exist simply by virtue of the statutory *capacity* of the Crown to proceed against the goods of the subject who declined to pay what turned out to be an invalid impost.[131] Another "device" before

126. *David Securities Pty Ltd v Commonwealth Bank of Australia* (1992) 175 CLR 353.
127. G Jones, "Restitution of Unconstitutional Tax" [1992] CLJ 29 at 30. Contrast *City of Rochester v Chiarella* 448 NE 2d (NYCA, 1983) where only protesting taxpayers recovered a tax later held invalid. There may also be differing consequences as regards limitation of actions: see *Commissioner of State Revenue (Vic) v Royal Insurance Australia Ltd* (1994) 182 CLR 51.
128. *R v Tower Hamlets LBC; Ex parte Chetnik Developments Ltd* [1988] AC 858; *Commissioner of State Revenue (Vic) v Royal Insurance Australia Ltd* (1994) 182 CLR 51 at 65.
129. See *Taxation (Administration) Act* 1987 (ACT), s 95D; *Recovery of Imposts Act* 1963 (NSW), s 3; *Property Law Act* 1969 (WA), s 124(2).
130. See *Mason and Carter*, op cit, § 416. There may be a critical distinction if the change is effected by statute with retrospective operation: cf *Commissioner of State Revenue (Vic) v Royal Insurance Australia Ltd* (1994) 182 CLR 51.
131. *Mason v New South Wales* (1959) 102 CLR 108 at 129 per Kitto J.

the fact/law mistake distinction was effectively swept away was the creation of a further exception to the rule that moneys paid under mistake of law were irrecoverable. Thus, it was suggested by Lord Bridge in *R v Tower Hamlets LBC; Ex parte Chetnik Developments Ltd*[132] that statutory bodies (including local government) were intended to act in the "same high principled way expected by the court of its own officers and not retain rates paid under a mistake of law" save in exceptional circumstances. This bold extension of a principle that previously applied to courts and those acting under the authority of a court order was foreshadowed by Vaisey J in *Sebel Products Ltd v Commissioners for Customs & Excise*.[133] Of course it relates only to mistaken payments, and not all who pay an impost that is not due can establish a causative mistake.

The force of the considerations favouring restitution was recognised by the English appellate courts in *Woolwich Equitable Building Society v Inland Revenue Commissioners*.[134] A building society paid tax on interest and dividends which the Revenue had demanded under a regulation. Woolwich disputed the regulation and successfully challenged its validity in proceedings commenced the day after payment. Its reasons for paying in the meantime included the desire to avoid the grave embarrassment from adverse publicity that would have accompanied proceedings by the Revenue to enforce the tax. Non-payment would also have risked penalties and interest charges which would have exceeded Woolwich's net return in investing the money. It can thus be seen that Woolwich laboured under no mistake, and that it did not make the payment with the intention of closing the transaction. Woolwich's judicial review proceedings challenging the regulation succeeded at first instance and, after a setback in the Court of Appeal, in the House of Lords.[135] The Crown thereupon repaid the tax plus interest from the date of the first instance judgment. Woolwich countered with a demand for interest from the date of its original payment, arguing that the Crown had been under a legal obligation to repay the money from the outset. The relevant statute[136] empowered the court to award interest on the judgment debt from the date the cause of action arose, so the critical question became whether the cause of action arose at the time the Crown received payment. Woolwich could not point to any entitlement based on duress or contract. However, it succeeded in persuading the Court of Appeal and the House of Lords to hold that the law of restitution should recognise a prima facie right of recovery based solely on payment of money pursuant to an ultra vires demand by a public authority. In each court Woolwich succeeded by a bare majority, with the judges dividing over whether or not it was appropriate that the old law should be changed in the light of constitutional and restitutionary principle. The majority in the House of Lords were Lord Goff, Lord Browne-Wilkinson and Lord Slynn. Lord Browne-Wilkinson and Lord Slynn agreed with Lord Goff although they also gave separate opinions.

132. [1988] AC 858 at 877.
133. [1949] CH 409 at 413.
134. [1993] AC 70.
135. *R v Inland Revenue Commissioners; Ex parte Woolwich Equitable Building Soc* [1990] 1 WLR 1400.
136. *Supreme Court Act* 1981 (UK), s 35A.

While acknowledging that his speech represented a new development in the law, Lord Goff relied principally on general restitutionary principles of unjust enrichment, notably the injustice of the Revenue retaining the interest earned on money to which it had never been lawfully entitled. There are indications that he regarded the unjust factor as the ultra vires impost that led to the receipt. However, a narrower, and more traditional, basis of recovery identified by the majority was absence of consideration for the payment.[137] The House of Lords also cited the constitutional principle enshrined in the *Bill of Rights* that taxes should not be levied without the authority of Parliament.[138] Lord Goff also pointed out that to refuse Woolwich's claim would penalise the good and trusting citizen who might suffer unpleasant economic and social consequences from refusing to pay in the first instance.[139] It was not necessary for him to determine whether the right of recovery applied outside imposts that were not due because of ultra vires, for example because the public authority had misconstrued a relevant statute or regulation.[140] Naturally the case did not involve an unconstitutional law, nor did the earlier decision in the *Woolwich* litigation invalidating the regulation amount to any sudden reversal of earlier precedent.

In reaching this position, English law chose not to follow the predominant view in North America. Courts in the United States have generally denied a common law right of recovery of an unconstitutional tax, even in jurisdictions which allow recovery based on mistake of law.[141]

This is also the prevailing view in Canada, although the position remains open. In *Air Canada v British Columbia*,[142] a case where it was not necessary for the Supreme Court to decide the point, La Forest J (Lamer and L'Heureux-Dube JJ concurring) recognised the general recoverability of moneys paid under mistake of law. Nevertheless he rejected a right of recovery in relation to an unconstitutional or ultra vires statute because of policy concerns relating to fiscal chaos. He argued that since government usually spends the taxes it raises during the current year, a right of recovery would disrupt public affairs:

137. [1993] AC 70 at 166 (Lord Goff), 197-198 (Lord Browne-Wilkinson), 201-202 (Lord Slynn). See *Westdeutsche Landesbank Girozentrale v Islington London Borough Council* [1994] 1 WLR 938. As to the application of this principle beyond failure of contractual reciprocation, see Birks, *An Introduction to the Law of Restitution* (rev ed, 1989), pp 223-226.
138. See pp 114-115, above.
139. [1993] AC 70 at 172-173. Cf also *Melbourne Tramway & Omnibus Co Ltd v Melbourne City Council* (1903) 28 VLR 647.
140. At 177. However, he, like Lords Jauncey (at 196), and Slynn (at 205) doubted any such distinction. The distinction is, however, recognised in Canada. See further pp 127-128, below.
141. See G E Palmer, *Law of Restitution*, 1978 §§ 9.16, 14.20; Oliver P Field, *The Effect of an Unconstitutional Statute* (1971), Ch 10; C Pannam, "The Recovery of Unconstitutional Taxes in Australia and the United States" (1964) 42 Texas L Rev 177; *Mercury Machine Importing Corp v City of New York* 154 NE 2d 400 (1957) (NYCA). Contrast *Atchison, Topeka and Sante Fe Railway Co v O'Connor* 223 US 280 (1912) (Holmes J). The American position is further tempered by its readiness to treat protest as proof of duress: *City of Rochester v Chiarella* 448 NE 2d (NYCA, 1983).
142. (1989) 59 DLR (4th) 161. See also *Regional Municipality of Peel v Canada* (1992) 98 DLR (4th) 140 at 143-144.

"The only practical alternative as a general rule would be to impose a new tax to pay for the old, which is another way of saying that a new generation must pay for the expenditure of the old. At best it is simply inefficient." [143]

He considered that to involve the courts in deciding whether recovery would disrupt public finances in a particular case would be unseemly and difficult. This limitation in favour of the Revenue did not, however, apply where a tax is extracted from a taxpayer through a misapplication of the law: it is confined to unconstitutional or ultra vires levies, especially where the statute is unconstitutional due to a technicality. [144] Most academic commentators have found the contrary view of Wilson J more persuasive. She disputed the justice of making the individual taxpayer, as opposed to taxpayers as a whole, bear the burden of the government's mistake. In *Woolwich Equitable Building Society v Inland Revenue Commissioners*, [145] Lord Goff expressed preference for this position. So too did Mason CJ in *Commissioner of State Revenue v Royal Insurance Australia Ltd*. [146]

The North American cases reflect concern about the disruption to public finances that would flow from too liberal a right of recovery. As indicated below, I believe that those concerns are better accommodated by enlarging the "defences" to this category of restitutionary claim, rather than denying it altogether.

In my view, the High Court will follow *Woolwich* when the opportunity presents itself. Apart from the persuasive reasoning in *Woolwich* itself (and the academic writing which presages it), the following are pointers to its adoption in Australia, perhaps with modification.

First, *Woolwich* represents a distinct but logical extension of the *colore officii* cases. [147] In *Sargood Brothers v Commonwealth*, [148] customs duty was demanded and paid under a change in legislation which was proposed and announced, but which at the relevant time had not yet come into force, and which did not eventually come into force. It was held that the duty was recoverable because it was demanded *colore officii* and therefore was paid under improper pressure. The case did not directly involve the nature of the claim for recovery. Nevertheless, some of the judgments discuss it, in differing terms. Some of the judgments appear to turn on a finding of duress because the exercise of Customs control over goods was impliedly threatened. [149] Others, perhaps foreshadowing a principle more akin to the *Woolwich* principle, seem to suggest that the mere unenforceability of the demand was sufficient to ground recovery. Thus O'Connor J, in a passage cited in *Woolwich Equitable Building Society v Inland Revenue Commissioners*, said:

143. At 195.
144. At 197. See further pp 128-130, below.
145. [1993] AC 70 at 175-176.
146. (1994) 182 CLR 51 at 68.
147. Generally as to the recovery of money extracted *colore officii*, see *Mason and Carter*, op cit, § 529.
148. (1910) 11 CLR 258. See also *Re Broughton* (1897) 18 LR (NSW) 247; *Kelly v The King* (1902) 27 VLR 522; *Werrin v Commonwealth* (1938) 59 CLR 150.
149. Eg Isaacs J at 287, 299.

"The principle of law applicable in such cases is well recognised. Where an officer of Government in the exercise of his office obtains payment of moneys as and for a charge which the law enables him to demand and enforce, such moneys may be recovered back from him if it should afterwards turn out that they were not legally payable even though no protest was made or question raised at the time of payment. Payments thus demanded *colore officii* are regarded by the law as being made under duress."[150]

It is arguable that the last sentence stretches the concept of demands *colore officii* well beyond previous bounds, although the facts are consistent with a more traditional case.

Mason v New South Wales[151] has generally been regarded as authority for the proposition that the mere making of an unlawful demand by a person in authority is insufficient to establish a right of recovery.[152] This interpretation has been challenged by Professor Birks.[153] In *Mason* the plaintiffs were Victorian carriers who had paid, under protest, licence fees demanded by New South Wales in relation to a licence to carry goods into that State. After the statute imposing the fee was held unconstitutional,[154] the plaintiffs sought recovery and their claim was upheld by the majority of the High Court. Regrettably, the precise ratio is elusive, because it is uncertain how far some of the judgments turn on the plaintiffs' apprehension that, if they did not obtain licences, their vehicle would be stopped and seized under powers purportedly conferred by the unconstitutional Act.[155]

What is clear is that Dixon CJ, Kitto J and perhaps Menzies J[156] suggest reservations about mechanically applying the private law of duress in this field. Kitto J in particular declined to place much weight on the evidence of the plaintiffs' subjective apprehensiveness. He found for the plaintiffs because the unconstitutional Act, with its penalties and powers of seizure, was coercive in itself.[157] These statements nevertheless fall short of the *Woolwich* principle because they still appear to require proof of compulsion, albeit it may be presumed from the statutory framework and perhaps independently of the subjective perception of the particular taxpayer.

Secondly, a general right of recovery accords with policy that the burden of an unlawful act should be spread evenly through the society that benefited from it. The policy is better expressed by Wilson J in *Air Canada v British Columbia*:

150. (1910) 11 CLR 258 at 276, cited in *Woolwich Equitable Building Soc v Inland Revenue Commissioners* [1993] AC 70 at 91 per Glidewell LJ. See also Griffith CJ at 263-264 and Higgins J at 308-309. See also *Payne v The Queen* (1901) 26 VLR 705 at 719; *Melbourne Tramway & Omnibus Co Ltd v Melbourne City Council* (1903) 28 VLR 647.
151. (1959) 102 CLR 108.
152. See, eg *Esso Australia Resources Ltd v Gas & Fuel Corp of Victoria* [1993] 2 VR 99.
153. In Finn, *Essays on Restitution*, pp 188-191.
154. In *Hughes & Vale Pty Ltd v New South Wales* (1954) 93 CLR 1.
155. See generally at 115-116 per Dixon CJ, 123-124 per Fullagar J, 129 per Kitto J, 130 per Taylor J, 133 per Menzies J.
156. At 117, 125-129 and 134-135 respectively.
157. Contrast however Kitto J's later views in *Bell Bros Pty Ltd v Shire of Serpentine-Jarrahdale* (1969) 121 CLR 137 at 145.

"Why should the individual taxpayer, as opposed to taxpayers as a whole, bear the burden of government's mistake? I would respectfully suggest that it is grossly unfair that X, who may not be (as in this case) a large corporate enterprise, should absorb the cost of government's unconstitutional act. If it is appropriate for the courts to adopt some kind of policy in order to protect government against itself (and I cannot say that the idea particularly appeals to me), it should be one that distributes the loss fairly across the public. The loss should not fall on the totally innocent taxpayer whose only fault is that it paid what the legislature improperly said was due." [158]

But, if Australian law follows England in preference to North America, the right of recovery should, I believe, be finely tuned to take account of the crippling disruption to State and federal revenues that would flow from an unrestricted right of recovery operating in the context of a changing Australian constitutional law. One claim may signal an avalanche of others.

Prospective overruling?

One judicial device that could be used in some situations to sidestep a remedy based on *Woolwich* would be the *prospective* overruling of an earlier precedent that upheld the validity or construction of the taxing law whose overturning is the basis for the refund application.

In *Woolwich Equitable Building Society v Inland Revenue Commissioners*, [159] there was no sudden switch in the law as regards the validity of the challenged impost, and the House of Lords merely noted the application of the principles of prospective overruling to taxes in Europe. [160]

Mason v New South Wales [161] involved a claim to recover from the State money collected at a time when the empowering statute was *generally* regarded as valid, in that the law on s 92 at the time the impost was paid would have sustained its validity. This "old" law was overturned in *Hughes & Vale Pty Ltd v New South Wales*. [162] Mr and Mrs Mason were held entitled to recover licence fees collected under the (invalid) statute. It may be critical that they paid under protest and at a time when "the attempt to obtain a reconsideration of the old decisions meant no weakening of the administrative enforcement of the law". [163]

---

158. (1989) 59 DLR (4th) 161 at 169, cited by Lord Goff in *Woolwich Equitable Building Soc v Inland Revenue Commissioners* [1993] AC 70 at 176. In *Commissioner of State Revenue (Vic) v Royal Insurance Australia Ltd* (1994)182 CLR 51 at 68 Mason CJ described these reasons as "compelling".

159. [1993] AC 70.

160. *Woolwich Equitable Building Soc v Inland Revenue Commissioners* ibid at 174, 200. For a fuller discussion, see Law Commission (UK), *Restitution: Mistake of Law and Ultra Vires Public Authority Receipts and Payments*, Law Com No 227, 1994, §§ 11.23-11.30.

161. (1959) 102 CLR 108.

162. (1954) 93 CLR 1 (a decision that was itself to be effectively reversed 24 years later in *Cole v Whitfield* (1988) 165 CLR 360).

163. Dixon CJ at 115.

The High Court has recently applied the practice of prospective overruling in appropriate cases (not necessarily constitutional cases).[164] If this remedial solution were adopted in relation to a sudden shift in the law that rendered earlier exactions of tax ultra vires or even unconstitutional, then respect for the rule of law would be achieved without massive disruption to government programs, although at the "cost" of conceding a controversial legislative role to the judiciary that it has already laid claim to in many areas. This is the role of deciding which situations merit the denial of the (usual) principle that new precedents operate retroactively, a topic which is the subject of strong debate in the United States.[165] The highest courts in the United States[166] and India[167] have already gone down this path, and the Supreme Court of Canada has already achieved the same result, albeit on grounds that are more debatable.[168] In Ireland[169] and the European Court of Justice[170] recovery of unconstitutional taxes is confined to those who have taken out proceedings before the statute was struck down.

As long as the declaratory theory of law held sway, no one questioned the right of recovery of those who paid at the time the law required it, but who launched a timely action for recovery when "it later transpired" that the statute was unconstitutional.[171] But, now that the declaratory theory has been abandoned in theory and practice,[172] the High Court freely concedes that it may and does "change" the law from time to time. Ironically, this is what the House of Lords readily acknowledged it was doing in England itself in *Woolwich Equitable Building Society v Inland Revenue Commissioners*.[173]

To date, Australian constitutional theory has generally proceeded upon the doctrine that once a court declares a statute invalid it is void ab initio, and cannot provide any justification for conduct in reliance upon it.[174] Nevertheless, pending a declaration of invalidity, the High Court itself applies something akin to a presumption of constitutional validity, and consistently denies interlocutory relief claimed on the basis of the invalidity

---

164. See, eg *McKinney v The Queen* (1991) 171 CLR 468. Generally, see Keith Mason, "Prospective Overruling" (1989) 63 ALJ 526.
165. See *American Trucking Assoc v Smith* 496 US 167 (1990); *Harper v Virginia Department of Taxation* 125 L Ed 2d 74 (1993).
166. See cases just cited, noting that the later case indicates a retreat.
167. *Synthetics & Chemicals Ltd v State of UP AIR* [1990] SC 1927. See Gareth Jones, *Restitution in Public and Private Law* (1991), p 56.
168. *Air Canada v British Columbia* (1989) 59 DLR (4th) 161, discussed above at pp 122-123.
169. *Murphy v Attorney-General* [1982] IR 241.
170. *Blaizot v University of Liege* [1989] 1 CMLR 57.
171. *Mason v New South Wales* (1959) 102 CLR 108 at 142 per Windeyer J.
172. See, eg *Giannarelli v Wraith* (1988) 165 CLR 543 at 584-586; *Polyukhovich v Commonwealth* (1991) 172 CLR 501 at 532-533.
173. [1993] AC 70.
174. *R v Brisbane Licensing Court; Ex parte Daniell* (1920) 28 CLR 23 at 29-30, 32; *Riverina Transport Pty Ltd v Victoria* (1937) 57 CLR 327 at 342; *South Australia v Commonwealth* (1942) 65 CLR 373 at 408; *Bank of New South Wales v Commonwealth* (1948) 76 CLR 1 at 230. See general discussion in *Peters v Attorney-General (NSW)* (1988) 16 NSWLR 24 at 38-40 (McHugh JA).

of the statute under challenge in substantive proceedings.[175] There are other traces of recognition that inoperative laws may still have limited effect.[176] If this theory of voidness ab initio were to be revisited, presumably in the context of a discussion about prospective overruling in constitutional matters, then this could affect the theoretical basis upon which the *Woolwich* principle might operate. For if the tax was "due" when it was paid, according to the law as it then stood, the right of recovery is definitely not axiomatic.[177]

Assuming Woolwich applies, what should be its scope in Australia?

In *Woolwich Equitable Building Society v Inland Revenue Commissioners*,[178] three Law Lords suggested that there is no distinction between misconstruction of a statute or regulation pursuant to which an impost is levied, and reliance upon an ultra vires statutory instrument. A similar view has been taken in Australia in the context of the "old law".[179] This distinction has, however, been embraced in Canada, with imposts under ultra vires statutes being held irrecoverable.[180] Although it can be argued that the *Bill of Rights* principle is not offended by a tax imposed with the sanction of Parliament, even if Parliament exceeds its constitutional powers,[181] it is, in principle, difficult to see why there is any difference, or why constitutional ultra vires should be treated more leniently than other grounds for rendering an impost invalid. In the converse situation of recovery *by* the Revenue, recovery will be permitted if the payment out of consolidated revenue is ultra vires a statute, regardless of how this comes about.[182]

In the English Court of Appeal in *Woolwich Equitable Building Society v Inland Revenue Commissioners*,[183] two judges indicated their view that the right to restitution should extend beyond the central Revenue and include at least local government bodies that purport to impose taxes, licence fees or other imposts. This seems an appropriate position, especially since it is in accord with the range of imposts amenable to the *colore officii* doctrine. Indeed, there appears to be no reason for stopping short of any

---

175. See *Richardson v Forestry Commission* (1988) 164 CLR 261 at 275-6; *Australian Capital Television v Commonwealth* (1992) 66 ALJR 214 at 217; H Burmeister, "The Presumption of Constitutionality" (1983) 13 Fed L Rev 277.
176. See L Katz, "Ex parte Daniell and the Operation of Inoperative Laws" (1976) 7 Fed L Rev 66.
177. See further p 116, above.
178. [1993] AC 70 at 177, 196, 205.
179. *Jax Tyres Pty Ltd v Commissioner of Taxation* (1986) 5 NSWLR 329 at 333.
180. See *Air Canada v British Columbia* (1989) 59 DLR (4th) 161 at 169 per Wilson J, cited by Lord Goff in *Woolwich Equitable Building Soc v Inland Revenue Commissioners* [1993] AC 70 at 176. See also *Allied Air Conditioning Inc v British Columbia* (1992) 76 BCLR (2d) 218.
181. See B C Wells, "Restitution from the Crown: Private Rights and Public Interest" (1994) 16 Adel LR 191 at pp 196-197.
182. See pp 109-111, above.
183. [1993] AC 70 at 79, 138.

compulsory impost, especially in the light of the very wide meaning of "tax" recently adopted by the High Court of Australia in *Australian Tape Manufacturers Association Ltd v Commonwealth*.[184] If the *Woolwich* principle is part of the law, there is no rationale for allowing any public authority to escape it, at least as regards exactions purportedly imposed by law, as distinct from negotiated contractual rights.[185] Not every action by a public authority will expose its receipts to the *Woolwich* principle. If those receipts are paid pursuant to a commercial contract, they will not be recoverable merely because the contract's terms (wrongly) presupposed the validity of an impost.[186]

However, particular imposts may more readily attract particular defences. For example, a licence fee paid for a monopoly right that is enjoyed before the licensee seeks recovery of the fee should not be recoverable in every case.[187] And for other taxes, the availability of a statutory regime which addresses the recovery of overpaid imposts may impliedly exclude the common law remedy.[188]

Legislative capacity to enact bars and defences

Since constitutional principles lie behind the *Woolwich* principle and since, in Australia, constitutional invalidity of a tax may be the trigger for recovery proceedings, it is necessary to consider at the outset the capacity of legislatures to bar or modify common law rights to restitution, whether flowing from *Woolwich* or the earlier law. I have already adverted to the general issue as to the Constitution as a direct source of remedies,[189] and the principles there discussed have similar application to defences.

In some situations State and federal parliaments have power to legislate to block restitution by sanctioning the retention of money erroneously collected under a taxing statute. Alternatively, recovery of taxes already paid may be restricted to those who satisfy conditions, such as proof that the tax has not been passed on. The circumstances in which this may be done include payments made under a valid taxing statute which, on its true construction, did not impose the tax levied and paid;[190] or payments made under an invalid taxing statute, provided at least that the source of

---

184. (1993) 176 CLR 480.
185. See Andrew Burrows, *The Law of Restitution* (1993), pp 353-354. Privatisation may present issues of characterisation: see Law Commission (UK), *Restitution: Mistake of Law and Ultra Vires Public Authority Receipts and Payments*, Law Com No 227, 1994, §§ 6.43-6.45, 8.10, 8.16-8.19.
186. *Esso Australia Resources Ltd v Gas & Fuel Corporation of Victoria* [1993] 2 VR 99. Cf also *Air India v Commonwealth* [1977] 1 NSWLR 449; *Commonwealth v Crothall Hospital Services* (Aust) Ltd (1981) 54 FLR 439; 36 ALR 567; *Woolwich Equitable Building Soc v Inland Revenue Commissioners* [1993] AC 70 at 79. See also P Birks, "Restitution from the Executive: A Tercentenary Footnote to the Bill of Rights" in Finn, *Essays on Restitution* (1990), p 195, n 163.
187. See further pp 134-135, below.
188. See further p 133, below.
189. See pp 104-107, above.
190. *Werrin v Commonwealth* (1938) 59 CLR 150.

invalidity was remediable in the sense that the tax could have been reimposed (retrospectively) in compliance with proper constitutional manner and form by the same legislature.[191]

An example of a "remediable" or "procedural" source of invalidity is failure to comply with s 55 of the Commonwealth Constitution, which requires laws imposing taxation to deal only with that subject, and for laws imposing certain types of taxation to deal only with that type of taxation. But this power is not available where the invalidity of the taxing statute had its origin in some want of legislative power or irremediable contravention of a constitutional prohibition.[192] For example, in *Antill Ranger & Co Pty Ltd v Commissioner for Motor Transport*,[193] the High Court declared invalid legislation that had been enacted by the Parliament of New South Wales to abolish the right of the plaintiffs to recover moneys which had been paid by interstate carriers. This money had been paid under legislation which the Privy Council subsequently held to be in breach of s 92 of the Constitution. Because s 92 withdrew the power to tax interstate carriers, it followed that it prohibited legislation which sought to prevent the recovery of money obtained in breach of s 92. On appeal to the Privy Council,[194] the Judicial Committee said that "[n]either prospectively nor retrospectively . . . can a State law make lawful that which the Constitution says is unlawful". The case represents an example of a constitutionally invalid attempt to do indirectly what could not be done directly. The ruling principle was pithily expressed by Dickson J in *Amax Potash Ltd v Government of Saskatchewan*.[195] "If a State cannot take by unconstitutional means it cannot retain by unconstitutional means".

In the case of a legislature, like the Commonwealth Parliament, that cannot "acquire" property otherwise than on just terms,[196] a mere legislative cancelling of any contractual or restitutionary obligation to refund risks being characterised as such an acquisition, and invalidated accordingly.[197]

191. *Mutual Pools & Staff Pty Ltd v Commonwealth* (1994) 179 CLR 155. See also *Anniston Manufacturing Co v Davis* 301 US 324 (1937). In *Mutual Pools*, the right extinguished was contractual, because the Commonwealth had previously agreed to repay the tax in the event, which happened, that the taxing statute was found to be invalid. But there is no reason why the same principles would not apply to the extinguishment of a *Woolwich*-based right, so long as it involved taxes that were not due for "remediable" reasons (as explained below). Brennan J recognised the possibility of parallel restitutionary rights: at 176.
192. *Mutual Pools & Staff Pty Ltd v Commonwealth* (1994) 179 CLR 155 at 167, 175, 183, 206, 212-216.
193. (1955) 93 CLR 83, affd (1956) 94 CLR 177; *Barton v Commissioner for Motor Transport* (1957) 97 CLR 633. See also *Amax Potash Ltd v Government of Saskatchewan* (1976) 71 DLR (3d) 1.
194. (1956) 94 CLR 177 at 179-180.
195. (1976) 71 DLR (3d) 1 at 12.
196. See Constitution, s 51(xxxi).
197. See *Georgiadis v Australian & Overseas Telecommunications Corp* (1994) 179 CLR 297. In *Mutual Pools & Staff Pty Ltd v Commonwealth* (1994) 179 CLR 155 the Commonwealth Act was characterised as a law that did not fall within s 51(xxxi) because it adjusted conflicting claims and obligations flowing from the invalidation of the taxing Act after pool builders had built the tax into the cost of the pools.

The critical distinction between the two categories of situation was expressed by Brennan J in *Mutual Pools & Staff Pty Ltd v Commonwealth*[198] as follows:

"[W]here a taxpayer is entitled to recover moneys exacted as a tax under a purported but invalid law, the question whether a legislature has power to enact a law which does no more than bar such recovery depends on whether the legislature had power to impose the purported tax (as in *Werrin v Commonwealth*)[199] or had no such power (as in *Antill Ranger & Co Pty Ltd v Commissioner for Motor Transport*)."[200]

But not every legislative qualification of the right of recovery does "no more than bar such recovery". And for both categories of constitutional invalidity, the High Court has recognised that rights of recovery may be qualified or made subject to (stringent) limitation requirements, as I discuss below.

Like their North American counterparts,[201] judges in Australia and England have recorded concerns about the impact of a belated discovery of invalidity on the finances of the public authority concerned, not necessarily being the central government.[202] In the Australian constitutional setting, these concerns have heightened impact. What is at issue goes beyond the inconvenience to government of a right of automatic recovery. It is concern about disruption to the primary function of the State, namely the capacity for coordinated action.[203]

The possibility of catastrophic disruption to treasuries (and what that would entail) by a blunt application of *Woolwich Equitable Building Society v Inland Revenue Commissioners*,[204] especially in the Australian constitutional context, is the primary reason why the prima facie right to restitution of moneys paid in response to an unauthorised tax assessment must necessarily be qualified. It certainly qualifies any prima facie case of unjust enrichment by the Revenue. At the very least, the concerns reflected in those cases need to be translated into a remedy that recognises the competing public interests involved. Hence the concern for defences. In other areas, the recognition of new or broader rights to restitution has led to greater attention to defences which perform the role of protecting the security of receipts.[205]

There are at least three additional reasons why there should not be an uncritical application of *Woolwich Equitable* in favour of taxpayers whose situation is clearly distinguishable from the obvious moral entitlement of

198. (1994) 179 CLR 155 at 175.
199. (1938) 59 CLR 150.
200. (1955) 93 CLR 83.
201. See pp 122-123, above.
202. See, eg *Sargood Brothers v Commonwealth* (1910) 11 CLR 258 at 303; *Werrin v Commonwealth* (1938) 59 CLR 150 at 163; *R v Tower Hamlets LBC; Ex parte Chetnik Developments Ltd* [1988] AC 858 at 879.
203. See pp 117-118, above.
204. [1993] AC 70.
205. See, eg *Barclays Bank Ltd v W J Simms Son & Cooke (Southern) Ltd* [1980] 1 QB 677 at 695; *David Securities Pty Ltd v Commonwealth Bank of Australia* (1992) 175 CLR 353 at 379.

the plaintiff in that case. These reflect the principles of unjust enrichment underpinning the law of restitution. First, if the law continues to adhere to the theory that an unconstitutional law is void ab initio,[206] the need for special defences is patent. Respect for the rule of law, which lies behind *Woolwich Equitable*, does not mandate recovery in all situations, especially where there is a shift in constitutional jurisprudence.[207] Secondly, restitution would be an instrument of injustice if the successful plaintiff were a member of a class that enjoyed the effective benefit of the impost before its invalidity was raised or established. And thirdly, a plaintiff who has passed on the burden of what turned out to be an invalid tax should not be allowed recovery in circumstances where that would be a windfall.

Defences

Because the *Woolwich* principle is itself part of the common law of restitution, and presumably will, if adopted, remain such in Australia,[208] it (like the earlier law) carries with it the standard restitutionary defences discussed elsewhere.[209] Since, however, some of these have received special attention in the case and statute law relating to claims against the Revenue, and since there is reason to believe that some special defences apply in this field, I will briefly address several defences and possible defences.[210]

(i) Compromise and payment with intention to close transaction

Just as with ostensibly mistaken payments, so also a taxpayer who compromises the Revenue's claim, with knowledge of the possibility of an argument about the validity of an assessment or the statute under which it was made, is not allowed later recovery if another and bolder taxpayer later establishes invalidity.[211] Similarly, the taxpayer who pays with an intention to close a particular transaction should not on general principle be entitled to reopen it.[212] Payment under protest will provide evidence of an intention not to close the transaction.[213]

206. See p 126 above. The likelihood of this changing through the device of prospective overruling is discussed at pp 125-127.
207. See *Regional Municipality of Peel v Canada* (1992) 98 DLR (4th) 140 at 143-144. See also *Arizona Governing Committee for Tax Deferred Annuity and Deferred Corp Plans v Norris* 463 US 1073, 1105-1107 (1983).
208. Cf pp 114-115, above.
209. See *Mason and Carter*, op cit, Pt VII.
210. For a fuller treatment, see *Mason and Carter*, op cit, §§ 2032-8.
211. *Commissioner of State Revenue (Vic) v Royal Insurance Australia Ltd* (1994) 182 CLR 51 at 87.
212. *McClintock v Commonwealth* (1947) 75 CLR 1 at 40-41; *South Australian Cold Stores Ltd v Electricity Trust of South Australia* (1957) 98 CLR 65 at 74-75; *Mason v New South Wales* (1959) 102 CLR 108 at 143; *Cam and Sons Pty Ltd v Ramsay* (1960) 104 CLR 247 at 272; *R v Tower Hamlets LBC; Ex parte Chetnik Developments Ltd* [1988] AC 858 at 881; *Woolwich Equitable Building Soc v Inland Revenue Commissioners* [1993] AC 70 at 100, 204. See generally *David Securities Pty Ltd v Commonwealth Bank of Australia* (1992) 175 CLR 353 esp at 373-374, 402-403.
213. *Woolwich Equitable Building Soc v Inland Revenue Commissioners* CLR 353 at 166. Generally as to protests see *Mason and Carter*, op cit, § 523.

(ii) Limitation statutes

In *Woolwich Equitable Building Society v Inland Revenue Commissioners*, [214] Lord Goff recognised the legislature's capacity to protect the Executive through the enactment of short time limits within which claims must be advanced. The constitutional validity of such enactments is clear, even when passed by legislatures that turn out to have lacked power to pass the taxing Act in question, so long at least as those limitation statutes allow a realistic period within which claims may be lodged. [215] On the other hand, if the statute simply extinguishes, retroactively, all civil liabilities arising out of acts done in pursuance of a prior statute which has been adjudged unconstitutional for irremediable lack of power it will be held to represent an invalid attempt to do what cannot be done directly. [216]

In each Australian jurisdiction there are special limitation statutes relating to restitutionary claims for the recovery of imposts. In New South Wales, the *Recovery of Imposts Act* 1963 [217] provides, in s 2: [218]

"2(1) No proceedings shall be brought to recover from the Crown or the Government or the State of New South Wales or any Minister of the Crown, or from any corporation, officer or person or out of any fund to whom or which it was paid, the amount or any part of the amount of any tax paid, under the authority or purported authority of any Act,—

(a) . . .

(b) subsequent to the commencement of this Act, after the expiration of twelve months after the date of payment.

(2) Subsection (1) shall not apply to any proceedings brought pursuant to any specific provision of any Act providing for the mode of challenging the validity, or for the recovery of the whole or any part of any tax actually paid.

(3) Without affecting the generality of this section, and for the avoidance of doubt, it is declared that this section applies to proceedings for the recovery of money (paid by way of tax or purported tax) on the ground of, or on grounds that include, the invalidity of taxation legislation."

Section 1A contains extended definitions of "invalidity", "pay", "proceedings" and "tax".

214. [1993] AC 70 at 174.
215. See *Antill Ranger & Co Pty Ltd v Commissioner for Motor Transport* (1955) 93 CLR 83 at 99-100, 103; *Barton v Commissioner for Motor Transport* (1957) 97 CLR 633 at 641, 650, 659-660, 662, 666. See also *McKesson Corp v Florida Alcohol & Tobacco Division* 496 US 18 at 50 (1990). The limitation statute must indicate with sufficient clarity that it applies to claims based upon constitutional invalidity, otherwise general and longer limitation periods will apply: cf *Commissioner of State Revenue (Vic) v Royal Insurance Australia Ltd* (1994) 182 CLR 51. See also *Woolwich Equitable Building Soc v Inland Revenue Commissioners* [1993] AC 70 at 141, 169-170.
216. See pp 128-130, above.
217. As amended by the *Limitation of Actions (Recovery of Imposts) Amendment Act* 1993.
218. Section 2(1)(a) deals with payments made before the commencement of the Act.

Other States and Territories have limitation statutes operating in this area. They prescribe a short limitation period for the recovery of invalid taxes or taxes paid under mistake of fact or law.[219] As might be expected, provisions of this sort will be construed fairly strictly, but it is no objection that they apply to limit recovery action brought in relation to an ultra vires enactment.[220]

The statutory rights of recovery of customs and excise duty paid under protest also have short limitation periods, and have been held to constitute codes when their procedure (payment under protest) is followed.[221] If, however, there is resort to a truly alternative statutory procedure (such as application for review to the Administrative Appeals Tribunal), appropriate common law causes of action will lie if and when the determination is set aside and the invalidity of the impost finally determined in the taxpayer's favour.[222]

(iii) Defence of failure to exhaust statutory remedies?

There is much to be said, in principle, for a general defence to a *Woolwich* claim that there has been a failure to exhaust statutory remedies. This would reflect the principles relating to judicial review of administrative action. It is supported by administrative convenience, and it reflects the principles lying behind decisions such as *Port of Melbourne Authority v Anshun Pty Ltd.*[223]

(iv) Change of position

As a general restitutionary defence, the defence of change of position[224] should be open to the Executive, all the more so since that would be the situation if the plaintiff relied upon mistake of law, as many could do.

---

219. ACT: *Limitation Act* 1985, s 21A (6 months); NT: *Limitation Act* 1981, s 35D (6 months); Qld: *Limitation of Actions Act* 1974, s 10A (12 months); SA: *Limitation of Actions Act* 1936, s 38 (6 months); Tas: *Limitation Act* 1974, s 25D (6 months); Vic: *Limitation of Actions Act* 1958, s 20A (12 months); WA: *Limitation Act* 1935, s 37A (12 months). In some cases longer periods apply in relation to taxes paid before 1993 amendments, or where special statutory schemes for recovery of overpaid valid taxes apply.
220. *Commissioner of State Revenue (Vic) v Royal Insurance Australia Ltd* (1994) 182 CLR 51. The current s 20A of the *Limitations of Actions Act* 1958 (Vic) is not the similarly numbered provision considered in this case.
221. *Customs Act* 1901 (Cth), s 167; *Excise Act* 1901 (Cth), s 154. See *Dahlia Mining Co Ltd v Collector of Customs* (1989) 17 NSWLR 688; *Comptroller-General of Customs v Kawasaki Motors Pty Ltd* (1991) 32 FCR 243; 103 ALR 637; *Chippendale Printing Co Pty Ltd v Deputy Commissioner of Taxation (No 2)* (1995) 130 ALR 699.
222. *Collector of Customs v Gaylor Pty Ltd* (1995) 127 ALR 641 (dismissing an appeal from *Dahlia Mining Co Ltd v Collector of Customs* (1989) 17 NSWLR 688). But resort to the alternative procedure must have first resulted in a successful re-determination: see *BHP Petroleum (Bass Strait) Pty Ltd v Jenkins* (1993) 115 ALR 179 (upheld on appeal, *BHP Petroleum (Bass Strait) Pty Ltd v Jenkins* (unreported, SC Vic App Div, 15 August, 1994).
223. (1981) 147 CLR 589. See generally Law Commission (UK), *Restitution: Mistake of Law and Ultra Vires Public Authority Receipts and Payments*, Law Com No 227, 1994, §§ 8.26-8.32, 9.15, 9.19-9.20. See also *Woolwich Equitable Building Soc v Inland Revenue Commissioners* [1993] AC 70 at 101 (Glidewell LJ).
224. Discussed in *Mason and Carter*, op cit, Ch 24.

English, Irish and Canadian authority supports this proposition. [225] In *Commissioner of State Revenue (Vic) v Royal Insurance Australia Ltd*[226] Mason CJ appeared to contemplate that the defence was capable of operating in favour of the State in relation to unauthorised receipts.

The real difficulty is the near impossibility of the Executive making out the defence, assuming it is bold enough to plead it. In the area of mistaken payments, a private litigant will not establish the defence merely by showing that he or she consumed a mistaken windfall in ordinary living expenses. [227] The State should be no better placed. [228] The defence may also fail if it entails an element of absence of fault and relevant fault is found. [229]

Assuming the *Woolwich* principle applies to local government, [230] the defence of change of position may be more accessible to a local government body that has put the unlawful impost into a fund for some specific purpose for which it was levied, such as the eradication of pests or weeds in an area. If the money has been spent, especially in aid of a class of persons that includes the plaintiff, it would be inequitable to order its recovery. [231]

(v) Defence of value directly received by taxpayer?

Based on analogous considerations, there should be a defence precluding claims by those who pay what turns out to be an invalid licence fee or other impost, who receive a direct and comparable benefit from a branch of the State, where the effective source of that benefit was the money which the taxpayer later seeks to recover. In some cases, the taxpayer who sues to recover an invalidly levied tax may already, directly, and as a member of a specific class of persons, have received, in the form of grants or services provided by government, the value of the benefit of the moneys paid. This could be the case with regard to statutory schemes whereby moneys are levied to fund the marketing of a primary product, or some local activity such as the eradication of a weed or pest, and where the taxpayer enjoys the benefit of the expenditure before suing for recovery. Similarly, certain types of licence may confer a valuable monopoly right in favour of a small class of persons. Recovery of the (invalid) licence fee after enjoyment of the right for which it was the consideration would result in unjust enrichment,

---

225. *Spiers & Pond Ltd v Finsbury Metropolitan Borough Council* (1956) 1 Ryde's Rating Cases 219; *Rural Municipality of Storhoaks v Mobil Oil of Canada Ltd* (1975) 55 DLR (3d) 1; *Murphy v Attorney General* [1982] 1 IR 241; *Westdeutsche Landesbank Girozentrale v Islington LBC* (1993) 91 LGR 323 at 387-97. See also P Birks in Finn, *Essays on Restitution*, pp 200-201; Law Commission (UK) *Restitution: Mistake of Law and Ultra Vires Public Authority Receipts and Payments*, Law Com No 227, 1994, §§ 11.10-11.17.
226. (1994) 182 CLR 51 at 65.
227. See *David Securities Pty Ltd v Commonwealth Bank of Australia* (1992) 175 CLR 353 at 386.
228. Cf *Rural Municipality of Storthoaks v Mobil Oil of Canada Ltd* (1975) 55 DLR (3d) 1 at 13.
229. Cf *Mason and Carter*, op cit, § 2419.
230. As to which see pp 127-128, above.
231. Cf *R v Tower Hamlets LBC; Ex parte Chetnik Developments Ltd* [1988] AC 858 at 879-880.

not its prevention. Sometimes ultra vires is the result of technical breaches and not fundamental absence of power. Respect for the constitutional principles underpinning the usual *Woolwich* situation does not require recovery in this limited class of cases.[232] It is especially unjust to allow a plaintiff to attack the validity of legislation upon which he or she had earlier relied and under which benefits were obtained.[233]

(vi) Passing on or windfall gain defence?

Taxpayers who have met or intend to meet a tax, such as an excise, customs duty or service tax may seek indemnity against its burden by adding the amount of tax to the price of goods or services. Such taxes are inherently capable of being passed on.[234] However, the High Court has effectively rejected the defence of passing on as an answer to a claim by the taxpayer to recoup an invalidly demanded impost.[235] This has been achieved by an insistence upon proof of enrichment *at the expense* of the plaintiff and by a somewhat uncharacteristic preference for form over substance in concluding that a plaintiff who has passed on the burden to its customers will nevertheless be the person at whose expense the enrichment occurred. This reasoning is understandably and openly affected by the acknowledgment that the taxpayer is more likely to seek recovery than its customers (who may individually have suffered only small losses), with the result that vindication of the constitutional principle involved is more likely to occur if the taxpayer can recover, whether or not it is bound to account to its customers for its own litigation windfall.[236]

Perhaps troubled by matters apart from the purity of restitutionary theory, the Commonwealth and several States have enacted legislation providing for a passing on defence.[237] In the Australian Capital Territory, New South Wales and Tasmania there are broadly expressed passing on defences which are available regardless of the nature of the restitutionary claim for recovery of the impost.[238]

232. Cf Oliver P Field, *The Effect of an Unconstitutional Statute*, pp 253-254. See also Law Commission (UK), *Restitution: Mistake of Law and Ultra Vires Public Authority Receipts and Payments*, Law Com No 227, 1994, §§ 10.44-10.48.
233. See L Katz, "Another Look at Davison's Case" (1977) 2 UNSWLJ 175.
234. *Capital Duplicators Pty Ltd v Australian Capital Territory (No 2)* (1993) 178 CLR 561 at 610 per Dawson J.
235. *Mason v New South Wales* (1959) 102 CLR 108 at 146; *Commissioner of State Revenue (Vic) v Royal Insurance Australia Ltd* (1994) 182 CLR 51.
236. This critique of the High Court's reasoning is more fully developed in *Mason and Carter*, op cit, § 2038.
237. See, eg *Sales Tax Assessment Act* 1992. (Cth), s 51 and Sch 1, Table 3 (CR1) (formerly, *Sales Tax Assessment Act* (No 1) 1930 (Cth) s 26(3)(c)); *Swimming Pools Tax Refund Act* 1992 (Cth) (considered in *Mutual Pools & Staff Pty Ltd v Commonwealth* (1994) 179 CLR 155); *Stamp Duties Act* 1920 (NSW), s 25c(5); *State Taxation (Amendment) Act* 1992 (Vic).
238. See *Taxation (Administration) Act* 1987 (ACT), s 95c; *Recovery of Imposts Act* 1963 (NSW), s 4; *Limitation Act* 1974 (Tas), s 25c.

Chapter 5

Constitutionally Protected
Individual Rights

Leslie Zines

The standard remark that the Australian Constitution lacks a Bill of Rights
has been challenged by Deane J in *Street v Queensland Bar Association*
(1989).[1] He said:

"It is often said that the Australian Constitution contains no Bill of
Rights. Statements to that effect, while literally true, are superficial
and potentially misleading. The Constitution contains a significant
number of express or implied guarantees of rights and immunities. The
most important of them is the guarantee that the citizen can be
subjected to the exercise of Commonwealth judicial power only by the
"courts" designated by Ch III (s 71). Others include: the guarantee
that the trial on indictment of any offence against any law of the
Commonwealth shall be by jury (s 80); the guarantees against
discrimination between persons in different parts of the country in
relation to custom and excise duties, and other Commonwealth taxes
and bounties (ss 51(ii), 51(iii), 86, 88 and 90); the guarantee of
freedom of interstate trade, commerce and intercourse (s 92); the
guarantee of direct suffrage and of equality of voting rights among
those qualified to vote (ss 24 and 25); the guarantee of the free exercise
of religion (s 116); and the guarantee against being subjected to
inconsistent demands by contemporaneously valid laws (ss 109
and 118)."

This is rather a strange mixture of matters, most of which would not be
regarded as the stuff of which Bills of Rights are made. They are all
described by Deane J, however, as serving "the function of advancing or
protecting the liberty, the dignity or the equality of the citizen under the
Constitution".[2]

Some of these "rights" are related to the nature of our federal system.
Those preventing the Commonwealth from discriminating against States or
parts of States or requiring geographical uniformity have the object of
ensuring that the Commonwealth does not play favourites among the
components of the federation. They might be described as group rights.
Section 92, in respect of trade and commerce, as an anti-discrimination and

1. 168 CLR 461 at 521-522.
2. Ibid at 522.

anti-protectionist provision, achieves a similar object in respect of both State and federal power. It is difficult to see the exclusive power of the Commonwealth in s 90 as a "right". To describe it as a right to be free of State taxes does not seem a very fruitful approach. Perhaps, so far as s 90 is concerned, Deane J saw it as a right of all manufacturers and traders to equality of treatment in the taxation of goods. A more usual manner of regarding the provision is as one enhancing the national common market or preventing any impairment of federal tariff policy, depending on which interpretation is accepted.

I have always regarded the statement that s 109 is a guarantee of the right not to be subjected to inconsistent laws as rather extraordinary. Any legal system will have a method of resolving the problem of inconsistent laws. If s 109 were not there, something similar would be implied from the Constitution as a whole or inferred from covering cl 5. The object seems to be more related to the coherence and integrity of the legal system than human rights or guarantees.

These comments of Deane J seem to get close to treating any limitation on power as a protection of the interests or rights of persons who would otherwise be exposed to the law's command. Indeed, it is sometimes said that a federal system enhances individual liberty by producing checks and balances in addition to those which result from the separation of powers. In a federation the national majority does not always win.

RIGHTS AND FEDERALISM

In *Modern Federalism*, Professor Sawer declared that:

"My own preference would be for a Bill of Rights state, but I would sooner live in a moderately incompetent affluent federalism than in any centralised system with no entrenched Bill of Rights at all."[3]

If, however, federalism acts as a protection of human rights in any particular case it will be, to some extent, accidental, depending on the way the powers are distributed and the source of the threat to the particular right. In the *Communist Party* case[4] the High Court held the *Communist Party Dissolution Act* 1950 (Cth) invalid as not coming within any subject matter of the federal legislative power. The case is rightly regarded as enhancing individual liberty. The same might be said of *Adelaide Company of Jehovah's Witnesses v Commonwealth*[5] which held that national security regulations purporting to dissolve the Jehovah's Witnesses were not authorised by the defence power. It followed from the reasoning in both of these decisions, however, that the particular law concerned could have been enacted by a State Parliament. Human rights were enhanced because the threat came only from the federal government. In Canada, for example, the opposite occurred. A Quebec law prohibiting the use of a house to propagate communism was held invalid because it came within the federal

3. Sawer G, *Modern Federalism* (Pitman Australia, 1976), p 153.
4. *Australian Communist Party v Commonwealth* (1951) 83 CLR 1.
5. (1943) 67 CLR 116.

exclusive power over "criminal law", rather than exclusive provincial power over "property and civil rights in the Province".[6]

The extent to which a federal system will protect human rights depends to a large degree, therefore, on particular circumstances. If a federal or State government has plenary power in a particular field it can pass laws in that field that are as draconian as any that could be passed by a unitary legislature. The most that can be said is that there are more opportunities for challenge, but this may not always enhance the cause of human rights.

If the view of the minority judges had prevailed in *Koowarta v Bjelke-Peterson*[7] and the Commonwealth's *Racial Discrimination Act* had been held invalid, it would have been difficult to argue that human rights had been vindicated as a result of the federal system producing limited central power.

When it comes to the powers of the Commonwealth, however, individual rights have intruded into the process of characterisation. This has occurred where the issue is whether a law is incidental to a subject power or where, otherwise, it is necessary to determine whether a law is capable of being reasonably regarded as appropriate or adapted to achieving a legitimate end.

The words "reasonably", "appropriate" and "adapted" require for their application a degree of personal judgment and, therefore, provide scope for inclusion of factors concerned with human rights.

Allied to this principle is the notion that a law will not be "appropriate" or "adapted" to a legitimate end if it is out of proportion to that end.[8] The concept of "proportionality" can, of course, be used to protect persons from laws regarded as harsh or oppressive.

In *Davis v Commonwealth*[9] it was held that the prohibition of the use of certain words without the consent of the Australian Bicentennial Authority was invalid as not being reasonably adapted to the purpose of facilitating and protecting the attainment of the legitimate object of commemorating the bicentenary of British settlement in Australia. Matters of degree were, of course, raised. Freedom of speech was, for the judges, clearly a factor in determining the issues. Mason CJ and Deane and Gaudron JJ spoke of the provisions as being "an extraordinary intrusion into freedom of expression".[10] Brennan J said that: "freedom of speech can hardly be an incidental casualty of an activity undertaken by the Executive government to advance a nation which boasts of its freedom".[11]

In *Davis's* case it was probably unnecessary to the court's decision to raise individual rights. On any view the prohibition was so absurd that it is difficult to see how it could be regarded as "appropriate" or "proportionate".

6. *Switzman v Elbling* [1957] SCR 286.
7. (1982) 153 CLR 168.
8. *Commonwealth v Tasmania* (1983) 158 CLR 1 at 260 (*Franklin Dam* case); *South Australia v Tanner* (1989) 166 CLR 161 at 165.
9. (1988) 166 CLR 79.
10. Ibid at 100.
11. Ibid at 116.

The issue was dealt with more clearly by Mason CJ and McHugh J in *Nationwide News Pty Ltd v Wills*,[12] which held invalid a provision making it an offence to use words calculated to bring the Industrial Relations Commission or a member of it into disrepute. The majority of judges relied on the implied freedom of communication arising from the institution of representative government. Mason CJ, Dawson and McHugh JJ, however, held that the provision could not be supported by the conciliation and arbitration power, Mason CJ and McHugh J relied on the fact that it was disproportionate to the object of protecting the authority of the Commission, because it protected it even against truthful and justified statements.

In coming to that conclusion, they held that in determining whether a provision is reasonably appropriate and proportionate to the object, the court should look at the consequences resulting in infringement of "fundamental values traditionally protected by the common law".[13] Mason CJ repeated this view in *Cunliffe v Commonwealth*.[14]

The determination of what is "appropriate", "adapted" or "proportionate" to an object involves questions of connection and degree. To hold that a law has a connection which is merely "tenuous" may be the result of comparing its slight relevance to the subject matter when compared with its great effect on other areas of social life. Also, in the upshot, the issue must be resolved in the context of our social ideas and values. But when all that is said, it still seems to me that it is not appropriate to take account in this area of interpretation of fundamental freedoms or rights as such. The federal system prescribed by the Constitution distributes total power between the Commonwealth and States, subject to constitutional guarantees and restrictions of power. In the absence of the latter, if a law is not within Commonwealth power it must be within State power. In the *Communist Party* case,[15] for example, it was recognised that (as stated above) if the Act was not within Commonwealth power, it came within State power. Similarly in *Polyukhovich v Commonwealth*[16] Dawson J supported the application of the external affairs power to matters outside Australia on this ground. As the States did not have any general power in this area he regarded an interpretation of the Constitution which denied the completeness of Australian legislative power as unacceptable in terms of constitutional theory and practice. He said: "Apart from express or implied constitutional prohibitions or limitations, it is not to be contemplated that there are laws which no Parliament has the power to pass."

On the basis, therefore, of a federal distribution of powers it is difficult to see in principle why individual rights should be a factor in characterisation. Also, that method of characterisation produces a lopsided freedom, that is, freedom from federal and not from State control, because it is hardly ever necessary to characterise a State law.

12. (1992) 177 CLR 1.
13. Ibid at 3 and 101.
14. (1994) 124 ALR 120 at 131.
15. (1951) 83 CLR 1.
16. (1991) 172 CLR 501 at 638. (See also *The Queen v Duncan; Ex parte Australian Iron and Steel Pty Ltd* (1983) 158 CLR 535 at 590.)

EXPRESS RIGHTS

The express provisions of the Constitution that seem most obviously designed to protect rights of individuals against governmental action are ss 80, 116, 117 and 51(xxxi).

It is perhaps significant of the general attitude of the founders of the Australian Constitution that s 116 and the relevant part of s 51(xxxi) are phrased as limitations on power rather than as a protection of the individual. Section 117, while the only provision which takes the individual expressly as the focus of attention, is concerned with ensuring that a State will not treat out-of-State residents as foreign nationals, rather than with the general issue of the protection of individual rights against the government. All these provisions, other than s 117, limit only Commonwealth power. Whether s 117 binds the Commonwealth is undecided. [17]

Until recent times, the High Court's treatment of ss 80, 117 and the relevant part of s 116 was widely denounced. The decisions made one wonder why anyone bothered to put those provisions in the Constitution at all. The High Court seemed to provide a fairly easy means for the legislatures and governments to avoid them. This led to the view that the general outlook of the Australian judiciary would prevent the effective interpretation and application of a Bill of Rights. In *Krygger v Williams*, [18] for example, the court held that a law for compulsory military training as applied to a person whose religion forbade him to take part in military activities was not in breach of s 116, which prevents the Commonwealth from making any law "for prohibiting the free exercise of any religion". Military training was said to have "nothing at all to do with religion". Similarly, in the *Jehovah's Witnesses* case, [19] although the regulations were held invalid as not being within the defence power, they were held not to be contrary to s 116. Many of the judges used very broad criteria to describe the permissible qualifications on freedom of religion, including "unsocial actions" [20] and acts which were "subversive", [21] contrary to "social order", and "dangerous to the common weal". [22]

As indicated below, this broad brush approach to the balancing of rights with other social interests has been replaced by a more searching examination of the purpose and effect of legislation and whether reasonable alternatives are available which do not impair the right or do so to a lesser extent.

17. Another provision which clearly protects rights, but is of a limited nature, is s 51(xxiiiA). This provision gives the Parliament power to make laws with respect to the provision of a number of social services and welfare payments, including "medical and dental services (but not so as to authorise any form of civil conscription)". This provision is examined in *British Medical Association v Commonwealth* (1949) 79 CLR 201 and *General Practitioners Society v Commonwealth* (1980) 145 CLR 532.
18. (1912) 15 CLR 366.
19. (1943) 67 CLR 116.
20. Ibid at 155.
21. Ibid at 149.
22. Ibid at 150.

The court's attitude to s 117 was, if anything, even narrower. In 1973 a majority of the court held to be consistent with s 117 South Australian rules for the admission of legal practitioners. Those rules required a period of residence in South Australia for admission. The judges held that they did not breach s 117 because all persons, whether permanently resident in South Australia or not, had to satisfy the residential requirements. A resident of South Australia, for example, might be temporarily residing in Melbourne. He or she would have to return to South Australia for a period in order to gain admission, in the same way as would a resident of Victoria. The majority of the court did not ask themselves why the founders took the trouble to put in the Constitution a provision which could be so easily evaded.[23]

Much of this approach has now changed. In many areas of constitutional law the judges have, in modern times, attacked past decisions as being "narrow", "formalistic", or as disregarding "practical reality". In many areas of constitutional law there has occurred more open application of policy considerations, examination of historical material and a general attack on "form" as against "substance".[24]

This new approach to constitutional interpretation, including the interpretation of constitutional guarantees, is illustrated by *Street v Queensland Bar Association*[25] which overruled the earlier decision of *Henry v Boehm*. The court held that s 117 prevented Queensland from denying a New South Wales lawyer a right to practise in Queensland on the sole ground that his residence or principal place of business was not in Queensland. The court construed s 117 as protecting the individual and promoting national cohesion and the establishment of a national citizenship. It declared that, in judging whether there was a disability or discrimination within the meaning of s 117, it was necessary to examine the object of the legislation and its effect on the applicant, whatever the formal criterion of operation in the Act.

This approach is bound to affect the interpretation and application of the "free exercise" aspect of s 116. In *Church of the New Faith v Commissioner of Payroll Tax (Vic)*[26] (a non-constitutional case) Mason CJ and Brennan J emphasised the importance of freedom of religion, which they described as "of the essence of a free society". In that case a broad meaning was given to "religious institution" for tax exemption purposes. Mason and Brennan JJ in interpreting that phrase regarded the freedom in s 116 as relevant.

The dual nature of the Commonwealth's power in s 51(xxxi) has been expressed in many cases. It is conferred as a subject of power, but its limitation of "just terms" constitutes a constitutional guarantee. It is regarded as warranting a liberal construction on both grounds. Seen as an individual right, it was not given the narrow or literal interpretation associated, in the past, with ss 80, 116 and 117.[27]

23. *Henry v Boehm* (1973) 128 CLR 482.
24. Zines L, *The High Court and the Constitution* (3rd ed, Butterworths, 1992), pp 359-362.
25. (1989) 168 CLR 461.
26. (1983) 154 CLR 120 at 130.
27. *Minister for State for Army v Dalziel* (1944) 68 CLR 261 at 276, 284-285. *Grace Bros Pty Ltd v Commonwealth* (1946) 72 CLR 269 at 290-291. *Australian Tape Manufacturers Association Ltd v Commonwealth* (1993) 176 CLR 480 at 509.

The limitation contained in the acquisition power ensures that, in the absence of any indication to the contrary, the power to make laws in respect of the acquisition of property for the requisite purpose is extracted from the proper construction of other powers. In the absence of s 51(xxxi) many of the other powers of the Commonwealth would have included, incidentally, the power to acquire property for the purpose of the subject of the power. To construe them in this way, however, would defeat one of the purposes of the acquisition power, namely, the right of the individual or State to compensation.[28]

Apart from s 122, there are some valid acquisitions of property that are not within s 51(xxxi) and which, therefore, come within other powers, free from the requirement of just terms. The examples that have been given in the cases are taxation and bankruptcy laws, penalties by way of forfeiture and the application of enemy property as war reparations.[29]

The status of the acquisition power as a guarantee has led to a broad interpretation being given to the terms "property" and, to a degree, to the concept of "acquistion". "Property" extends beyond those interests that in general law are designated as proprietary, to cover "innominate and anomalous interests" such as possession for an indefinite period.[30] Gummow J, in the Federal Court of Australia, held that, having regard to the object of s 51(xxxi) as a constitutional guarantee, and looking "to the substance of the matter", confidential information protected by equitable doctrines and remedies was "property" within the acquisition power.[31] A majority of the High Court considered that the statutory entitlement of a doctor to payment from the Commonwealth under the *Health Insurance Act* 1973 (Cth) was property for purposes of that paragraph.[32]

A number of cases have contrasted the language of s 51(xxxi), with its reference to "acquisition", with the Fifth Amendment of the United States Constitution which prevents property from being "taken" without just compensation. This led to the conclusion that a mere deprivation of rights relating to property, without any corresponding benefit, cannot be an acquisition.[33]

Many of the difficulties involved with this power have come about because of the accumulation of, and tension between, a number of factors. These include:

(a) the importance of s 51(xxxi) as a constitutional guarantee;

(b) the need to ensure governmental authority to regulate matters within its given powers;

28. *Attorney-General (Cth) v Schmidt* (1961) 105 CLR 361. *Trade Practices Commission v Tooth and Co* (1979) 142 CLR 397.
29. *Mutual Pools and Staff Pty Ltd v Commonwealth* (1994) 119 ALR 577 at 585-587. *Georgiadis v Australian and Overseas Telecommunications Corp* (1994) 119 ALR 629 at 635. *Franklin Dam* case (1983) 158 CLR 1 at 281-283.
30. *Bank of New South Wales v Commonwealth* (1948) 76 CLR 1 at 349. *Army Minister v Dalziel* (1944) 68 CLR 261.
31. *Smith Kline and French v Secretary, Department of Community Services and Health* (1990) 95 ALR 87.
32. *Health Insurance Commission v Peverell* (1994) 119 ALR 675.
33. *Franklin Dam* case at 145. *Mutual Pools v Commonwealth* (1994) 119 ALR 577 at 588, 597, 626.

(c) the holding that s 51(xxxi) extends to laws authorising compulsory acquisition by persons other than the Commonwealth; and

(d) the modern emphasis on "substance" as against mere "form".

For example, while the extinguishing of rights does not, in itself, constitute acquisition of them, such an act will usually benefit someone else. A chose in action is property and can, of course, be compulsorily acquired, but if it is extinguished, there is not in general law an acquisition of the chose by the debtor. Nevertheless the debtor has benefited to the extent of the creditor's loss. As the concepts of "property" and "acquisition" are not confined to the meaning those terms have at common law and equity, it can be argued that there has been "in substance" an acquisition of property which is invalid without provision for just terms.

A majority of the High Court did hold that a law extinguishing a tortious chose in action against the Commonwealth, as an incident of a new compensation scheme for Commonwealth employees, constituted an acquisition of property which was invalid because of the lack of just terms.[34]

To extend this line of reasoning, on the ground that constitutional guarantees should be interpreted liberally, could considerably reduce the powers of the Commonwealth to regulate matters within its control. This has been recognised by many of the judges and has acted as a motive in adopting certain interpretations. The effect of a broad interpretation on the general regulating power of the Commonwealth concerned Murphy J in *Trade Practices Commission v Tooth and Co* when he rejected the view (that the majority accepted) that the acquisition power extended to acquisitions by citizens. He said:

"Many federal laws provide for alteration of property rights and obligations between citizens without any intended use of the property by the executive governments or its agents. If such alterations were to be regarded as acquisitions of property within s 51(xxxi) there would be some remarkable results."[35]

It was this concern, also, that, in part, supported Dawson and Toohey JJ's view, in dissent, that money was not "property" for purpose of the paragraph.[36] Similarly, Brennan J has said that: "It would be erroneous to elevate the constitutional guarantee of just terms to a level which would so fetter other legislative powers as to reduce the capacity of parliament to exercise them effectively."[37]

Whereas other "rights" are limited by reference to external factors such as an "orderly community" and important social needs and interests, similar ends have been achieved in respect of s 51(xxxi) by the interpretation given to the terms of the paragraph. In *Georgiadis*, for example, Mason CJ, Deane and Gaudron JJ said that the position in that case might have been

34. *Georgiadis v Australian and Overseas Telecommunications Corp* (1994) 119 ALR 629 (Mason CJ, Brennan, Deane and Gaudron JJ; Toohey and McHugh JJ dissenting).
35. (1979) 142 CLR 397 at 434.
36. *Mutual Pools* at 610.
37. Ibid at 594.

different if the cause of action had not arisen under the general law, but had no existence apart from statute.[38] Similarly, an acquisition or extinguishing of rights that was an incident of achieving an object that was not acquisition of property might be regarded as outside s 51(xxxi) on the basis that it is not a law *with respect to* acquisition. *Georgiadis* was regarded by the majority as a borderline case in this regard. Mason CJ, Deane and Gaudron JJ suggested that the legislation might have had a different character if it had applied to employers and employees generally.

The chief manner in which the constitutional guarantee has been adjusted to the general power of the Commonwealth to regulate has been by declaring that laws which are a means of adjusting competing and conflicting claims of individuals or which regulate their relationships are not laws that have as their subject matter the acquisition of property for the prescribed purpose. The same is true where the extinguishing or acquisition is "an element in a regulatory scheme for the provision of welfare benefits from public funds".[39]

Section 80 of the Constitution is one case where literalism seems to have prevailed. In *R v Archdall and Roskruge; Ex parte Carrigan and Brown*[40] the High Court held that Parliament was not required to provide trial by jury in respect of an offence which had a maximum penalty of one year's imprisonment. It was held that all this section did was to say that if there was an indictment there must be a jury, "but there is nothing to compel procedure by indictment". In 1938 this approach was attacked by Dixon and Evatt JJ in a joint judgment.[41] They said that it was "a queer intention to ascribed to a constitution" and that "a cynic might suggest the possibility that s 80 was drafted in mockery; its language was carefully chosen so that the guarantee it appeared on the surface to give should be in truth illusory". The literal interpretation has, however, been upheld in recent times over the vigorous protest of Deane J that s 80 should be interpreted as guaranteeing an important individual right and basic traditional institution.[42] It may be that in this instance the language of the provision and to some extent the historical evidence might be seen as a barrier to a more substantive interpretation. Isaacs warned the Melbourne Convention that Parliament could avoid trial by jury by substituting a procedure other than an indictment.[43]

Nevertheless, although it can be avoided by Parliament quite easily, the guarantee in s 80 has been strengthened in those cases where an indictment is prescribed. In *Cheatle v R*[44] it was held that s 80 precluded a verdict of guilty "otherwise than by agreement or consensus of all the jurors". The court purported to rely on the historical principles and values that produced the common law institution in order to determine its "meaning" in 1900.

---

38. At 634. Justice Finn's paper refers to some flaws in the reasoning, or at any rate the language, of the court in this respect.
39. *Health Insurance Commission v Peverell* (1994) 119 ALR 675 at 680, *Mutual Pools* at 587, 601.
40. (1928) 41 CLR 128.
41. *R v Federal Court of Bankruptcy; Ex parte Lowenstein* (1938) 59 CLR 556 at 581-582.
42. *Kingswell v The Queen* (1985) 159 CLR 264.
43. Constitutional Debates Melbourne, 1898, pp 352 and 1895.
44. (1993) 177 CLR 541.

If one concentrates on s 80 as a guarantee, the decision in *Brown v The Queen*[45] is rather strange. A majority held that the requirement of trial by jury in s 80 could not be waived (Brennan, Deane and Dawson JJ; Gibbs CJ and Wilson J dissenting). Why should the accused be held to have "a right" which he or she does not want? The answer given was that, unlike the Sixth Amendment to the United States Constitution, s 116 was not a mere "right", but was concerned with an institution in which the community had an interest. The jury trial was referred to as "the chief guardian of liberty under the law and the community's guarantee of sound administration of criminal justice".[46] Deane J thought that it reflected "a deep-seated conviction of free men and women about the way in which justice should be administered in criminal cases."[47]

In *Brown*, Dawson J pointed to the fact that the Constitution, and Ch III in particular, "almost without exception, deals with the structure and relationships of government rather than individual rights or freedoms".[48] Similarly, in *Street* he referred to the unique form of s 117 in having the individual as the recipient of a right.[49] In fact, many of the rights and freedoms or immunities that have been held to arise under the Australian Constitution have been based on the existence of institutions and structures. The right has been seen as a necessary incident or element of an institution or of the governmental framework. The two most important involve the separation of the judicial power of the Commonwealth and the institution of representative government.

RIGHTS AND THE SEPARATION OF POWERS[50]

There have been frequent judicial remarks in recent years of the importance of Ch III in relation to freedom and the rule of law. Brennan and Toohey JJ have said that the provisions of Ch III guarantee freedom under the law.[51] Deane J has referred to that Chapter as the Constitution's only guarantee of due process. It is likely that for the future the separation of judicial power will provide a rich source of rights, including many which in other constitutions and in international conventions are the subject of express guarantee. Like many of the express guarantees in the Australian Constitution, however, the separation of judicial power limits only the power of the Commonwealth.

It is likely that those common law rules of evidence and procedure that the court considers fundamental will be regarded as entrenched. Rules of evidence which make it difficult for a party to adduce evidence or which in

---

45. (1986) 160 CLR 171.
46. Ibid at 197 per Brennan J.
47. Ibid at 201-202.
48. Ibid at 208.
49. (1989) 168 CLR 461 at 541.
50. See, generally Winterton, "The Separation of Judicial Power as an Implied Bill of Rights" in Lindell (ed) *Future Directions in Australian Constitutional Law* (Sydney Federation Press, 1994), pp 185-208.
51. *Re Tracey; Ex parte Ryan* (1989) 106 CLR 518 at 574.

some circumstances reverse the onus of proof in an unjust manner may be regarded as preventing the court from carrying out its functions in a judicial way. Laws which prevent or impair a "fair trial" may be seen in the same light. It is doubtful, for example, whether the Commonwealth Parliament could do as the Victorian Parliament has done and override the decision in *Dietrich v The Queen*[52] requiring a judge to grant a stay of proceedings in the trial of an indigent person accused of a serious offence who is not provided with counsel. (Deane and Gaudron JJ were of that view.) The decision was based on the notion of a fair trial and it is unlikely that the High Court would countenance the Commonwealth requiring a court in federal jurisdiction to conduct an unfair trial. The same argument applies to the decision in *McKinney v The Queen*[53] holding that a warning should be given to a jury about the unreliability of a confession made in a police station without the assistance of a lawyer or other persons.

In *Polyukhovich v Commonwealth*[54] it was generally agreed that Ch III prevented an Act from providing what in the United States Constitution is referred to as a Bill of Attainder, which has been interpreted to mean a law which judges a person or members of a group to be guilty of an offence or which punishes them. The holding that one cannot have, consistently with Ch III, a legislative judgment is of course consistent with the principle going back to the early years of federation that only a court can conclusively determine disputes as to existing rights and duties. This principle was recently affirmed in *Brandy v Human Rights and Equal Opportunity Commission*[55] which held that a determination of the Commission could not, on registration with the Federal Court, be enforced as a default judgment. The law did not guarantee a *de novo* hearing by the court.

The principle against having a legislative judgment or punishment, however, raises difficult issues of whether a provision is in breach of that principle. It was said by three judges (Brennan, Deane and Dawson JJ) that, subject to the usual exceptions (such as dealing with persons with infectious or mental diseases or accused persons awaiting trial), Parliament cannot invest the Executive with the power to hold citizens in custody notwithstanding that the detention is not, on the face of the Act, a consequence of any criminal guilt. The judges said that (apart from the exceptions) custody by the state was always penal and punitive in character and, therefore, exists only as an incident of the judicial power.[56]

If this view were accepted, it would raise the question of when laws which deal harshly with particular individuals or groups should be regarded as a judgment of guilt or as punishment. The *Communist Party Dissolution Act* could probably be regarded as within this category, but such a conclusion is assisted by the preamble which constitutes clear legislative findings of guilt. The Act was in fact referred to by Fullagar J in *Marcus Clarke and Co Ltd v Commonwealth*[57] as imposing "what were really penalties". But

52. (1992) 174 CLR 455.
53. (1991) 171 CLR 468.
54. (1991) 172 CLR 501.
55. (1995) 127 ALR 1.
56. *Lim v Minister for Immigration* (1992) 176 CLR 1 at 27.
57. (1952) 87 CLR 177 at 253.

what if federal law prevented members of various groups, for example fascist, communist or racial supremacist organisations from being granted a broadcasting licence, an export licence or from becoming a member of the defence forces? Issues arise as to the distinction between prophylactic measures and punishment.

In *Mutual Pools and Staff Pty Ltd v Commonwealth*[58] Dawson and Toohey JJ suggested that a federal levy on particular persons which did not constitute "taxation" for the purposes of the taxation power, because the criterion was not sufficiently general, in some circumstances "may even amount to a Bill of Attainder or of pains and penalties and so constitute a usurpation of judicial power in contravention of s 71 of the Constitution". While other judges would probably regard such a levy as running foul of s 51(xxxi), the example given by Dawson and Toohey JJ illustrates the scope for future argument as to what is a legislative judgment of guilt.

Also awaiting resolution is the view of Deane and Gaudron JJ in *Polyukhovich v Commonwealth*[59] holding the *War Crimes Act* invalid on the ground that a retroactive criminal law is a declaration of legislative guilt. Toohey J, while upholding the legislation, made it clear that in other circumstances he might agree with Deane and Gaudron JJ. Mason CJ, Dawson and McHugh JJ expressed the opposite view. Brennan J held the Act invalid as not authorised by the external affairs power, and did not, therefore, express any opinion on this point.

The matter, therefore, awaits determination. For the judges who regard retroactive legislation as unconstitutional, there is no relevant difference between the War Crimes legislation and an Act which prescribed punishment for all persons who had been members of the Gestapo. In each case the only function of the court is, in their view, to determine whether a person before the court was a member of a group of persons that Parliament had determined to punish.

In the War Crimes legislation, however, the onus of proof, the degree of proof and the necessary elements of *actus reus* and *mens rea* were all exactly the same as where a trial of a person for a crime under a prospective statute was involved. (Of course, a retroactive criminal law might for other reasons amount to a pronouncement of legislative guilt.)

Both Deane J and Gaudron J attempted to distinguish retrospective civil liability from criminal liability. I find the reasons they give either difficult to understand or unconvincing. Ultimately the distinction they make can, in my opinion, be based only on the importance given to social values and historical considerations. In many of the judgments there are extensive references to the constitutions of other countries, international treaties, judgments and historical works proscribing, or expressing abhorrence of, ex post facto criminal laws.

Should the views of Deane J and others prevail, Australia will have acquired by implication a guarantee expressly provided for in Art 1, s 9 of the United States Constitution (but confined to the Commonwealth Parliament) preventing passage of a Bill of Attainder or ex post facto law.

58. (1994) 119 ALR 577 at 611.
59. (1991) 172 CLR 501.

RIGHTS AND REPRESENTATIVE GOVERNMENT

The most striking decisions relating to rights in recent times were *Australian Capital Television Pty Ltd v Commonwealth*[60] and *Nationwide News Pty Ltd v Wills*.[61] A majority of the court held that the Constitution required freedom of communication on political and public affairs. This conclusion was derived mainly from ss 7 and 24 of the Constitution, providing that Senators and Members of the House of Representatives shall be "directly chosen by the people". As a result of this principle there was declared invalid legislation prohibiting the broadcasting of political advertising during election periods, and a provision making it an offence to use words that would bring the Industrial Relations Commission or a member of it into disrepute.

All the judges accepted that ss 7 and 24 require that the electors shall have a true choice at elections and that a degree of free speech was essential to provide that. The majority, however (all except Dawson and McHugh JJ), took the matter rather further. They held that the purpose of the provisions was a general system of representative government. Representative government meant that the people were "sovereign"[62] and had "the ultimate power of governmental control". Such a system requires more than a right of people to know the views of candidates for election. It involves freedom of communication on all public affairs at all times and among all persons. It was held in later cases that the law of defamation, whether statutory or common law, needed to be accommodated to the principle of representative government. Generally speaking, it was held (Mason CJ, Deane, Toohey, Gaudron JJ; Brennan, Dawson and McHugh JJ disenting) that a communication protected under the principle will not be actionable under the law of defamation if the defendant establishes that it (usually it is a company) was unaware of the falsity of the material, did not publish it recklessly, that is, not caring whether it was true or false, and that it was reasonable in the circumstances.[63]

Deane J would have held that the institution of representative government precluded the imposition of liability for damages for publication of statements about the official conduct or suitability of a Member of Parliament or other holder of high office. In order to provide a majority in the two cases, however, he supported the answers given by Mason CJ, Toohey and Gaudron JJ.

Although, once again, the institution from which the freedoms are derived is confined by the Constitution to the Commonwealth sphere, the court held in *Australian Capital Television* that the Commonwealth could not prohibit communication about State political or public affairs because of the interaction of those affairs and federal matters as evidenced by federal parliamentary debates, national political parties and

60. (1992) 177 CLR 106.
61. (1992) 177 CLR 1.
62. Mason CJ at 137.
63. *Theophanous v Herald and Weekly Times Ltd* (1994) 124 ALR 1; *Stephens v West Australian Newspapers Ltd* (1994) 124 ALR 80.

Commonwealth influence and practical control (for example, by s 96 grants) over matters for which it cannot directly legislate. As freedom to communicate on any public affairs was a necessary element in the Commonwealth's system of representative government, it followed, as held in *Stephens*, that State Parliaments could not restrict any area of political communication.

The extent of the area of free speech can be gauged by the decision in *Cunliffe v Commonwealth*[64] where the court upheld a provision of the *Migration Act* 1958 (Cth) prohibiting the giving of advice or assistance to immigrants except by persons registered under the Act. (Brennan, Dawson, Toohey and McHugh JJ; Mason CJ, Deane and Gaudron JJ dissenting.) A majority were, however, of the view that the type of communication prohibited by the Act came within the implied freedom, that is, the dissenting judges and Toohey J. It is clear that for representative government to exist there must be other freedoms such as some degree of freedom of movement, association and assembly. It may be that processions, demonstrations and lobbying cannot be subject to a broad discretion of police and officials. It remains to be seen whether the High Court will follow the example of the United State Supreme Court in admitting to the ranks of "political speech" such acts as picketing and flag burning.

Whatever the extent of the freedoms that derive from representative government, the nature of that institution provides limits. Several judges (Mason CJ, Brennan, Dawson and McHugh JJ) have declared that the framers rejected the model of the United States Bill of Rights. Mason CJ said it was, therefore "difficult, if not impossible, to establish a foundation for the implication of general guarantees of fundamental rights and freedoms".[65] The joint judgment in *Theophanous* emphasised that the implied freedom was limited and did not extend to *all* communication. They pointed out that commercial advertising was not, as such, prohibited.[66] But, as the amendments that were made to the tobacco advertising legislation show, it may not always be easy to disentangle the political from the commercial.

The principles enunciated in the representative government cases may lead to the constitutional conventions that support the system of responsible government being considered as rules of law implied in the Constitution. Indeed, in the *Engineers'* case the Constitution was referred to as "permeated through and through" with the institution of responsible government.[67] The latter was said to be "interwoven in its texture".[68] It is not unlikely, therefore, that a Governor-General might be held legally bound by ministerial advice in most situations. This does not, however, raise the issue of "rights" or freedoms to the same extent as the broader concept of representative government.

64. (1994) 124 ALR 120.
65. *Australian Capital Television Pty Ltd v Commonwealth* (1992) 177 CLR 106 at 136.
66. Ibid, at 14.
67. *Amalgamated Society of Engineers v Adelaide Steamship Co Ltd* (1920) 28 CLR 129 at 147.
68. Ibid at 146.

RIGHTS AND THE SOVEREIGNTY OF THE PEOPLE

The statements that representative government involves the sovereignty of the people and that the people have the ultimate power of governmental control raise questions whether any rights should be implied from that new legal principle. It is, of course, difficult to define the concept "people" for purposes of that principle. Clearly, the people does not, and cannot, exercise its sovereign power in the manner in which the old sovereign, the United Kingdom parliament did, nor can it initiate any change to the Constitution as the British Parliament could, theoretically, do. In any case, it is difficult to say who among the actual population are guaranteed any "right" to take part in exercising the people's sovereign power, whatever it is.

It is clear that the sovereignty of the people is not a substitute for the sovereign British parliament, but something quite different. For example, it was said in *Australian Capital Television* that the parliamentary representatives are accountable to the people for what they do and have a responsibility to take into account the views of those on whose behalf they act. The Commonwealth Parliament, however, owed no such duty to the British Parliament. The Commonwealth Parliament was not exercising delegated power of that body, although it was bound by its relevant enactments. Indeed, as applied in *Australian Capital Television* and in the other implied rights cases, particularly *Theophanous*, there is no reason to limit the doctrine of the sovereignty of the people to a period when British sovereignty over Australia ceased. If "sovereignty" is regarded as a wrong word to use for the people of a colony, there is no reason why the Commonwealth parliament and government could not, from its beginnings, have been regarded as subject to a people that was, within the limits of colonial status, "supreme", and with all the implied freedoms that representative government requires. Indeed this seems to be the view taken in the joint judgment of Mason CJ, Toohey and Gaudron JJ when, in *Theophanous*, they said that, if the content of the freedom so requires, "the common law must be taken to have adapted to it in 1901".[69] If, as stated in *Australian Capital Television*, representative government rests on the sovereignty of the people and implied rights flowed from that sovereignty at 1901, it is clear that sovereignty of the people has a meaning different from the legal fundamental source of the Constitution.

In *McGinty v Western Australia*[70] a number of judges said that the concept of representative government and "chosen by the people" was to be interpreted in accordance with modern perceptions.[71] It seems clear from these judgments that the Constitution requires adult universal suffrage, subject to exceptions that one finds in modern legislation in respect of resident requirements, unsoundness of mind and so on. The high constitutional object of representative government that the majority of the High Court found in the cases referred to above would, today, be regarded

69. (1994) 124 ALR 1 at 15.
70. (1996) 134 ALR 289.
71. Ibid at 293, 320-321, 337, 388.

as inconsistent with the electoral qualifications one found in 1900 and highly unequal electorates. In *Cheatle v R*[72] concerning the notion of a jury as representative of the community, the court referred to the fact that in 1900 the exclusion of women and unpropertied men from the jury "was presumably seen as justified in earlier days by a then current perception that the only true representatives of the wider community were men of property". They went on to say "in contemporary Australia, the exclusion of females and unpropertied persons would itself be inconsistent with such a requirement."[73] The majority of *McGinty* held that equality of voting power was not an essential element of representative government. A number of judges said, however, that relative equality of voting power was an important factor in the modern notion of representative government and popular sovereignty. Other matters were also relevant, such as community of interest, which could be taken into account.

However, I do not think it is necessary to resort to the notion of popular sovereignty for the above purposes. The concept of representative government would do. The idea of a sovereign of any sort is not essential.

If, however, the concept of popular sovereignty is regarded as an overarching theoretical explanation of our system, it might have an effect on the interpretation of governmental powers that goes beyond the requirements of representative government. It could mean that the provisions of the Constitution should be considered on the basis that the governments and parliaments must act for their benefit. Such a view would be very similar to that expounded by Street CJ in *Builders Labourers Federation of New South Wales v Minister for Industrial Relations*[74] that it was for a court to determine whether New South Wales legislation was for the "peace", the "welfare" and the "good government" of the State. Nevertheless, it is a view pressed to a certain degree by Deane J in *University of Wollongong v Metwally*[75] where s 109 was treated as a "right" of individuals not to be subject to inconsistent laws. The Commonwealth, of course, argued that s 109 was designed to ensure Commonwealth supremacy of laws. Deane J replied that:

> "the submission fails adequately to acknowledge that the Australian federation was and is a union of people and that, whatever may be their immediate operation, the provisions of the Constitution should properly be viewed as ultimately concerned with the governance and protection of the people from whom the artifical entities called Commonwealth and States derive their authority."[76]

In the result, however, the decision in *Metwally*, as is nearly always the case, benefited some people at the expense of others. Outside the object of representative government, the idea of interpreting the Constitution for the benefit or protection of the people as a whole is so vague that it invites the application of a wide choice of political and social theories that are not

72. (1993) 177 CLR 541.
73. Ibid at 561.
74. (1986) 7 NSWLR 372.
75. (1984) 158 CLR 447.
76. Ibid at 476-477.

readily discernible in the Constitution. Inherent in the idea of acting for the people's benefit is the balancing and adjustment of conflicting social interests, a process that is at the heart of the work of the executive and the legislature.

This approach may, however, have an intimate connection with the theory that relies on the common law as a check on Parliament. This is dealt with below.

ENTRENCHED COMMON LAW RIGHTS

There have been suggestions in a number of judicial statements in recent years to the effect that the Constitution may presuppose the equality of the people of the Commonwealth, which in turn would limit the power of the federal Parliament and possibly the State Parliaments. An early reference to this issue was that of Deane J in *Queensland Electricity Commission v Commonwealth*[77] where he suggested that the implied rule prohibiting Commonwealth discrimination against the States might be part of a wider restraint arising from "the underlying equality of the people of the Commonwealth under the law of the Constitution". He said that the implication "was not explored in argument", thus inviting future argument. Toohey J made a similar comment in *Street v Queensland Bar Association*[78] where he said that "Australia was to be a commonwealth in which the law was to apply equally to all its citizens". Apart from these remarks and the broader view of rights expressed by Murphy J, I do not think that such a constitutional principle had ever been raised let alone judicially suggested. It had to meet formidable textual difficulties, namely, the existence of express provisions prohibiting discrimination or preference or requiring uniformity in relation to specific subjects of legislative power, for example, ss 51(ii), (iii), 88, 99, 102 and 117. It also had to contend with the clear historical fact that the framers expressly and intentionally deleted from the draft Constitution in 1898 a provision which would have guaranteed "equal protection of the laws".[79]

These considerations, however, did not deter some judges in *Leeth v Commonwealth*[80] from finding an implication of equality in the Constitution. The issue was the validity of a Commonwealth provision that, generally speaking, required a court, in sentencing convicted persons for a federal offence, to follow the law of the State or Territory in which the offender was convicted in respect of the period to be served before there was eligibility for parole. The result was that there were different minimum periods of imprisonment for federal offenders. A majority held the legislation valid (Mason CJ, Brennan, Dawson and McHugh JJ; Deane, Toohey and Gaudron JJ dissenting). However, the differing reasoning among the majority and minority judges leaves unresolved the issue of

77. (1985) 159 CLR 192 at 247-248.
78. (1989) 168 CLR 461 at 554.
79. La Nauze, *The Making of the Australian Constitution* (MUP, 1972), pp 229-232.
80. (1992) 174 CLR 455.

whether there is an implied right to equality in the Australian Constitution and, if so, what is its scope. Mason CJ, Dawson and McHugh JJ rejected the doctrine pointing to the express provisions in the Constitution. Deane and Toohey JJ embraced it, but the other dissenting judge, Gaudron J, relied on the separation of powers in Ch III and did not express a view on "equality" as a general implication. Brennan J, a majority judge, accepted the doctrine but found the legislation valid in any event.

Deane and Toohey JJ relied on several grounds. They began with the implied restriction on federal power preventing discrimination against the States. The States, they said, are merely "artificial entities", whereas the parties to the federal compact were the people of the colonies. As the court should be concerned with substance rather than form, it followed that it was absurd to protect the artificial States from discriminatory treatment, but not the real people who constitute them.

This reasoning illustrates, in my view, some of the distortions that can occur by too great emphasis on the people being either the masters or beneficiaries of the Constitution. The implied restriction prohibiting the States from discrimination is based on the federal principle. However "artificial" the States may be, there would be no federal system without them. The doctrine does away with the motive behind the old doctrine of immunities to prevent the Commonwealth or States from trying to destroy each other. Without discrimination, the only way the Commonwealth can destroy the States is if it had the unlikely aim of destroying everyone else. These policies and principles based on the federal system have nothing to do with the equality of citizens.

Those judges also thought that equality was inherent in the agreement of the people recited in the preamble to unite in a Commonwealth, and in the provisions of covering cl 5 making the Constitution and federal laws binding on the people of every State.

In addition, the separation of judicial power was considered to require judges to give equal justice.

The main ground for their decision, however, seemed to be that the Constitution had to be interpreted consistently with fundamental rights under the common law. In their view "the essential and underlying theoretical equality of all persons under the law and before the courts" was such a fundamental right. (They admitted that to reach that view it was necessary to put "to one side the position of the Crown and some past anomalies, notably discriminatory treatment of women".)

The equality doctrine was, of course, subject to any indication of a contrary intention, such as the nature of a particular subject of power, for example, the acquisition and race powers. Brennan J in stating that the notion of equality was inherent in the Constitution referred only to the constitutional unity of the Australian people flowing from the first preamble. It may be, therefore, that his concept is confined to preventing the Commonwealth having different rules for the people of the different States, but that is uncertain.

If the view is finally accepted that the Parliaments of Australia are bound by a doctrine of equality in the absence of indication to the contrary, it will make the High Court the judges of whether the different treatment of people and groups that exists in nearly all laws is relevant or justified or, in the words of Deane and Toohey JJ, whether the grounds of any discrimination "are reasonably capable of being seen as proving a rational and relevant basis for discriminatory treatment".[81] This will constitute a very considerable transfer of power from the legislatures to the courts and despite the textual aspects which run counter to the implication.

The most radical of the grounds for finding a right to equality, however, is that the legislative power of the Commonwealth (and perhaps the States) is limited by the "fundamental principles of the common law". This view was repeated by Deane and Toohey JJ in *Nationwide News*, where this time they added a temporal factor. They referred to those common law rights recognised "at the time the Constitution was adopted as the compact of the Federation".[82] This principle, if accepted, would present two main difficulties, namely, what rights are "fundamental" and which ones were recognised in 1901. The reference to 1901 is particularly troublesome in relation to common law principles because of the traditional view of the common law as an evolving process and because later courts may regard earlier decisions as wrong or undesirable. What principles are "fundamental" would, of course, be for the judiciary to determine, thus giving it power, in effect, to create a Bill of Rights.[83]

This approach is all the more remarkable when regard is had to the fact that the supremacy of Parliament is a basic common law rule. As Jeffrey Goldsworthy has said, the colonial legislatures were held to possess a similar sovereignty to that of the United Kingdom Parliament within the limits of their written constitutions.[84] This was reinforced by the *Colonial Laws Validity Act* 1865. It is true that the courts are required to determine what are fundamental rights for purposes of the rule that statutes are to be interpreted so as not to impair them, unless Parliament clearly indicates otherwise.[85] But, if this rule is applied to the interpretation of the Constitution, the legislatures will be limited by the judiciary's view of what is required for a good society. As Doyle CJ has pointed out, the creation, extension and restriction of rights at common law is a judicial function. We should not assume that tradition or evolution will be characteristic of that judicial process. In his chapter on "Common Law Rights and Democratic Rights",[86] written before his appointment to the Bench, Doyle CJ said:

> "We are so accustomed to speaking of common law rights that it hardly occurs to us to question the terminology. No doubt it reflects the fact that the rights or interests or values which we identify in this way are located in the common law. Calling them common law rights not only indicates this origin, and perhaps their subjection to statute law, but also lends an air of antiquity and authority to the rights referred to. This is probably beneficial.

81. Ibid at 488.
82. 177 CLR at 69.
83. Doyle, "Common Law and Democratic Rights" in Finn (ed), *Essays on Law and Government Vol 1* (LBC, 1995), Ch 6, pp 155-156.
84. "Implications in Language, Law and Constitution" in Lindell (ed), *Future Directions in Australian Constitutional Law*, pp 174-178.
85. *Coco v The Queen* (1994) 120 ALR 415.
86. Finn (ed), *Essays on Law and Government Vol 1*, Ch 6.

However the terminology also carries the implication, due to attitudes to and beliefs about the common law, that the rights simply exist as a kind of closed class, and have always been there waiting to be uncovered. For this reason the terminology tends to divert our attention from the important issue of what common law rights we need and should have, and what is the criterion by which we answer that question.

If we simply refer to fundamental rights, freedoms and immunities we are forced to confront these issues. What are they, how does the court identify them, should it create new ones as society changes? These are real and important issues, and need to be considered. The problem with our terminology of 'common law rights' is that it tends to obscure these issues, and in particular the judicial responsibility to attune the common law to the needs of society."

This passage, in my view, not only sums up accurately the modern view of common law rights, but makes clear the broad function and discretion the High Court would have in shaping our society if these "rights", as the court created and developed them, were to limit legislative and executive power.

THE BALANCING OF RIGHTS AND INTERESTS

The issue of adjusting individual rights to other important social interests was often in the past either avoided by a process of dogmatic characterisation or by the unsophisticated process of declaring that an interest or right prevailed over another. The latter occurred in *Adelaide Company of Jehovah's Witnesses v Commonwealth*[87] in relation to the "free exercise" clause in s 116. Phrases such as "preservation of the community", "opinions or practices dangerous to the common weal",[88] "unsocial actions or action subversive of the community",[89] "prejudicial to the defence of the Commonwealth",[90] "subversive of good government" and "serious menace"[91] were treated as decisive. There was no attempt to examine the extent to which the Jehovah's Witnesses impaired the war effort or whether other methods might have been used to attain the defence object.

When s 92 was regarded as a right of the individual to trade interstate, subject to that degree of regulation necessary to an orderly community, the balancing process was obscured by dogmatic declarations that a particular law was a "regulation" of the trade or alternatively "burdened it". For example, in *McCarter v Brodie*[92] Fullagar J, in explaining why rules of the road, safety devices and maximum speeds were consistent with the

87. (1943) 67 CLR 116.
88. Ibid at 149-150 per Rich J.
89. Ibid at 165 per Starke J.
90. Ibid at 157 per McTiernan J.
91. Ibid at 160 per Williams J.
92. (1950) 80 CLR 432 at 496.

individual's right to trade and move interstate, said that "commonsense" provided the answer. "The reason is that they cannot fairly be said to impose a burden on the trader or deter him from trading." He then went on to say that some rules of that type would be contrary to s 92, for example, a speed limit of one mile an hour. The reason for invalidity would be that it would be a burden on the trader by making the journey economically impossible.

There seems no consciousness of the fact that the issue was the right to trade versus public safety and how much restriction of the former might be required to achieve the latter object. In the last few years the limit that must be placed on rights in the light of other rights and social interests has been more carefully considered. Interestingly, the vehicle for achieving this has been the formula of Marshall CJ in *McCulloch v Maryland*[93] designed to take a broad view of federal powers by including what, in Australia, is referred to as an implied incidental power or the implied incidental area of a power:

> "Let the end be legitimate, let it be within the scope of the Constitution, and all means which are appropriate, which are plainly adapted to that end, which are not prohibited, but consist with the letter and spirit of the Constitution, are constitutional."

This principle has also played a part in respect of the application of the external affairs power in respect of treaties and the defence power. The concept of proportionality became associated with that principle when it formally entered our constitution law in the judgment of Deane J in the *Franklin Dam* case,[94] where he referred to "a reasonable proportionality between the designated purpose or object and the means which the law embodies for achieving or procuring it". In my view the concept of proportionality has always been inherent in the "appropriate and adapted" formula. It has always been recognised that whether a provision is appropriate and adapted or "reasonably necessary" to achieve an object is a matter of degree.[95] If the means are disproportionate to the end either they will not be "appropriate" or "reasonably necessary" or, alternatively, the law will be seen as having an object other than the alleged (legitimate) object. In other jurisdictions, such as that of the European Court of Human Rights and the European Court of Justice, in applying the European Convention and the European Communities Treaties, respectively, and the Supreme Court of Canada in relation to the Charter, the principle of proportionality has been, and is being, used in respect of the balancing of social interests that inevitably occurs where there are constitutional guarantees. In Australia this was expressly done in respect of s 92.

In *Castlemaine Tooheys Ltd v South Australia*[96] the facts showed that the South Australian legislation had destroyed the market share of a Western Australian brewer and so advantaged domestic brewers. The State pleaded the necessity to deal with an environmental problem. The joint

93. 7 US 316 at 421 (1819).
94. (1983) 158 CLR 1 at 260.
95. *Burton v Honan* (1952) 86 CLR 169. *Victoria v Commonwealth* (1957) 99 CLR 575.
96. (1990) 169 CLR 436.

judgment of five judges declared that the issue was whether the provisions were appropriate and adapted either (a) to the protection of the community from a real danger or threat or (b) to the enhancement of its welfare. The judges, after referring to the implementation of treaties, said that "if the means . . . are disproportionate to the object to be achieved, the law has not been considered to be appropriate to the achievement of the object." They went on to say that there was a compelling case for taking a similar approach to the problem under consideration in that case.

The difference in the use of these concepts in characterisation cases and in s 92 and "rights" cases is that, in respect of the latter, the object is whatever pressing social problem the legislature chooses to tackle. In respect of treaties and the various powers of the Commonwealth, the object must be one within the treaty or within the subject of a power. Also in respect of s 92 and rights the existence of the object of free trade or the particular right or institution from which it is derived provides an available standard to judge whether the means of dealing with the problem are disproportionate. The issue is whether other reasonable means were available which would have less impact on free trade or on the right.

The same formula and concepts were used in respect of the implied rights proclaimed in *Nationwide News Ltd v Wills*[97] and *Australian Capital Television Pty Ltd v Commonwealth*.[98] Having found the implied freedom of political communication, it became necessary to balance that constitutional interest with the problems that were said to be the concern of the legislation. The main objects of Parliament were said to be the prevention of political corruption and equality of treatment for those who cannot afford the high cost of broadcasting political advertisements.

All those judges who supported the implied freedom regarded their task as determining whether the law was appropriate and adapted to the achievement of the declared object, which involved determining whether the means were disproportionate to those objects.[99] A similar approach was taken in balancing the protection of reputation in *Theophanous v Herald and Weekly Times Ltd*[100] and *Stephens v West Australian Newspapers*[101] and the protection of immigrants in *Cunliffe v Commonwealth*.[102]

The use of the "appropriate and adapted" test and the accompanying proportionality concept in characterisation may differ in one other respect from its use in balancing rights and other interests. The principle as stated by Deane J in *Franklin Dam* was whether the law was "*capable* of being reasonably considered to be appropriate and adapted".[103] This involved, he said "a reasonable proportionality between the objects and the means". Other judges such as Mason J tended to state the issue as whether the law was appropriate and adapted (rather than "capable of being reasonably considered"). Nothing much seemed to turn on this difference of language.

97. (1992) 177 CLR 1.
98. (1992) 177 CLR 106.
99. See Mason CJ at 143-144 and Brennan J at 155-162.
100. (1994) 124 ALR 1.
101. (1994) 124 ALR 80.
102. (1994) 124 ALR 120.
103. (1983) 158 CLR 1 at 260. The emphasis has been added.

Although Deane J used a test more favourable to legislative discretion, he found that most of the provisions in the legislation considered in *Franklin Dam*, in respect of the external affairs power, did not conform to the treaty. Mason J held that they did.

It seems, nevertheless, that in respect of characterisation of laws, where object or purpose is relevant, the formulation of Deane J has been accepted.[104] It has been suggested, however, that the principle operates differently in the case of constitutional freedoms. Mason CJ in *Cunliffe v Commonwealth* said that in the case of characterisation "a certain margin is available to the legislature" and, therefore, the principle is that stated above.

But, in applying an implied freedom or constitutional guarantee, the court must determine for itself whether the freedom "is reasonably appropriate and adapted" etc. Deane and Gaudron JJ expressed similar views.[105]

Brennan J, has used the same principle for both purposes and has in many cases emphasised Parliament's "margin of appreciation". What all this comes down to is the degree of deference that should be paid to the policies of Parliament and the Executive where rights are concerned.

It is clear that the principles applied by the court require a close examination of the social consequences of a challenged law in the light of its ostensible object and the existence of the constitutional right, express or implied. There must also be an examination of alternative methods, if any, of achieving the object, which have less impact on the right. Much of this will require, at times, evidence as to social or economic facts relating to a social problem that the legislature is concerned to control. In this area it may be that a greater "margin of appreciation" should be permitted the legislature when facts of this sort have been investigated and found by legislative committees or advisory commissions.[106]

104. For example *Richardson v Forestry Commission* (1988) 164 CLR 261 at 283 per Mason CJ and Brennan J.
105. Ibid at 163-164, 201-202.
106. Compare Burmester, "The Presumption of Constitutionality" (1983) 13 FLRev 277 regarding legislative findings and the presumption of validity.

Chapter 6

Criminal Procedure and the Fair Trial Principle

Mark Weinberg QC[1]

INTRODUCTION

An accused person has the right to a fair trial. Courts throughout the common law world recognise this right, and are becoming increasingly explicit in articulating it. The High Court, in particular, has described the right to a fair trial as the central prescript of our criminal law. The Crown, too, is said to be entitled to a fair trial. Whether or not there is potential for conflict between these mutual "entitlements" is, of course, a nice question.

The fact that modern jurists and, in particular, the current justices of the High Court, are prepared to speak so openly and directly of "rights" is, in part, a reflection of broad changes to the theory and manner of judicial reasoning. It is the search for principles which underlie legal rules and, indeed, the search for values which underlie such principles, that dominates such reasoning at the highest appellate level.

This is not to say that the judges of the past were altogether reluctant to articulate the principle that an accused person has a right to a fair trial. In *Mraz v The Queen*[2] Fullagar J considered the meaning to be accorded to the proviso to s 6(1) of the *Criminal Appeal Act* 1912 (NSW), and observed:

> "It is very well established that the proviso to s 6(1) does not mean that a convicted person, on an appeal under the Act, must show that he ought not to have been convicted of anything. It ought to be read, and it has in fact always been read, in the light of the long tradition of the English criminal law that every accused person is entitled to a trial in which the relevant law is correctly explained to the jury and the rules of evidence are strictly followed. If there is any failure in any of these respects, and the appellant may thereby have lost a chance which was fairly open to him of being acquitted, there is, in the eye of the law, a miscarriage of justice. Justice has miscarried in such cases, because the appellant has not had what the law says that he shall have, and justice is justice according to law. It is for the Crown to make it clear that there is no real possibility that justice has miscarried."[3]

1. Barrister-at-Law, former Commonwealth Director of Public Prosecutions 1988-91, Dean, Faculty of Law, University of Melbourne 1984-85.
2. (1955) 93 CLR 493.
3. Ibid at 514. See also *Davies and Cody v The King* (1937) 57 CLR 170 at 180.

His Honour did not refer, in terms, to the right of an accused to a "fair" trial. He did, of course, come close to asserting the existence of such a right when he referred to the appellant not having had "what the law says that he shall have". It may be thought that his Honour was saying, by implication at least, that what "the law says that he shall have" must be something akin to a "fair trial". Judges of an earlier era avoided speaking in such sweeping generalities. One will find few, if any, references in past judgments of the High Court to "rights" of the kind which have, in recent years, come to dominate the discourse of that court.

The most general expression of the rights of an accused is the right to a fair trial. That right is commonly invoked as a basis for seeking evidential and procedural relief. Examples include severance of counts in an indictment,[4] the granting of separate trials,[5] the adjournment of a trial to overcome unduly prejudicial publicity,[6] the exclusion of evidence the probative value of which is said to be outweighed by its likely prejudicial consequences[7] and the exclusion of evidence said to have been "unfairly" obtained.[8]

In some cases, nothing that a trial judge can do by rulings of this kind will prevent the trial from being unfair. The remedy which is now invariably sought in such circumstances is the grant of a permanent stay. The doctrinal basis for such a remedy is the broad rubric of "abuse of process".

The current edition of a leading text which deals with, inter alia, criminal procedure, summarises recent developments in this area as follows:

"The circumstances giving rise to a stay of proceedings to prevent an abuse of process vary enormously, for example where:

- an accused who is facing charges for serious indictable offences is without legal representation: *Dietrich v R* (1992) 177 CLR 292 (see also *Crimes Act* 1958 (Vic), s 360A);

- the prosecution has used an ex officio indictment to avoid committal proceedings: *Barton v R* (1980) 147 CLR 75;

- a trial has been preceded by unfair committal proceedings: *R v Basha* (1989) 39 A Crim R 337 (NSW CCA);

- a private prosecution is brought for an improper purpose: *Williams v Spautz* (1992) 174 CLR 509;

- pre-charge and post-charge delay is likely to prevent a fair trial: *Jago v District Court* (NSW) (1989) 168 CLR 23 (applied in *Adler v District Court (NSW)* (1990) 19 NSWLR 317);

- pre-trial publicity is likely to prevent a fair trial: *R v Connell (No 3)* (1993) 8 WAR 542;

---

4. See generally M Weinberg, "Multiple Counts and Similar Fact Evidence" in *Well and Truly Tried*, E Campbell and L Waller (eds) (Law Book Co 1982), p 250.
5. See generally M Weinberg, "Joint Trials—The Problem of Reciprocal Blame" (1984) 8 Crim LJ 197.
6. *R v Glennon* (1992) 173 CLR 592 (discussed below).
7. R Pattenden, *Judicial Discretion and Criminal Litigation* (2nd ed, Clarendon Press, Oxford 1990), pp 232-239.
8. Ibid at 264-281.

- entrapment practices have been used by law enforcement officers: *R v Steffan* (1993) 30 NSWLR 633 (NSW CCA); *R v Taouk* (1992) 65 A Crim R 387 (NSW CCA);

- a multiplicity of charges or a repetition of prosecutions creates unfairness: *Connelly v DPP* [1964] AC 1254; *Walton v Gardiner* (1993) 177 CLR 378;

- the accused has been unlawfully or improperly extradited: *R v Horseferry Road Magistrates' Court; Ex parte Bennett* [1994] 1 AC 42; *Levinge v Director of Custodial Services* (1987) 9 NSWLR 547."[9]

It can be seen from this passage alone just how many circumstances may give rise to an application for a permanent stay of criminal proceedings. The list set out above is by no means exhaustive. The case law upon the subject is growing at an appreciable rate.

This paper seeks to trace the development of a "fair trial" principle through various rulings of appellate courts and, in particular, the High Court. That principle seems to have emerged almost as a by-product of that court's treatment of the doctrine of abuse of process. Indeed, the wider discourse of "rights", now almost routinely invoked by that court, is said by some of its members to be derived from the federal Constitution. It is further sustained by principles of international law. This mode of analysis can reasonably be regarded as revolutionary, at least in the context of our system of criminal justice.

THE POWER TO STAY AS AN ABUSE OF PROCESS

The power of a court to stay proceedings as an abuse of process is said to involve an exercise of judicial discretion.[10] The abuse of process doctrine operates right across the board, in civil and criminal matters. Its pedigree in civil litigation is well established. In 1885, Lord Blackburn observed:

"from early times (I rather think, though I have not looked at it enough to say, from the earliest times) the court had inherently in its power the right to see that its process was not abused by a proceeding without reasonable grounds, so as to be vexatious and harassing—the court had the right to protect itself against such an abuse . . . by a summary order to stay the action which was brought under such circumstances as to be an abuse of the process of the court; and in a proper case they did stay the action."[11]

The power to stay proceedings as an abuse of process was one of two powers exercisable by a court in its inherent jurisdiction. The other was the

9. M Aronson and J Hunter, *Litigation—Evidence and Procedure* (5th ed, Butterworths 1995), p 473.
10. AL Choo, *Abuse of Process and Judicial Stays of Criminal Proceedings* (Clarendon Press, Oxford, 1993), p 1. The nature of that discretion, and whether it is "strong" or weak in the Dworkin sense has yet to be definitively resolved. See RM Dworkin, 'Is Law a System of Rules?' in *The Philosophy of Law* (1977), pp 53-54.
11. *Metropolitan Bank v Pooley* (1885) LR 10 App Cas 210 at 220-221.

power to punish for contempt of court. [12] These powers were "inherent". The jurisdiction did not derive from any statute, or rule of law, but from the nature of the court as a superior court of law. [13]

Civil cases

The inherent discretion to stay civil proceedings is given more precise expression, and a statutory basis, in the various Supreme Court Rules which authorise the stay of an action shown by the pleadings to be "frivolous or vexatious". [14] The term "abuse of the process of the court" did not appear in the English rules until they were revised in 1962. [15] It may be said, however, that the adoption of this expression does not appear to have altered the established body of doctrine built up throughout the previous century.

There are many different situations which can give rise to a claim that there has been an abuse of process. These include proceedings which constitute a sham, or where the process of the court is being employed for some ulterior or improper purpose or, in an improper way, proceedings which are manifestly groundless, and multiple or successive proceedings which cause, or are likely to cause, improper vexation or oppression. [16] Though there will be overlap between the principles governing abuse of process in civil cases, and their application in criminal cases, it cannot be assumed that either the principles, or their application, will in all respects be identical. Plainly, different considerations apply in criminal trials.

Criminal cases—the English beginnings

It was not until 1964 that, in the field of criminal law, the discretion to stay proceedings as an abuse of process received any real attention. In *Connelly v DPP*[17] the House of Lords affirmed the power of a trial judge to stay a criminal prosecution, at least in circumstances which amounted to a violation of the rule against double jeopardy.

The facts of *Connelly* are important to an understanding of the statements of principle adopted by their Lordships. The appellant and three other men were each charged with murder and robbery. The offences occurred in November 1962. In accordance with prevailing practice, the indictment for murder was tried alone. The appellant's defence to the charge of murder was (a) alibi, and (b) if contrary to (a) he was present,

12. AL Choo, op cit p 2.
13. K Mason, "The Inherent Jurisdiction of the Court", (1983) 57 ALJ 449; *R v Forbes; Ex parte Bevan* (1972) 127 CLR 1 at 7 per Menzies J.
14. See for example, Rules 23.01(1) and (2) of the Victorian Supreme Court Rules. The Federal Court analogue is to be found in Order 20, Rule 2 of the Federal Court Rules. See generally *Dey v Victorian Railways Commissioners* (1949) 78 CLR 62, and for a recent, and unusual application of the doctrine, *Second Life Decor Pty Ltd v Comptroller of Customs* (1994) 53 FCR 78.
15. Order 25, Rule 4 of the 1883 Supreme Court Rules became Order 18, Rule 19 and included the concept of "abuse of process" for the first time.
16. AL Choo, op cit p 4.
17. [1964] AC 1254.

no intent to murder. The jury convicted all four accused of murder. At the conclusion of the trial, the judge directed that the indictment for robbery should remain on the file but that it should be marked "not to be proceeded with without leave of this court, or of the Court of Criminal Appeal".

The appellant appealed against his conviction for murder. The primary question considered by the Court of Criminal Appeal was whether the evidence, and the directions to the jury on the question whether or not he had been present at the scene of the crime, were satisfactory. That court considered that there had been a fundamental misdirection, and that the conviction must be quashed. This necessitated the direction of a verdict of acquittal. The court thereafter granted leave to the Crown to proceed with the prosecution of the appellant on the second indictment for robbery. When the matter came before the trial judge, the appellant raised a plea of autrefois acquit. The trial judge was also asked to exercise a discretion to prevent the Crown from proceeding on the second indictment. The trial judge held that the only discretion which he had in such circumstances was to express an opinion, which he was prepared to express, that it would be wrong for the Crown to proceed. The Crown elected to proceed with the prosecution. A month later the appellant was tried and convicted on the indictment for robbery. The Court of Criminal Appeal dismissed his appeal against conviction.

The five Law Lords who considered this matter held widely differing views about the ability of a court to stay a criminal prosecution as an abuse of process. Lords Reid, Devlin, and Pearce, in separate speeches, each acknowledged a residual discretion in a trial judge to prevent an abuse of process. [18] Lord Devlin observed:

> "Are the courts to rely on the Executive to protect their process from abuse? Have they not themselves an inescapable duty to secure fair treatment for those who come or are brought before them? To questions of this sort there is only one possible answer. The courts cannot contemplate for a moment the transference to the Executive of the responsibility for seeing that the process of law is not abused." [19]

Lord Pearce agreed with Lord Devlin that proceedings which put an accused in double jeopardy could be stayed as an abuse of process, even if, for technical reasons, the pleas of autrefois acquit and autrefois convict, were unavailable. [20]

Lords Morris and Hodson took a much narrower view of the power of a trial judge to interfere in what was perceived to be essentially a prerogative of the Crown. As Lord Morris noted:

> "once an indictment is before the court the accused must be arraigned and tried thereon unless (on a motion to quash or demurrer pleaded) the indictment is held to be defective in substance or form and is not amended, or unless matter in bar is pleaded and the plea is tried or

18. Lord Reid delivered a short speech at 1295-1296, and agreed, in terms, with the views of Lords Devlin and Pearce.
19. Ibid at 1354.
20. See particularly 1362.

confirmed in favour of the accused or unless (after the indictment is found) the Attorney-General enters a nolle prosequi or unless the court has no jurisdiction to try the offence disclosed by the indictment."[21]

Lord Morris said he knew of no power in the court to quash an indictment merely because it was anticipated that the evidence would not support the charge. His Lordship recognised that a court endowed with a particular jurisdiction had powers necessary to enable it to act effectively within such jurisdiction, and that such powers were inherent. His Lordship observed:

"A court must enjoy such powers in order to enforce its rules of practice and to suppress any abuses of its process and to defeat any attempted thwarting of its process."[22]

His Lordship concluded, however, that the preferment in this case of the second indictment could not be characterised as an abuse of the process of the court.

Lord Hodson agreed with Lord Morris in doubting the existence of a discretion to stay a prosecution where the pleas in bar were unavailable. His Lordship observed, pungently:

"If there were such a discretion, I do not understand why so many cases have been decided and so much learning has been expended in considering the doctrine of autrefois convict and autrefois acquit. Has all this been a waste of judicial time?"[23]

In 1977 the House of Lords again dealt with the principles governing a stay of proceedings in a criminal trial. In *DPP v Humphrys*[24] the issue before their Lordships was whether the doctrine of issue estoppel could be invoked in a criminal case. The respondent had been charged with driving whilst disqualified. His defence at his trial had been that he was not the driver of the vehicle on the day in question. In evidence, the respondent denied driving any motor vehicle throughout the entire year in which the offence was allegedly committed. He was acquitted. Later he was charged with perjury, there being evidence that he had driven a motor vehicle at some stage during that year. The respondent raised a plea of issue estoppel in seeking to prevent the police officer who had given evidence of the respondent having driven on the particular day which gave rise to the first prosecution from being led. That submission was rejected, and the respondent was convicted. The Court of Appeal allowed his appeal against conviction. On appeal by the Crown, the House of Lords determined that the doctrine of issue estoppel had no place in English criminal law. The mere fact that an issue had been determined in favour of the accused at his first trial was no bar to the admissibility at his second trial of evidence given at the first trial directed to establishing perjury at that trial. Lord Salmon recognised the existence of a judicial power to stay a prosecution:

"a judge has not and should not appear to have any responsibility for the institution of prosecutions; nor has he any power to refuse to allow a prosecution to proceed merely because he considers that, as a matter

21. Ibid at 1300.
22. Ibid at 1301.
23. Ibid at 1337.
24. [1977] AC 1.

of policy, it ought not to have been brought. It is only if the prosecution amounts to an abuse of the process of the court and is oppressive and vexatious that the judge has the power to intervene. Fortunately, such prosecutions are hardly ever brought but the power of the court to prevent them is, in my view, of great constitutional importance and should be jealously preserved. For a man to be harassed and put to the expense of perhaps a long trial and then given an absolute discharge is hardly from any point of view an effective substitute for the exercise by the court of the power to which I have referred."[25]

Lord Edmund-Davies stated:

"While judges should pause long before staying proceedings which on their face are perfectly regular, it would indeed be bad for justice if in such fortunately rare cases as . . . their hands were tied and they were obliged to allow the further trial to proceed."[26]

Viscount Dilhorne took a much narrower view of the power, emphasising the traditional distinction between the functions of the Executive, and the judiciary:

"A judge must keep out of the arena. He should not have or appear to have any responsibility for the institution of a prosecution. The functions of prosecutors and of judges must not be blurred. If a judge has power to decline to hear a case because he does not think it should be brought, then it soon may be thought that the cases he allows to proceed are cases brought with his consent or approval.

If there is the power which my noble and learned friends think there is to stop a prosecution on indictment *in limine*, it is in my view a power that should only be exercised in the most exceptional circumstances."[27]

In recent years, English courts have tended to confine the operation of the abuse of process power to what have been described as "conventional categories".[28] There have, however, been some interesting developments in the fields of illegal extradition[29] and destruction of exhibits.[30]

Criminal cases—abuse of process as developed in New Zealand

From its modest beginnings in *Connelly*, the seed that was planted germinated, and eventually took root. The New Zealand Court of Appeal

25. Ibid at 46.
26. Ibid at 54.
27. Ibid at 26.
28. See generally D Paciocco, "The Stay of Proceedings as a Remedy in Criminal Cases: Abusing the Abuse of Process Concept" (1991) 15 A Crim LJ 315 at 322. The author makes the valid point that the English approach to this doctrine is characterised by a somewhat timorous duo of cases—*R v Sang* [1980] AC 402 (no discretion to stay, or even to exclude evidence, because of entrapment) and *R v Heston-Francis* [1984] QB 278 (unlawful seizure of privileged documents from accused).
29. *R v Bow St Magistrates; Ex parte Mackeson* (1982) 75 Cr App R 24.
30. *R v Lord and Fraser* [1983] Crim L R 191. An Australian application of this doctrine is to be found in *R v Reeves* (1994) 122 ACTR 1.

had cause to examine the principles underlying the doctrine of abuse of process in *R v Hartley*,[31] a case involving illegal extradition from Australia. Broad statements of principle were articulated by each of Richardson and Woodhouse JJ, in *Moevao v Department of Labour*.[32] These statements of principle came later to be cited with approval by the High Court, in *Jago v District Court of New South Wales*.[33]

Barton v The Queen—the first stirrings of a fair trial principle in the High Court

In Australia, the High Court first recognised the ability of a trial judge conducting a criminal trial to stay proceedings as an abuse of process in *Barton v The Queen*.[34] *Barton* raised the question whether an exercise of power by the Attorney-General to ex officio indict an accused was subject to review. The court concluded that the function performed by the Attorney-General in commencing prosecutions was one that was not subject to judicial review. This did not, however, conclude the matter. There are passages in the various judgments of the members of the court which indicate that what the court would not countenance directly, it would permit to be done indirectly. De facto judicial review could be achieved by the exercise of the power of a trial judge to stay a trial to prevent an abuse of process. In the joint judgment of Gibbs ACJ and Mason J (with whom Aickin J agreed), their Honours observed:

> "It is one thing to say that the filing of an ex officio indictment is not examinable by the courts; it is quite another thing to say the courts are powerless to prevent an abuse of process or the prosecution of a criminal proceeding in a manner which will result in a trial which is unfair when judged by reference to accepted standards of justice. The courts exercise no control over the Attorney-General's decision to commence criminal proceedings, but once he does so, the courts will control those proceedings so as to ensure that the accused receives a fair trial."[35]

Their Honours went on to say:

> "There is ample authority for the proposition that the courts possess all the necessary powers to prevent an abuse of process and to ensure a fair trial. The exercise of this power extends in an appropriate case to the grant of a stay of proceedings so as to permit a preliminary examination to take place."[36]

Their Honours expressed strong views concerning the importance of committal proceedings as an element in our system of criminal justice. They said:

31. [1978] 2 NZLR 199.
32. [1980] 1 NZLR 464.
33. (1989) 168 CLR 23 at 30 per Mason CJ.
34. (1980) 147 CLR 75.
35. Ibid at 95-96.
36. Ibid at 96.

"They constitute such an important element in the protection of the accused that a trial held without antecedent committal proceedings, unless justified on strong and powerful grounds, must necessarily be considered unfair."[37]

The remaining three members of the court, Stephen, Murphy and Wilson JJ did not accept the bald proposition that the fair trial of an accused required, as a general proposition, that it should be preceded by a committal hearing. Stephen J did note that the absence of committal proceedings will always call for a careful evaluation by the trial court of all the circumstances, in order to ensure that any consequent prejudice to the accused should not be such as to have deprived him of a fair trial.[38] Murphy J accepted that every court hearing criminal proceedings has power to control those proceedings in order to avoid injustice. His Honour stated:

"Trial by jury without previous committal proceedings can and should be stayed until the accused has been given discovery by proper particulars and notice of the evidence to be tendered against him. But this does not entitle any court to decline to proceed on an indictment filed by the Attorney-General until there have been committal proceedings. This would be to deny in substance the Attorney-General's right to file an ex officio indictment."[39]

His Honour went on to indicate a radically different view of the utility of committal proceedings to that which found favour with Gibbs ACJ, Mason and Aickin JJ:

"The desirability of committal proceedings in modern times is doubtful, at least in certain kinds of cases. A trend has developed in New South Wales in which conspiracy, fraud, and various corporate charges become delayed because of committal proceedings which go on for months or years. These are often interrupted with excursions into the Supreme Court for rulings on points of law or procedure. This not only tends to improperly frustrate prosecutions, but also can result in embarrassment and oppression to defendants. While I do not criticise the magistrates who unfortunately have to preside over them, such committal proceedings have become a disgrace to the administration of criminal justice in New South Wales."[40]

Wilson J found "much wisdom" in the words of Viscount Dilhorne in *Humphrys* concerning the judge's duty to "keep out of the arena". His Honour went on to observe:

"I would add, in the interest of clarity in the present context, that in my opinion the concept of abuse of process carries with it the inference of a trial which if allowed to proceed must necessarily be unfair to the accused. It is a fundamental defect which goes to the root of the trial, of such a nature that nothing that a trial judge can do in the conduct of the trial can relieve against its unfair consequences. A defect of this kind will ordinarily reside in the nature and content of the charge or

37. Ibid at 100. Aickin J, at 109 agreed with the reasons and conclusions arrived at by Gibbs ACJ and Mason J.
38. Ibid at 105.
39. Ibid at 107.
40. Ibid at 108.

charges contained in a particular indictment in the circumstances of the case. I find it more difficult to conceive of an abuse of process arising in cases based, not on a criticism of the charge itself, but on procedures that either have been or are proposed to be followed.''[41]

Wilson J was unable to comprehend how the mere absence of committal proceedings, of itself, could ever sustain an allegation of abuse of process.[42]

The court determined, ultimately, to remit certain of the proceedings to the Supreme Court of New South Wales to decide whether a stay should be granted, but otherwise dismissed the appeals. The case left the law in a state of uncertainty, but opened many doors, few of which were left unentered.

STAY OF PROCEEDINGS BASED UPON UNDUE DELAY

What occurred thereafter, in Australia, was that there developed, in New South Wales especially, a willingness on the part of the Supreme Court and, in particular, the Court of Appeal, to stay criminal prosecutions as an abuse of process because of the very significant delays that had become almost routine in the trial of criminal matters in that State. Such delays occurred both before charge, and between the date of charge, and the date of trial.

Similar developments occurred in England where the abuse of process discretion soon become the chief mechanism invoked by defendants complaining of the prejudice brought about by undue delay.[43] Somewhat surprisingly, Magna Carta came to be invoked as a relevant statute in this context. It was contended that such delays as were occurring were prohibited by cl 29 of the 1225 (Henry III) and 1297 (Edward I) versions of Magna Carta to the effect that "we will not deny, or defer, to any man, either justice or right".[44]

In a number of New South Wales cases, McHugh JA (as he then was) held that cl 29 embodied the right to a speedy trial.[45] His Honour relied, in part, on Coke's observation, in his First Institute, that Magna Carta was merely a confirmation of the common law. Some would regard this as a bold, and unhistoric, interpretation of the statute.

By this time the issue was ripe for consideration by the High Court. That court had referred to the "right to a fair trial" in *Barton*, but had only sparingly, and somewhat elliptically, addressed that concept prior to that case.[46] The reluctance to embrace the concept openly was about to end.

---

41. Ibid at 111.
42. Ibid at 114.
43. See generally, A Choo, op cit at 47-57. See also *Attorney-General's Reference (No 1 of 1990)* [1992] QB 630; *R v Derby Crown Court; Ex parte Brooks* (1984) 80 Cr App R 164; *R v Telford Justices; Ex parte Badhan* [1991] 2 QB 78.
44. The argument was given short shrift by Lord Lane CJ in *Attorney-General's Reference (No 1 of 1990)* at 640.
45. *Herron v McGregor* (1986) 6 NSWLR 246 at 252; *Aboud v Attorney-General (NSW)* (1987) 10 NSWLR 671 at 691; *Jago v The District Court of New South Wales* (1988) 12 NSWLR 558 at 583 and ff.
46. See the discussion of *Mraz v The Queen* (1955) 93 CLR 493, and in particular the celebrated passage from the judgment of Fullagar J at 514, above.

Jago's case—A New Beginning

On 12 October 1989 the High Court delivered judgment in *Jago v The District Court of New South Wales.*[47] The case raised a number of important questions of principle. It required the court to consider the circumstances in which the power permanently to stay criminal proceedings may be exercised. Perhaps the leading judgment was that of Mason CJ, who expressed the principle in these terms:

> "To justify a permanent stay of criminal proceedings, there must be a fundamental defect which goes to the root of the trial 'of such a nature that nothing that a trial judge can do in the conduct of the trial can relieve against its unfair consequences': *Barton* (1980) 147 CLR 75 at 111 per Wilson J. Where delay is the sole ground of complaint an accused seeking a permanent stay must be 'able to show that the lapse of time is such that any trial is *necessarily unfair* so that any conviction would bring the administration of justice into disrepute'." (emphasis added)[48]

Mason CJ had earlier determined that there was not, in New South Wales, a right at common law to the speedy trial of a criminal charge, separate from the right to a fair trial. All other members of the High Court specifically endorsed this conclusion, thus returning Magna Carta to something akin to its former, more arcane, status.

In addressing the "fairness" of the trial process, Mason CJ noted that the power to prevent an abuse of process derived from the public interest: "first that trials *and the processes preceding them* are conducted fairly"[49] (emphasis added).

However, the yardstick was not simply fairness to the particular accused, but also the misuse of the court process by those responsible for law enforcement.[50] His Honour observed:

> "The continuation of processes which will culminate in an unfair trial can be seen as a 'misuse of the court process' which will constitute an abuse of process because the public interest in holding a trial does not warrant the holding of an unfair trial."[51]

The power to grant a permanent stay "will be used only in most exceptional circumstances".[52] The "touchstone" in every case is fairness.[53] The test of fairness which must be applied involves:

> "a balancing process, for the interests of the accused cannot be considered in isolation, without regard to the community's right to expect that persons charged with criminal offences are brought to trial

47. (1989) 168 CLR 23. See generally R Fox, "Jago's Case: Delay, Unfairness and Abuse of Process in the High Court of Australia" [1990] Crim L R 554.
48. Ibid at 34.
49. Ibid at 30. The extension of the fairness principle to pre-trial investigative and other processes may yet prove to be more significant than has thus far been realised.
50. Ibid.
51. Ibid at 30-31.
52. Ibid.
53. Ibid at 33.

. . . At the same time . . . the community expects trials to be fair and to take place within a reasonable time after a person has been charged."[54]

Deane J addressed the question of a fair trial in the following terms:

"The central prescript of our criminal law is that no person shall be convicted of crime otherwise than after a fair trial according to law . . . As a matter of ordinary language it is customary to refer in compendious terms to an 'accused's right to a fair trial'. I shall, on occasion do so in this judgment. Strictly speaking, however, there is no such directly enforceable 'right' since no person has the right to insist upon being prosecuted or tried by the State. What is involved is more accurately expressed in negative terms as a right not to be tried unfairly or as an immunity against conviction otherwise than after a fair trial."[55]

His Honour went on to point out that the general notion of fairness which has inspired much of the traditional criminal law of this country defies analytical definition. Whether a particular trial has been deprived of the quality of fairness must be determined on a case by case basis, and involve an undesirably, but unavoidably, large content of "essentially intuitive judgment". His Honour gave some examples of circumstances which would render a particular trial unfair, including impropriety on the part of the prosecution concealing from the accused important exculpatory evidence, and calculated and unreasonable delay on the part of the prosecution in bringing proceedings to trial. His Honour went on to observe:

"An unfair trial is not a nullity. An acquittal after such a trial is ordinarily final and decisive. So, unless it is impeached on an appeal, is a conviction. Nonetheless, an unfair trial represents a miscarriage of the curial process. If circumstances exist in which it can be seen in advance that the effect of prolonged and unjustifiable delay is that any trial must necessarily be an unfair one, the continuation of the proceedings to the stage of trial against the wishes of the accused will constitute an abuse of that curial process. In such a case, the continuation of proceedings to the stage of trial will inevitably infringe *the right not to be tried unfairly* and a court which possesses jurisdiction to prevent abuse of its process, possesses jurisdiction, at the suit of the accused, to stay the proceedings pursuant to that power."[56] (emphasis added)

Toohey and Gaudron JJ resolved the question before the court in language which was more cautiously expressed. Their Honours agreed, in general, with the views of Mason CJ.

---

54. Ibid.
55. Ibid at 56-57. It is submitted, with respect, that his Honour's "more accurate" expression in "negative terms" was scarely necessary. The fact that no person has the right to insist upon being prosecuted or tried by the State has nothing whatever to do with whether, once the State has elected to bring a person to trial, that person has a right to a trial which is fair.
56. Ibid at 57-58.

In many ways, the judgment of Brennan J (as his Honour then was) can properly be described as a dissenting view, though his Honour arrived at the same conclusion, ultimately, as the others members of the court, in dismissing the appeal. After joining in rejecting the contention that there was a common law right to a *speedy trial*, his Honour turned to the notion of a *fair trial*, and specifically, to the doctrine of abuse of process. Brennan J found the doctrine, and the concomitant remedy of a permanent stay, less attractive than did the other members of the court. His Honour's judgment merits careful consideration. His Honour noted:

> "A power to ensure a fair trial is not a power to stop a trial before it starts. It is a power to mould the procedures of the trial to avoid or minimise prejudice to either party."[57]

His Honour then proceeded:

> "Obstacles in the way of a fair trial are often encountered in administering criminal justice. Adverse publicity in the reporting of notorious crimes . . . adverse revelations in a public inquiry . . . absence of competent representation . . . or the death or unavailability of a witness, may present obstacles to a fair trial; but they do not cause the proceedings to be permanently stayed. Unfairness occasioned by circumstances outside the court's control does not make the trial a source of unfairness. When an obstacle to a fair trial is encountered, the responsibility cast on a trial judge to avoid unfairness to either party but particularly to the accused is burdensome, but the responsibility is not discharged by refusing to exercise the jurisdiction to hear and determine the issues."[58]

His Honour was, of course, well aware of the need to protect the process of the court, whether that process be civil or criminal. His Honour was, however, more restrained in his view of what might constitute an abuse of process. He observed:

> "An abuse of process occurs when the process of the court is put in motion for a purpose which, in the eye of the law, it is not intended to serve or when the process is incapable of serving the purpose it is intended to serve. The purpose of criminal proceedings, generally speaking, is to hear and determine finally whether the accused has engaged in conduct which amounts to an offence and, on that account, is deserving of punishment. When criminal process is used only for that purpose and is capable of serving that purpose, there is no abuse of process."[59]

Brennan J did not accept that a trial was not capable of serving its true purpose when some unfairness had been occasioned by circumstances outside the court's control. His Honour was critical of the plethora of applications for permanent stays based on alleged abuse of process which had been witnessed in New South Wales in the years leading up to *Jago*. As his Honour noted:

57. Ibid at 46-47.
58. Ibid at 47.
59. Ibid.

"It is understandable that, when one party to litigation appears to be prejudiced by the conduct of the other, the court would wish to grant a remedy and, if there be no remedy available, to create a new remedy to avoid the prejudice. In this way, new manifestations of injustice stimulate new growth in the law. In creating new remedies, there is a natural tendency to graft the novelty onto an established rule and to bring the principles governing the new remedy under an old rubric. That course of judicial innovation is facilitated when the old rubric is expressed in terms which defy exhaustive definition. 'Abuse of process' is such a term."[60]

While recognising the serious delays which had frustrated the administration of criminal justice in New South Wales and in other States, and the prejudice suffered by accused persons thereby, his Honour rejected as inappropriate the remedy of a permanent stay to mark the court's disapproval of the failure of other branches of government to furnish the resources necessary to cope with an accumulation of criminal cases awaiting trial. The permanent stay was described, unflatteringly, as "a radical discretionary power", and one which involved an abdication of the court's duty to try the case. His Honour cautioned:

"If it be said that judicial measures cannot always secure perfect justice to an accused, we should ask whether the ideal of perfect justice has not sounded in rhetoric rather than in law and whether the legal right of an accused, truly stated, is a *right to a trial as fair as the courts can make it*. Were it otherwise, trials would be prevented and convictions would be set aside when circumstances outside judicial control impair absolute fairness. . . . If permanent stay orders were to become commonplace, it would not be long before courts would forfeit public confidence. The granting of orders for permanent stays would inspire cynicism, if not suspicion, in the public mind."[61] (emphasis added)

His Honour decried the notion that not only were the categories of case in which the power to grant a permanent stay should be exercised not closed, but the power was available "whenever it would be unfair to the accused to permit the prosecution to proceed".[62] Indeed, his Honour asserted:

"In practice, so broad a power does not fall far short of a power which is incompatible with the rule of law. Of course, one finds in these cases the qualification that a permanent stay will be ordered only in an "exceptional" case, but that is an ineffectual qualification to place upon so broad a power."[63]

He concluded:

"In the onward march to the unattainable end of perfect justice, the court must not forget those who, though not represented, have a

---

60. Ibid at 48.
61. Ibid at 49-50.
62. Ibid at 53.
63. Ibid. His Honour was, with respect, making an important point in this aspect of his reasoning. It is difficult to see why a power to stay a trial which will *necessarily be unfair* should only be exercised in exceptional cases. What more, if anything, is required to make such a case exceptional?

legitimate interest in the court's exercise of its jurisdiction. In the broadening of the notion of abuse of process, however, the interests of the community and of the victims of crime in the enforcement of the criminal law seem to have been depreciated, if not overlooked. How has this occurred? The notion of abuse of process was pressed into service as the means of constraining prosecuting authorities to eliminate delays. But it will not do. It involves the courts in extraordinary evaluations of the investigative process and of the resources of law enforcement agencies which, in my view, the courts are unfitted to undertake . . . and which the courts refused to undertake when they were invited to review the exercise of the discretion to prosecute."[64]

It is instructive to trace the derivation of the permanent stay as a remedy for abuse of process in the context of delays in criminal proceedings in this country prior to *Jago*. An analysis of the cases reported in the *Australian Criminal Reports* demonstrates only sporadic reference to the doctrine until 1986 when Vol 26 of that series reports two such cases, Vol 27 two more (though two other cases reported in that volume raise the question of abuse of process), Vol 28 four more such cases, and then a steady, and ever increasing stream thereafter. New South Wales certainly generated far and away the greatest number of permanent stay applications. It may be said that, until *Jago*, the prospects in that State of successfully obtaining a stay (based upon what was described as "presumptive prejudice" arising from undue delay) were at least reasonable.

In Australia, *Jago* was seen as representing a restraining influence upon the earlier willingness of courts to grant permanent stays arising from prosecutorial delay. Paradoxically, in England, *Jago* was seen as a more radical judgment, moving the common law away from its traditional reluctance to permit judicial scrutiny of the decision to prosecute.

THE QUEEN v GLENNON—ABUSE OF PROCESS AND PREJUDICIAL PUBLICITY

The High Court next dealt with the principles governing the grant of a permanent stay of criminal proceedings in *The Queen v Glennon*.[65] The respondent, a Roman Catholic priest, had been convicted in 1978 of a sexual offence. In 1985 he was a witness in a case in which he was cross-examined about his earlier conviction and about an alleged homosexual rape of one of the accused. Extensive publicity was given to the allegation. He was subsequently charged with a number of offences and appeared before a Magistrates' Court in November 1985. The following day a well-known radio commentator launched a series of attacks upon the priest in three broadcasts, the last of which was in March 1986. The commentator was convicted of contempt of court in respect of those broadcasts. The contempt proceedings received extensive publicity.

64. Ibid at 54.
65. (1992) 173 CLR 592.

The respondent was charged with 17 counts of sexual offences against young people who were members of a youth group of which he was the founder and director. His trial was listed for hearing on 1 August 1988. The trial judge dismissed an application by the respondent for a permanent stay of proceedings on the basis that he would be unable to receive a fair trial because of the prejudicial effect of the pre-trial publicity. The respondent then sought a stay in the Supreme Court, invoking the supervisory and original jurisdiction of that court. Crockett J, in the Supreme Court, dismissed the originating summons. The trial proceeded in May/June 1991. The respondent was convicted on five counts and acquitted on the remaining 12. An appeal by the respondent to the Court of Criminal Appeal was allowed, by majority. The Crown sought special leave to appeal to the High Court.

The court by a 4 to 3 majority determined that special leave should be granted, and that the Court of Criminal Appeal had erred in allowing the respondent's appeal. In a joint judgment, Mason CJ and Toohey J noted that a permanent stay will only be ordered in an "extreme" case[66] and reiterated that there must be a fundamental defect of such a nature that nothing that a trial judge can do in the conduct of the trial can relieve against its unfair consequences.

Brennan J referred to the earlier finding of the court that the radio commentator had committed a contempt of court. His Honour noted that some degree of risk, albeit not a substantial risk, to the integrity of the administration of criminal justice is accepted as the price which has to be paid to allow a degree of freedom of public expression when it is exercised in relation to a crime that is a topic of public interest.[67] His Honour went on to say: "Clearly enough, though the fairness of a criminal trial may be at some risk in such a case, the trial proceeds."[68]

After referring to the judgment of Crockett J at first instance, Brennan J noted:

> "In my respectful opinion, his Honour's conclusion was clearly right either on the ground that the present case is not an "extreme case" or on the ground—which, in my respectful opinion, is a ground better founded on principle and more realistic in practice—that the trial of the applicant, provided it was as fair as the court could make it, would produce no miscarriage of justice."[69]

Deane, Gaudron and McHugh JJ determined that special leave to appeal should be refused. Their Honours concluded that the threshold requirement that there be "very exceptional circumstances" (a requirement imposed upon the Crown when seeking special leave from a decision of an intermediate appellate court quashing a conviction, but not imposed upon other applicants) had not been overcome.[70] Their Honours repeated the now familiar statement:

66. Ibid at 605.
67. Ibid at 613.
68. Ibid at 613.
69. Ibid at 616.
70. Ibid at 618.

"The central prescript of our criminal law that no person shall be convicted of a crime otherwise than after a fair trial according to law dictates that an accused is entitled to be protected from an unacceptable and significant risk that the effect of prejudicial pre-trial publicity will preclude a fair trial." [71]

Their Honours went on to say that ordinarily that risk will be obviated by appropriate and thorough directions and, if the circumstances warrant, a temporary stay for the minimum period adjudged necessary for the pre-trial publicity to date. Their Honours would not, however, exclude the possibility that, in an extreme case, a permanent stay might be the only remedy which could prevent a miscarriage of justice. [72]

WILLIAMS v SPAUTZ—IMPROPER PURPOSE AS ABUSE OF PROCESS

In *Williams v Spautz*, [73] the court dealt with the principles governing abuse of process, and the remedy of a permanent stay, in a context other than one of delay. A lecturer had commenced an action against a university for wrongful dismissal. He later laid informations against various officers of the university, alleging a number of criminal offences, including criminal conspiracy to defame him. On the application of some of those university officers for declarations that the prosecutions were an abuse of process, the trial judge found that the lecturer's predominant purpose in instituting and maintaining the criminal proceedings was to exert pressure upon the university to reinstate him and/or to agree to a favourable settlement of his case for wrongful dismissal. The trial judge stayed the prosecutions permanently. The Court of Appeal of New South Wales allowed the appeal, and the university officers appealed to the High Court. A majority of the court determined that the appeal should be allowed, and that the trial judge's decision to permanently stay the criminal proceeding should be restored.

The majority of the court held that the power to grant a permanent stay is not confined to those circumstances in which an accused claims that he is being subjected to an unfair trial. A stay may be sought to stop a prosecution which has been instituted and maintained for an improper purpose even if there is a prima facie case that the offences have been committed, and no basis for believing that there cannot be a fair trial.

The majority were conscious of the need to ensure that courts should exercise, rather than refrain from exercising, their jurisdiction, especially their jurisdiction to try persons charged with criminal offences. The majority accepted that it was well established that the onus of satisfying the court that there is an abuse of process lies upon the party alleging it, and that the onus is "a heavy one". The power to grant a permanent stay is to be exercised only in the most exceptional circumstances. [74]

71. Ibid at 623.
72. Ibid at 624.
73. (1992) 174 CLR 509.
74. Ibid at 529.

Brennan J delivered a separate concurring judgment, treating the improper purpose with which Dr Spautz had commenced and maintained the proceedings against other university officers as justifying the granting of a stay. Deane and Gaudron JJ dissented. Deane J held that the mere existence of a predominant subjective purpose on the part of the informant that was not directed towards the punishment of a defendant, or the protection of the public, did not of itself lead to the conclusion that the proceedings were an abuse of process which should be stayed. Gaudron J adopted an analysis of "improper purpose" which produced a similar result.

DIETRICH v THE QUEEN—THE RIGHT TO A FAIR TRIAL

In *Dietrich v The Queen*[75] a majority of the court determined that, while an accused had no right at common law to be provided with counsel at public expense, the courts have power to stay proceedings that will result in an unfair trial. The power to grant a stay extends to a case in which representation of the accused by counsel is essential to a fair trial. Such representation will be so regarded in most cases in which an accused is charged with a serious offence. Absent exceptional circumstances, a judge faced with an application for an adjournment, or a stay, by an indigent accused charged with a serious offence who, through no fault of his own is unable to obtain legal representation, should adjourn, postpone or stay the trial until legal representation is available.

In the joint judgment of Mason CJ and McHugh J, the right to a fair trial is described as "a central pillar of our criminal justice system".[76] Their Honours observed: "The right of an accused to receive a fair trial according to law is a fundamental element of our criminal justice system."[77]

The joint judgment then noted that Deane J had correctly pointed out in *Jago* that the accused's right to a fair trial is more accurately expressed in negative terms as a right not to be tried unfairly. It was said to be "convenient" and "not unduly misleading" to refer to an accused's positive right to a fair trial. The right was described as being manifested in rules of law and of practice designed to regulate the course of the trial—and reference was made to *Bunning v Cross*,[78] the seminal authority dealing with the exclusion of evidence illegally or improperly obtained. In an important statement of principle, their Honours went on to say:

"There has been no judicial attempt to list exhaustively the attributes of a fair trial. That is because, in the ordinary course of the criminal appellate process, an appellate court is generally called upon to determine, as here, whether something that was done or was said in the

75. (1992) 177 CLR 292. For subsequent developments see *R v Small* (1994) 33 NSWLR 575 and *R v Batiste* (1994) 35 NSWLR 437. See also the seminal ruling of Hunt CJ at CL in *R v Milat* (unreported, Supreme Court of New South Wales Criminal Division, 11 August 1995) applying *Dietrich* as requiring an appropriate level of competent representation in the context of a complex murder trial.
76. Ibid at 298.
77. Ibid at 299.
78. (1978) 141 CLR 54.

course of the trial, or less usually before trial, resulted in the accused being deprived of a fair trial and led to a miscarriage of justice. However, various international instruments and express declarations of rights in other countries have attempted to define, albeit broadly, some of the attributes of a fair trial. Article 6 of the European Convention for the Protection of Human Rights and Fundamental Freedoms ('the ECHR') enshrines such basic minimum rights of an accused as the right to have adequate time and facilities for the preparation of his or her defence and the right to the free assistance of an interpreter when required. Article 14 of the International Covenant on Civil and Political Rights ('the ICCPR') to which instrument Australia is a party contains similar minimum rights, as does s 11 of the Canadian Charter of Rights and Freedoms. Similar rights have been discerned in the "due process" clauses of the Fifth and Fourteenth Amendments to the United States Constitution."[79]

Mason CJ and McHugh J rejected the appellant's contention that there was to be found in Australia's international obligations, including conventions ratified by the Executive, a source of the right to have counsel provided by the State. Ratification of such conventions as an executive act had no direct legal effect upon domestic law; the rights and obligations contained in those conventions were not incorporated into Australian law unless, and until, specific legislation was passed implementing the provisions.[80] It might be correct to say that in construing domestic legislation which is ambiguous, Australian courts would presume that Parliament intended to legislate in accordance with its international obligations. Such resort to international obligations might also be permissible in order to help resolve uncertainty or ambiguity in judge-made law. There was, however, no such uncertainty or ambiguity in the domestic law under consideration in *Dietrich*, because what the court was being asked to do was to declare that a right which had hitherto never been recognised should now be taken to exist.

Having rejected the principal submission advanced by the appellant, one might have expected their Honours to dismiss the appeal. What their Honours did, however, was to provide an indirect means of achieving that for which the law did not provide. Their Honours, having accepted that Australian law did not recognise that an indigent accused, on trial for a serious criminal offence, had a right to the provision of counsel at public expense, went on to hold that Australian law acknowledged that an accused had the right to a fair trial. Depending upon the circumstances of the particular case, lack of representation may mean that an accused is unable to receive, or did not receive, a fair trial. The idea that Mason CJ and McHugh J were recommending no more than an examination of the particular circumstances of each case was soon dispelled. They went on to say:

79. *Dietrich v The Queen* (1992) 177 CLR 292 at 300.
80. Note, however, the treatment accorded to international treaties and conventions, ratified but not incorporated into Australian domestic law, in *Minister for Immigration v Teoh* (1995) 128 ALR 353. The "legitimate expectation" that consideration will be given to the terms of such treaties and conventions by administrative decision makers has since been legislatively negated.

"For our part, the desirability of an accused charged with a serious offence being represented is so great that we consider that the trial should proceed without representation for the accused in exceptional cases only." [81]

Deane J commenced his judgment by asserting that the fundamental prescript of the criminal law, that no person be convicted of a crime except after a fair trial according to law, found its source, in relation to federal crime at least, in the constitutional principle embodied in the separation of powers doctrine, in Ch III of the Constitution. This was an observation of profound importance, elevating the right to a fair trial on a charge of an offence against a law of the Commonwealth to a constitutional right, seemingly incapable of being legislatively abrogated. The requirement of fairness was said to transcend the content of more particularised legal rules, and principles, and to provide the ultimate rationale and touchstone of the rules and practices which the common law required to be observed in the administration of the substantive criminal law. [82]

His Honour then analysed earlier statements by the court of the overriding common law requirement that a criminal trial be fair, including reference to the views of each of the six justices in *Barton v The Queen* [83] and other similar statements of principle. His Honour noted that in *McKinney v The Queen* [84] a majority of the court had recognised as the central thesis of the administration of criminal justice the entitlement of an accused person to a fair trial, according to law.

Deane J recognised that the practical content of the requirement that a criminal trial be fair may vary with changing social standards and circumstances. [85] His Honour cited *Barton* as representing, in effect, the first occasion upon which the court had correctly asserted the authority, and duty, of the courts to take all steps necessary, including the grant of a stay of proceedings, to prevent the abuse of process involved in an unfair trial. This interpretation of *Barton*, and the broader principles underlying that decision, enabled the earlier decision of the court in *McInnis v The Queen* [86] to be at least distinguished, if not overruled.

His Honour found in *Barton* express or implicit support for the proposition that the courts possess all necessary powers to ensure a fair trial. He also found in *Barton* a recognition of the duty of courts to determine the essential pre-requisites of a fair trial in the context of contemporary standards and circumstances. [87]

It is in the judgment of Deane J in *Dietrich* that one finds perhaps the highest judicially formulated expression of the right to a fair trial. His Honour concluded:

81. Ibid at 311.
82. Ibid at 326. Hunt CJ at CL went at least as far in *Milat*, and described the right to a fair trial as "an inseparable part of every system of law which makes any pretension to civilization": see judgment at p 3.
83. (1980) 147 CLR 75.
84. (1991) 171 CLR 468 at 478.
85. *Dietrich v The Queen* (1992) 177 CLR 292 at 328.
86. (1979) 143 CLR 575.
87. *Dietrich v The Queen* (1992) 177 CLR 292 at 332.

"It follows from the foregoing that, as a general proposition and in the absence of exceptional circumstances, a trial of an indigent person accused of serious crime will be unfair if, by reason of lack of means and the unavailability of other assistance, he is denied legal representation."[88]

Toohey J spoke of the right to a fair trial as being "engrained in our legal system". His Honour recognised that the concept of a fair trial is one that is impossible, in advance, to formulate exhaustively, or even comprehensively. His Honour cited with approval the observations of Deane J in *Jago* to the effect that the central prescript of our criminal law is that no person shall be convicted of crime otherwise than after a fair trial according to law. [89]

Gaudron J also accepted that it is fundamental to our system of criminal justice that a person should not be convicted of an offence save after a fair trial according to law. She observed:

"The expression 'fair trial according to law' is not a tautology. In most cases a trial is fair if conducted according to law, and unfair if not. If our legal processes were perfect that would be so in every case. But the law recognises that sometimes, despite the best efforts of all concerned, a trial may be unfair even though conducted strictly in accordance with law. *Thus the overriding qualification and universal criterion of fairness*!" (emphasis added)[90]

Gaudron J agreed with Deane J in finding the fundamental requirement that a trial be fair entrenched in the Commonwealth Constitution by Chapter III's implicit requirement that judicial power be exercised in accordance with the judicial process. In her Honour's view, the right to a fair trial, at least in federal matters (though her Honour did not state this limitation) does not emanate from the common law, but rather derives directly from implications derived from structure of the Constitution. The requirement of "fairness" was both independent from, and additional to the requirement that a trial be conducted in accordance with law. And it was "intrinsic" and "inherent". Her Honour stated:

"Speaking generally, the notion of 'fairness' is one that accepts that, sometimes, the rules governing practice, procedure and evidence must be tempered by reason and common sense to accommodate the special case that has arisen because, otherwise, prejudice or unfairness might result."[91]

She observed that the notion of a fair trial, and the inherent powers which exist to serve that end do not permit of "idiosyncratic notions of what is fair and just", any more than do other general concepts which carry broad powers or remedies in their train. However, what is fair very often depends on the circumstances of the particular case, and notions of fairness are inevitably bound up with prevailing social values. [92] Acknowledging the

88. Ibid at 337.
89. Ibid at 361.
90. Ibid at 362.
91. Ibid at 363.
92. Ibid at 364.

force of the views of Brennan J in *Jago*, her Honour accepted that a trial is not necessarily unfair because it is less than perfect. She added, however, that a trial is unfair if it involves a risk of the accused being improperly convicted. Indeed, she opined that if the only trial that can be had is one which involved a risk of that kind, "there can be no trial at all".[93]

Both Brennan and Dawson JJ dissented. They accepted the desirability of according an entitlement to legal aid in serious criminal matters. The point of difference between their views, and those of the other members of the court, was whether the court could, and should, translate such desirability into a rule of law, or a rule of practice, governing the conduct of criminal proceedings. The dissentients concluded that the court could not properly create such a rule.

The transition from the somewhat tentative, if not cautious, expressions surrounding the right to a fair trial in *Jago*, to the powerful, broadly expressed, statements of the majority in *Dietrich* demonstrates just how far the High Court had moved in its thinking on this subject over a period of no more than three years. The importance of Ch III of the Constitution as a source of individual rights and liberties has developed separately from, though concurrently with, the implications accorded to it in *Dietrich*.[94] The role accorded to Ch III in requiring a trial which is in all relevant senses "fair" by Deane and Gaudron JJ in *Dietrich* carries with it profound implications for the development of the criminal law, and not merely at federal level. Is the right to a fair trial, insofar as it finds its source in Ch III, capable of more general application? Can it be said to underlie the trial of purely State offences?[95] If so, how? Will the "equality" principle particularly developed in *Leeth v The Commonwealth*[96] sustain this transition? Developments are awaited, with interest.

WALTON v GARDINER—EXPLAINING THE DOCTRINE OF ABUSE OF PROCESS

The next occasion on which the court pronounced upon the doctrine of abuse of process, and the use of the remedy of a permanent stay, did not arise in the context of the criminal law. In *Walton v Gardiner*[97] the issue was whether the New South Wales Court of Appeal had acted correctly in ordering a permanent stay of certain complaints made against three medical practitioners. Related complaints had previously been the subject of consideration by the Medical Tribunal, and had previously been stayed as an abuse of process. A Royal Commission had subsequently reported

---

93. Ibid at 365. This must, with respect, be somewhat of an overstatement. Many, if not all, trials involve a risk of the accused being improperly convicted. It is not the risk which vitiates the trial, but the eventuality, should it be established. The statutes governing the circumstances in which criminal appeals may be allowed require no less.
94. See *Polyukhovich v Commonwealth* (1991) 172 CLR 501 at 606-614 per Deane J, and at 697-707 per Gaudron J; *Lim v Minister for Immigration* (1992) 176 CLR 1 at 26-29 per Brennan, Deane and Dawson JJ, at 66-74 per Gaudron J.
95. See *John Fairfax Publications Pty Ltd v Doe* (1995) 130 ALR 488 at 515 per Kirby P for a suggestion that this might be so.
96. (1992) 174 CLR 455.
97. (1993) 177 CLR 378.

adversely on the conduct of the practitioners. In 1991, five years after the earlier complaints had been stayed, fresh complaints were made against them. These new complaints arose out of the same pattern of professional conduct as had given rise to the earlier complaints. The court, by a three to two majority, held that the proceedings had been properly stayed.

The issue which gave rise to the grant of special leave was whether the grounds upon which a permanent stay may be granted are limited to cases where the proceedings have been brought for an improper purpose, or where there is no possibility of the tribunal affording the affected party a fair hearing. The court determined that there was no such limitation upon the power to grant a permanent stay. In the joint judgment of Mason CJ, Deane and Dawson JJ the principles were stated in the following broad terms:

"The inherent jurisdiction of a superior court to stay its proceedings on grounds of abuse of process extends to all those categories of cases in which the processes and procedures of the court, which exist to administer justice with fairness and impartiality, may be converted into instruments of injustice or unfairness. Thus, it has long been established that, regardless of the propriety of the purpose of the person responsible for their institution and maintenance, proceedings will constitute an abuse of process if they can be clearly seen to be foredoomed to fail. Again, proceedings within the jurisdiction of a court will be unjustifiably oppressive and vexatious of an objecting defendant, and will constitute an abuse of process, if that court is, in all the circumstances of the particular case, a clearly inappropriate forum to entertain them. Yet again, proceedings before a court should be stayed as an abuse of process if, notwithstanding that the circumstances do not give rise to an estoppel, their continuance would be unjustifiably vexatious and oppressive for the reason that it is sought to litigate anew a case which has already been disposed of by earlier proceedings."[98]

The width of this statement of principle has already produced an interesting and, it may be said, novel application. In *R v Smith*[99] the Crown appealed against orders staying proceedings permanently against five police officers who had been charged with murder. The trial judge, at the outset of the trial, had ordered a permanent stay upon the basis that the prosecution case was fundamentally flawed, and was clearly "foredoomed to fail", after a trial which was estimated to be likely to run for the best part of a year. The Full Court of the Supreme Court allowed the appeal, though it was accepted that civil or criminal proceedings would be an abuse of process if it could be said of them that it was quite clear that they must inevitably fail.

The sequel to this case occurred in the High Court where in *Smith v The Queen*[100] it was determined that the Full Court lacked jurisdiction to entertain an appeal from the decision of a trial judge granting a permanent stay. The decision of the High Court, in effect, restored the decision at first instance, thereby staying the prosecution.

98. Ibid at 392-393.
99. [1995] 1 VR 10.
100. (1994) 181 CLR 338.

ROGERS v THE QUEEN—A NEW SOLUTION TO THE ISSUE ESTOPPEL DILEMMA

In *Rogers v The Queen*,[101] the facts were that at a trial in 1989 on an indictment containing four counts of armed robbery, the prosecution sought to rely on admissions in several records of interview made by the accused. The trial judge rejected the tender of those records of interview upon the basis that they were not made voluntarily. In 1992, the accused was indicted on a further eight counts of armed robbery. The prosecution sought to rely upon one of the records of interview which had previously been excluded in the first trial. That record of interview contained admissions relating to some of the eight counts which the accused was now facing (as well as two of the counts for which he had previously been tried). The court determined by a majority of three to two that the tender of the records of interview amounted to a direct challenge to the 1989 ruling, and, in the circumstances, would be an abuse of process. Mason CJ referred to the authorities governing this doctrine, and concluded:

> "In the present case, a weighing of these considerations inevitably compels the conclusion that a stay should be ordered. The public interest in securing the convictions of the appellant is clearly outweighed by other relevant considerations. The tendering of the confessions by the prosecution was vexatious, oppressive and unfair to the appellant in that it exposed him to re-litigation of the issue of the voluntariness of the confessional statements in the records of interview. This issue had already been conclusively decided in the appellant's favour because the confessions sought to be tendered— though relating to different crimes—were made at the same time and in exactly the same circumstances as the confessions that were the subject of the *voir dire*. Re-litigation in subsequent criminal proceedings of an issue already finally decided in earlier criminal proceedings is not only inconsistent with the principle that a judicial determination is binding, final and conclusive . . . but is also calculated to erode public confidence in the administration of justice by generating conflicting decisions on the same issue."[102]

Deane and Gaudron JJ referred to the harm which would be caused to public confidence in the administration of justice if a determination were now to be made that the confessions were made voluntarily. This would undermine the "incontrovertible correctness"[103] of the verdicts of acquittal entered in 1989.

Brennan J regarded the abuse of process argument as misconceived. His Honour noted that there was nothing to suggest that the tender was for any purpose other than proof of the issues in the second trial. He went on to say:

> "There is no abuse of process in the *bona fide* prosecution of a person for a criminal offence. The tender of evidence that is probative of the

101. (1994) 181 CLR 251.
102. Ibid at 257.
103. Ibid at 280.

offence charged is not an abuse of process merely because its admissibility is challenged. If the evidence is rejected, the trial simply proceeds without it.'' [104]

His Honour, together with McHugh J, would have dealt with the matter by recognising that the doctrine of issue estoppel is applicable to criminal proceedings. McHugh J, however, dissented in holding that, in the particular circumstances of this case, that doctrine had no application.

RIDGEWAY v THE QUEEN—FURTHER AVENUES FOR PERMANENT STAYS?

The culmination of the post *Jago* High Court approach to the doctrine of abuse of process, and the use of the stay as a remedy for such abuse, is the recent decision of the court in *Ridgeway v The Queen*. [105] The appellant had been convicted of having had in his possession, contrary to s 233B of the *Customs Act* 1901, a prohibited import, namely 140.4 grams of heroin. The circumstances giving rise to the conviction were that the Australian Federal Police became aware of the appellant's interest in importing heroin into Australia, and his dealings with a man named Lee who was, unbeknown to the appellant, a registered police informer. The police, acting in conjunction with the Malaysian police, set up a "controlled" importation and delivery of heroin.

Lee, accompanied by a man named Chong, purchased heroin in Malaysia. Subsequently, the two men flew with it to Australia. Australian Customs had been notified in advance of the arrival of the heroin, and permitted it to be imported. Chong and Lee were met at the airport by officers of the Australian Federal Police, and delivery to Ridgeway was organised. Shortly after the appellant took possession of the heroin, the Australian Federal Police arrested him. In truth, the whole of the unlawful importation was arranged by and under the auspices of the Australian Federal Police, with complete involvement on the part of those in a high level of command.

On the appeal the Crown conceded that those members of the Australian Federal Police who had facilitated the importation of the heroin had committed a serious criminal offence pursuant to s 233B(1)(d) of the Act. The maximum penalty for each of the offences committed by Chong, and by members of the Australian Federal Police, was imprisonment for 25 years, and a fine of $100,000. The appellant contended:

(a) that the common law recognised a substantive defence of entrapment;

(b) that, by analogy with the *Bunning v Cross* discretion to exclude illegally procured evidence, there was a discretion to exclude evidence of an offence or an element of an offence procured by unlawful conduct on the part of law enforcement authorities;

104. Ibid at 270.
105. (1995) 129 ALR 41.

(c) that the appropriate immediate remedy in a true entrapment case was a stay of proceedings on the ground that they amount to an abuse of process.

The court unanimously rejected contention (a). Four members of the court, Mason CJ, Deane, Dawson and Brennan JJ rejected contention (c), while the remaining three members of the court, Toohey, Gaudron and McHugh JJ favoured its adoption. All members of the court save McHugh J accepted contention (b) as encapsulating the relevant principles, and held that the particular circumstances of this case required discretionary exclusion on public policy grounds.

In dealing with the question of a stay of prosecution based upon abuse of process, Mason CJ, Deane and Dawson JJ stated the following principle:

"Once it is concluded that our law knows no substantive defence of entrapment, it seems to us to follow that the otherwise regular institution of proceedings against a person who is guilty of a criminal offence for the genuine purpose of obtaining conviction and punishment is not an abuse of process by reason merely of the circumstance that the commission of the offence was procured by illegal conduct on the part of the police or any other person. To the contrary, to institute and maintain proceedings in a competent criminal court for that purpose is to use the process of that court for the very purpose for which it was established. [106]

Their Honours noted, however, that the "appropriate ultimate relief" in a case where the commission of the charged offence had been procured by illegal police conduct may well be a permanent stay of further proceedings, but via a more circuitous route. Once the decision is taken to exclude the evidence on public policy grounds, it may become apparent that it would be an abuse of process for the Crown to proceed with the trial. The abuse would arise from the fact that the proceedings will necessary fail with the consequence that a continuance of them would be oppressive and vexatious. Short of that position, however, the remedy of a stay has no application.

Brennan J reiterated what he had said in *Jago* in declining to follow the approach taken by some Australian courts that prosecution of an offender entrapped in the commission of an offence is an abuse of process enlivening a judicial discretion to stay the prosecution. [107] In determining that the *Bunning v Cross* discretion required discretionary exclusion of the evidence, his Honour felt constrained to comment: "This result is manifestly unsatisfactory from the viewpoint of law enforcement." [108]

Toohey J favoured dealing with entrapment upon the basis that it produces an abuse of process. [109] His Honour observed:

"The concept of abuse of process is not a precise one. Nor can it be; it gives effect to a concern on the part of courts that may arise in a variety of circumstances. But at the heart of the concept lies the

106. Ibid at 55.
107. Ibid at 62.
108. Ibid at 66.
109. Ibid at 69.

legitimate power of the courts to stay prosecutions brought in exercise of the prerogative of the Crown . . . Generally, abuse of process derives from a concern that judicial process be not invoked for an improper purpose (the issue in *Williams v Spautz*) and that the process be not abused in a way that interferes with the conduct of a fair trial (the issue in *Jago v District Court of NSW* and *Walton v Gardiner*). There are distinct aspects of abuse of process in that proceedings may be stayed if it appears they have been brought for an improper purpose even though there is no reason to doubt that the accused will receive a fair trial. Equally, an accused may not receive a fair trial, by reason of delay for instance, though there is no improper purpose in bringing the proceedings. But the power of a superior court to stay its proceedings on grounds of abuse of process is not confined to those situations. A stay of criminal proceedings gives effect to the view that it 'would offend the courts' sense of justice' if the accused had to stand trial in those circumstances.''[110]

Toohey J noted that the facts of *Ridgeway* did not disclose an indictment having been filed for an improper purpose. Nor did the appellant complain that he did not receive a fair trial. The reason given by his Honour for favouring a stay was that the charge against the appellant was the result of actions by police officers involving breaches of the law. To proceed against the appellant in those circumstances brought the administration of justice into disrepute.

Gaudron J, who also favoured utilising the remedy of a permanent stay in response to entrapment, commented:

"Abuse of process cannot be restricted to 'defined and closed categories' because notions of justice and injustice, as well as other considerations that bear on public confidence in the administration of justice, must reflect contemporary values and, as well, take account of the circumstances of the case. That is not to say that the concept of 'abuse of process' is at large or, indeed, without meaning. As already indicated, it extends to proceedings that are instituted for an improper purpose and it is clear that it extends to proceedings that are 'seriously and unfairly burdensome, prejudicial or damaging' or 'productive of serious and unjustified trouble and harassment'.''[111]

Her Honour went to reject the proposition that whether a prosecution based on entrapment can constitute an abuse of process depends solely upon whether the accused can receive a fair trial. She went on to say:

"Public confidence could not be maintained if the courts were to permit prosecutions to proceed in circumstances where a fair trial was impossible. However, and although there is a clear public interest in ensuring that the courts exercise their criminal jurisdiction rather than refrain from so doing, it is simply not possible to say that, so far as criminal proceedings are concerned, the inability of a court to ensure a fair trial is the only matter which could or might adversely affect public confidence.''[112]

110. Ibid at 71.
111. Ibid at 83.
112. Ibid at 84.

Gaudron J concluded that the administration of justice would inevitably be brought into question, and public confidence in the courts necessarily diminished, where the illegal actions of law enforcement agents culminate in the prosecution of an offence which results from their own criminal acts.

It is illuminating to note how McHugh J, in his dissent, came to precisely the opposite conclusion. While agreeing that the ultimate question must always be whether the administration of justice will be brought into disrepute (because the processes of the court are being used to prosecute an offence that was artificially created by the misconduct of law enforcement authorities), his Honour determined that the prosecution of the accused in *Ridgeway* would not have that consequence. Indeed, his Honour went on to say:

> "The prosecution of the appellant does not bring the administration of justice into disrepute. On the contrary, I think that the administration of justice will speedily fall into disrepute if courts stay prosecutions based on facts similar to the facts in this case." [113]

A cynic might be tempted to suggest that the majority in *Ridgeway* intended to send a clear message to the Commonwealth Parliament that if the police were to engage in "controlled importations and deliveries", legislation should be enacted to permit this to occur. The courts should not be expected to condone what would otherwise be serious breaches of the criminal law. [114]

If so, the message has been noted, and heeded. Such legislation was introduced into the Parliament on 29 June 1995, within two months of the decision of the court. [115] The Bill provides that a law enforcement officer who, for the purpose of a "controlled operation" (defined in cl 15H), engages in conduct which would otherwise constitute an offence under s 233B of the *Customs Act*, is not liable for that offence. In effect, *Ridgeway* is legislatively abrogated, subject only to appropriate statutory safeguards being met.

CONCLUSION

It is clear to anyone who reads the judgments of the High Court over the past decade that there has been a fundamental change in its mode of reasoning. This change has not been confined to the constitutional arena, though constitutional theory has been at the forefront of development. As Professor Zines notes:

> "There has been a general attack on past rules and formulae as being 'formalistic', deserting 'practical reality', ignoring social consequences and relying on 'form' rather than 'substance'." [116]

113. Ibid at 97.
114. See the judgment of Brennan J at 66.
115. See Crimes Amendment (Controlled Operations) Bill 1995. South Australia enacted the *Criminal Law (Undercover Operations) Act* 1995. The Act is not limited to drug offences, but is designed to overcome the wider implications of *Ridgeway*.
116. L Zines, "*Cole v Whitfield*—Most significant case of the Mason High Court", Vol 30, No 5, *Australian Lawyer*, p 18.

In a sense, the court has provided a working illustration of the Hart-Dworkin debate about the way judges function "at the margin of rules and in the fields left open by the theory of precedent".[117] There now seems to be far greater willingness to depart from established authority, and to search for appropriate principles to resolve given questions. When relevant principles conflict, the court seems inclined to weigh them, and to apply those which best accord with the court's perception of actual, and appropriate, community values and standards.

The willingness of the High Court to engage in the new discourse of rights has inevitably seen the court placed in a more activist role. The flow-on effect of some of the court's judgments dealing with the right to a fair trial have already begun to affect significantly the manner in which criminal trials are conducted. This may, however, prove to be a mixed blessing. The administration of criminal justice, and the daily conduct of criminal trials, is, at the best of times, a difficult process. Any uncertainty created by a more flexible approach towards the use of remedies, such as the permanent stay, invites such applications to be made. This may in turn lengthen proceedings, produce more appeals and, perhaps worst of all, lead to fragmentation of the criminal justice system, particularly through collateral review. Such fragmentation already occurs frequently enough through the use of judicial review in the Federal Court arising out of major prosecutions for corporate and revenue fraud. The interests of the community are scarcely served by opening up new avenues for delay and obfuscation.

On the positive side, the willingness of courts at all levels to recognise as fundamental the right to a fair trial represents a welcome move in the direction of strengthening the rule of law. The decisions of the High Court since *Jago* have provided a powerful stimulus for legal debate. That debate undoubtedly will continue as the courts strive to balance the competing claims of the State, and those unwillingly facing its most obviously coercive manifestation.

117. H Hart, *The Concept of Law* (New York, 1961), p 132.

Chapter 7

Procedural Fairness

John Griffiths*

INTRODUCTION

The High Court took less than 12 months after the 1994 Law and Government Seminar to demonstrate that the former Solicitor-General and now Chief Justice of the Supreme Court of South Australia could have pursued a highly successful career as a soothsayer. At that seminar, J J Doyle QC predicted that common law rights would be used more often and with increased rigour to limit government power and also that as pressure mounted for the High Court to apply and extend the list of common law rights, the role of that court itself would come under greater critical scrutiny.[1] The decision of the High Court in *Minister for Immigration and Ethnic Affairs v Teoh*,[2] delivered on 7 April 1995, has given realisation to each of those predictions, albeit in an administrative law setting rather than the constitutional law context which the legal clairvoyant may primarily have had in mind.

The rules of procedural fairness are among our best known common law rights. A series of High Court decisions commencing in the mid-1970s, most of them involving divided courts, saw those rules extended significantly, not only in terms of their application to a broader range of government activities than previously, but also in relation to the content of the rules.[3] *Teoh* continues the expansionist trend; however, its true significance lies not so much in that fact but in how administrative law and international law principles combined to reveal a novel dimension to common law procedural fairness requirements in Australia.

The *Teoh* decision and the government's swift and critical reaction to it provide a convenient framework within which to examine some of the key

---

* A Sydney Barrister.
1. "Common Law Rights and Democratic Rights" in P D Finn (ed), *Essays on Law and Government*, Vol 1, 1995.
2. (1995) 128 ALR 353.
3. *Twist v Randwick Municipal Council* (1976) 136 CLR 106; *Salemi v MacKellar (No 2)* (1977) 137 CLR 396; *Heatley v Tasmanian Gaming and Racing Commission* (1977) 137 CLR 487; *FAI Insurances Ltd v Winnecke* (1982) 151 CLR 342; *Kioa v West* (1985) 159 CLR 550; *South Australia v O'Shea* (1987) 163 CLR 378; *Haoucher v Minister for Immigration and Ethnic Affairs* (1990) 169 CLR 648; *Attorney-General (NSW) v Quin* (1990) 170 CLR 1; *Annetts v McCann* (1990) 170 CLR 596; *Ainsworth v Criminal Justice Commission* (1992) 175 CLR 564; *Johns v Australian Securities Commission* (1993) 178 CLR 408.

topical issues affecting procedural fairness and consultative duties in Australian law. They include:

1. the continuing challenge confronting courts in striking an appropriate balance between safeguarding individual rights, interests, and expectations while not erecting unacceptable barriers to efficient and effective public administration;

2. whether the doctrine of legitimate expectations which has been developed by the courts over the last 25 years to expand natural justice requirements provides a sufficiently coherent and acceptable basis for curial intervention;

3. the role of international law in the further development and application of procedural fairness; and

4. the potential for procedural fairness to operate partly to redress what has been described as the "present imbalances in the citizen-state relationship at least where a person is induced to rely upon the representations, etc of government".[4]

THE HIGH COURT'S DECISION IN TEOH

The case involved a judicial review challenge under the ADJR Act to decisions made by the Minister's delegate to refuse Mr Teoh's application for resident status and to deport him. Mr Teoh was serving a lengthy prison sentence for importation and possession of heroin. He was married to an Australian citizen and was father or step-father to seven children, all of whom were Australian citizens. The effect of Mr Teoh's deportation on his family was at the heart of the case.

Having failed at first instance, Mr Teoh appealed to the Full Court of the Federal Court.[5] His appeal succeeded on two new grounds added during the hearing of the appeal. First, that the Minister's delegate had failed to give proper consideration to a relevant factor to which she was bound to have regard, namely the effect of Mr Teoh's deportation on his family's future welfare. Secondly, that Australia's accession to the United Nations Convention on the Rights of the Child (the Convention) had generated a legitimate expectation on the part of the Teoh children that the terms of the Convention would be implemented in determining their father's application for resident status. Article 3(1) of the Convention provided that in all actions concerning children, including those taken by administrative bodies, "the best interests of the child shall be a primary consideration". It was held that because of the legitimate expectation so generated, procedural fairness obliged the delegate to make appropriate inquiries into the impact of Mr Teoh's deportation on the children's future welfare.

Although the reasoning of the Full Court, below, was not fully endorsed by the High Court, the Minister's appeal was rejected by a majority of four

---

4. Paul Finn and Kathryn Jane Smith, "The Citizen, the Government and 'Reasonable Expectations' " (1992) 66 ALJ 139 at 147.
5. (1994) 121 ALR 436.

to one. Significantly, however, the High Court majority agreed that ratification of the Convention enlivened a legitimate expectation deserving of procedural protection through application of common law procedural fairness rights. In a joint judgment, Mason CJ and Deane J held that even though the Convention was not part of Australian municipal law and did not provide a direct source of individual rights and obligations, ratification of the Convention gave rise to a legitimate expectation that its provisions would be implemented by administrative decision-makers exercising discretions under Australian law, including migration legislation. This was because:

> "ratification by Australia of an international Convention is not to be dismissed as a merely platitudinous or ineffectual act, particularly when the instrument evidences internationally accepted standards to be applied by courts and administrative authorities in dealing with basic human rights affecting the family and children. Rather, ratification of a Convention is a positive statement by the Executive government of this country to the world and to the Australian people that the Executive government and it agencies will act in accordance with the Convention. That positive statement is an adequate foundation for a legitimate expectation, absent statutory or executive indications to the contrary, that administrative decision-makers will act in conformity with the Convention and treat the best interests of the children as a 'primary consideration'. It is not necessary that a person seeking to set up such a legitimate expectation should be aware of the Convention or should personally entertain the expectation; it is enough that the expectation is reasonable in the sense that there are adequate materials to support it."[6]

Accordingly, Mason CJ and Deane J held that the rules of procedural fairness operated to provide procedural protection to that legitimate expectation by requiring the Minister's delegate to give notice and the opportunity of a hearing to the children (or their father acting on their behalf) in circumstances where the delegate proposed to depart from Art 3(1) of the Convention. Their Honours gave emphasis to the procedural nature of that protection and contrasted it with the court's inability to provide substantive relief to compel compliance with the Convention. Moreover, it was because the legitimate expectation did not constitute a binding rule of law that their Honours held that the expectation could be defeated by statutory or executive indications to the contrary.[7]

In separate reasons for judgment, Toohey J agreed with Mason CJ and Deane J on the effect of the interrelationship between the Convention and procedural fairness or legitimate expectation requirements in the circumstances of the *Teoh* case, including their finding that the doctrine of

---

6. (1995) 128 ALR 353 at 365. That approach is reminiscent of that of Cooke P in *Tavita v Minister for Immigration* [1994] 2 NZLR 257 at 266 where, in responding to an argument that a Minister could ignore unincorporated international instruments, his Honour said: "That is an unattractive argument, apparently implying that New Zealand's adherence to the international instruments has been at least partly window-dressing."

7. Ibid.

legitimate expectation did not depend on the subjective state of mind of the persons asserting the expectation. His Honour also indicated in obiter dicta that he may have been prepared to go further than his brethren (including Gaudron J),[8] in requiring the decision-maker to initiate inquiries and obtain reports. His Honour did not make clear under which head of review such duty might arise, but the candidates would include procedural fairness as well as substantive heads of review, such as the duty to have proper regard to relevant considerations or Wednesbury unreasonableness.[9]

While agreeing that procedural fairness rules applied in the circumstances of the case, Gaudron J went much further than the other majority judges. Her Honour agreed that the children had an expectation that their interests would be taken into account as a primary consideration and that such expectation was protected procedurally in the manner found by the other majority judges, but her Honour described the Convention itself as being of only "subsidiary significance" in this regard.[10] Gaudron J based the children's expectations on what she described as a common law right of child citizens to have their interests taken into account as a primary consideration in all discretionary decisions by government departments and agencies which directly affect a child's individual welfare.[11] Her Honour's reliance on one common law right to found the expectation upon which another common law right operated, that of procedural fairness, represents a radical new approach. Moreover, it provides an interesting "double-barrelled" example of the expansion of common law rights to limit, in a procedural way, the exercise of government powers.

McHugh J delivered a strongly worded dissenting judgment. His Honour found that the effect of the majority's judgment was to extend procedural fairness into the forbidden area of providing substantive, as opposed to procedural, protection to a legitimate expectation; that ratification of the Convention did not generate any legitimate expectation that an application for resident status would be decided in accordance with Art 3(1); that the doctrine of legitimate expectations does not require a decision maker to inform a person affected of an intention to depart from a rule when there is no obligation to apply that rule and no undertaking has been given to apply the rule; and that in any event on the facts the delegate did comply with the Convention and had had regard to the children's best interests as a primary consideration. The depth of McHugh J's disagreement with the majority's approach is reflected in the following statement:

> "It seems a strange, almost comic, consequence if procedural fairness requires a decision-maker to inform the person affected that he or she does not intend to apply a rule that the decision-maker cannot be required to apply, has not been asked or given an undertaking to apply, and of which the person affected by the decision has no knowledge."[12]

8. Ibid at 376.
9. Ibid at 374.
10. Ibid at 375.
11. Ibid.
12. Ibid at 383.

THE AFTERMATH OF TEOH

Scarcely four weeks after the High Court delivered its judgment, on 10 May 1995 a Joint Ministerial Statement was issued by the Minister for Foreign Affairs and the Attorney-General. The express object of the joint statement was to prevent any future application of the majority's reasoning in *Teoh* by declaring on behalf of the government that no person should have any legitimate expectation that the provisions of a treaty to which Australia was a party, either now or in the future, necessarily would be applied in administrative decision-making. [13]

Not content merely to rely on an executive statement designed to defeat legitimate expectations which would otherwise arise from the act of ratification, the government has also moved to introduce legislation as foreshadowed in the joint statement noted above. In the explanatory memorandum to the Administrative Decisions (Effect of International Instruments) Bill 1995, it is stated that:

"The purpose of the Bill is to eliminate any expectation which might exist that administrative decisions, whether at the Commonwealth, State or Territory level, will be made in conformity with the provisions of ratified but unimplemented treaties, or, that if a decision is to be made contrary to such provisions, an opportunity will be given for the affected person to make submissions on the issue."

While acknowledging the distinction drawn in *Teoh* between procedural and substantive protection, the explanatory memorandum records the government's view that the effect of the High Court's decision was "to give to ratified but unimplemented treaties a force in domestic law which was previously assumed to be dependent upon parliamentary action". The object of the Bill is to "restore the situation which existed before *Teoh*, which, if there were to be changes to procedural or substantive rights in Australian law resulting from adherence to a treaty, they would be made by parliamentary and not executive action." Another stated object of the Bill is to remove the "uncertainty" which is said to be created by allowing decisions to be challenged on the ground that decision-makers did not properly give effect to legitimate expectations based on international instruments not forming part of Australian law.

The key position of the Bill which seeks to achieve those objects is cl 5, which provides as follows:

"5. The fact that Australia is bound by, or a party to, a particular international instrument, or that an enactment reproduces or refers to a particular international instrument, does not give rise to a legitimate expectation, on the part of any person, that:

(a) an administrative decision will be made in conformity with the requirements of that instrument; or

(b) if the decision were to be made contrary to any of those requirements, any person affected by the decision would be given

13. The core passage is cited at (1995) 17 Syd LR 204 at 237.

notice and an adequate opportunity to present a case against the taking of such a course."

The legal effect of the Bill will be examined further below. [14]

THE SCOPE OF PROCEDURAL FAIRNESS

It is not surprising that the High Court in *Teoh* was attracted by the principles of procedural fairness as providing a basis for judicial intervention, as opposed to one of the substantive heads of judicial review, such as failure to heed relevant considerations as relied upon in part in the court below. There is an obvious difficulty, as implicitly acknowledged by Mason CJ and Deane J, [15] in reconciling the notion that the terms of an international treaty not incorporated into Australian domestic law constitute a relevant consideration which a decision-maker is bound to take into account, with the orthodox position that such treaties do not provide a direct source of individual rights and obligations. [16] But the preference for procedural fairness as the basis for judicial intervention probably goes deeper than that. It reflects a stronger judicial confidence in reviewing administrative action on procedural grounds where questions of the legitimacy of judicial review itself are normally less acute than is the case with review on substantive grounds. The latter may operate in practice to create insurmountable legal impediments to the making of particular administrative decisions whereas the former rarely if ever have that effect. Difficult issues relating to estoppel and fettering the future exercise of statutory discretions or duties are also substantially avoided by limiting relief to procedural protection. [17]

What is perhaps more surprising about *Teoh* is that the High Court should insist that procedural fairness requirements operated because of the doctrine of legitimate expectations, a doctrine which itself has been subjected to considerable criticism by virtually all members of the High Court and one which itself involves some difficult issues concerning the legitimacy of judicial review. [18]

The last 20 years has seen a steady expansion in the requirements of procedural fairness affecting public administration not only in Australia but in other common law jurisdictions, including the United Kingdom, Canada, and New Zealand. [19] With only a few exceptions, such as the High Court's peculiar refusal in 1985 in *Public Service Board of New South Wales v Osmond* [20] to endorse a general requirement for administrators to

14. See below, pp 206-208.
15. (1995) 128 ALR at 364-365.
16. Ibid at 361 and see *R v Secretary of State for the Home Department; Ex parte Brind* [1991] 1 AC 696.
17. See below, pp 208-213.
18. See below, pp 202-206. It may prove significant that the *Teoh* court did not comprise either Brennan or Dawson JJ, two of the court's strongest critics of the doctrine.
19. See Sir Robin Cooke, "Has Administrative Law Gone Too Far?", paper delivered at International Bar Association Biennial Conference, Melbourne, October 1994.
20. (1985) 159 CLR 656. Contrast the recent decision of the House of Lords in *R v Home Secretary; Ex parte Doody* [1994] 1 AC 531.

give reasons for their decisions (a decision handed down only weeks after the High Court's landmark procedural fairness decision in *Kioa*), the trend in Australia has been towards greater transparency and openness in public decision-making. The trend probably commenced in *Randwick Municipal Council v Twist*,[21] where a majority of the High Court resurrected the common law roots of procedural fairness. The consequence was to subtly change the role of the courts in determining procedural fairness requirements from being an exercise in statutory construction with its primary focus on divining legislative intent to one which, of necessity, seeks to accommodate parliamentary supremacy, but gives much greater emphasis to common law requirements and the need to safeguard the interests of individuals in the absence of a clear and unambiguous contrary legislative intention. The leading cases are too well-known to be recited in detail here. Their effect can be summarised as follows:

Application: As to the threshold question of the application of procedural fairness to public administration:

• There is a strong presumption in favour of the common law duty to act fairly applying to the making of administrative decisions which affect rights, interests and expectations, subject only to a clear manifestation of a contrary statutory intention;[22]

• That presumption applies to both statutory and non-statuory governmental executive decision-making, at least insofar as the exercise of justiciable non-statutory powers are concerned, that is, those which have a direct and immediate impact on the rights or interests of persons in their individual capacities;[23]

• In the case of statutory powers, the presumption is not displaced merely by the high status of the decision-maker involved, such as the Crown's representative or Cabinet;[24]

• Procedual fairness does not apply generally to the making or changing of legislative or quasi-legislative instruments which do not directly affect the rights, interests and expectations of persons in their individual capacities, but rather affect them in their capacities as members of the general public or members of a class of the public;[25]

21. (1976) 136 CLR 106.
22. *Kioa* (1985) 159 CLR 550 at 584 per Mason J; *Annetts* (1990) 170 CLR 596 at 598 per Mason CJ, Deane and McHugh JJ.
23. *Haoucher* (1990) 169 CLR 648 at 653 per Deane J; *Minister for the Arts, Heritage and Environment v Peko-Wallsend Ltd* (1987) 15 FCR 274; *Victoria v Master Builders' Association of Victoria* [1995] 2 VR 121; *Waters v Acting Administrator of the Northern Territory* (1993) 46 FCR 462.
24. *FAI* (1982) 151 CLR 342 at 364-366; *O'Shea* (1987) 163 CLR 378 at 386 per Mason CJ; *C O Williams Construction Ltd v Blackman* [1995] 1 WLR 102.
25. *Salemi (No 2)* (1977) 137 CLR 396 at 452 per Jacobs J; *O'Shea* (1987) 163 CLR at 387 per Mason CJ; at 410-411 per Brennan J and 417-418 per Deane J; *Kioa* (1985) 159 CLR 550 at 609 per Brennan J and 632 per Deane J; *Western Australia v Bropho* (1991) 5 WAR 75. But see *Bread Manufacturers of NSW v Evans* (1981) 38 ALR 93, where participation in a public inquiry leading up to the making of a quasi-legislative order was critical in attracting natural justice obligations.

- By the same token, procedural fairness requirements do not generally apply to the making or changing of policies, [26] absent circumstances of a special kind; [27]

- The law is uncertain as to when, if ever, procedural fairness requires a decision maker to disclose the terms of a policy for comment by a person affected by the application of the policy. Traditionally, a distinction has been drawn between adverse factual matters, which must be revealed, and adverse policies, which generally need not. [28]

That distinction has clear potential to cause injustice. In particular, it is not easily reconciled with the long-established principle that while a decision-maker is entitled to have regard to a policy as a relevant consideration as long as the individual merits of a particular case are considered [29] and an affected person has an entitlement to argue that the policy does not apply to her or his case or that an exception to it should be made. [30] Those entitlements are meaningless if the affected person is not aware of the existence or proposed application of the policy.

Content: As to the content of the requirements of procedural fairness:

- That content is highly variable such that the exercise of the same power may give rise to different procedural fairness requirements depending on the circumstances and the content may even contract to nothingness in an appropriate case; [31]

- The requirements of procedural fairness may also change with the passage of time, both in general and in their application to decisions of a particular type; [32]

- At the heart of the subject of procedural fairness lies the question what is "fair and just" in all the circumstances. [33] Accordingly no semantic formula or linguistic label will provide a mechanical answer to the content of procedural fairness in an individual case. [34] A pragmatic approach is essential in order to weigh up a range of potentially relevant

26. *Quin* (1990) 170 CLR 1 at 17 per Mason CJ, at 39-40 per Brennan J and at 61 per Dawson J; *O'Shea* (1987) 163 CLR 378; *Peninsula Anglican Boys' School v Ryan* (1985) 7 FCR 415; *West Australian Field and Game Association Inc v Pearce* (1992) 27 ALD 38.
27. See *R v Liverpool Corp; Ex parte Liverpool Taxi Fleet Operators' Association* [1972] 2 QB 299; *Council of Civil Service Unions v Minister for the Civil Service* [1985] 1 AC 374; *R v Secretary of State for Transport; Ex parte Richmond upon Thames London Borough Council* [1994] 1 WLR 74 at 93 per Laws J.
28. *Peninsula Anglican Boys' School v Ryan* (1985) 7 FCR 415 at 429 per Wilcox J.
29. *Re Drake and Minister for Immigration and Ethnic Affairs (No 2)* (1979) 2 ALD 634.
30. *British Oxygen Co Ltd v Minister of Technology* [1971] AC 610; *R v Port of London Authority; Ex parte Kynoch Ltd* [1919] 1 KB 176.
31. *Kioa* (1985) 159 CLR 550 at 616 per Brennan J.
32. *R v Secretary of State for the Home Department; Ex parte Doody* [1994] 1 AC 531 at 540 per Lord Mustill and *Johns v Release on Licence Board* (1987) 9 NSWLR 103.
33. *Haoucher* (1990) 169 CLR 648 at 652 per Deane J.
34. As Deane J said in *O'Shea* (1987) 163 CLR 378 at 416:
    "The common law rules of natural justice or procedural fair play are not susceptible of being expressed in terms of logical syllogism or precise comprehensive formula. They reflect minimum standards of basic fairness which the common law requires to be observed in the exercise of government (and, in some cases, non-government) authority or power."
    To similar effect, see *Teoh* (1995) 128 ALR 353 at 371 per Toohey J.

factors, including the context of the statute (if any) which creates an administrative discretion, [35] the subject matter, [36] the impact on the affected person, [37] the nature of the decision-making process, [38] and other matters such as the practical implications of imposing procedural requirements on efficient administration; [39]

- The principles governing bias in administrative decision-making seem relatively well-settled and need not be summarised here; [40]

- The other limb of procedural fairness (audi alteram partem) is more volatile and uncertain. This is not only understandable, it is probably unavoidable. Fundamental differences between judicial and administrative processes have required judicial review courts to modify and adapt procedural fairness requirements which traditionally applied to adversarial hearings familiar in the judicial system. In the administrative justice system content rules have to accommodate the variable nature of contemporary public administration, involving as it does the exercise of a diverse range of legislative and non-legislative powers and functions, by an array of departments, agencies, tribunals and officials, which affect in differing ways and degrees a broad spectrum of individual rights, interests and entitlements. The courts are effectively developing codes of administrative practice, albeit in a piecemeal fashion depending on the opportunities presented by individual judicial review cases;

- Consequently, modern procedural fairness requirements in the administrative justice system may involve implementation of procedural steps which extend well beyond the traditional indicia of a fair hearing in an adversarial adjudicative context. For example, in particular circumstances a public administrator may be obliged by procedural fairness to take positive steps to assist an applicant in identifying "the critical issue" at stake, [41] possibly to initiate independent inquiries or reports, [42] to draw an applicant's attention to a fundamental flaw in an application or the need to obtain corroborative material, [43] to provide applicants with equal access to relevant departmental publications to

---

35. A good illustration of this trite proposition is *West Australian Field and Game Association Inc v Pearce* (1992) 27 ALD 38 where the terms of the *Worldlife Conservation Act* 1950 were held to be inconsistent with an alleged legitimate expectation of consultation prior to the enunciation of a new policy on the controversial subject of duck shooting.
36. See Lord Tucker LJ's classic statement in *Russell v Duke of Norfolk* [1949] 1 All ER 109 at 118.
37. *Kioa* (1985) 159 CLR 550 at 582 per Mason J.
38. *Zhang de Yong v Minister for Immigration* (1993) 118 ALR 165.
39. See below, pp 198-200.
40. See, for example, *Livesey v NSW Bar Association* (1983) 151 CLR 288 and *Laws v Australian Broadcasting Tribunal* (1990) 170 CLR 70.
41. *Kioa* (1985) 159 CLR 550 at 587 per Mason J; *Broussard v Minister for Immigration, Local Government and Ethnic Affairs* (1989) 98 ALR 180 at 189 per Gummow J; *Commissioner for ACT Revenue v Alphaone Pty Ltd* (1995) 127 ALR 699.
42. *Videto v Minister for Immigration, Local Government and Ethnic Affairs* (1985) 69 ALR 342 at 353 per Toohey J and *Fares Rural Meat and Livestock Co Pty Ltd v Australian Meat and Livestock Corp* (1990) 96 ALR 153 at 172 per Gummow J; but see *Teoh* at 364 per Mason CJ and Deane J, at 376 per Gaudron J and at 388-389 per McHugh J.
43. *Broussard* (1989) 98 ALR 180 at 588 per Gummow J.

enable proper completion of pro forma applications,[44] or to refrain from providing misleading or erroneous advice or information relevant to a person's application or interests.[45]

The extent of the adaptation of procedural fairness requirements from their historical origins in the judicial system to the modern administrative justice system is illustrated by the recent decision of Justice Lockhart in *Consolidated Press Holdings Ltd v Federal Commissioner of Taxation.*[46] Certain taxpayers had provided confidential information about their financial affairs to the Australian Taxation Office in support of their applications for extension of time for payment of tax and other relief under taxation legislation. There was a series of telephone conversations and correspondence between the taxpayers' representative and the ATO and their solicitors. Unbeknownst to the taxpayers, the ATO had instructed their solicitors to engage an external accounting expert to analyse the taxpayers' information and that information was forwarded to the expert for that purpose. The taxpayers argued inter alia that they had a legitimate expectation that the ATO would not divulge or communicate information concerning their affairs to persons outside the ATO without first consulting with the taxpayers. Justice Lockhart agreed that based on the evidence of the course of dealings with the ATO and their solicitors the taxpayers had been led to believe that the information was being examined solely by the ATO. Even though the external consultant was held to be bound by the secrecy provisions in taxation legislation, Justice Lockhart held that, because of the taxpayers' legitimate expectation, procedural fairness required that the ATO consult with the taxpayers on the following matters before the information was divulged to the accounting expert:[47]

- why such information needed to be sent to persons external to the ATO and their legal advisers at all;

- the identity of the proposed accounting expert, in case the taxpayers wished to comment on any issue of conflict of duty or interest;

- whether the taxpayers preferred to withdraw their applications altogether rather than have the information divulged;

- whether the taxpayers may wish to seek restriction on the scope of information divulged; and

- whether the identities of the taxpayers and their tax file numbers should be disclosed.

Justice Lockhart's decision represents a guarded but appropriate response to what appears to be an increasing tendency on the part of the ATO to turn to the private sector for expert non-legal advice to assist in complex tax audits and other taxation matters. The court was not prepared to hold that the ATO was powerless to engage such external assistance but

---

44. *Hamilton v Minister for Local Government and Ethnic Affairs* (1995) 35 ALD 205 at 212-214 per Beazley J (reversed on a different point—see (1994) 53 FCR 349).
45. *Minister for Immigration, Local Government and Ethnic Affairs v Hamilton* (1994) 53 FCR 349 at 362 per Burchett J; *R v Secretary of State for Transport; Ex parte London Borough of Richmond upon Thames, TLR,* 20 December 1994.
46. (1995) 129 ALR 443.
47. Ibid at 453.

was concerned to ensure the taxpayers were treated fairly in a procedural sense. As with all administrative law decisions, the particular facts of the case together with the statutory context in which those facts arose (particularly the presence of strict statutory secrecy provisions) were of critical importance, as Justice Lockhart emphasised. [48] While it may not be possible to extract from the case a general duty of consultation in all cases prior to the ATO retaining external consultants, the presence in taxation legislation of tight secrecy provisions, the importance of maintaining public confidence in the proper administration of revenue statutes and the general expectation of taxpayers based on past custom that their tax information will be kept strictly confidential to the ATO, mean that there is ample scope for the doctrine of legitimate expectations to operate in many other fact situations to give rise to a similar duty of consultation.

COST-BENEFIT CONSIDERATIONS

Procedural fairness requirements, such as those listed above, plainly come at some cost to public administration. An issue which arises is whether courts should be influenced by cost-benefit considerations in determining the content of procedural fairness requirements. Such matters have at times been candidly addressed by certain judges. The high water mark is probably Kirby P's judgment in *Johns v Release on Licence Board*, in the context of the question whether procedural fairness required the Board to provide oral hearings to prisoners whose releases on licence were revoked. His Honour said:

> "Words of such generality, 'the duty to act fairly', have the advantage of flexibility and the capacity to adapt with changing community attitudes and expectations and the differing circumstances of particular cases. But they present a very practical problem to statutory bodies such as the Board and to administrators generally. Provided with no specific guidance by Parliament as to what they should do in particular cases, the somewhat vague injunction of the common law to proceed with fairness as the case requires may lead to uncertainty and error, even where there is a will to act fairly. In part, this is inescapable. Different courts at different times may consider that different requirements should be observed. But courts within the one jurisdiction do well to endeavour to reduce confusion by adopting, as far as differing legislation permits, consistent approaches to the elaboration of the requirements of procedural fairness. They also do well to spell out those requirements with due regard to the practicalities, including the costs involved, having regard to the benefits which stand to be gained." [49]

Although the New South Wales Court of Appeal was not persuaded in *Johns* by the material tendered on behalf of the government highlighting the alleged practical and economic burdens of the Board providing oral

48. Ibid at 454.
49. (1987) 9 NSWLR 103 at 109.

hearings, similar considerations have weighed more heavily in other cases to shape the nature of the requirements of procedural fairness.[50]

There is no systematic or consistent judicial approach to these matters. In *Teoh*, for example, Justice Toohey alone among the majority judges expressly considered the practical impact of the court's ruling on administrators. His Honour rejected the argument that the ruling created an "impossible task" for decision makers, noting that the ruling did not fetter substantive decision-making and commenting that each area of public administration should be familiar with relevant conventions affecting their activities.[51]

Both common sense and public confidence in the judicial system dictate that courts must be mindful of the practical implications of imposing particular procedural requirements on the public administration, but there would be obvious difficulties in adopting a cost-benefit approach in procedural fairness cases generally. Even if the costs of burdens for public administration were readily quantifiable (which is doubtful) the benefits of procedural fairness are intangible and difficult to quantify in any meaningful or admissible way. As Justice French has commented:

"Value judgments must be made of the importance of the private interest affected by the decision on the one hand and the burden to the administrative process of adopting a particular set of procedures on the other. These are factors generally not capable of quantification and, in any event, are qualitatively different."[52]

The benefits procedural fairness requirements bring to the administrative process include not only the giving effect to individual justice but also the administrative efficiencies which flow from adherence to objective legal standards. As Professor H W R Wade has said:

"Lawyers are a procedurally minded race, and it is natural that administrators should be tempted to regard procedural restrictions, invented by lawyers, as an obstacle to efficiency. It is true that the rules of natural justice restrict the freedom of administrative action and that their observance costs a certain amount of time and money. But time and money are likely to be well spent if they reduce friction in the machinery of government; and it is because they are essentially rules for upholding fairness and so reducing grievances that the rules of natural justice can be said to promote efficiency rather than impede it. Provided that the courts do not let them run riot, and keep them in touch with the standards which good administration demands in any case, they should be regarded as a protection not only to citizens but also to officials. A decision which is made without bias, and with proper consideration of the views of those affected by it, will not only be more acceptable; it will be of better quality. Justice and efficiency

50. See, for example, *Zhang de Yong* (1993) 118 ALR 165 at 191, where Justice French said: "In my opinion, courts should be reluctant to impose in the name of procedural fairness, detailed rules of practice, particularly in the area of high volume decision-making involving significant use of public resources."
51. (1995) 128 ALR 353 at 373.
52. *Zhang de Yong* (1993) 118 ALR 165 at 190.

go hand in hand, so long at least as the law does not impose excessive refinements."[53]

A related issue is whether, even if procedural fairness requirements cannot or should not be determined according to a strict cost-benefit evaluation, the courts' attitude should be influenced by the extent to which, statistically, compliance with procedural fairness produces a different administrative decision. That issue was raised by Sir Anthony Mason extracurially when he suggested that if the proportion of different decisions was insignificant "then it may be undesirable to expend too much of our resources in these cases".[54]

The question requires detailed examination but, even if it transpired that the number of cases was insignificant, it is submitted that appropriate recognition would still need to be given to the wider role played by procedural fairness in enhancing the legitimacy of public decision-making. Both public and individual confidence in the integrity of executive government and administrative processes is enhanced by the adoption of procedures which are, and are seen to be, fair and just in all the circumstances.

Procedural fairness is fundamentally about people having a say concerning matters which affect them individually. That opportunity should exist even if their views do not ultimately prevail, as the courts have generally recognised.[55] That does not mean that the same opportunities should apply uniformly across the spectrum of public administration. However, the highly variable content of modern procedural fairness equips courts with the ability to tailor requirements according to the particular circumstances. It may well be that in an area of high volume decision-making and minimal discretion that the rules will contract to very basic requirements.[56]

Apart from varying the content of the rules, courts also retain the discretion to withhold judicial review relief in appropriate cases, even if procedural unfairness is established. The availability of an adequate alternative remedy is one ground upon which relief may be withheld.[57] Another is futility, that is where ordering reconsideration of a decision to be conducted in accordance with procedural fairness requirements would be pointless because no other decision is legally open to be made in the circumstances.[58]

---

53. H W R Wade and C Forsyth, *Administrative Law*, 7th ed, 1994, p 414.
54. "The Increasing Importance of Judicial Review of Administrative Action", paper delivered on 9 June 1994 to the Administrative Law Section of the Law Institute of Victoria, p 9.
55. See, for example, *Annamunthodo v Oilfields Workers' Trade Union* [1961] AC 945 at 956 per Lord Denning.
56. As was the case in *Zhang de Yong* (1993) 118 ALR 165.
57. See generally, M Allars, *Introduction to Australian Administrative Law*, 1990, paras 6.93-6.96 and Bingham, "Should Public Law Remedies be Discretionary?" (1991) Public Law 64; *R v Marks; Ex parte Australian Building Construction Employees and Builders Labourers' Federation* (1981) 147 CLR 471 at 484-485 per Mason J; *Marine Hull and Liability Insurance Co Ltd v Hurford* (1986) 67 ALR 77 at 91-92 per Wilcox J and *Gudgeon v Black* (unreported, FC SC WA, 10 November 1994).
58. See, for example, *Mobil Oil Canada Ltd v Canada Newfoundland Offshore Petroleum Board* (1994) 111 DLR (4th) 1.

LEGITIMATE EXPECTATIONS

The considerable expansion in the reach and content of procedural fairness requirements over the last 30 years has coincided with the development and application of the doctrine of legitimate expectations. That doctrine was originally created as a tool for enabling procedural fairness to operate beyond the rigid mould of "existing legal rights and interests", to which the rules of natural justice were traditionally confined.[59] As McHugh J observed in *Haoucher*,[60] the "justice and wisdom of extending procedural fairness to legitimate expectations as well as to existing rights and interests seems obvious". That is because the practical impact on an individual of the loss of an expected substantive benefit or privilege, such as the renewal of a licence, will often be just as devastating as the revocation of an existing licence.

But the doctrine of legitimate expectations quickly outgrew its origins and came to be employed in a wider category of cases to ground procedural fairness requirements, not only because of the nature of the benefit or privilege involved, but also because of the conduct or actions of the public officials leading up to the exercise of executive power. The two limbs of legitimate expectations which emerged are described and illustrated in the following extract from McHugh J's judgment in *Haoucher*:

"A legitimate expectation may arise from the conduct of the person proposing to exercise the power or from the nature of the benefit or privilege enjoyed: *Kioa*. In *Attorney-General (Hong Kong) v Ng Yuen Shiu*, the Privy Council held that a policy announcement that illegal immigrants would be interviewed and their cases considered on their merits gave rise to a legitimate expectation that an immigrant would not be deported without the policy being implemented. *Ng Yuen Shiu* is an illustration of an undertaking giving rise to a legitimate expectation. *Heatley v Tasmanian Racing and Gaming Commission* is an illustration of a course of conduct creating a legitimate expectation. In *Heatley*, this court held that members of the public had a legitimate expectation that they would continue to receive the customary permission to go on to racecourses upon the payment of the stated fee to the racecourse owner. *FAI Insurances Ltd v Winnecke*, on the other hand, is an illustration of the nature of the benefit or privilege enjoyed giving rise to a legitimate expectation. Because an insurer does not set up an insurance business on the basis that it will only last one year, this court held that, where an insurer had been given approval to conduct an insurance business, there was a legitimate expectation that its approval would be renewed each year unless there was a good reason for refusing it.

A legitimate expectation that a person will obtain or continue to enjoy a benefit or privilege must be distinguished, however, from a

59. See generally Tate, "The Coherence of 'Legitimate Expectations' and the Foundations of Natural Justice" (1988) 14 Mon LR 15 and Forsyth, "The Provenance and Protection of Legitimate Expectations" [1988] CLJ 238.
60. (1990) 169 CLR 648 at 680.

mere hope that he or she will obtain or continue to enjoy a benefit or privilege. A hope that a statutory power will be exercised so as to confer a benefit or privilege does not give rise to a legitimate expectation sufficient to attract the rules of natural justice: *South Australia v O'Shea*. To attract the operation of the rules of procedural fairness, there must be some undertaking or course of conduct acquiesced in by the decision-maker or something about the nature of the benefit or privilege which suggests that, in the absence of some special or unusual circumstance, the person concerned will obtain or continue to enjoy a benefit or privilege."[61]

The doctrine of legitmate expectations has not been without its critics, even among those who would generally support the current extended ambit of procedural fairness, yet the courts persist with its use, as *Teoh* exemplifies. The difficulties with the doctrine are well known and may be summarised as follows:

1. The doctrine arguably undermines the legitimacy of judicial review because the notion of "legitimate" compels the court to evaluate the sufficiency of the reasonableness of the source of the expectation in order to determine whether the expectation is "legitimate" and, therefore, deserving of judicial review protection.[62]

2. The doctrine contains "no explicable legal principle" and is established merely by evaluation of particular facts, leaving wide scope for judicial discretion.[63]

3. While the sources of an expectation may assist in determining the content of requirements of procedural fairness in a particular case, such sources ought not to determine the threshold question. This is because, in Brennan J's words, the "only sound foundation for judicial review is, in my opinion, the statute which creates the power, construed to include any terms supplied by the common law".[64]

4. Several difficulties arise when the doctrine is used in the context of the giving of an assurance of a particular procedure. First, the doctrine provides no criterion by which the court may determine whether the expectation should be fulfilled.[65] Secondly, even if a legitimate expectation is engendered by such an assurance, procedural fairness may be satisfied by lesser or different procedures than those promised.[66] Thirdly, it is potentially confusing to apply the doctrine in those circumstances because the real basis for procedural fairness in such cases is the need to be just and fair because the assurance has been made.[67]

61. (1990) 169 CLR 648 at 681-682.
62. Significantly, the doctrine of legitimate expectations was first employed in *Schmidt v Secretary of State for Home Affairs* [1969] 2 Ch 149 to deny procedural fairness to foreign students on the grounds that as visitors they did not have a legitimate expectation of having their visitors' entry permits extended. See also *Annetts* (1990) 170 CLR 596 at 605 per Brennan J.
63. Ibid at 607 per Brennan J.
64. Ibid at 606.
65. Ibid.
66. *Haoucher* (1990) 169 CLR 648 at 660 per Dawson J.
67. *Quin* (1990) 170 CLR 1 at 57 per Dawson J.

5. The doctrine may distort the proper scope of judicial review, not only by drawing the courts into granting relief in inappropriate cases, but also by risking the denial of relief in circumstances where procedural fairness is required even though no legitimate expectation can be identified.[68]

6. The word "legitimate" tends to suggest entitlement to the substance of the expectation "whereas the true entitlement is to the observance of procedural fairness before the substance of the expectation is denied".[69]

7. The phrase "legitimate expectation", in common with other phrases such as "natural justice" and "procedural fairness", encourages the view that it is a label or mechanical formula "somehow determining the outcome of a particular matter".[70]

Legitimacy of judicial review: The essence of many of these criticisms is a lingering concern that the doctrine of legitimate expectations may provide an inadequate jurisprudential foundation for judicial review in comparison with other principles. Such concerns are perhaps readily understood because a peculiar feature of the doctrine of legitimate expectations is its capacity to operate substantially independently of the statute or other legal source of power pursuant to which an administrative decision is made. The point is best illustrated by contrasting the operation of the doctrine with the court's approach to one of the most popular substantive heads of review, namely failure to take into account relevant considerations. It is trite law that where a statute fails to identify the relevant considerations to which the decision-maker must have regard, the court must determine those relevant considerations according to the subject matter, scope and purpose of the statute conferring the relevant power.[71] The ambit of the court's inquiry is thereby ultimately constrained by the relevant statutory framework. The framework operates as an anchor for judicial review by restraining the court from embarking on a subjective and idiosyncratic exercise of compiling a list of relevant considerations to which a decision-maker ought ideally to have regard.

Critics of the doctrine of legitimate expectations claim that it does not provide an equivalent framework to guide and restrain the court. Thus the full ambit of the doctrine is left quite unclear. This is because the matter which generates the legitimate expectation can arise independently of the exercise of the power which is the subject of the judicial review proceedings. The problem is seen to be most acute when the alleged legitimate expectation is said to stem from a source which is unrelated to the nature of the interest or benefit affected by the challenged administrative decision. There are several potential sources of legitimate expectation which have little or nothing to do with the nature of an applicant's interest or benefit. Conduct on the part of a public official, such as by the giving of an

---

68. *Haoucher* (1990) 169 CLR 648 at 652 per Deane J and *Annetts* (1990) 170 CLR 596 at 606 per Brennan J.
69. *Haoucher* (1990) 169 CLR 648 at 651-652 per Deane J.
70. *Teoh* (1995) 128 ALR 353 at 371 per Toohey J.
71. See *Water Conservation and Irrigation Commission (NSW) v Browning* (1947) 74 CLR 492 at 505 per Dixon J and *Minister for Aboriginal Affairs v Peko-Wallsend Ltd* (1986) 162 CLR 24 at 40 per Mason J.

assurance or representation, constitutes one such category already recognised by law. But the category effectively operates as a sub-set of a potentially wider category of principles of "good administration". That category has already been drawn on in some cases and its full potential is likely to be tested further. In *Ng Yuen Shiu*, for example, Lord Fraser held:

> "When a public authority has promised to follow a certain procedure, it is in the interests of good administration that it should act fairly and should implement its promise, so long as implementation does not interfere with its statutory duty."[72]

Similarly, in *Consolidated Press Holdings Ltd*,[73] Justice Lockhart linked the course of conduct engaged in by the ATO which grounded the taxpayers' legitimate expectations of consultation to what he described as taxpayers' confidence in "the proper administration" of taxation legislation. His Honour said:

> "In the long run the duty of the Commissioner to accord procedural fairness to the applicants is directly referable to the proper administration of the Act because it is not conducive to the confidence of taxpayers if highly sensitive and important information about their finances and affairs may be revealed to persons or bodies outside the ATO, in particular chartered accountants who may act for competitors of the taxpayers themselves, without taxpayers having some say on the five points to which earlier reference has been made."[74]

The notion of good administration also underlies *Teoh*. Good administration is not observed if, having taken the considered and public step of ratifying an international treaty and thereby accepting the responsibility to conduct public affairs in accordance with its terms, the Executive government retains a broad if not unfettered discretion to act inconsistently with that responsibility and without providing an opportunity to those affected by its actions to have a direct say in the matter, subject only to monitoring by the Human Rights and Equal Opportunities Commission. As Associate Professor Margaret Allars has persuasively argued, the issue is fundamentally one of the courts properly seeking to promote integrity in government by procedural fairness requirements. In her view:

> "The common law right of fair procedure is a right to know more about the decision-making process and to participate in it. *Teoh's* case requires administrators to be conscious of implications of their decisions for human rights and to permit the individuals whose human rights are affected to have a say with regard to that aspect of the decision . . . integrity in government will be well secured by a decision which precludes a secret or unarticulated application of policy involving non-compliance with international obligations which the Australian government has publicly undertaken to respect."[75]

72. [1983] 2 AC 629 at 636.
73. (1995) 129 ALR 443. See also *Kelson and McKernan v Forward* (1996) 39 ALD 303.
74. Ibid at 453.
75. "One Small Step for Legal Doctrine, One Giant Leap Towards Integrity in Government: Teoh's Case and the Internationalisation of Administrative Law" (1995) 17 Syd LR 204 at 235.

That all makes good sense, but it is also important to note that a majority in *Teoh* did not go so far as to say that procedural fairness requirements potentially applied with equal force to all the terms of the hundreds of unincorporated treaties ratified by Australia. Mason CJ and Deane J, in particular, went to some lengths in their joint judgment to deny such a sweeping proposition. Consistently with the pragmatic approach customarily adopted in determining the content of procedural fairness requirements, their Honours insisted that each case would need to be looked at individually and that much:

> "would depend upon the nature of the relevant provision, the extent to which it has been accepted by the international community, the purpose which it is intended to serve and its relationship to the existing principles of our domestic law".[76]

Accordingly, the subject matter of the particular Convention in *Teoh* and its manifestation of what were described as "internationally accepted standards to be applied by courts and administrative authorities in dealing with basic human rights affecting the family and children" were critical matters influencing Mason CJ and Deane J.

Those particular matters did not appear to weigh so heavily with Toohey J. Although his Honour's judgment does not contain any express statement to the effect that procedural fairness requirements attach to all unincorporated international treaties (subject to contrary or executive actions[77]), there are some signs that his Honour may have been prepared to go that far.[78]

Putting to one side for the moment the somewhat different approach adopted by Justice Gaudron, it can be seen that while the majority judgments in *Teoh* unquestionably break new ground in the nexus drawn between international law and administrative law, the joint judgment of Mason CJ and Deane J does so in a conspicuously measured way which reflects an underlying concern to balance the temptation for courts to formulate and enforce general standards of good administration with the need to preserve the legitimacy of judicial intervention.

More difficult questions regarding legitimacy of judicial review are presented by Justice Gaudron's approach in *Teoh* which identifies common law rights as another potentially significant category source for legitimate expectations attracting procedural protection. What may prove to be important in the longer term is not whether her Honour was correct in holding that Australian child-citizens enjoyed a common law right of the type described by her Honour,[79] but rather the opening up of a vast and uncertain range of other common law rights to ground legitimate expectations in future cases. Such rights could include not only existing common law rights, but other rights which could emerge in the future as foreshadowed by J J Doyle QC.[80] Traditional common law rights or

76. (1995) 128 ALR 353 at 363.
77. Ibid at 374.
78. ibid at 371 and 373.
79. Ibid at 375 and see Allars (1995) 17 Syd LR at 225.
80. See n 1, above.

freedoms associated with human rights affecting such matters as freedom of speech, assembly and association spring readily to mind as being potentially relevant foundations for legitimate expectations. But there are many other common law rights and freedoms, including some of an economic nature, which have equal potential to figure prominently in future administrative law litigation in giving rise to legitimate expectations warranting procedural protection if Justice Gaudron's approach gains wider support. They include the common law freedom to trade or set up a viable business[81] and the established common law right to prepare goods for sale overseas and to export them.[82] In some instances the scope for procedural requirements to come into play based on legitimate expectations may be affected by existing or future legislation regulating and derogating from a particular common law right or freedom. The courts would then be called upon to determine the extent to which the common law right or freedom survives such legislation and grounds a relevant legitimate expectation (unlike a legitimate expectation arising from an executive act, such as the ratification of a treaty, which is capable of being extinguished by another executive act, legislation would be required to defeat a legitimate expectation arising from a common law right).

Self-evidently, there is considerable scope for judicial discretion and consequent uncertainty associated with Justice Gaudron's approach, not only in the identification and possible development of relevant common law rights or freedoms attracting procedural protection, but also in the determination of the extent to which any such rights or freedoms are affected by legislation. In those circumstances, it can confidently be expected that the role of the courts would come under close scrutiny.

THE LEGAL EFFECT OF THE "ANTI-TEOH" BILL

The government has apparently drawn little comfort from the limited nature of the procedural protection resulting from the majority's approach in *Teoh* and, as noted above, has moved swiftly to take both executive and legislative action to remove unincorporated international treaties from the category of potential sources for legitimate expectations.

Professor Allars has raised several doubts regarding the effectiveness of the Joint Ministerial Statement to achieve its intended objective of removing the legitimate expectations which attracted procedural protection in *Teoh*.[83] Those doubts include:

- the inability of an executive statement to defeat legitimate expectations generated by common law rights, as relied upon by Justice Gaudron;

---

81. See, for example, *Northland Milk Vendors Association Inc v Northern Milk Ltd* [1988] 1 NZLR 530 (NZ CA).
82. See *Mudginberri Station Pty Ltd v Langhorne* (1985) 7 FCR 482 at 489-491 and *Fares Rural Meat and Livestock Co Pty Ltd v Australian Meat and Livestock Corp* (1990) 96 ALR 153 at 155 per Gummow J.
83. (1995) 17 Syd LR at 239-241.

- the inability of a policy statement to restrict the general availability of procedural fairness as a common law head of judicial review;

- uncertainty whether a policy statement of the kind represented by the joint ministerial statement is a sufficient act to extinguish the *Teoh* legitimate expectation or whether nothing short of deratification of the Convention would suffice; and

- uncertainty about whether the joint ministerial statement will be effective to defeat legitimate expectations arising from the ratification of future treaties given such subjective ratification may impliedly override the statement.

It might be thought that the Bill (which lapsed with the announced federal election) would put all these matters beyond doubt. That is probably the case with the third and fourth points raised above, but the position is not so clear with the remainder. The reason for such continuing doubts relates to the issue of whether the doctrine of legitimate expectation was the only basis upon which the High Court could have concluded that procedural fairness applied in the circumstances of *Teoh*. That issue assumes critical importance because the core provision in the Bill, cl 5, focuses exclusively on defeating the legitimate expectation specifically identified by the majority judgments in *Teoh* as the foundation for procedural fairness, rather than on the requirements of procedural fairness themselves irrespective of the source of their operation. Although the majority found it convenient to utilise the terminology of legitimate expectation, it seems that it would have been equally open to have used the language of "interests" associated with the orthodox doctrine of procedural fairness. The interchangeability of "legitimate expectations" and "interests" in a procedural fairness context was expressly acknowledged by Justice Brennan in *Quin* when he observed that:

"The objects properly sought by invoking the notion of legitimate expectation can be attained in any event within the orthodox framework of administrative law . . . a person who entertains a legitimate expectation is, ex hypothesi, a person whose interests are so affected."[84]

In that vein, Professor Allars has argued that the principle of *Teoh* is capable of expression in the following terms which do not require recourse to the language of legitimate expectation:

"Ratification by Australia of an international Convention is a positive statement by the Executive government of the country to the world and to the Australian people that the Executive government and its agencies will act in accordance with the convention and is an adequate foundation, absent statutory or Executive indications to the contrary, for an interest of individuals that administrative decision-makers will act in conformity with the convention when making decisions which affect rights and freedoms of the individual which would have been protected by the convention, or at least not depart from the convention without giving the individual a hearing."[85]

---

84. (1990) 170 CLR 1 at 40.
85. (1995) 17 Syd LR at 223-224.

On that basis, it is arguable that the Bill is ineffective in preventing procedural fairness requirements arising on the basis of orthodox principles concerning the protection of rights and interests, quite apart from legitimate expectations. In view of the courts' insistence that clear and unambiguous words be used to oust common law procedural fairness, [86] it is difficult to see how the Bill could be regarded as meeting that stringent test because of its exclusive concentration on defeating legitimate expectations rather than interests. There is no ambiguity or obscurity in the Bill to justify reference to extrinsic materials. Even if there were, there must be some prospect that a court would follow the approach adopted by Mason CJ, Wilson and Dawson JJ in *Re Bolton; Ex parte Beane*[87] where, in response to a submission that the second reading speech of the Minister was a relevant aid to statutory construction of extradition legislation, their Honours said:

"That speech quite ambiguously asserts that Pt III relates to deserters and absentees whether or not they are from a visiting force. But this of itself, while deserving serious consideration, cannot be determinative; it is available as an aid to interpretation. The words of a Minister must not be substituted for the text of the law. Particularly is this so when the intention stated by the Minister but unexpressed in the law is restrictive of the liberty of the individual. It is always possible that through oversight or inadvertence the clear intention of the Parliament fails to be translated into the text of the law. However unfortunate it may be when that happens, the task of the court remains clear. *The function of the court is to give effect to the will of Parliament as expressed in the law.*" (emphasis added)

LEGITIMATE EXPECTATIONS AND THE PRINCIPLE OF INALIENABILITY

Ironically, *Teoh* confirms the potential of the doctrine of legitimate expectation but also exposes its limitations. The doctrine has no application to cases involving legal rights or obligations. To apply it to such cases would be to invite public officials to avoid discharge of their obligations in connection with a legal right by the simple device of giving notice to the beneficiary of the right and providing an opportunity to be heard on why the legal right should not be enjoyed. It was because the Convention did not give rise to a binding legal right that the majority in *Teoh* resorted to the doctrine of legitimate expectations as a foundation for procedural fairness.

The development of the doctrine has occurred at a time when courts are searching for appropriate remedies for individuals who act to their

---

86. See, for example, *Commissioner of Police v Tanos* (1958) 98 CLR 383 at 396 per Dixon CJ and Webb J and *Annetts* (1990) 170 CLR 596 at 598 per Mason CJ, Deane and McHugh JJ.

87. (1987) 162 CLR 514 at 518. To similar effect see *Barry Liggins Pty Ltd v Comptroller-General of Customs* (1991) 32 FCR 112 at 120 and *Brennan v Comcare* (1993) 50 FCR 555 at 574-575.

detriment in reliance upon representations or assurances made by public officials. The doctrine has the potential to provide some relief in those circumstances, but its confinement to according procedural protection alone leaves much of the potential injustice unanswered. In private law, individuals might be able to take advantage of developments in the law of estoppel to obtain substantive relief.[88] But the orthodox principle of inalienability, that a public authority cannot by contract or representation fetter itself in the future exercise of statutory duties or discretions,[89] operates to create in public law an imbalance in the remedies available to private individuals.[90] The essence of the problem is that the principle of inalienability governing the unfettered exercise of public duties and discretions operates to facilitate the disregard of the very matters which the doctrine of legitimate expectations is designed to protect.[91] From the individual's viewpoint there is a manifest inequity in the current situation whereby public officials are substantially immune from equitable and other remedies which are available in private law.

The reluctance of courts to apply the doctrine of estoppel against public officials is grounded on three fundamental concerns.[92] First, a concern not to undermine the doctrine of ultra vires by allowing public officials to extend their legal powers by their own acts or representations. Secondly, a public policy concern not to hinder the free exercise of statutory duties or discretions given that the public are the ultimate beneficiaries of the ultra vires doctrine. Thirdly, a concern that estoppel in public law could operate to prejudice the interests of third parties who have not been heard. But as has been pointed out, while the logic of the doctrine may be beautiful, the injustice is ugly.[93]

Despite various attempts the common law has yet to develop a satisfactory answer to the problem. Lord Denning saw some scope for a form of estoppel to operate against a public body in circumstances where instead of properly using its powers, it abuses or misuses them.[94] That approach involves the court in weighing or balancing competing public and private interests. Justice Gummow has criticised Lord Denning's approach on two grounds.[95] First, that it draws the court into the forbidden province of the administrator in determining the merits of administrative action. Secondly, that if the representation or conduct upon which the estoppel is allegedly based is itself ultra vires, that fact alone precludes any judicial balancing exercise.

Although these criticisms were noted by Mason CJ in *Quin*, his Honour gave his qualified endorsement to the essence of Lord Denning's approach when he said:

---

88. See, for example, *Waltons Stores (Interstate) Ltd v Maher* (1988) 164 CLR 387 and the discussion in *Commonwealth v Verwayen* (1990) 170 CLR 394.
89. See *Quin* (1990) 170 CLR 1 at 17-18 per Mason CJ and *Minister for Immigration and Ethnic Affairs v Kurtovic* (1990) 92 ALR 93 at 108-117 per Gummow J.
90. See n 4, above.
91. See M Fordham, *Judicial Review Handbook*, 1994, p 253.
92. See P P Craig, *Administrative Law*, 1983, p 559.
93. See B Schwartz, *Administrative Law*, 1976, p 134.
94. See *Laker Airways Ltd v Department of Trade* [1977] QB 643 at 707.
95. *Kurtovic* (1990) 92 ALR 93 at 121-122 per Gummow J.

"What I have just said does not deny the availability of estoppel against the Executive, arising from conduct amounting to a representation, when holding the Executive to its representation does not significantly hinder the exercise of the relevant discretion in the public interest. And, as the public interest necessarily comprehends an element of justice to the individual, one cannot exclude the possibility that the courts might in some situations grant relief on the basis that a refusal to hold the Executive to a representation by means of estoppel will occasion greater harm to the public interest by causing grave injustice to the individual who acted on the representation than any detriment to that interest that will arise from holding the Executive to its representation and thus narrowing the exercise of the discretion: see the observations of Lord Denning in *Laker Airways v Department of Trade*; but see also the criticism of this approach by Gummow J in *Kurtovic*."[96]

Those observations seem to contemplate the possibility in a particular case of an estoppel operating against a public authority even if an ultra vires act is involved but the position in Australia remains uncertain on that point. There is, however, some Australian authority in support of the proposition that an estoppel may operate where intra vires conduct is involved and it would be unfair on the individual affected by such conduct and contrary to the public interest to allow the public authority to renege on its conduct.[97]

Apart from these sporadic judicial developments, it remains the case in Australia that no doctrine of administrative estoppel has emerged, as Justice Brennan noted in *Annetts*.[98] Meanwhile, in overseas jurisdictions, Lord Denning's balancing approach seems to have provided the genesis for the development of a new head of judicial review concerned with substantive unfairness. The availability of that head of review has now been firmly ackowledged and accepted by courts in both the United Kingdom[99] and New Zealand.[100] The capacity for substantive unfairness to provide more than procedural protection to individuals who rely detrimentally on the conduct of public officials is illustrated by the decision of the Divisional Court in *R v IRC; Ex parte MFK Underwriting Agents Ltd*.[101] The case involved judicial review proceedings by taxpayers who had taken certain investment action in reliance upon discussions with revenue officials as to how particular transactions would be treated. The taxpayers argued that the

96. (1990) 170 CLR 1 at 18.
97. See *Keenan v Minister for Immigration, Local Government and Ethnic Affairs* (unreported, Federal Court, Einfield J, 16 April 1993) and *Maiorana v Minister for Immigration and Ethnic Affairs* (1993) 42 FCR 119 at 122-123 per Einfield J. And see also *Metropolitan Transit Authority v Waverley Transit Pty Ltd* [1991] 1 VR 181.
98. (1990) 170 CLR 596 at 605.
99. See, for example, *HTV v Price Commission* [1976] ICR 170 at 189 per Scarman LJ; *Re Preston* [1985] AC 835 at 865 per Lord Templeman and see generally Wade and Forsyth, *Administrative Law*, pp 418-420.
100. See, for example, *Thames Valley Electric Power Board v NZFP Pulp and Paper Ltd* [1994] 2 NZLR 641 (NZ CA) and *Northern Roller Milling Co Ltd v Commerce Commission* [1994] 2 NZLR 747 at 750-754 per Gallen J.
101. [1990] 1 WLR 1545.

Inland Revenue acted so unfairly in resiling from the advice given to the taxpayers that its conduct amounted to an abuse of power. It was argued that a public body was obliged to "recognise and give effect to the legitimate expectation of those who deal with it, in matters both of procedure and decision". [102] The court held that on the facts the Inland Revenue had given no clear and unambiguous assurances and that its advice fell short of constituting a statement of official policy. Significantly, however, the court contemplated the possibility of judicial review for abuse of power based on unfairness to the individual in an appropriate case giving rise to an order restraining the Inland Revenue from departing from its advice. The court enunciated certain preconditions to such relief and, in so doing, was plainly influenced by elements of the law of estoppel. Those conditions were that:

- the taxpayer must make full disclosure of all relevant facts and also make clear that he seeks a fully considered ruling which will be relied upon; and
- the ruling must be unambiguous.

Bingham LJ said:

"In so stating these requirements I do not, I hope, diminish or emasculate the valuable, developing doctrine of legitimate expectation. If a public authority so conducts itself as to create a legitimate expectation that a certain course will be followed it would often be unfair if the authority were permitted to follow a different course to the detriment of one who entertained the expectation, particularly if he acted on it. If in private law a body would be in breach of contract in so acting or estopped in so acting a public authority should generally be in no better position. The doctrine of legitimate expectation is rooted in fairness. But fairness is not a one-way street. It imports the notion of equitableness, of fair and open dealing, to which the authority is as much entitled as a citizen. The revenue's discretion, while it exists, is limited. Fairness requires that its exercise should be on the basis of full disclosure." [103]

Judge J said:

"In the present case the revenue promulgated a number of guidelines and answered questions by or on behalf of taxpayers about the likely approach to a number of given problems. The revenue is not bound to give any guidance at all. If however the taxpayer approaches the revenue with clear and precise proposals about the future conduct of his fiscal affairs and receives an unequivocal statement about how they will be treated for tax purposes if implemented, the revenue should in my judgment be subjected to judicial review on grounds of unfair abuse of power if it peremptorily decides that it will not be bound by such statements where the taxpayer has relied on them. The same statement should apply to revenue statements of policy." [104]

102. Ibid at 1566.
103. Ibid at 1569-70.
104. Ibid at 1574-75.

It can be expected that Australian courts will come under increasing pressure to adopt substantive unfairness as a head of judicial review both generally and specifically as a surrogate for estoppel. It seems, however, that in the near future, the doctrine of legitimate expectations is likely to be seen by Australian courts as a more attractive, although more circumscribed, remedy than substantive unfairness in seeking to provide some balance in the relationship between individuals and government. Australian courts are attracted by the limited procedural nature of the protection available under the doctrine, as well as by the fact that its operation does not depend on elements necessary to establish an estoppel, such as detrimental reliance and a knowing state of mind. [105] Australian courts have generally been alert to the danger of allowing the doctrine to become a vehicle for substantive relief and thereby threatening the principle of inalienability. *Haoucher* is a good example. Two legitimate expectations were present in that case arising from the Ministerial policy statement tabled in the Parliament concerning criminal deportations:

- an expectation that a person would not be deported unless their conduct fell within the terms of the policy;

- an expectation that the Minister would accept a recommendation of the Administrative Appeals Tribunal that a deportation order be revoked unless there were "exceptional circumstances and only when strong evidence can be produced to justify" rejection.

The protection accorded to those expectations was procedural, not substantive. Procedural fairness required the Minister to notify the deportee of the matters which constituted "exceptional circumstances" and "strong evidence" and to provide an opportunity for representations to be made as to why the Tribunal's recommendation should be adopted. The court emphasised that the deportee was not entitled to any substantive protection which would fetter the Minister's powers of deportation. [106]

The dichotomy between substantive and procedural to a legitimate expectation provided one of the grounds for Justice McHugh's dissent in *Teoh*:

> "A legitimate expectation may give rise to a requirement of procedural fairness but it does not give substantial protection to any right, benefit or privilege that is the subject of the expectation. So even if the respondents had a legitimate expectation concerning the Convention, the delegate was not obliged to apply the Convention." [107]

It is difficult to understand this criticism of the majority's reasoning since its effect was not to provide substantive protection. The majority expressly acknowledged that the Convention was not binding in Australian domestic law and no order was made compelling its implementation. Rather, the majority held that because of the respondent's legitimate expectation that the terms of the Convention would be relevantly applied in the exercise of statutory powers affecting the interests of children, procedural fairness

105. See *Haoucher* (1990) 169 CLR 648 at 669-670 per Toohey J.
106. (1990) 169 CLR 648 at 652 per Deane J.
107. (1995) 128 ALR 353 at 383.

required that the respondent be notified and heard if the Minister's delegate intended to act otherwise than in accordance with the relevant terms of the Convention and thereby defeat the respondent's expectation of implementation. Accordingly, the majority was providing similar relief to that given in *Haoucher*, in which Justice McHugh formed part of the majority.

CONCLUSION

Speaking extra-curially in 1986, Sir Gerard Brennan stated that the "imprecision in the content of 'natural justice' and the ex posto facto declaration of that content is one of the unsolved problems of administrative law and practice".[108] Although some progress has been made over the last decade towards greater simplicity in the law relating to the threshold question of whether or not procedural fairness rules apply at all, the uncertainty surrounding the content of those rules substantially remains. That position is unlikely to change dramatically in the future. The further the courts move away from the model of judicial decision-making with the familiar trappings of adversarial litigation, the greater the need for flexibility and variability in the content of procedural fairness requirements in order to accommodate the diversity which is inherent in any sophisticated public administrative system.

The rules of procedural fairness have traditionally been analysed on the basis that their object is to ensure a fair and just hearing for individuals adversely affected by administrative action. Such terminology is inapt in the context of the contemporary administrative justice system. It is more accurate nowadays to speak in that context of procedural fairness rules operating to provide an opportunity for fair and effective participation in administrative decision-making which affects people individually. This may involve the taking of steps beyond those normally associated with the conduct of a hearing.

The uncertainty associated with procedural fairness is not simply a product of a diverse and complex administrative justice system. It also reflects the nature of judicial review and the haphazard way in which legal issues arise for judicial determination. A judicial review court's immediate concern is to dispose of the case before it, rather than to formulate general guidelines for administrative decision-making in other cases. Of course standards may and do emerge as a matter of deduction from decided cases but it is rare for a single judicial decision to be wholly prescriptive of such standards.

A degree of uncertainty seems inevitable, unpalatable though that may be to some administrators who yearn, perhaps unrealistically, for a high level of certainty. If the courts are to maintain the legitimacy of judicial intervention on procedural fairness grounds, it is important that there at

---

108. "The Purpose and Scope of Judicial Review", in M Taggart (ed), *Judicial Review of Administrative Action in the 1980's*, 1986, p 28.

least be clear identification of the range of factors which are taken into account in shaping the requirements of procedural fairness in individual cases. Otherwise, the courts expose themselves to the criticism that procedural fairness rules are formulated not according to objective criteria but by operation of idiosyncratic discretion or judicial whim.

Up to a point, courts were less vulnerable to such criticisms when their approach to natural justice was said to be driven by the application of mechanical formulae such as whether a body was under a duty to act judicially or whether express procedural requirements were mandatory or directory. The contemporary approach to procedural fairness has seen the courts move away from rigid legal categories and labels to an overall evaluation of what is fair and reasonable in all the circumstances of a particular case. Such an approach tends to merge heads of judicial review on substantive and procedural grounds. It also carries with it an increased judicial responsibility to rationalise and fully explain the basis for judicial intervention.

In discharging that responsibility courts should draw confidence that their insistence on procedural fairness accords with contemporary community values and standards. The importance attached to participation in public decision-making is reflected in various ways. For example, the widespread inclusion of duties of consultation in federal and state legislation dealing with subject matters such as the environment and planning, local government and management of primary resources reflects the acceptance by parliaments of the value and importance of public participation in the making of quasi-legislative instruments and the like. [109] Notably, the Commonwealth might join some of the states in enacting legislation which specifically requires formal public notice and consultation procedures prior to the making of certain subordinate legislation. [110] Finally, the fundamental importance attached to opportunities for public participation in public affairs is given express recognition in cl 25 of the *International Covenant on Civil and Political Rights*, which constitutes Sch 2 to the *Human Rights and Equal Opportunities Act* 1986 (Cth).

Developments such as these play an important role in establishing and confirming contemporary values and standards which in turn may be taken into account and influence the courts in their development of common law principles of procedural fairness. [111]

The government's reaction to *Teoh* reminds us, however, that issues of legitimacy are never far away when it comes to judicial review of administrative action, even where that review is limited to procedural matters and represents a logical step in the continuing evolution of the common law principles of procedural fairness.

---

109. See T Sherman, "Administrative Law—The State of Play" (1991) 66 *Canberra Bulletin of Public Administration* 63 and Report No 35 by the Administrative Review Council, "Rule Making by Commonwealth Agencies", 1992.

110. See Legislative Instruments Bill 1994 (Cth); *Subordinate Legislation Act* 1962 (Vic) and *Subordinate Legislation Act* 1989 (NSW).

111. See *Mabo v Queensland (No 2)* (1992) 175 CLR 1 at 44 per Brennan J (with whom Mason CJ and McHugh J agreed) and *Dietrich v The Queen* (1992) 177 CLR 292 at 321 per Brennan J and at 360 per Toohey J.

Chapter 8

Principles of Statutory Interpretation Relating to Government

Susan Kenny

INTRODUCTION

Statutory interpretation is a large topic and there may be different views as to its essentials. Fortunately, this paper is not concerned with statutory interpretation in any general sense. Instead, what follows is an excursus into the principles which courts follow in construing statutes dealing with the powers and duties of government and governmental bodies.

The difficulties which the rules of statutory interpretation are intended to overcome are general in the sense that they most often arise from the limitations of language and legislative imagination, rather than from difficulties of the particular subject matter. Regardless of its subject, a statutory provision may be ambiguous, or obscure (as in *Hepples v Commissioner of Taxation (No 2)*[1]). Even when the statutory terms are clear, their operation in the particular circumstance may be uncertain, perhaps because the legislature did not imagine that the circumstance might occur. As one writer has said:

> "Nature has a nasty habit of creating situations in which the applicability of a statute is unclear. But even if nature were not unkind, the meaning of statutes would still be problematic because language is inherently imprecise and because rational political actors, having numerous competing ways to occupy their time, would never devote the effort necessary to minimise the indeterminacy of statutory language."[2]

On this view, the basic role of the courts is to complete the task which Parliament has left undone. The relation of Parliament and the courts is to be seen as a co-operative one and, by reason of this relation, the courts inherit some democratic legitimacy in performing the task.

---

1. (1992) 173 CLR 492.
2. McNollgast, "Legislative Intent: the Use of Positive Political Theory in Statutory Interpretation" (1994) 57 *Law and Contemporary Problems* 1 at 13.

The call "to fill in the gaps"[3] is, as Justice McHugh has noted,[4] tending greatly to increase; and this tendency is particularly apparent in the area of statutory regulation of government and governmental bodies. Moreover, in this particular context, statutory specificity provides no guaranteed cure.[5]

Some principles of statutory interpretation express the courts' understanding of their basic constitutional position. Some of these principles are of general application. The first of these is that, subject to constitutional limitations, the will of Parliament must prevail. Hence, statutory interpretation can be seen to involve what one commentator has called the "method of imagination" by which "the judge should put himself in the shoes of the enacting legislators and figure out how they would have wanted the statute applied".[6] Secondly, the task of construing a statute and giving the final decision as to its meaning is a fundamental responsibility of the courts and cannot be diminished by agreement between the parties,[7] nor can it altogether be taken away.[8]

In interpreting statutory provisions which give power to, or impose duties on government and its instrumentalities, the courts have developed particular rules of statutory interpretation which tell even more about the courts' understanding of their constitutional responsibilities and of the constitutionally appropriate relation for themselves and Parliament and, especially, for themselves and the Executive.

I discuss these rules and this understanding first, in relation to the conferral of decision-making power on administrative bodies; secondly, in relation to the conferral of limited decision-making power on the courts; thirdly, in relation to privative and conclusive evidence clauses; fourthly, in relation to the rights and freedoms of natural persons; and fifthly, in relation to the immunities and privileges of the Crown.

(A) CONFERRAL OF DECISION-MAKING POWER ON ADMINISTRATIVE BODIES

The number of statutes which grant to administrators the authority to make decisions affecting individual interests, both legal and otherwise, is enormous. The courts have traditionally acted upon the assumption that any such exercise of statutory power by an administrator, or an administrative body will be subject to court supervision unless the relevant statute clearly indicates a contrary intention.[9] The nature and extent of this supervision is very much the outcome of statutory interpretation.

3. Ibid.
4. Justice M H McHugh, "The Growth of Legislation and Litigation" (1995) 69 ALJ 37.
5. *Hunt v Minister for Immigration and Ethnic Affairs* (1993) 41 FCR 380 at 386 per Gummow J.
6. Richard A Posner, "Statutory Interpretation—in the Classroom and in the Courtroom" (1983) 50 *University of Chicago Law Review* 800 at 817.
7. *Accident Towing and Advisory Committee v Combined Motor Industries Pty Ltd* [1987] VR 529 at 548; *Cherwell District Council v Thames Waterboard* [1975] 1 WLR 448 at 452.
8. See the discussion of ouster clauses below.
9. Some constitutional limits upon statutory attempts to exclude this supervision are discussed below.

In Australia, though not perhaps in England, courts will ordinarily intervene in the decision-making process of an administrative body if there is shown to have been some jurisdictional error on the part of that body. The courts will sometimes intervene in the event of non-jurisdictional error, providing the error appears on the face of the record. To state the well-known rule in different terms, unless jurisdictional error is shown, the courts will not grant the remedies afforded by the prerogative writs of prohibition, mandamus and certiorari (other than certiorari for error of law on the face of the record).

The position is commonly said to be different in England as a result of the decision in *Anisminic Ltd v Foreign Compensation Commission*.[10] In that case, the House of Lords held that a court might quash a decision for error, even though made in the process of exercising the relevant statutory power. Errors made in that process could include the following: asking the wrong question, bad faith, failure to consider relevant matters or to observe the requirements of natural justice, and the consideration of irrelevant matters.[11] Notwithstanding their adherence to the distinction between jurisdictional and non-jurisdictional error,[12] however, Australian courts have reached a similar outcome to that in England by treating an error as jurisdictional if, in committing it, the administrative body strayed too far from the supervisory court's understanding of what Parliament intended that body to do under the relevant statutory power. Accordingly, whether an alleged error is jurisdictional or not will almost invariably depend upon the relevant court's construction of the governing statute.

As to matters of jurisdiction

If the governing statute provides that the decision-making authority of an administrative body exists only in, or in relation to, a specific state of fact, there is a long-entrenched reluctance on the part of courts to accord that administrative body any final authority to decide whether or not such state of fact exists. A statute will almost invariably be construed so as to authorise the court to inquire into and decide such a matter independently.

Potter v Melbourne and Metropolitan Tramways Board[13] is a straightforward example of the orthodox approach. The *Melbourne and Metropolitan Tramways Act* 1928 (Vic) set up, in s 17(5), an appeal board to hear and determine "all appeals by officers, servants and employees of the Melbourne and Metropolitan Tramways Board against dismissals, fines, deductions from wages, reductions in rank, grade or pay or other punishments".

Victor Potter had been a one-man-bus operator, but because he had consistently failed to keep to the timetable of his route, he had been

10. [1969] 2 AC 147.
11. Ibid at 171 per Lord Reid; at 195 per Lord Pearce.
12. *R v Gray; Ex parte Marsh* (1985) 157 CLR 351 at 371-373 per Gibbs CJ; at 390 per Deane J; at 394 per Dawson J. *Public Service Association (SA) v Federated Clerks' Union of Australia (SA Branch)* (1991) 173 CLR 132 at 141 per Brennan J; at 148-152 per Deane J; at 163 per Dawson and Gaudron JJ; at 164-165 per McHugh J.
13. (1957) 98 CLR 337.

demoted to the position of conductor. The appeal board found that this was a punishment. The judge at first instance disagreed. On appeal, the High Court held:

> "The provision uses no words which justify the inference that the authority of the appeal board was to extend to anything which appeared to that tribunal to amount to a dismissal, deduction from wages, reduction in rank, grade or pay or other punishment inflicted so that, notwithstanding that the appeal board had travelled outside its province, the tramways board should be governed by its decisions. The words do not relate to what the appeal board supposes to fall within the category. There is, we think, no warrant for construing s 17(5) as authorising the appeal board to deal with anything which in fact falls outside the conception of punishment."[14]

In relation to administrative bodies, courts also assert, by a similar process of statutory construction, the power to make independent inquiry and determination as to whether a body was lawfully constituted[15] and, if lawfully constituted, as to whether the body asked itself the very question which Parliament had by statute directed.[16]

Jurisdictional error in the course of decision-making

In the case of jurisdictional error in the course of a decision-making process, a court's inquiry as to whether or not a case of jurisdictional error is shown begins with the governing statute. That statute circumscribes the inquiry. There will, for example, be no jurisdictional error simply because the decision maker did not take every relevant factor into account. Jurisdictional error will arise only if the decision maker failed to consider a factor which the statute insisted must be taken into account, either expressly or by necessary implication.[17] Such an implication can only arise if the terms of the statute, its subject matter, scope and purpose permit it to be drawn. Similarly, a factor will only be irrelevant if the statute says so, either expressly or by necessary implication.[18] Staying within these principles, a court will not permit itself to interfere in an administrative decision simply because it thinks that the administrator has made the wrong decision.

Two assumptions

It is, therefore, true to say, as courts consistently do, that in deciding whether there has been jurisdictional error courts have regard to the terms, subject matter, purpose and scope of the relevant statute. But there is an

14. Ibid at 344.
15. *R v Murray; Ex parte Proctor* (1949) 77 CLR 387.
16. *Re Racal Communications Ltd* [1981] AC 374 at 382-383; *BHP Petroleum Pty Ltd v Balfour* (1987) 180 CLR 474 at 480-481.
17. *Minister for Aboriginal Affairs v Peko-Wallsend Ltd* (1986) 162 CLR 24 at 39 per Mason J.
18. Ibid at 40 per Mason J; at 55-57 per Brennan J.

incomplete description of the process, if it leaves out of account the assumptions on which the courts proceed. The process of interpretation of a statutory grant of power to an administrative body is based upon the assumption that Parliament did not intend the grant to be used other than reasonably, having regard to all the circumstances. There is a further assumption that the statute was intended to operate in the context of the conventions of democratic, responsible government.

Two examples

BHP Petroleum Pty Ltd v Balfour[19] is an example of how the first assumption can be employed by the courts as means of deciding between competing interpretations, both of which would be consistent with the relevant statutory language. The case concerned the application of a provision describing the method of calculating royalty payments in respect of petroleum, a task entrusted to the designated Authority under the *Petroleum (Submerged Lands) (Royalty) Act* 1967 (Cth) and counterpart Victorian legislation. Under the relevant legislation, the Authority was required to fix the well-head in relation to petroleum recovered from wells in Bass Strait. The relevant well, Cobia No 2, was located about four kilometres from a platform called Mackerel A. Equipment, including outlets and valves designed to control the production of petroleum, was located on the sea bed immediately above the well. The relevant legislation provided that "the well-head, in relation to any petroleum, is such valve station as is agreed . . . , or, in default of agreement . . . is such valve station as is determined by the Designated Authority as being that well-head".

BHP Petroleum challenged the decision of the designated Authority to choose two safety valves on the Mackerel A platform as the well-head. The Authority had chosen this valve station as, in its opinion, the choice resulted in an adequate basis upon which the actual cost of exploration and production could be apportioned. The Authority relied upon the unqualified terms of the definition of "well-head" to support its argument that, for the purposes of the statute, it might select such valve station as it saw fit. This argument was rejected by the High Court which held that the Authority was bound to select a valve station which "fairly accords with the description of well-head".[20] Wherever this might be, it was not on the Mackerel A platform because the platform was too far from the well.

The process of deciding what question Parliament had set the designated Authority did not entirely depend in the *BHP Petroleum* case upon the terms of the statute. Another element was the court's assumption that Parliament did not intend to grant an arbitrary power and, in particular, did not intend the power to be exercised so as to effect an unreasonable result.

The decision of the High Court in *Minister for Aboriginal Affairs v Peko-Wallsend Ltd*[21] illustrates not only the application of the assumption

19. (1987) 180 CLR 474.
20. Ibid at 480.
21. (1986) 162 CLR 24 per Mason J.

of reasonableness but also the assumption that conventions of responsible government can properly form part of the process of statutory interpretation.

The question was whether, in deciding if land ought to be granted to a Land Trust for the benefit of certain Aboriginals, the Minister was bound to consider information given by the company to his predecessor in office, notwithstanding that the Minister had no personal knowledge that the company had given this information to his predecessor. The information was to the effect that the company had found large deposits of uranium within the relevant area.

The answer was reached by a process of statutory construction which included examination of the terms, subject matter, purpose and scope of the legislation. It was noted that the statute in substance directed that before the matter could be considered by the Minister, consideration was to be given to the detriment to others if the proposed land grant were made.[22] This fact alone could not, however, decide the question, because the statute did not in terms direct the Minister to consider the matter. The balance of the interpretative process proceeded upon the assumption that the legislature intended the statute to operate reasonably *and* in accordance with the conventions of responsible government. Given the significance of the decision to grant land and its potential to cause injury to the valuable interests of others, it was consistent with an assumption of reasonableness to find, as the court did, that the legislature did not intend a finding as to detriment to be reached upon out-of-date information.[23] It was, as Mason J said, but "a short and logical step" for the court to hold that the Minister was bound to consider the information addressed to his predecessor and in the possession of his Department.[24] The latter flows from conventions governing Ministers, their portfolio departments and Parliament.

The assumptions are necessary

When an issue of jurisdictional error arises, it is usually because there is a need for the relevant statute to be interpreted authoritatively. The need may arise because the statute is unclear in terms, or because circumstances have arisen which make its application uncertain. In neither case is it likely that resort to the terms, subject matter, scope and purpose of the statute will prove enough to decide the meaning of the provision or its operation. Assumptions of the kind mentioned are essential to the process, but courts are sometimes reluctant to acknowledge this fact.

It is not infrequently said, at least by administrators, that in construing statutory grants of power courts exceed their strictly supervisory function. It would, however, be a mistake to see court supervision of administrative decision-making as either trespassing into areas given by Parliament to administrators, or as so irremediably subjective as to lack legitimacy. The

22. Cf ibid at 44 per Mason J.
23. Ibid at 45-46, 65-66, 71.
24. Ibid at 44.

criticism appears to arise from a misunderstanding of the task of the courts and the processes they employ. This in turn may stem partly from the failure of the courts to identify sufficiently the assumptions which they use in construing statutory provisions conferring power on government and its instrumentalities. In the *BHP Petroleum* case, for example, the court did not in any sense step into the shoes of the Designated Authority: it simply told the Authority that it could not fix as a well-head a point distant from the well, and that it was required to fix a point which might rationally be seen to constitute a well-head within the accepted meaning of that word. That left for the Authority the area of decision-making which the statute had described. The court did not, however, expressly acknowledge the nature of the assumptions which informed its judgment.

Natural justice as an expression of the assumption of reasonableness

The rules of natural justice are in essence rules of statutory construction and, as such, they can be seen as an expression of the basic assumption of reasonableness. Unless a statute provides to the contrary, whether expressly or by necessary implication,[25] a statutory grant of power to decide matters affecting the interests of others is construed so as to impose upon the decision maker a duty to act in accordance with the requirements of procedural fairness—to act without the actuality or appearance of bias and to accord affected persons an opportunity to be heard. Breach of the duty constitutes an error of law which will vitiate the decision.

The specific content of the obligation to which the relevant statute gives rise varies depending on the terms of the statute, its subject matter, its scope and purpose, and the circumstances of the individual case.[26] But, considered as an expression of the assumption of reasonableness underlying the process of statutory interpretation, the rules of natural justice may also be seen, as Justice Deane has noted,[27] as encompassing what is sometimes referred to as the "Wednesbury principle". Possibly too, as Justice Deane has proposed, the assumption of reasonableness might permit the principles of natural justice to be construed as principles of statutory construction encompassing virtually all jurisdictional errors. Thus, in *Australian Broadcasting Tribunal v Bond* Justice Deane said:

> "If a statutory tribunal is required to act judicially, it must act rationally and reasonably. Of its nature, a duty to act judicially (or in accordance with the requirements of procedural fairness or natural justice) excludes the right to decide arbitrarily, irrationally or

25. The existence of a full statutory right of appeal may, for example, exclude the right to challenge a decision upon the ground of denial of natural justice: see *Twist v Randwick Municipal Council* (1976) 136 CLR 106; *R v Ross-Jones; Ex parte Beaumont* (1979) 141 CLR 503; *R v Marks; Ex parte Australian Building Construction Employees and Builders Labourers' Federation* (1981) 147 CLR 471. Cf *R v The Judges of the Federal Court of Australia; Ex parte The Western Australian National Football League (Incorp)* (1979) 143 CLR 191.
26. *Russell v Duke of Norfolk* [1949] 1 All ER 109 at 118.
27. *Australian Broadcasting Tribunal v Bond* (1990) 170 CLR 321 at 367.

unreasonably. It requires that regard be paid to material considerations
and that immaterial or irrelevant considerations be ignored. It excludes
the right to act on preconceived prejudice or suspicion. Arguably, it
requires a minimum degree of "proportionality" (cf the *CCSU Case*
[1985] AC 374 p 410). When the process of decision-making need not
be and is not disclosed, there will be a discernible breach of such a duty
if a decision of fact is unsupported by probative material. When the
process of decision-making is disclosed, there will be a discernible
breach of a duty if findings of fact upon which a decision is based are
unsupported by probative material and if inferences of fact upon which
a decision is based cannot reasonably be drawn from such findings of
fact. Breach of a duty to act judicially constitutes an error of law which
will vitiate the decision." [28]

As Justice Deane acknowledged, not all would agree with this analysis. [29]
For my part, a not insignificant virtue of his analysis is that it sets out and
acknowledges as such one of the fundamental assumptions underlying the
process of construing statutory grants of power to administrative bodies.

Natural justice, legitimate expectations and international treaties

The provisions of an international treaty to which Australia is a party do
not form part of Australian law unless those provisions have been validly
incorporated into law by statute. This principle, as the Chief Justice and
Justice Deane recently noted, has its origins in the fact that in the Australian
constitutional system, the making and ratification of treaties is for the
Executive in the exercise of its prerogative whilst the making of law is for
Parliament. [30] Nonetheless, ratification may carry certain consequences for
Australian law even without specific legislation. In particular, courts will
construe a statute in a way which accords with a treaty to which Australia
is a party if the statute is ambiguous in a relevant respect, at least where the
statute is "enacted after, or in contemplation of, entry into, or ratification
of, the relevant international instrument". [31]

The recent decision of the High Court in *Minister for Immigration v
Teoh* [32] extended this rule significantly. The decision can be seen as
attributing primacy to the assumption of reasonableness, considered in the
context of responsible government. The case concerned a decision of the
Immigration Review Panel to refuse an application for resident status made
by a Malaysian citizen with responsibility in Australia for a number of
children. The majority decided that the ratification by Australia of the
United Nations *Convention on the Rights of the Child* gave rise to a
legitimate expectation (absent statutory provision or Executive statement to
the contrary) that administrative decision makers such as the Panel would

28. Ibid at 367.
29. Cf *Council of Civil Service Unions v Minister for the Civil Service* [1985] AC 374 at
410-411, 414-415.
30. *Minister for Immigration v Teoh* (1995) 69 ALJR 423 at 430 and the cases there cited.
31. Ibid at 430; *Chu Keng Lim v Minister for Immigration* (1992) 176 CLR 1 at 38.
32. (1995) 69 ALJR 423.

act in conformity with the Convention.[33] The Convention required that the best interests of children be treated as a primary consideration. Accordingly, if the decision-maker proposed to make a decision inconsistent with that legitimate expectation, persons affected were, by reason of the rules of natural justice (or procedural fairness), entitled to an opportunity to persuade the decision-maker to the contrary.[34] The act of ratification was, according to the majority, to be characterised as "a positive statement by the Executive government of this country to the world and to the Australian people that the Executive government and its agencies will act in accordance with the Convention".[35]

In effect, *Teoh's* case decided that it was to be implied in every statutory grant of administrative decision-making power that the power would be exercised in conformity with obligations arising under international instruments ratified by the Executive, always providing that Parliament and the Executive might indicate to the contrary. In drawing this implication, the court, in my view, gave effect to the assumption of reasonableness. An aspect of the assumption of reasonableness is the expectation that government will act consistently—not only in the exercise of particular statutory powers but more generally. By its act of ratification, the executive government undertook to observe the terms of the treaty. If it were to act consistently (and therefore reasonably), the Executive would act in conformity with this undertaking wherever it might lawfully choose to do so. It was in that sense that ratification gave rise to the relevant legitimate expectation.

Given that the Executive remains responsible to Parliament for acts of ratification, the acknowledgment of such a rule of construction did not offend any constitutional principle. In particular, it did not, even in a practical sense, amount to attributing to an act of ratification the effect of amending the law.[36]

Parliament, however, appears likely to reject the proposed rule of construction.[37]

(B) THE CONFERRAL OF DECISION-MAKING POWERS ON COURTS

Statutes also confer decision-making authority on courts and, of course, the issues of statutory interpretation which may arise in this regard may resemble those which arise in relation to administrative decision-making.

33. Ibid at 432 per Mason CJ and Deane J; at 438-439 per Toohey J; at 440 per Gaudron J.
34. Ibid at 433, 438-439, 440.
35. Ibid at 432 per Mason CJ and Deane J; also at 438 per Toohey J; at 440 per Gaudron J.
36. McHugh J, dissenting, took a contrary view: see ibid at 447.
37. See Administrative Decisions (Effect of International Instruments) Bill 1995. The Commonwealth Attorney-General and the Minister for Foreign Affairs issued a Joint Statement on 10 May 1995 intended to establish a contrary intention sufficient to displace the implication. The Bill excludes any legitimate expectation which arises from Australia's adherence to any international treaty, in the absence of legislation incorporating the agreement into Australian law. It is proposed that the new law apply to administrative decisions made on or after 10 May 1995, including decisions reviewing or determining an appeal in respect of decisions made at an earlier date.

Courts have, however, adopted a significantly different approach to the interpretation of statutory grants of authority to courts.

The basic rule is the same: the remedies of prohibition, mandamus and certiorari (other than certiorari for error of law on the face of the record) are available for jurisdictional error, subject to discretionary considerations.[38] In relation to the former Court of Conciliation and Arbitration an error was not said to be jurisdictional in the relevant sense, however, if it was made in the course of deciding an application which the court was authorised by statute to entertain in proceedings regularly before it.[39] In relation to courts, the High Court has said that the authority given by statute to decide includes the authority to decide wrongly.

As to matters of jurisdiction

As in the case of administrative bodies, Parliament may make some fact or circumstance the condition precedent to a court's authority to decide. Where Parliament has done so, however, the High Court has been especially alive to what Justice Mason referred to as "the adverse consequences of so conditioning the jurisdiction of a court, even an inferior court".[40]

The High Court has therefore treated the issues of jurisdictional fact affecting a court's jurisdiction quite differently from jurisdictional fact affecting administrative bodies. Frequently cited and applied are the observations made by Justice Dixon in *Parisienne Basket Shoes Pty Ltd v Whyte* to the effect that:

> "if the legislature does make the jurisdiction of a court contingent upon the actual existence of a state of facts, as distinguished from the court's opinion or determination that the facts do exist, then the validity of the proceedings and orders must always remain an outstanding question until some other court or tribunal, possessing power to determine that question, decides that the requisite state of facts in truth existed and the proceedings of the court were valid. Conceding the abstract possibility of the legislature adopting such a course, nevertheless it produces so inconvenient a result that no enactment dealing with proceedings in any of the ordinary courts of justice should receive such an interpretation unless the intention is clearly expressed."[41]

In consequence, the presumption is very strong that Parliament intended a court to decide for itself the facts upon which its jurisdiction depends.

38. See, eg, *R v The Commonwealth Court of Conciliation and Arbitration; Ex parte Amalgamated Engineering Union* (1953) 89 CLR 636.
39. See, eg, ibid at 648; *R v Evatt; Ex parte The Master Builders' Association of New South Wales* (1974) 132 CLR 150. The same approach has been adopted in relation to the Federal Court of Australia: see *R v Judges of the Federal Court of Australia and McDowell Pacific Ltd; Ex parte Pilkington ACI (Operations) Pty Ltd* (1978) 142 CLR 113.
40. *Ex parte Pilkington ACI (Operations) Pty Ltd* (1978) 142 CLR 113 at 125.
41. (1938) 59 CLR 369 at 391-392.

It is not only in relation to issues of jurisdictional fact that courts have emphasised the difference between the presumptions which apply in relation to them and those which apply in relation to tribunals. In *Re Racal Communications Ltd* Lord Diplock referred to:

"the presumption that where Parliament confers on an administrative tribunal or authority, as distinct from a court of law, power to decide particular questions defined by the Act conferring the power, Parliament intends to confine that power to answering the question as it has been so defined".[42]

The High Court specifically assented to this proposition in the *BHP Petroleum* case.[43]

Why different rules of construction apply to courts

What is the rationale, if any, for the presumption to which Lord Diplock referred and why should the presumption apply in relation to tribunals and not courts? Why should a want of finality in relation to jurisdictional facts be seen as a greater problem for courts than administrative bodies?

The answer lies, it seems, in the courts' perception that there is some relevant constitutional difference between them and administrative bodies, whether in the nature of the power they wield, the manner of its exercise, or in their respective compositions and responsibilities.

The difference cannot, however, lie in the difference between judicial and administrative power. First, it has proved difficult to define the content of judicial power at all and in particular, to define in what precise way it differs from administrative power.[44] In any event, the doctrine of the separation of powers is confined in its operation to the Commonwealth Constitution.[45] State courts can and do regularly exercise administrative as well as judicial power.[46] As the presumptions in question apply as much in State as in Commonwealth jurisdictions, the relevant constitutional difference cannot depend upon the difference in the nature of judicial and administrative power.

Nor can the difference be justified by reference to the "general" jurisdiction of the courts and the "limited" or "special" jurisdiction of tribunals: there are some courts, like the Federal Court of Australia, which derive their power from statute.[47] Nor does it seem likely that differences in judicial and administrative decision-making processes could constitute a relevant difference. Subject to constitutional constraints, these processes

42. [1981] AC 374 at 382-383.
43. See *BHP Petroleum Pty Ltd v Balfour* (1987) 180 CLR 474 at 480-481.
44. See, eg, *Precision Data Holdings Pty Ltd v Wills* (1991) 173 CLR 167 at 188-189.
45. The reasoning in the *Boilermakers' Case* (1956) 94 CLR 254; (1957) 95 CLR 529; [1957] AC 288 has not been applied in relation to State Constitutions. See, eg, *City of Collingwood v Victoria* [1994] 1 VR 652 at 663.
46. This can give rise to significant problems where a State court is called on to exercise power in respect of federal offences in its federal jurisdiction: see, eg, *Grollo v Bates* (1994) 125 ALR 492.
47. See, eg, *Sen v The Queen* (1991) 30 FCR 174 at 175 (discussing the statutory nature of the right to appeal to the Full Court).

are variable—the statutory framework being a matter for Parliament to determine. In the Commonwealth context, the adversarial mode adopted in the Administrative Appeals Tribunal contrasts with the inquisitorial mode of the Immigration Review Tribunal and the Refugee Review Tribunal. The approach appropriate to an exercise of native title jurisdiction in the Federal Court differs from that elsewhere in the court's jurisdiction.[48]

The reason for the difference in the presumptions which apply to statutory grants of power to courts as compared with administrative bodies lies, it seems, in the different composition of the bodies themselves and in their ultimate responsibilities. I do not mean that the relevant difference lies in the personal and professional characteristics of judge and administrator. These may be virtually identical. The differences lies, it seems, partly in the tenured nature of judicial appointments, tenure being designed to secure independence in fact and in perception from executive government and other interests.[49] Administrators may, of course, enjoy tenure by reason of statute and contract, but the tenure of judges of the High Court and of the Federal Court is constitutionally protected.[50] In the States, the tenure of judges of the Supreme Court is also specially protected.[51] Tenure and the independence it is intended to ensure cannot be the whole explanation, however: in the States, judges of lower courts do not invariably have such special protection. The balance of the explanation must lie in the fact that courts alone are responsible for giving final, authoritative decisions on the meaning and application of statute.

In summary, the presumptions applying to statutory grants of power to courts and administrative bodies express the courts' perception as to the differences in constitutional responsibility of courts and administrators. These differences are supported, in the case of courts, by special provisions to secure independence. In any event, administrators, whether departmental or agency officers or members of statutory tribunals, cannot be entirely independent of the constraints of the Executive government of which they form part, and cannot therefore properly assume responsibility for the authoritative interpretation of statute.

Administrators have, of course, other responsibilities. The rules of statutory construction which apply in deciding whether there has been jurisdictional error do not permit the supervising court to inquire into the merits of a decision. Leaving Commonwealth constitutional considerations aside, there is no rule of statutory construction to the effect that, absent a contrary legislative intent, persons affected have a right of appeal on the merits from an administrative decision made in exercise of statutory power. As Justice Mason said in the *Peko-Wallsend* case:

> "The limited role of a court reviewing the exercise of an administrative discretion must constantly be borne in mind. It is not the function of the court to substitute its own decision for that of the administrator by

---

48. See, eg, *Native Title Act* 1993 (Cth) and Federal Court Rules, O 75.
49. Cf *Shell Co of Australia Ltd v Commissioner of Taxation* (1930) 44 CLR 530 at 545-546; *New South Wales v Commonwealth* (1915) 20 CLR 54 at 61-62, 93, 109.
50. Commonwealth Constitution, s 72.
51. *Constitution Act* (SA), s 75; *Constitution Act* (Qld), s 16; *Constitution Act* (WA), s 55; *Constitution Act* (Vic), s 77; *Supreme Court Act* 1970 (NSW), s 27(2); *Supreme Court (Judges Independence) Act* 1857 (Tas).

exercising a discretion which the legislature has vested in the administrator. Its role is to set limits on the exercise of that discretion, and a decision made within those boundaries cannot be impugned."[52]

The rules of statutory construction and the presumptions and assumptions which apply in this context serve to maintain the distinction between inquiring into the lawfulness of a decision and inquiring into its merits.

(C) OUSTER AND CONCLUSIVE EVIDENCE CLAUSES

For many good reasons, including the interests of efficient and speedy decision-making, the avoidance of costs and unnecessary formality and technicality, legislatures regularly seek to exclude or substantially limit the power of the courts to examine the decision-making processes which supposedly take place under the authority of statute. Courts now and in the past have proved reluctant to accept that the Parliament could have intended to prevent the courts' independent scrutiny of administrative decisions. This reluctance is reflected in judicial approaches to statutory interpretation of privative clauses.

Constitutional constraints on privative clauses

Even before questions of statutory interpretation arise, there may well be issues of validity. Under the Commonwealth Constitution, statutory attempts to regulate the way in which a court is to exercise its power (or to prevent it from exercising power at all) may be invalid by reason of Chapter III. *Chu Keng Lim v Minister for Immigration*[53] is illustrative. In that case, the High Court held unlawful the attempt, by s 54R of the *Migration Act* 1958 (Cth), to prevent a court from ordering a detainee's release from unlawful detention. The provision was, as Justices Brennan, Deane and Dawson said: "a direction by the Parliament to the courts as to the manner in which they are to exercise their jurisdiction".[54]

Their Honours added that:

"It is one thing for the Parliament, within the limits of the legislative power conferred upon it by the Constitution, to grant or withhold jurisdiction. It is a quite different thing for the Parliament to purport to direct the courts as to the manner and outcome of the exercise of their jurisdiction."[55]

The position under the States' constitutions is less rigorous.[56]

52. *Minister for Aboriginal Affairs v Peko-Wallsend Ltd* (1986) 162 CLR 24 at 40-41.
53. (1992) 176 CLR 1.
54. Ibid at 36-37; see also at 53 per Gaudron J.
55. Ibid at 36-37.
56. Cf *Building Construction Employees and Builders Labourers' Federation of New South Wales v Minister for Industrial Relations* (1986) 7 NSWLR 372, at 375-378, 394-395 and *City of Collingwood v Victoria* [1994] 1 VR 652 at 666-668.

The High Court has also held that whilst the Commonwealth Parliament can validly limit the circumstances in which the remedies referred to in s 75(v) of the Constitution are available,[57] the Parliament cannot validly abrogate the jurisdiction conferred on the High Court by s 75(v). Further, unless the Commonwealth Parliament expressly or by necessary implication indicates to the contrary, the same is true of s 39B of the *Judiciary Act* 1903, conferring a jurisdiction on the Federal Court which is to all intents and purposes the same as that conferred on the High Court by s 75(v).[58]

The decision in *Deputy Commissioner of Taxation (Cth) v Richard Walter*[59] has highlighted that, by reason of Ch III of the Commonwealth Constitution, the validity of conclusive evidence provisions in Commonwealth statutes cannot be assumed in every case.

Conclusive evidence provisions are commonplace in taxing legislation. In the Commonwealth sphere, s 177 of the *Income Tax Assessment Act* 1936 (Cth), considered by the court in the *Richard Walter* case, is probably the most well-known example (at least amongst lawyers and accountants). Provisions in the same form as s 177 exist in the *Taxation (Unpaid Company Tax) Assessment Act* 1982,[60] *Fringe Benefits Tax Assessment Act* 1986,[61] *Petroleum Resource Rent Tax Assessment Act* 1987,[62] *Child Support Act* 1988,[63] *Training Guarantee (Administration) Act* 1990,[64] *Superannuation Guarantee (Administration) Act* 1992,[65] and *Sales Tax Assessment Act* 1992.[66] On one analysis, conclusive evidence provisions such as this can give rise to virtually the same difficulties as ouster clauses—at least that was the view adopted by Justice Brennan, and to a lesser extent Chief Justice Mason, in *Deputy Commissioner of Taxation v Richard Walter*.[67]

Section 177(1) of the *Income Tax Assessment Act* 1936 (Cth) provides that the production of a notice of assessment or of a copy:

> "shall be conclusive evidence of the due making of the assessment and, except in proceedings under Pt IVC of the *Taxation Administration Act* 1953 on a review or appeal relating to the assessment, that the amount and all the particulars of the assessment are correct".

That provision falls to be read in the context of section 175 which provides that the validity of an assessment "shall not be affected by reason that any of the provisions of this Act have not been complied with".

---

57. *Ince Bros and Cambridge Manufacturing Co Pty Ltd v Federated Clothing and Allied Trades Union* (1924) 34 CLR 457 at 464; *Deputy Commissioner of Taxation (Cth) v Richard Walter Pty Ltd* (1995) 69 ALJR 223 at 228, 235.
58. *Richard Walter* ibid at 228, 235.
59. (1995) 69 ALJR 223.
60. Section 23.
61. Section 126.
62. Section 106.
63. Section 116.
64. Section 97
65. Section 75
66. Section 116.
67. (1995) 69 ALJR 223 at 257; also at 230.

A majority in the *Richard Walter* case upheld the validity of s 177(1) although there was little consensus as to the precise basis for so doing. Three bases found favour; it was variously said that the provision was valid because:

(a) it operated only upon the evidence in the particular case, without diminishing the jurisdiction of the High Court under s 75(v) of the Constitution;[68]

(b) it effected a substantive rule that any requirement that a decision maker act in conformity with described procedures is directory only;[69] and

(c) the legislative scheme in which the provision was contained permitted the *Hickman* principle to be applied.[70]

This lack of agreement and the fact that two members of the court dissented, holding the provision invalid, tends to indicate that other conclusive evidence provisions in Commonwealth legislation may not withstand scrutiny. Moreover, it seems that under the Constitution a provision such as s 175 is crucial to the validity of a conclusive evidence provision in the form of s 177. It was the presence of s 175 which provided the basis for the conclusion reached by Chief Justice Mason and Justice Brennan that the decision-making procedures set out in the statute were to be regarded as directory only, not mandatory.[71] This in turn led to their decision that the provision was valid.

What is clear is that a conclusive evidence provision would invalidly diminish the High Court's jurisdiction under s 75(v) of the Constitution if it would effectively determine the very matters in issue between the parties *for all purposes*.[72]

It is also possible that a conclusive evidence provision which was invalid because it purported to diminish the High Court's jurisdiction under s 75(v) of the Constitution would fail in the Federal Court, because it would be read as inconsistent with s 39B of the *Judiciary Act* 1903 which is, it would seem, to be given paramount effect, unless there is manifest a clear contrary statutory intent.[73]

Ouster provisions are narrowly construed

Legislation which defines the occasion for the exercise of jurisdiction, or attaches legal consequences to some act, fact or circumstance is not ordinarily seen as an invalid ouster of jurisdiction.

If constitutional limits are not overstepped, the fact remains that in this country as elsewhere in the common law world the courts have narrowly construed statutory provisions which seek to exclude or diminish their

68. (1995) 69 ALJR 223 at 251 per Dawson J; at 259 per Toohey J.
69. Ibid at 231 per Mason CJ; at 264-265 per McHugh J.
70. Ibid at 237 per Brennan J. This principle is discussed below.
71. Ibid at 232, 238.
72. Ibid at 251 per Dawson J; cf at 237 per Brennan J; at 245 per Deane and Gaudron JJ dissenting.
73. See ibid at 228, 235, 247 and 249.

jurisdiction to supervise the decision-making of administrative bodies. The construction is made by reference to the presumption that the legislature could not have intended to deprive the citizen of access to the courts, other than to the extent expressly stated or necessarily to be implied. [74]

Legislatures have sought to exclude or diminish the jurisdiction of the courts in a number of ways, including by statutory statement that a factual prerequisite to power shall be sufficiently established if established "in the opinion" or "to the satisfaction of" the decision maker; or by statutory statement that the decision be final and not open to question, appeal or review; or by statutory statement that the remedies of mandamus, prohibition or certiorari are excluded; or by statutory statement that an instrument or an act shall be conclusive of the matters upon which the authority to make the decision depends. Whatever the means Parliament has sought to employ, the courts have consistently adopted the same presumption, leading to a narrow construction of the relevant provision.

There are many illustrations of this fundamental approach: *Hockey v Yelland*[75] is one such case. The *Workers Compensation Act* 1916 (Qld) provided, in s 14C(11), that a decision of the Neurology Board established under that Act was to be "final and conclusive". Notwithstanding this, Mr Hockey sought to challenge the Board's decision to reject his claim in respect of alleged work injury, seeking an order nisi for certiorari to quash the Board's decision for error of law on the face of the record. Because the critical words of exclusion were insufficiently specific, the High Court held the "final and conclusive" provision did not oust the court's jurisdiction to grant the remedy sought. Chief Justice Gibbs said:

> "It is a well recognised principle that the subject's right of recourse to the courts is not to be taken away except by clear words. If the subsection had provided that the determination should not be 'quashed or called in question' it would have been effective to oust certiorari for errors of law not going to jurisdiction, . . . but although the formula is by no means unfamiliar to the Queensland legislature, it is not used in s 14C(11)."[76]

Even when the critical words are used, the exclusion of the court's jurisdiction is ordinarily only partially successful. Statutory privative provisions which state that the relevant decision is final *and* which exclude its quashing or calling into question are, absent constitutional constraints, ordinarily effective only to exclude review for non-jurisdictional error upon application for certiorari on the face of the record.[77]

But what of jurisdictional error? A general privative clause of this kind is not effective to exclude review for jurisdictional error, whether

---

74. *Public Service Association (SA) v Federated Clerks' Union (SA)* (1991) 173 CLR 132 at 160 per Dawson and Gaudron JJ.
75. (1984) 157 CLR 124.
76. Ibid at 130; also at 142 per Wilson J. For a much earlier statement, see *Clancy v Butchers' Shop Employees Union* (1904) 1 CLR 181 at 204 per O'Connor J.
77. *Houssein v Under Secretary, Department of Industrial Relations and Technology (NSW)* (1982) 148 CLR 88; *Public Service Association of South Australia v Federated Clerks' Union of Australia* (1991) 173 CLR 132 at 141 per Brennan J.

constituted by want or excess of jurisdiction, or a failure to exercise jurisdiction.[78] If, however, the relevant privative provision excludes from its coverage errors in the nature of "excess or want of jurisdiction", the exclusion will not cover a wrongful failure or refusal to exercise jurisdiction.[79]

Statutory attempts to exclude the courts' jurisdiction (almost) entirely

Undeterred by judicial censure, legislatures have sometimes eschewed general language and, by statute, specifically excluded what they might reasonably have believed to be the entirety of the court's supervisory jurisdiction. The *National Security (Coal Mining Industry Employment) Regulations* considered in *R v Hickman; Ex parte Fox*[80] established a Local Reference Board "to settle disputes as to any local matter likely to affect the amicable relations of employers and employees in the coal mining industry". The regulations further provided that the Board's decision "shall not be challenged, appealed against, quashed or called into question, or be subject to prohibition, mandamus or injunction, in any court on any account whatever".

Faced with a privative provision of this kind the courts have nonetheless declined to be shut out from exercising responsibility for the final and authoritative determination of the meaning and operation of the statute governing the administrative decision-maker. They have reduced the occasion for independent inquiry and determination whilst not abandoning the task entirely.

The rationale for continued court supervision despite the introduction of an apparently exhaustive privative clause has been said to lie in the need:

> "to reconcile the prima facie inconsistency between a statutory provision which appears to limit the powers of a tribunal and the privative clause which appears to contemplate that the tribunal's order will operate free from any restriction."[81]

In *Hickman's* case Justice Dixon sought to reconcile this perceived inconsistency by a rule of construction. The privative clause was to be given effect, providing the purported exercise of power was:

(a) a bona fide attempt to exercise the power;

(b) related to the subject matter of the power; and

(c) was reasonably capable of reference to the power given to the body purporting to exercise it.[82]

---

78. *Public Service Association of South Australia v Federated Clerks' Union of Australia* ibid at 142 per Brennan J; at 160 per Dawson and Gaudron JJ.
79. Ibid at 142, 160-161.
80. (1945) 70 CLR 598.
81. *Deputy Commissioner of Taxation (Cth) v Richard Walter Pty Ltd* (1995) 69 ALJR 223 at 228 per Mason CJ; *R v Coldham; Ex parte Australian Workers' Union* (1983) 153 CLR 415 at 418 per Mason CJ and Brennan J; *O'Toole v Charles David Pty Ltd* (1991) 171 CLR 232 at 248-249, 304.
82. *R v Hickman* (1945) 70 CLR 598 at 615.

The High Court has since consistently applied this so-called rule of construction.[83]

There may be a further condition—namely, that the decision must not transgress "inviolable limitations or restraints" which the statute imposes. This fourth condition has been mentioned by Mason CJ and Brennan J in *R v Coldham; Ex parte Australian Workers' Union*[84] and by Brennan J in *O'Toole v Charles David Pty Ltd.*[85] In *Coldham's* case, this expression was used to refer to a jurisdictional fact, the existence of which was not a matter for the decision-maker's opinion, first because the statute did not purport to make it so, and secondly because Ch III of the Commonwealth Constitution prevented any person but a court from finding the jurisdictional fact conclusively. None but a court could decide the jurisdictional fact, at least in the Commonwealth jurisdiction, because the jurisdictional fact involved the finding of entitlement (as to employees' eligibility to join a trade union).[86]

But for the fact that Justice Dixon (and later judges) have presumed that Parliament would not have intended validity to inhere in decisions made beyond power, the problem of inconsistency would not have arisen. An alternative view of a *Hickman*-style privative clause would be to regard it as amounting to a statutory rule that acts of an administrative decision maker are valid, whether or not within power. Such an approach would rely upon the administrator to recognise and respect the limits of his own authority, subject of course to the ultimate responsibility of the Executive to Parliament.

The inherent difficulty with such an approach is not its impracticability, but that it involves depriving the courts of responsibility for the interpretation of legislation. This might be seen as constituting a fundamental interference with the judicial function. Perhaps such an idea lies at the bottom of Chief Justice Mason's observation in *O'Toole v Charles David Pty Ltd* that:

> "The *Hickman* interpretation of s 60 [of the *Conciliation and Arbitration Act* 1904 (Cth)] does not depend upon the s 75(v) jurisdiction of this court; the *Hickman* interpretation has its origins in the supremacy of the Constitution and the judicial power. The provisions of the Constitution, with all their limits, are binding 'on the courts, judges and people, of every part of the Commonwealth': covering cl 5 of the Constitution. The courts are the arbiters of constitutionality and the legislature cannot shackle the jurisdiction of the courts to determine questions of constitutional validity, though the legislature can define the jurisdiction of particular courts pursuant to s 77."[87]

---

83. *R v Commonwealth Conciliation and Arbitration Commission; Ex parte Amalgamated Engineering Union (Australian Section)* (1967) 118 CLR 219 at 252-253; *R v Coldham; Ex parte Australian Workers' Union* (1983) 153 CLR 415 at 418; cf *O'Toole v Charles David Pty Ltd* (1991) 171 CLR at 249-250, 275 and *Deputy Commissioner of Taxation (Cth) v Richard Walter Pty Ltd* (1995) 69 ALJR 223 at 228, 236.
84. (1982) 153 CLR 415 at 419.
85. (1991) 171 CLR 232 at 274-275.
86. *R v Coldham; Ex parte Australian Workers' Union* (1983) 153 CLR 415 at 419 per Mason CJ and Brennan J; at 428 per Deane and Dawson JJ.
87. (1991) 171 CLR 232 at 251.

These observations are in terms addressed to the situation which arises under the Commonwealth Constitution when facts are necessary for constitutionality. If, however, the *Hickman* interpretation has its origins in judicial power, it also has its origins in issues of general jurisdictional fact. That is, *R v Hickman* did not concern issues of constitutional jurisdictional fact of the kind agitated in *O'Toole v Charles David Pty Ltd*. Accordingly, if the Chief Justice's observations are to be given a consistent application, they properly extend beyond the Commonwealth constitutional context to matters of statutory interpretation.

Application of the *Hickman* principle means that an act of an administrative body cannot be shielded from attack when it exceeds the power which can be constitutionally given to it.[88] The application of the *Hickman* principle also means that an act of an administrative body will be found to be invalid if it is not referable to any power given to the body. Hence in *McDonald v Commissioner of Business Franchises*,[89] the High Court held that s 19(E)(2) of the *Business Franchise (Tobacco) Act* 1974 (Vic) had no application to the assessment in question, because as a result of repeal, the Victorian legislation contained no power which could have supported the making of an assessment of the relevant kind. In light of the decision in the *Richard Walter* case, it seems that conclusive evidence provisions are also subject to the *Hickman* principle, although it is not altogether clear how the principle would operate in relation to them.

There remain other areas in which the scope of the *Hickman* principle is unclear. The High Court itself has not agreed upon whether, in determining the bona fides of a decision maker, a court can examine the decision-maker's subjective intentions, or whether the court is confined to the objective considerations appearing on the face of the record. In *O'Toole v Charles David Pty Ltd*, Chief Justice Mason, Justices Brennan and Dawson (with whom Justice Toohey agreed) favoured the wider view,[90] but Justices Deane, Gaudron and McHugh favoured the narrower view.[91] In light of the decision of the court in *Richard Walter* case[92] the wider would now appear to be the preferred view.

(D) PROTECTION FOR RIGHTS AND FREEDOMS

In addition to the *Hickman* principle as applied to ouster clauses, there are numerous other well-accepted rules of statutory construction which are, broadly speaking, protective of individual rights and freedoms. The rationale of all such rules is said to lie in the assumption that the Parliament would not intend to diminish the rights and liberties of individuals unless it has stated its intention with utmost clarity.[93] Underlying this assumption

---

88. *O'Toole v Charles David Pty Ltd* (1991) 171 CLR 232 at 250, 270; *Re Australian Railways Union; Ex parte Public Transport Corp* (1993) 67 ALJR 904 at 910.
89. (1992) 175 CLR 472.
90. (1991) 171 CLR 232 at 232, 249, 305 and 309.
91. Ibid at 287.
92. (1995) 69 ALJR 223.
93. *Bropho v Western Australia* (1990) 171 CLR 1 at 18.

is the courts' perception that, constitutionally speaking, they are bound to show special solicitude for certain fundamental principles protective of the individual in the modern state.

First amongst these rules are those which require clear and unambiguous words to abolish or curtail fundamental common law principles or rights.[94] *R v Fuller*[95] is one recent example. In that case the New South Wales Court of Criminal Appeal was called upon to construe s 413B of the *Crimes Act* 1990 (NSW). That provision reads:

> "(1) In any proceedings an accused person may:
>
> > (a) personally or by his counsel ask questions of any witness with a view to establishing directly or by implication that the accused is generally or in a particular respect a person of good disposition or reputation;
> >
> > (b) himself give evidence tending to establish directly or by implication that the accused is generally or in a particular respect such a person; or
> >
> > (c) call a witness to give any such evidence,
>
> but where any of these things has been done, the prosecution may call, and any person jointly charged with the accused person may call, or himself give, evidence to establish that the accused person is a person of bad disposition or reputation, and the prosecution or any person so charged may in cross-examining any witness (including, where he gives evidence the accused person) ask him questions with a view to establishing that fact."

The Crown submitted that, when read literally, the provision contrasted evidence adduced from a witness other than the accused (where the questions were to be asked "with a view" to establishing good disposition or character) and evidence adduced by the accused himself (where the evidence need only tend to establish good character) before the Crown might be permitted to prove the bad character of the accused by way of rebuttal. The Crown submitted that, in relation to a witness other than the accused, the provision reflected the common law, according to which the Crown becomes entitled to adduce such evidence only where a question is asked, or evidence given, with the intention of putting the accused's character in issue. In relation to the accused, however, the provision no longer required such an intention, it being sufficient for the evidence to have the requisite tendency, whether intended or not.

The court held that s 413B did not abrogate the fundamental rule of the common law at all. Referring to *Atwood v The Queen*[96] Justice Hunt said:

94. See, eg, *Benson v Northern Island Road Transport Board* [1942] AC 520 at 526-527; *Potter v Minahan* (1908) 7 CLR 277 at 304; *Ex parte Walsh and Johnson; Re Yates* (1925) 37 CLR 36 at 93; *American Dairy Queen (Qld) Pty Ltd v Blue Rio Pty Ltd* (1981) 147 CLR 677 at 682-683; *Baker v Campbell* (1983) 153 CLR 52 at 96-97, 123; *Corporate Affairs Commission (NSW) v Yuill* (1991) 172 CLR 319 at 322, 338; *Re Bolton; Ex parte Beane* (1987) 162 CLR 514 at 523; *Bropho* (1990) 171 CLR 1 at 17-18; *R v Fuller* (1994) 34 NSWLR 233 at 237-238; *Coco v The Queen* (1994) 179 CLR 427 at 437-438.
95. (1994) 34 NSWLR 233.
96. (1960) 102 CLR 353 at 359-360.

"Evidence of bad character is otherwise excluded not because it is irrelevant to the accused's guilt but as a matter of policy ('policy deeply rooted in principle') in fairness to the accused."[97]

After referring to the presumption that the legislature does not intend to abrogate a common law right or privilege unless a contrary intention is clearly expressed or necessarily implied, Justice Hunt added:

"There is nothing in s 413B which expressly states an intention to abrogate the common law as I have expressed it. The only basis upon which such an intention could possibly be implied is the contrast between adducing evidence from a witness other than the accused (where the questions have to be asked 'with a view' to—that is, with the intention of—establishing good character) and evidence given by the accused himself (where the evidence need only tend—that is, intentionally or otherwise—to establish good character). That contrast is a very flimsy basis for a necessary implication. The requirement that the implication necessarily arise imports a high degree of certainty as to the legislative intention: *Hamilton v Oades* (1989) 166 CLR 486 at 495. There is no such certainty here."[98]

In *Coco v The Queen*[99] a question arose as to whether section 43(2)(c) of the *Invasion of Privacy Act* 1971 (Qld) conferred authority on a judge of the Supreme Court to authorise entry onto premises for the purposes of installing and maintaining listening devices in circumstances where the entry would otherwise have amounted to a trespass. Section 43(1) of the Act made it an offence to use "a listening device to overhear, record, monitor or listen to a private conversation", but s 43(2)(c) provided that s 43(1) did not apply:

"to or in relation to the use of any listening device by—

(i) a member of the police force acting in the performance of his duty if he has been authorised in writing to use a listening device by—

(a) the Commissioner of Police;

(b) an Assistant Commissioner of Police; or an officer of Police of or about the rank of Inspector who has been appointed in writing by the Commissioner to authorize the use of listening devices,

under and in accordance with an approval in writing given by a judge of the Supreme Court in relation to any particular matter specified in the approval."

The court decided the question by reference to the presumption that a general statutory statement was insufficient to interfere with a basic freedom. The majority[100] stated:

"The insistence on express authorization of an abrogation or curtailment of a fundamental right, freedom or immunity must be

---

97. *Fuller's* case (1994) 34 NSWLR 233 at 237.
98. Ibid at 238. Bruce and Dowd JJ agreed with him.
99. (1994) 179 CLR 427.
100. Mason CJ, Brennan, Gaudron, and McHugh JJ.

understood as a requirement for some manifestation or indication that the legislature has not only directed its attention to the question of the abrogation or curtailment of such basic rights, freedoms or immunities but has also determined upon abrogation or curtailment of them. The courts should not impute to the legislature an intention to interfere with fundamental rights. Such an intention must be clearly manifested by unmistakable and unambiguous language. General words will rarely be sufficient for that purpose if they do not specifically deal with the question because, in the context in which they appear, they will often be ambiguous on the aspect interference with fundamental rights.''[101]

The majority added:

"At the same time, curial insistence on a clear expression of an unmistakable and unambiguous intention to abrogate or curtail a fundamental freedom will enhance the parliamentary process by securing a greater measure of attention to the impact of legislative proposals on fundamental rights.''[102]

Because the Queensland Act did not contain express words conferring power upon a judge to authorise otherwise tortious conduct, the court held that a judge had no power to authorise members of the police force to enter premises to install listening devices in a way which would otherwise amount to a trespass.

The presumption against interference with basic rights has been applied to protect "the right of every [person] born in Australia, and whose home is in Australia, to remain in, depart from, or re-enter Australia" at will;[103] common law rights of a periodical tenant;[104] and the right to claim legal professional privilege.[105]

Courts have continued to require that there be a manifest intention to exclude the privilege against self-incrimination before the privilege is lost.[106] The rule of construction is the same where the privilege against self-exposure to a civil penalty is in question.[107]

Further, when an investigative power to require the giving of information is conferred by statute, it will ordinarily be construed as exhausted when any criminal proceedings to which the information relates have been commenced. The investigative power is presumed to be conferred for the performance of the administrative function of determining whether

---

101. At 437.
102. Ibid at 437-438.
103. *Potter v Minahan* (1908) 7 CLR 277 at 304; cf *Ex parte Walsh and Johnson; Re Yates* (1925) 37 CLR 36 at 93.
104. *American Dairy Queen (Qld) Pty Ltd v Blue Rio Pty Ltd* (1981) 147 CLR 677 at 682-683.
105. *Baker v Campbell* (1983) 153 CLR 52 at 96-97; *Corporate Affairs Commission of NSW v Yuill* (1991) 172 CLR 319 at 322, 338.
106. *Pyneboard Pty Ltd v Trade Practices Commission* (1983) 152 CLR 328 at 347; *Sorby v Commonwealth* (1983) 152 CLR 281 at 289; *Controlled Consultants Pty Ltd v Commissioner for Corporate Affairs* (1985) 156 CLR 385 at 396; *R v Zion* [1986] VR 609 at 613; *Hamilton v Oades* (1989) 166 CLR 486 at 500-501, 516; *Balog v Independent Commission Against Corruption* (1990) 169 CLR 625; Cf *Environment Protection Authority v Caltex Refining Co Pty Ltd* (1993) 178 CLR 477 at 503, 506 per Mason CJ, Toohey J; at 517 per Brennan J; at 533-534 per Deane, Dawson, Gaudron JJ.
107. *Pyneboard Pty Ltd v Trade Practices Commission* (1983) 152 CLR 328 at 347.

proceedings should be instituted and that purpose is spent when proceedings are begun.[108] The power to compel testimony of relevant facts is said to be inconsistent with the accused's right of silence at the pending trial.[109] In the Commonwealth context, the rule of construction is also affected by Ch III considerations.

Another important presumption protective of individual rights and freedoms is the presumption that Parliament does not intend a statute to operate retrospectively unless it unambiguously says so.[110] Nor is a statute to be construed so as to deprive a person of property without compensation, unless that intention is very clearly stated.[111] Indeed, statutes are generally construed by reference to the presumption that Parliament did not intend to interfere with proprietary rights at all,[112] although it seems that this rule of construction does not extend (or perhaps applies with less force)[113] to the alteration of existing statutory rights—rights of this kind being "inherently susceptible of variation".[114]

(E) CROWN IMMUNITIES AND PRIVILEGES

Over the past decade, the so-called privileges and immunities of the Crown have been significantly reduced by modifications in the rules of statutory construction relating to them. One reason lies in the change which has taken place in Australian governmental administration. Corporatisation and commercialisation of governmental activities has altered the very basis upon which the law relating to Crown immunity and privilege was once framed. The term "government business enterprise" is now commonplace and is frequently applied to bodies which, although subject to some control by the Crown, have legal personalities separate from the Crown and engage in commercial activities like any private entity. Telstra Corporation and the Australian Postal Commission are well-known examples. The second

108. *Huddart, Parker and Co Pty Ltd v Moorehead* (1909) 8 CLR 330 at 384-385; *Melbourne Steamship Co Ltd v Moorehead* (1912) 15 CLR 333 at 341, 343, 346, 347, 350; *Trade Practices Commission v Pioneer Concrete (Vic) Pty Ltd* (1981) 55 FLR 77 at 94-95; 36 ALR 151 at 166-167; *Pioneer Concrete (Vic) Pty Ltd v Trade Practices Commission* (1982) 152 CLR 460 at 474; *Hammond v Commonwealth* (1982) 152 CLR 188; *EPA v Caltex* (1993) 178 CLR 477 at 516-517 per Brennan J; at 557-558 per McHugh J.
109. *EPA v Caltex* ibid at 516-517 per Brennan J.
110. *Maxwell v Murphy* (1957) 96 CLR 261 at 267; *Fisher v Hebburn Ltd* (1960) 105 CLR 188 at 194; *Geraldton Building Co Pty Ltd v May* (1977) 136 CLR 379; *Rodway v The Queen* (1990) 169 CLR 515 at 518; *Polyukhovich v Commonwealth* (1991) 171 CLR 501 at 642.
111. *Attorney-General v De Keyser's Royal Hotel* [1920] AC 508.
112. *Clissold v Perry* (1904) 1 CLR 363 at 373; *Colonial Sugar Refining Co Ltd v Melbourne Harbour Trust Commissioners* (1927) 38 CLR 547 at 559; *Wade v New South Wales Rutile Mining Co Pty Ltd* (1970) 171 CLR 177 at 181, 182; *Clunies-Ross v Commonwealth* (1984) 155 CLR 193 at 199-200; *Mabo v Queensland* (1986) 166 CLR 186 at 213, 223.
113. *Georgiadis v Australian & Overseas Telecommunications Corporation* (1994) 179 CLR 297 at 305-306; *Health Insurance Commission v Peverill* (1994) 1979 CLR 226 at 237.
114. *HIC v Peverill* ibid at 237 per Mason CJ, Deane and Gaudron JJ.

reason for change in the relevant rules of construction is the courts' determination that rules of statutory construction should accord with the actualities of government.

Before *Bropho v Western Australia*[115] a statute was construed as inapplicable to the Crown unless the intention to bind the Crown was manifest from the very terms of the statute.[116] The presumption was not confined to the Sovereign herself, but extended to confer immunity upon governmental instrumentalities or agents acting in the course of their functions or duties as such.[117] The presumption did not, however, apply to benefits arising by reason of statute: the Crown could take the benefit of statute although not bound by it.[118]

The justification for the pre-*Bropho* statement of the rule lay principally, it seems, in a sense of what was fitting:

> "in a regard for the dignity and majesty of the Crown; concern to ensure that any proposed statutory derogation from the authority of the Crown was made plain in the legislative provisions submitted for the royal assent; and, the general proposition that, since laws are made by rulers for subjects, a general description of those bound by a statute is not to be read as including the Crown".[119]

In *Bropho's* case, however, the High Court acknowledged that these considerations were of limited relevance to the Australian government in the late 20th century. The court said:

> "[T]he historical considerations which gave rise to a presumption that the legislature would not have intended that a statute bind the Crown are largely inapplicable to conditions in this country where the activities of the executive government reach into almost all aspects of commercial, industrial and developmental endeavour and where it is commonplace for governmental commercial industrial and developmental instrumentalities and their servants and agents, which are covered by the shield of the Crown either by reason of their character as such or by reason of specific statutory provision to that effect, to compete and have commercial dealings on the same basis as private enterprise."[120]

Given these changes in governmental administration,[121] the test of "manifest intent", as the court noted, was out-of-step. So fundamental and

---

115. (1990) 171 CLR 1.
116. *China Ocean Shipping Co v South Australia* (1979) 145 CLR 172 at 199, 221, 240; *Brisbane City Council v Group Projects Pty Ltd* (1979) 145 CLR 143 at 169; *Province of Bombay v Municipal Corporation of Bombay* [1947] AC 58 at 61.
117. (1990) 171 CLR 1 at 16.
118. *McGraw-Hinds (Aust) Pty Ltd v Smith* (1979) 144 CLR 633 at 656 per Mason J. The extent to which the Crown is bound by statute in civil proceedings is the subject of specific legislation in the Commonwealth and States: see *Judiciary Act* 1903 (Cth), s 64, *Crown Proceedings Act* 1988 (NSW), s 5(2), *Crown Proceedings Act* 1980 (Qld), s 9(2), *Crown Proceedings Act* 1992 (SA), s 5, *Crown Proceedings Act* 1993 (Tas), s 5, *Crown Proceedings Act* 1958 (Vic), s 25, *Crown Suits Act* 1947 (WA), s 5.
119. (1990) 171 CLR 1 at 18.
120. Ibid at 19.
121. The court also referred in this regard to the *Judiciary Act* 1903, s 64 and like provisions in State legislation.

extensive had these changes been that, as the court noted, it would in many cases simply not have occurred to Parliament to indicate by manifest intent that a statute should apply to the Crown. Its application would have been assumed. Accordingly, the High Court in *Bropho* declined to apply the earlier "necessary intendment" rule. It held that whilst the presumption remained, it might much more readily be displaced by a legislative intention—which might be other than an intention manifest from the statute's very terms.[122] Following *Bropho's* case the question, whether or not the Crown is bound by a statute, is to be answered by considering all the relevant circumstances, including the terms of the statute, its subject matter, purpose, policy *and* the circumstance that there remains a presumption against it being bound.[123]

Prior to *Bropho's* case, it had been accepted that a statutory instrumentality may be entitled to immunity from one statute, but not another.[124] *Bropho's* case also contemplates that a legislative intention to bind the Crown may apply to some but not all provisions of the same statute; and that a statute may manifest an intention to bind the Crown in one, or some, but not all capacities.[125] There is therefore the possibility that a statute may bind neither the Sovereign in her personal capacity, nor a particular Crown instrumentality, but may bind the employees or agents of the Crown and of the instrumentality.

Presumptions are less rigid than rules of law. They generally reflect the courts' understanding of the constitutional realities and ideals of the day. The decision in *Bropho's* case is an example of an attempt to match an understanding of changing constitutional realities and ideals to the manner in which courts construe statutes. But the court remained fully conscious of historical considerations, including precedent.

The court proposed that decisions as to the meaning and application of a particular statutory provision which depended upon the earlier formulation of the presumption should not be disturbed. In other words, past constructions of particular statutory provisions abide.[126] Not all statutory provisions enacted at the time when the earlier formulation of the presumption prevailed have been the subject of judicial decision, however. A relevant consideration in construing such statutes would be the manner in which the presumption was formulated at the time of their enactment.[127] However, as to statutes which, as in *Bropho's* case, were enacted before *Bropho* but at a time when the circumstances giving rise to the *Bropho* reformulation were in existence, they would be construed according to the reformulated *Bropho* version of the presumption.[128] As

---

122. *Bropho* at 21-22.
123. Ibid.
124. *Superannuation Fund Investment Trust v Commissioner of Stamps (SA)* (1979) 145 CLR 330 at 340; *Australian Securities Commission v SIB Resources NL* (1991) 30 FCR 221 at 228.
125. *Bropho* at 24.
126. Ibid at 22.
127. Ibid at 23.
128. Prior to *Bropho's* case, the *Acts Interpretation Act* 1954 (Qld), s 13, and the *Acts Interpretation Act* 1931 (Tas), s 6(6) provided that the Crown is not bound by statute unless by express words. This continues to be the position in those States. The *Acts Interpretation Act* 1915 (SA), s 20, provides that statutes passed after 20 June 1990 will be taken to bind the Crown unless a contrary intention appears.

to statutory provisions enacted after *Bropho's* case, the *Bropho* formulation of the presumption would apply. [129]

Servants and Agents of the Crown

In what circumstances are servants and agents of the Crown entitled to the benefit of the Crown's immunity? As a general rule they may take the benefit of the Crown's immunity from statute only if the interests of the Crown would be prejudiced if they were bound. [130] The decision in *Registrar, Accident Compensation Tribunal v Commissioner of Taxation* [131] is illustrative. That case concerned the Registrar appointed under the *Accident Compensation Act* 1985 (Vic) and involved the question whether the Registrar stood in the same position as the Crown in his administration of the Accident Compensation Tribunal Fund. The High Court held that whilst some of the Registrar's functions were performed on behalf of the Victorian government, including the task of administering the Accident Compensation Tribunal, the Registrar could not be described as a servant or agent of the Crown for all purposes. In particular, he could not be so described in relation to his administration of the Fund, because the Registrar administered the Fund as trustee for private individuals, not the Crown. In his capacity as trustee, the Registrar was not entitled to the immunity of the Crown. The court said:

> "Given the purposes which, historically, were served by the assumption that the Crown is not bound by statute, there is now no basis, if there ever was any, for applying a presumption that the Crown is not bound unless the provision or provisions in question would operate so as to have some effect upon the 'interests or purposes of the Sovereign', or more accurately, the government concerned." [132]

Statutory instrumentalities and agencies

From time to time, statutory instrumentalities and agencies seek the benefit of Crown immunity. For more than a decade, however, courts have proved reluctant to extend the benefit of Crown immunity to them. In *Townsville Hospitals Board v Townsville City Council*, Chief Justice Gibbs set out what has become the general rule:

> "All persons should prima facie be regarded as equal before the law, and no statutory body should be accorded special privileges and immunities unless it clearly appears that it was the intention of the legislature to confer them. It is not difficult for the legislature to

129. *Bropho* at 23.
130. *Bradken Consolidated Ltd v Broken Hill Pty Co Ltd* (1979) 145 CLR 107 at 123-124, 129, 137-138; *Registrar, Accident Compensation Tribunal v Commissioner of Taxation* (1993) 178 CLR 145 at 171-172.
131. (1993) 178 CLR 145.
132. Ibid at 171-172 (footnotes omitted). For a more recent example, see *Paul Dainty Corporation Pty Ltd v National Tennis Centre Trust* (1990) 22 FCR 495 at 522.

provide in express terms that a corporation shall have the privileges and immunities of the Crown, and where it does not do so it should not readily be concluded that it had that intention."[133]

Unless Parliament has dealt with the issue expressly,[134] whether or not an instrumentality is entitled to the benefit of Crown immunity is entirely a matter of statutory construction. The most important factor to consider in that process is the extent of the statutory ability of the Crown to control the instrumentality. This factor was crucial in *Superannuation Fund Investment Trust v Commissioner of Stamps (SA)*.[135] In that case, the High Court held that the Investment Trust could not take the benefit of immunity from statute, principally because the members of the Trust were not subject to Ministerial or other control in exercising their functions as expert investors of the money of the Trust. On the contrary, they exercised independent judgment.[136]

Financial accountability to the Crown is not sufficient. In the *Townsville Hospitals Board* case, the Board was subject to financial control by the Crown, but the court held that it did not by reason of that fact obtain immunity from statute.[137]

Nor is it sufficient that an instrumentality holds property on behalf of the Crown. In the *Townsville Hospitals Board* case, for example, the relevant legislation, the *Hospitals Act* 1936 (Qld), provided that, although land should be vested in the Board for the purpose of building a hospital, the land should remain Crown land. This was not, in the court's view, sufficient itself to entitle the Board to the immunity of the Crown.[138] On the other hand, the fact that an instrumentality does not hold property for the Crown can be a disqualifying factor. In the *Accident Compensation Tribunal* case, the court, as already noted, attached much weight to the fact that the Registrar administered the Accident Compensation Fund as trustee for those private individuals entitled to compensation, and not for the Crown.[139]

Another matter which has in the past been considered relevant is the extent to which the functions of the instrumentality are "governmental" in character.[140] Given the changes in governmental administration already

---

133. (1982) 149 CLR 282 at 291.
134. Where a statute expressly refers to the Crown, it is presumed that it only refers to the Executive of the legislating jurisdiction. See *Superannuation Fund Investment Trust* (1979) 145 CLR 330 at 355, 357; *Bradken Consolidated Ltd v Broken Hill Pty Co Ltd* (1979) 145 CLR 107. The extent to which the Commonwealth may bind State Executives and the States bind the Commonwealth Executive or the Executives of another State is subject to constitutional regulation, although it seems that the presumption against a statute binding the Crown cannot be confined to the Crown in right of the community of the enacting legislature: *Bradken* at 136, 121-123, 129; *Rogers v Moore* (1993) 41 FCR 301 at 305-306 per Black CJ; at 323 per Sheppard J.
135. (1979) 145 CLR 330.
136. Ibid at 342, 347-348 per Stephen J; at 365, 372 per Aiken J.
137. 149 CLR 282 at 291-292.
138. Ibid at 282.
139. See (1993) 178 CLR 145 at 170.
140. *Superannuation Fund Investment Trust v Commissioner of Stamps (SA)* (1979) 145 CLR 330 at 355, 365, 371; *Bradken Consolidated Ltd v Broken Hill Pty Co Ltd* (1979) 145 CLR 107 at 115.

noted, it has, however, proved increasingly difficult to maintain the distinction between essentially governmental activities and the other activities carried on by governments, whether commercial, or otherwise. In consequence, the criterion is of little, if any, assistance in deciding whether an instrumentality is entitled to immunity from statute. [141]

CONCLUSION

Statutes are by their nature sometimes (if not always) [142] ambiguous and frequently uncertain in their application to particular circumstances. The presumptions which the courts employ to resolve the dilemma of uncertain meaning and operation are the logical expression of the courts' understanding of their ultimate constitutional responsibility and of their proper relation to Parliament and the Executive. The assumptions which the courts employ—whether as to reasonableness of a statute's operation, or as to its conformity with principles of responsible government—are unexceptional but they are necessary. Without them, there would in many cases be no possibility of rational solution. The presumptions and assumptions which the courts employ in statutory construction permit the courts to distinguish between Don Quixote's giants and Sancho Panza's windmills.

---

141. *Townsville Hospitals Board v Townsville City Council* (1982) 149 CLR 282 at 288-289 per Gibbs CJ; *Bropho* (1990) 171 CLR 1 at 19; *Deputy Commissioner of Taxation (Cth) v State Bank of New South Wales* (1992) 174 CLR 219 at 231-232; *Re Australian Education Union; Ex parte Victoria* (1995) 69 ALJR 451 at 463-464.
142. Justice M H McHugh, "The Growth of Legislation and Litigation" (1995) 69 ALJ 46.

Chapter 9

Public Interest Privileges and Immunities

T M Gault* †

INTRODUCTION

Citizens of a modern democratic state expect that litigation of disputes will be conducted in the courts in the manner best designed to establish the truth and give an impartial decision. They expect the courts to be open and accessible and to be presided over by an independent judiciary prepared where necessary to decide cases against the government. They expect, in an open society, that all relevant evidence will be available to be placed before the court—how else can justice be done? Yet sometimes all relevant evidence is not available. A greater interest than in achieving justice in a particular case demands that evidence be excluded.

Spouse cannot be compelled to give evidence against spouse. An accused person cannot be compelled to give evidence by way of self-incrimination. A juror cannot give evidence of what has been said in the jury room. A lawyer cannot, without consent of the client, divulge information received from a client or advice given. Discussions by way of negotiation cannot be the subject of evidence of what concessions a party to a dispute may have been prepared to make to achieve resolution. Rules such as these are justified as serving a greater public interest than would be served by requiring the evidence to be given. They have evolved as reflective of accepted public values. Inter-spousal communications should be open and unguarded. There must be no incentive to pressure suspects into confessing. Jurors must be protected against recriminations and publicity. Clients must be able to disclose problems candidly to legal advisers to obtain proper advice. Parties are to be encouraged to attempt to compromise disputes without risk. The benefit of some rules is in the nature of a privilege capable of waiver. A client can consent to disclosure by the lawyer. Other rules such as that relating to jury deliberations confer absolute immunity, regardless of the desire of the person concerned to disclose. These rules are applied without the need in each case to prove the underlying public interest.

Of primary concern here are rules under which the question of whether or not information should be disclosed turns upon proof in the particular case of where the public interest lies. They relate to information held by the

* A Judge of the Court of Appeal of New Zealand.
† Assistance of the Court of Appeal Judges' Clerks is gratefully acknowledged.

government and its agencies. Some of it will be regarded as secret, such as military information or as yet unannounced economic policy. Some of it will be information collected by government departments or agencies in carrying out their functions (for example, a tax department) and which has been supplied under compulsion and in the expectation that it will not be disclosed. Some of it, if disclosed, might put people at great risk, such as those who secretly provide information to the police about criminal conduct. Some of it may be capable, if disclosed, of greatly embarrassing the government. Even with the trend towards more open societies the need for some secrecy is to be recognised. But, at the same time, the need to expose corruption and other misconduct by public officials must not be hampered by legally-sanctioned secrecy. The need to achieve justice in individual cases may outweigh the advantage in maintaining secrecy that is not of greater value.

It is regarded as desirable that there be immunity from disclosure, even in court proceedings, of documents or evidence when the interests of the litigants and of the community as a whole in open justice are outweighed by the greater interest of the community in having official secrets preserved. Because of the wide range of circumstances in which these competing interests may arise there can be no fixed rule to cover them all. Instead, in each case there is an examination of whether it is in the public interest that the litigants be denied relevant material. This may occur at an early stage in litigation when a party seeks discovery and production by other parties of relevant documents. It may occur when an official is summoned to give evidence or where, in the course of evidence, there is asked a question the answer to which would require disclosure. There will be a claim that in the public interest there should not be disclosure and the court will rule upon it. Disclosure of official information might be required from officials in cases where the state is a party to the litigation or in cases where, in litigation between private litigants, evidence is required from state officials. Also, there may be cases in which there is in the hands of a party to private litigation sensitive information affecting government that should not be disclosed without opportunity being given to the government to claim immunity. The history and scope of this public interest immunity will be reviewed.

It will be seen that the desire of the courts to ensure parties to litigation have access to relevant material and the conflicting desire of Executive government to ensure it is withheld have created tensions in the course of the development of the relationship between the courts and the Executive in the evolution of the modern democratic state as we now know it.

Comparison between developments in Commonwealth countries, where the concepts of open government and freedom of access to official information have been more readily embraced, and those in England are informative. English judicial methods have led to complexities in the application of what should be straightforward principles which have given less trouble in the antipodes, where greater judicial freedom has been evident. In addition to the development of the common law, there has been legislative activity which, with some exceptions, has been broadly in conformity with judicial developments. A review of these developments shows that there remain unresolved the boundaries within which public interest immunity operates, particularly with reference to public authorities beyond central government. Future changes may be related to developments in the ways in which the courts treat confidential information more generally, and the emergence of broader judicial discretions to exclude evidence. Whatever the direction, the further exclusion of relevant evidence without good reason shown in each particular case is surely undesirable.

CROWN PRIVILEGE

From 1688 sovereignty in England and her colonies rested with the King or Queen and Parliament. There developed parliamentary democracy in which, by degrees, a growing proportion of the people came to share. The monarch's prerogative powers which constituted the Executive authority continued, except as gradually confined or extinguished by the laws enacted by the Parliament. The Crown, perceived as a corporation sole as distinct from the monarch, and acting through Ministers and their departments, represented the nation or state, enjoying all residual prerogative powers, privileges and immunities, holding property, conducting foreign relations and defending the realm. In the United States the doctrine of sovereignty was perceived differently. Ultimate sovereignty was vested in the general populace and the legislature was subject to the law. Whereas in the United States the Executive enjoyed such powers as were granted by the people, in England the people enjoyed such rights as were conferred by the state. This fundamental difference underlies much of the American thinking on open government and the entitlement of the people to official information.[1]

The development in England of representative government with its concomitant accountability was not immediately accompanied by increasing availability of, or access to, information in the hands of government. Indeed, criticism of the government was a criminal offence. Seditious libel was established by the Star Chamber and it was not until 1843 that truth became a defence.[2] Government was not the business of the people. Holt CJ said it all in *Tuchin's* case:[3]

> "If men should not be called to account for possessing the people with an ill opinion of the government, no government can subsist; for it is very necessary for every government, that the people should have a good opinion of it. And nothing can be worse to any government than to endeavour to procure animosities as to the management of it."

The *Official Secrets Acts* bound government agents to secrecy. There was little encouragement for those who might want documents or information in the hands of government for political purposes or to assist them in legal proceedings.

1. Goldman, "Combating the Opposition: English and United States Restrictions on the Public Right of Access to Governmental Information" (1985) 8 Hastings Int & Comp L R 249.
2. Ibid at 258, n 42.
3. Cited ibid at 256.

In litigation between private parties there developed in equity the right of each party to discovery of relevant documents in the possession of the other party. If the action was against the Crown on petition of right, the Crown enjoyed immunity from the obligation to give discovery.[4] This immunity appears to have been regarded as a prerogative power and, while of historical importance—if only as a source of confusion—it was abolished by the *Crown Proceedings Acts*, under which the Crown as a party or third party in proceedings can be required to answer interrogatories and give discovery of documents.[5] That is subject to the right to claim immunity on the ground that disclosure would be contrary to the public interest.[6]

The withholding of official documents or evidence in the public interest was known as crown privilege. It was available not only where the Crown was a party to proceedings but also in proceedings between private parties where documents or evidence were sought from the Crown and when in proceedings between private litigants the Crown objected to disclosure of official information they might have. There appears to be no single origin of this crown privilege. Probably it grew up as the Crown, although not bound to make discovery, voluntarily did so, but only to the extent regarded as appropriate, rationalising that stance as in the public interest.

Protection of the identity of informers was insisted upon and recognised by the courts from very early times.[7] Information about criminal offending and tax evasion was protected. Initially, this extended not just to the identity of the informer but also to the information received. It was treated as a secret of state to be disclosed at the discretion of the government. This was an absolute rule without case by case justification on public interest grounds, but that clearly was the rationale for it. An exception soon emerged under which disclosure would be required if that was necessary for an accused person to establish innocence.[8] This could be classed as a competing and superior public interest.

Another possible source may have been early libel cases in which one of the parties sought disclosure of official communications between

4. *Deare v Attorney-General* (1835) 1 Y & C Ex 197; 160 ER 80. The relevant cases are reviewed by Linstead, "The Law of Crown Privilege In Canada and Elsewhere" (1968) *Ottawa Law Review* 80 at 87.

5. In Australia the statutes which deal with Crown Proceedings are not as full as the New Zealand *Crown Proceedings Act* 1950 and so many of them do not explicitly discuss discovery against the Crown. However, many of them do contain a provision such as s 64 of the *Judiciary Act* 1903 (Cth) which provides that where the Act applies to a case "the rights of the parties shall as nearly as possible be the same . . . as in a suit between subject and subject." This has been read to mean that discovery is available against the Crown in proceedings to which the Act applies: see *Cth v Baume* (1905) 2 CLR 405 (HCA) and *Cth v Miller* (1910) 10 CLR 742 (HCA)—there are State authorities to similar effect. The Crown has the ability to object to discovery on any grounds open to an ordinary subject, and has the further ability to object where a claim of public interest immunity is available: see *Morissey v Young* (1896) 17 NSWR (Eq) 157.

6. The entitlement for the Crown to withhold documents and information on the ground that disclosure would be contrary to the public interest is to be distinguished from the former historical immunity from giving discovery at all, though it seems to have been frequently confused with it.

7. *Worthington v Scribner* 109 Mass 487 at 488 (1872).

8. *Marks v Beyfus* (1890) 25 QBD 494.

government agents or officers. The assertion of public interest in such cases has some of the flavour of the modern principle of qualified privilege in defamation proceedings. Its wider application became part of the development of the rule of evidence by which in any proceedings disclosure of official communications could be resisted on the grounds that because of the circumstances in which they were made disclosure would not be in the public interest.

Recognised aspects of public interest outside the informant cases were the safety of the realm and the confidentiality of official communications by or with government or its agents, together with the unarticulated premise that the business of government would not be intruded upon by the courts.

Two matters emerged quite early upon which judicial differences became apparent. One was whether the courts should accept without inquiry government claims to withhold documents or evidence.[9] The other was whether the courts should examine documents in the course of deciding whether they should be disclosed.[10] In these 19th century cases there can be found early signs of the potential for tension between the courts and the Executive as the right to justice for individual litigants came to be recognised as truly in competition with the interests of government in suppression. In these cases there is also language indicating that the right to withhold documents or information in the public interest was regarded at times as a privilege and at times as an immunity.

The House of Lords came to consider the issue in 1942 in *Duncan v Cammell Laird & Co*.[11] Representatives of persons who lost their lives when the new submarine *Thetis* sank during trials sued the builders and others in negligence. The defendants objected on the ground of crown privilege to production on discovery of certain relevant documents relating to the design, construction and performance of the submarine. This was supported by an affidavit from the First Lord of the Admiralty asserting that disclosure would be contrary to the public interest. Seven members sat but the decision was given in a single speech of Viscount Simon LC.[12] It was treated as a case of high constitutional importance because it involved a claim by the Executive to restrict the material which might otherwise be available to the court.

9. *Home v Bentinck* (1820) 8 Price 225; 146 ER 1185; and *Beatson v Skene* (1860) 5 H & N 838; 157 ER 1415. In the latter case Pollock CB referred to the administration of justice being only part of the general conduct of the affairs of any state or nation and subordinate to the general welfare of the community. It is notable however that in a dissenting judgment in that case Martin B asserted that whenever a judge was satisfied that the document might be made public without prejudice to the public interest production might be compelled despite ministerial objection. Pollock CB indicated that that could only be in extreme cases however.

10. In *Hennessy v Wright* (1888) 21 QB 509 the plaintiff in a libel case objected to the production of reports made by him in his capacity as Governor of Mauritius to the Colonial Secretary. It was held that these confidential communications should not be disclosed but Field J said that even if a proper objection to production of documents at trial is taken, the Judge should have the right to satisfy himself, by examining the documents if necessary, that the objection is properly based. In some subsequent cases documents were examined, eg *Asiatic Petroleum Co Ltd v Anglo-Persian Oil Co Ltd* [1916] 1 KB 822 (CA) and *Spigelman v Hocken* (1934) 150 LTR (NS) 256 (KBD).

11. [1942] AC 624.

12. The Lord Chancellor of course was also a member of the government.

There was a review of earlier authorities. Cases upholding the protection of informers were relied on as embodying the same general principles. This review subsequently has been demonstrated[13] in part to have been deficient, particularly in its consideration of Scottish cases and of a decision of the Privy Council on appeal from South Australia.[14] The conclusion was drawn that in every civil case relevant documents must not be produced if the public interest requires that they should be withheld and that the test could be found satisfied having regard either to the contents of a particular document or because the documents belong to a class which must be withheld from production. The principle was likened to an immunity and said to be unhappily described as crown privilege, because even if the documents were in the hands of a private litigant they could not be produced, a litigant could not waive the right and permit disclosure and the judge should if necessary insist on non-disclosure even if no objection is taken. The protection from production of documents by class was said to be necessary on the ground of the need for candour and completeness in communications with or within public departments.

Importantly, without apparently limiting the decision to classes based on national security, it was held that the objection when properly taken by the appropriate Minister or, in her or his absence, departmental head must be treated by the courts as conclusive. Suggestions in earlier cases of power to inspect documents to assess the claim were firmly rejected. The same principles were to apply to the exclusion of oral evidence. In view of the finding that ministerial claims were to be treated as conclusive the following passage at the end of the speech must be noted for its optimism:

"It is not a sufficient ground that the documents are 'State documents' or 'official' or are marked 'confidential'. It would not be a good ground that, if they were produced, the consequences might involve the department or the government in parliamentary discussion or in public criticism, or might necessitate the attendance as witnesses or otherwise of officials who have pressing duties elsewhere. Neither would it be a good ground that production might tend to expose a want of efficiency in the administration or tend to lay the department open to claims for compensation. In a word, it is not enough that the Minister of the department does not want to have the documents produced. The Minister, in deciding whether it is his duty to object, should bear these considerations in mind, for he ought not to take the responsibility of withholding production except in cases where the public interest would otherwise be damnified, for example, where disclosure would be injurious to national defence, or to good diplomatic relations, or where the practice of keeping a class of documents secret is necessary for the proper functioning of the public service."[15]

Of course, having ruled as it did, the House of Lords ensured that the courts would not know whether Ministers had acted as they were urged to do.

13. *Conway v Rimmer* [1968] AC 910 (HL).
14. *Robinson v South Australia (No 2)* [1931] AC 704.
15. [1942] AC 624 at 642.

THE CONTEXT OF THE DECISION IN CONWAY v RIMMER

Conway v Rimmer[16] generally is referred to as the primary authority for the modern rule of public interest immunity. In fact, it merely brought the English law into conformity with that of other common law countries. Still, that case, its effect and its subsequent treatment provide an interesting example of how judicial development of the law is unsystematic and erratic.

It was said that *Conway v Rimmer* was an early instance of the House of Lords exercising its newly found power to depart from its earlier decisions and that it overruled *Duncan v Cammell Laird & Co*. But of course no-one has ever suggested that the actual decision in the *Duncan* case was wrong. It was plainly right. It upheld a claim to crown privilege against disclosure in civil litigation during wartime of design and other documents relating to a new navy submarine that had sunk while on trial. It was held that the documents belonged to a class in respect of which the mere claim on behalf of the government that they be suppressed should be accepted as conclusive.

Unfortunately, the single opinion of the House of Lords was expressed in terms broader than necessary for the decision in that case. It was treated as providing refuge for officials at all levels anxious to avoid scrutiny. Such expressions referring to circumstances in which disclosure should be withheld as "where the practice of keeping a class of documents secret is necessary for the proper functioning of the public service" were irresistible attractions. Quite naturally such a broad formulation of the rule led to claims that were plainly defeating justice without good reason[17] but which were upheld by English courts apparently unprepared to identify the true ratio decidendi of the *Duncan* case and preferring to accord the dicta status approaching that of statute.[18] In 1956 the Lord Chancellor gave directions[19] which were intended to limit unjustified claims. Those directions included reference to circumstances in which crown privilege should not be claimed[20] and can be contrasted with some of the views expressed in the English judgments to the effect that the immunity must be claimed and cannot be waived. But it was not until *Conway v Rimmer* that the law in England was restated.

Commonwealth courts were not so easily diverted. As already mentioned, the Privy Council had addressed the issue in 1931 in *Robinson v South Australia (No 2)*. The claim to privilege in that case related to government documents produced in the course of the discharge of its responsibilities in the storage and marketing of wheat. The Privy Council referred to the privilege as a narrow one to be sparingly exercised. The case was referred

16. [1968] AC 910 (HL).
17. See eg *Ellis v Home Office* [1953] 2 QB 135; *Broome v Broome* [1955] P 190; *Gain v Gain* [1962] 1 All ER 63.
18. A recurring process: see similar criticism by the Privy Council in *Royal Brunei Airlines v Philip Tan Kok Ming* (unreported, Privy Council, 24 May 1995, Appeal 52 of 1994), p 6.
19. Reported in part in the argument in *Conway v Rimmer* [1968] AC 910 at 922.
20. See Jacob, "From Privileged Crown to Interested Public" [1993] *Public Law* 121 for a fascinating review of the extra-curial debate in the period between *Duncan's* case and *Conway v Rimmer*.

back to the Supreme Court of South Australia to investigate the basis for the claim and, if thought appropriate, to inspect the documents. Having regard to the quite different fact situation, the House of Lords in the *Duncan* case had no need to cast doubt on the *Robinson* decision, which had no national security content, but nevertheless it was disapproved. It was regarded more favourably by the Supreme Court of Canada,[21] the House of Lords on a Scottish appeal[22] and the Court of Appeal of New Zealand.[23] Those courts preferred the more robust view that ministerial claims to immunity from disclosure in the public interest should not be accepted as conclusive and that where necessary documents should be inspected. The same view had been taken earlier by the High Court of Australia in *Marconi's Wireless Telegraph Co Ltd v Commonwealth (No 2)*[24] and later in *Sankey v Whitlam*.[25]

In the *Conway* case the Home Secretary claimed in the public interest immunity from disclosure of probationary reports on the plaintiff, a former policeman, and a further report on his alleged involvement in a theft. That was in a proceeding he was bringing against a police superintendent for malicious prosecution. It was claimed that these reports were within classes of documents respectively comprising confidential reports by police officers to chief officers of police relating to the conduct, efficiency and fitness for employment of individual police officers, and reports by police officers to their superiors concerning investigations into the commission of a crime (in the specific case being that for which the plaintiff had been acquitted). These facts were some distance from the national security at issue in the *Duncan* case but, so broadly had that decision been expressed, that it was regarded as a conflicting precedent. In reaching its decision the House of Lords chose to confront head-on for the second time the issue of the tension between the courts and the Executive government—between government perception of the public interest and the court's perception of the public interest, after weighing also the public interest in securing justice for litigants. The outcome was the clear affirmation that it is for the court to determine whether or not a claim for suppression will be allowed on the ground of public interest; that in determining that it will balance in the particular case the claimed public interest in suppressing a document against the competing public interest in the proper and open administration of justice; and that, in appropriate cases, to facilitate the task, the courts may inspect the documents. In *Conway v Rimmer* the documents were duly inspected and there was an order that they be produced to the plaintiff.

The Lord Chancellor's directions of 1956 notwithstanding, the Attorney-General had intervened and argued that in the absence of good faith, mistake or misdirection the Executive had the sole right to determine whether communications with and between servants and officers of the Crown should be disclosed and that the courts must accept as conclusive a

---

21. *R v Snider* [1954] 4 DLR 483; *Gagnon v Quebec Securities Commission* (1964) 50 DLR (2d) 329.
22. *Glasgow Corp v Central Land Board* [1956] SC 1 (HL(Sc)).
23. *Corbett v Social Security Commission* [1962] NZLR 878 (CA).
24. (1913) 16 CLR 178.
25. (1978) 142 CLR 1.

statement that disclosure would be contrary to the public interest. This blunt challenge may explain the deferential terms in which the opinions were expressed. Nevertheless, to their credit, their Lordships rejected the argument and did not even seek a middle ground of accepting conclusiveness of ministerial certificates of the need in the public interest for suppression in such fields as national defence and (perhaps) diplomatic relations, while reserving the right to review the justification for the claim in respect of less sensitive classes of documents. That was essentially the position in the United States of America.[26] The House of Lords clearly determined that in all cases, while a ministerial certificate should be given the fullest consideration, the courts must decide where the balance of public interest lies and in doing so may inspect the documents. To the credit of the government no legislation followed overriding the decision.

It is doubtless significant that *Ridge v Baldwin*[27] had been decided just four years before, *Padfield v Minister of Agriculture, Fisheries and Food*[28] just two weeks before and *Anisminic Ltd v Foreign Compensation Commission* soon afterwards.[29] A considerable adjustment was taking place in the relationship between the courts and the Executive.

The *Conway v Rimmer* principles seemed clear. It was necessary to weigh the competing public interest in suppressing the documents by reference to such matters as the circumstances in which they were made, the degree of sensitivity, the reasons advanced for non-disclosure, their contents so far as known on the one hand against the nature of the litigation in which disclosure was sought and the significance of the documents to that litigation on the other. That the claim was for immunity for documents as a class was to be only one factor in the balancing. It was to be a factual assessment and judgment in all the circumstances of the particular case. Those factors suggest that the decision in one case would have little precedent value in another.

APPLICATION OF THE CONWAY v RIMMER DECISION

To trace some developments in England since *Conway v Rimmer* and draw comparisons with other jurisdictions is an instructive way to examine the scope and utility of the modern rule of public interest immunity.

In the application of the principles established by *Conway v Rimmer* in subsequent cases, the process that had followed the *Duncan* case began again. Statements used in the course of the reasons in *Conway v Rimmer* were seized upon and adopted as rules in themselves to the point where the principles became over-refined and lost effectiveness. This can be said especially of some of the deferential expressions that had been used. This continued until reigned in again by the House of Lords in *R v Chief Constable of West Midlands Police; Ex parte Wiley*.[30]

26. *United States v Reynolds* 345 US 1 (1953).
27. [1964] AC 40 (HL).
28. [1968] AC 997 (HL).
29. [1969] 2 AC 147 (HL).
30. [1995] 1 AC 274.

Protection of candour, confidentiality and the supply of information

The candour rationale for the rule had been mentioned by Lord Simon in *Duncan's* case and in earlier cases. He referred to a class of communications with or within a public department to be protected from disclosure on the ground that the candour and completeness of such communications might be prejudiced if they were liable to be disclosed.[31] A good deal of cold water was poured on this reasoning in *Conway v Rimmer*, particularly in relation to low level government communications, but it was preserved by Lord Reid who referred to the courts' ability to assess the likelihood of any class of documents being less full and candid because of knowledge of possible disclosure.[32] Arguments based on candour continued to be advanced. They met a mixed reception but little analysis. Not surprisingly, the contention that public servants would be less candid in their communications unless protected by the assurance of secrecy attracted little sympathy,[33] but the argument was said by Lord Wilberforce[34] to have received an excessive dose of cold water. The same lack of unanimity can be seen in the decisions in Australia and New Zealand.[35]

The argument for protection to ensure candour has tended to be merged with arguments based on the need to protect confidentiality to ensure the flow of information.[36] They do, however, raise quite separate issues and they were properly differentiated by Lord Keith in *Burmah Oil v Bank of England*.[37] The need to ensure candour generally has been advanced in relation to policy formulation and advice to, and deliberations of, government. The need to protect the flow of information has been relied upon to justify withholding information supplied by third parties to government agencies. Of course not everyone who provides such information can reasonably expect that it will never be disclosed in legal proceedings.

The need for protection from disclosure of the identity of police informers has long been recognised.[38] Generally, this has been so without any public interest inquiry, but subject to the clear exception that disclosure will be required if it is necessary to enable an accused to prove innocence. But, it has been held consistently that, merely because information is communicated in confidence, does not give rise to immunity from

31. [1942] AC 624 at 635.
32. [1968] AC 910 at 952.
33. Eg, "This contention must now be treated as having little weight, if any" per Lord Keith of Kinkel in *Burmah Oil Co v Bank of England* [1980] AC 1090 at 1132.
34. Ibid at 1112.
35. *Sankey v Whitlam* (1978) 142 CLR 1 at 63 per Stephen J, but contrast at 40 per Gibbs ACJ; *Konia v Morley* [1976] 1 NZLR 455 at 464 per McCarthy P; *Brightwell v Accident Compensation Corp* [1981] 1 NZLR 132 at 158 per McMullin J, reiterating that "advisers should be made of sterner stuff".
36. They are examined together by Zaltman, "Public Interest Immunity in Civil Proceedings: Protecting the Supply of Information to the Public Authority" [1984] PL 423.
37. [1980] AC 1090 at 1133.
38. *Marks v Beyfus* (1890) 25 QBD 494.

disclosure in legal proceedings. [39] There must be shown to be a sufficient public interest in suppression. The need to protect the flow of information of value in carrying out official functions has been sufficient. This was held to be the case in respect of allegedly libellous letters to the Gaming Board responsible for licensing gaming clubs, production of which was sought by an unsuccessful application for a licence. [40] There was the same outcome when a mother sought the identity of the informant from a society empowered by statute to bring proceedings for the welfare of children (but significantly not itself a public authority) which had learned (wrongly) that she had been mistreating her child. [41] That decision of the House of Lords reflected a willingness to uphold public interest immunity when claimed by a society that was neither part of government nor a crown agency. Further, the decision would have been the same even if the information had been provided maliciously—it fell within a protected class. It perhaps fits more comfortably into the informer category of cases. On the other hand, disclosure was ordered of documents that would indicate the identity of the importer of a chemical compound alleged to infringe a patent. [42] It was not seen as likely to prejudice the future provision of such information to customs officials.

An area in which the claimed need for secrecy in the interests of confidentiality, candour and the need to ensure co-operation was permitted to go too far was in connection with documents prepared in the course of police complaints procedures. Persons who had been involved in those procedures and thereafter wished to bring civil proceedings were denied access to the documents—even records of their own evidence. [43] A series of Court of Appeal decisions finally was over-ruled by the House of Lords in Ex parte Wiley. [44] The proper application of the principles of Conway v Rimmer was re-affirmed and the virtually automatic immunity for police complaints procedure documents rejected in favour of a proper balancing of the competing public interests case by case.

Class and contents claims

In the Duncan case the House of Lords referred to the two bases on which privilege might be claimed. They were either that the disclosure of the contents of a document would injure the public interest, for example in national defence or diplomatic relations, or that the document, irrespective of its contents, fell within a class which should not be disclosed. It was the second category for which secrecy was said to be necessary for the proper functioning of the public service. In Conway v Rimmer that dichotomy was entrenched. That case was dealt with as a class claim and there was

39. Alfred Crompton Amusement Machines Ltd v Customs and Excise Commissioners (No 2) [1974] AC 405 at 429.
40. R v Lewes Justices; Ex parte Home Secretary [1973] AC 388.
41. D v National Society for the Protection of Cruelty to Children [1978] AC 171.
42. Norwich Pharmacal Co v Custom and Excise Commissioners [1974] AC 133.
43. Neilson v Laugharne [1981] QB 736; Hehir v Commissioner of Police of the Metropolis [1982] 1 WLR 715; Makanjuola v Commissioner of Police of the Metropolis [1992] 3 All ER 617; Halford v Sharples [1992] 1 WLR 736.
44. [1995] 1 AC 274.

expressed a greater need in such cases for the courts to examine the assertion of public interest against disclosure. Class claims still were made thereafter—and it is a fair bet that some may have been so formulated because of difficulty in advancing a credible claim against disclosure of the contents. There is a clear explanation of the differences between the two categories in the judgment of Lord Wilberforce in *Burmah Oil Co Ltd v Bank of England*.[45] But perhaps the difference is more semantic than real. A claim to immunity for a class of documents is made because of the contents of documents of that class.

Justification for class claims generally has been by reference to candour and protection of the supply of information. Judicial attitudes to them have tended to reflect opinion as to the merits of those reasons. The distinction, in practice, between class and contents claims in many instances may depend on little more than the degree of generality with which the common contents of documents are described.[46]

It might have been expected that once the courts resolved to scrutinise class claims those that were upheld would diminish and be confined to classes of documents such as security records and diplomatic communications, the records of police operations and the like. On the contrary, the English courts upheld claims in respect of an increasingly wide range of classes of documents. Records of police complaints proceedings, a child welfare society and a gambling control authority were protected as already mentioned. On the other hand, in a libel action the New Zealand Court of Appeal was not prepared to recognise as a class of documents attracting immunity statements made by persons interviewed by police in connection with a suspected crime.[47] In Australia, the High Court, in a private prosecution brought against a former Prime Minister and three of his Ministers alleging conspiracy to effect an unlawful purpose, considered state papers relating to a loan proposal that had not proceeded should be produced.[48] The court inspected the documents. In *Alister v The Queen*[49] in an appeal against convictions for conspiracy to murder, the High Court rejected a claim that to disclose whether or not certain documents existed and were in the possession of the Australian Security Intelligence Organisation was contrary to the public interest. In *Commonwealth v Northern Land Council*[50] in a civil case, but one involving allegations of unconscionable conduct on the part of the Commonwealth, privilege was upheld for notes recording Cabinet deliberations there being no exceptional circumstances warranting inspection by the court or disclosure. All three cases involved class claims.

Presumably because of the perceived over-generous acceptance of class claims, with the consequent undervaluing of the interests of justice, Lord Templeman in *Ex parte Wiley*[51] said that if public interest immunity is

45. [1980] AC 1090 at 1111.
46. Ibid at 1132 per Lord Keith.
47. *Tipene v Apperley* [1978] 1 NZLR 761 at 768; see also *Konia v Morley* [1976] 1 NZLR 455.
48. *Sankey v Whitlam* (1978) 142 CLR 1.
49. (1983) 50 ALR 41.
50. (1993) 176 CLR 604.
51. [1995] 1 AC 274 at 281.

approached by every litigant on the basis that a relevant and material document must be disclosed, unless the disclosure will cause substantial harm to the public interest, the distinction between a class claim and a contents claim loses much of its significance. The majority were more guarded, however, and left the door open to class claims in appropriate cases. [52]

Cabinet documents and minutes

The example selected by Lord Reid in *Conway v Rimmer* [53] of a class of documents that should be accorded immunity regardless of contents was that of Cabinet minutes and the like, until such time as they are only of historical value. He clearly applied this also more generally to the business of government, extending to all documents concerned with policy making within departments, including minutes and the like by quite junior officials. That view was reiterated by Lord Scarman in *Burmah Oil Co Ltd v Bank of England*. [54] Collective responsibility and the need for candour were reasons given as justifying complete immunity. It was perhaps inevitable that with the increase in government activities, particularly in commercial areas, and the expanding scope of judicial review jurisdiction, such a stance would be eroded. By 1983, in the face of overseas decisions, it had been modified to "while Cabinet documents do not have complete immunity, they are entitled to a high degree of protection from disclosure". [55] Fully embracing the broad principle of judicial control, the High Court of Australia had no hesitation in concluding that, even in respect of Cabinet documents, the privilege is not absolute and the court still must undertake the balancing exercise. [56] The Supreme Court of Canada [57] and the New Zealand Court of Appeal [58] similarly were uninhibited. Also, their Lordships would have become fully aware of the rejection by the Supreme Court in the United States of the claim by Nixon to immunity for the Presidential tapes. [59]

In making reference to Cabinet documents in *Conway v Rimmer*, Lord Reid said that the most important reason for protecting them from disclosure was that they could create or fan ill-informed or captious public or political criticism. [60] Even with modern notions of accountability of representative government and collective Cabinet responsibility, there is recognition of the need for secrecy in policy formulation, at least while it is being formulated. But the potential for employing the terms of the judgment expansively to justify withholding information for the real purpose of avoiding criticism is obvious. There was perhaps some

52. See also *Commonwealth v Northern Land Council* (1993) 176 CLR 604 at 617.
53. [1968] AC 910 at 952.
54. [1980] AC 1090 at 1121.
55. *Air Canada v Secretary of State for Trade* [1983] 2 AC 394 at 432 per Lord Fraser of Tullybelton.
56. *Sankey v Whitlam* (1978) 142 CLR 1 at 41.
57. *Carey v The Queen* (1986) 35 DLR (4th) 161.
58. *Environmental Defence Society Inc v South Pacific Aluminium Ltd (No 2)* [1981] 1 NZLR 153; *Fletcher Timber Ltd v Attorney-General* [1984] 1 NZLR 290.
59. *Nixon v United States* 418 US 683.
60. [1968] AC 910 at 951.

acknowledgment of this by Lord Keith in *Burmah Oil Co Ltd v Bank of England*,[61] noting that "[t]here can be discerned in modern times a trend towards more open government methods than were prevalent in the past". Yet, a little over a decade after that, England was shaken by the *Matrix Churchill* affair.

Three directors of the company were prosecuted for exporting machine tools to Iraq in breach of published government export guidelines. In their defence they wished to show that government Ministers and MI6 knew and that the exports were authorised. They sought discovery of documents. Four Ministers signed certificates claiming public interest immunity for various categories of documents at a time when the government well knew the defences were correct, as emerged on the admission of one of the Ministers in the course of evidence. The prosecution then collapsed. But, plainly, in claiming the immunity in the circumstances, the government must have been prepared to see the accused wrongly convicted. In fact, the judge ordered production of most of the documents on a sensible application of the *Conway v Rimmer* principles, but the very claims to public interest immunity greatly embarrassed the government and led to the hasty appointment of an inquiry by Scott LJ.

Once exposed, the claims to immunity were justified by assertions on behalf of the government that the law required public interest immunity to be claimed and that it could not be waived. This gave rise to much debate.[62] It rested on certain dicta in earlier cases generally offered in the context of the distinction between a privilege and an immunity. It had been said by Lord Reid in *Conway v Rimmer*[63] that it is the duty of the court to prevent disclosure even without any claim by a Minister.[64] In *R v Lewes Justices; Ex parte Home Secretary*[65] Lord Reid had referred to the duty of the Gaming Board to raise the matter of immunity. It was regarded as a corollary of the function of the courts to balance the competing public interests that the public interest against disclosure must be presented. It was also said that while a privilege may be waived, an immunity cannot.[66] It does not seem to have been reasoned that if circumstances would justify waiver it could not be said that there is a public interest in suppression. Again, the over-reaching use of dicta caused problems—in this case the attempted cover up by government of embarrassing duplicity in trade policy.

The *Matrix Churchill* matter was not expressly mentioned in the speeches in the House of Lords in *Ex parte Wiley*, but Lord Woolf, who delivered the leading opinion, did refer to the scope and impact of public interest immunity being "controversial at the present time".[67] He did take the

---

61. [1980] AC 1090 at 1134.
62. Tompkins, "Public Interest Immunity after Matrix Churchill" [1993] PL 650; Ganz, "Matrix Churchill and Public Interest Immunity" (1993) 56 MLR 564; Bradley, Justice, "Good Government and Public Interest Immunity" [1992] PL 514.
63. [1968] AC 910 at 950.
64. See also *Burmah Oil Co Ltd v Bank of England* [1980] AC 1090 at 1147 per Lord Scarman.
65. [1973] AC 388.
66. *Makanjuola v Commissioner of Police of the Metropolis* [1992] 3 All ER 617 at 623 (CA).
67. [1995] 1 AC 274 at 287.

opportunity to dispose of the alleged duty to claim, and inability to waive, the immunity. The whole of that part of the judgment on these points[68] repays reading but, bearing in mind the timing, the following passage is poignant:

> "If a Secretary of State on behalf of his department as opposed to any ordinary litigant concludes that any public interest in documents being withheld from production is outweighed by the public interest in the documents being available for purposes of litigation, it is difficult to conceive that unless the documents do not relate to an area for which the Secretary of State was responsible, the court would feel it appropriate to come to any different conclusion from that of the Secretary of State."[69]

Lord Woolf disposed also of the related contention that the immunity extends to prevent use of knowledge obtained from the documents.[70]

The decision in *Ex parte Wiley* may well reflect more than a response to the *Matrix Churchill* affair and more than a re-clarification of muddled principles. It follows quite closely the enormously significant decision of the House of Lords in *M v Home Office*,[71] going to the very heart of the separation of powers. The leading opinion in that case also was written by Lord Woolf, who has said extra-judicially recently that it is becoming increasingly clear that there are no areas in the exercise of the Prerogative which are unreviewable by the courts.[72] *M v Home Office* and *Ex parte Wiley*, together with other recent judgments of their Lordships,[73] can be seen as reflecting judicial willingness to scrutinise immunities which, if wider than necessary, can impede the pursuit of justice.

Judicial inspection

There remains one aspect in which the courts in England have grafted on to the *Conway v Rimmer* principles an obstacle to persons seeking disclosure of documents. When disclosure is resisted in the public interest, the court may inspect the documents to assist the assessment as to whether the claimed public interest should yield to the interests of justice. Out of concern that litigants will embark upon fishing expeditions among official documents, there has been constructed a threshold to the determination by the court to inspect. It has been variously expressed but, as attributed to the majority of the House of Lords in the headnote to *Air Canada v Secretary of State for Trade*,[74] it is that the court should not inspect until satisfied that the documents contain material that would give substantial support to the contention of the party seeking disclosure on an issue in the case.

68. Ibid at 295-299.
69. Ibid at 296.
70. Ibid at 306.
71. [1994] 1 AC 377.
72. Lord Woolf of Barnes, "Separation of Powers in the United Kingdom" in Gray, McClintock (eds), *Courts and Policy: Checking the Balance* (1995), p 167.
73. *Pepper v Hart* [1993] AC 593; *Prebble v Television New Zealand Ltd* [1994] 3 NZLR 1.
74. [1983] 2 AC 394 at 395.

No such requirement had been imposed in *Conway v Rimmer*, in which private inspection by a judge had given no concern on grounds of denial to parties of open justice or potential improper influence upon the trial judge. However, there might have developed a concern to minimise the burden which could fall on first instance judges in particular of inspecting vast piles of documents without the assistance of counsel as to their significance. This could operate as a real incentive not only to restrict judicial inspection but also to recognise classes of documents for which immunity should be upheld. Whatever the reason, there was imposed upon the party without knowledge of the contents of documents (otherwise their production would not be needed) the obligation to satisfy the court that they contain material that will assist her or his case. In principle, it might be thought that the fact that the existence of the documents had been disclosed in compliance with an order for discovery should be sufficient indication of the relevance of the contents in the proceedings. This threshold requirement has not yet been resiled from in England. It has not been adopted in Canada[75] or in New Zealand.[76]

Reading the English cases leaves the impression that, though there are repeated expressions of the importance of full and open justice, the pervading attitude, at least until very recently, is as captured in this brief passage:

"In a case where the considerations for and against disclosure appear to be fairly evenly balanced the courts should I think uphold a claim to privilege on the ground of public interest and trust to the head of the department concerned to do whatever he can to mitigate the ill-effects of non-disclosure."[77]

Following the decision in *Ex parte Wiley*, it might be said that after a century of cases in which trends in favour of suppression has been arrested by historic decisions at timely intervals, the position today in England is not too different from what it was in 1888 after the decision in *Hennessy v Wright*.[78]

Why has England had so much trouble?

The rather tortuous path taken by the English cases can be contrasted with what can be said to be a more direct and robust approach to be found in the antipodean decisions. To venture explanations is perilous; some even may be without controversy. In England the influence of history is more direct than in countries whose colonists tended to retain only that which was perceived as of practical utility in their new worlds. A fresh start enabled

75. *Carey v The Queen* (1986) 35 DLR (4th) 161 at 194 (SCC).
76. *Fletcher Timber Ltd v Attorney-General* [1984] 1 NZLR 290. The ground upon which the *Air Canada* decision was distinguished has since disappeared but it is broadly thought that the conclusion would still be the same: see also the view of Toohey J (dissenting) in *Commonwealth v Northern Land Council* (1993) 176 CLR 604 at 635.
77. *Alfred Crompton Amusement Machines Ltd v Customs and Excise Commissioners (No 2)* [1974] AC 405 at 434 per Lord Cross of Chelsea.
78. (1888) 21 QB 509.

provides for conclusiveness of certificates of Ministers or the Clerk of the Privy Council as to non-disclosure of information constituting a confidence of the Queen's Privy Council for Canada, defined in substance as federal Cabinet proceedings not more than 20 years old. The federal legislation has not been adopted in the provinces where the common law position continues to apply.

The New Zealand Law Commission is undertaking a comprehensive review of the law of evidence. Its discussion paper on privilege[95] includes a chapter on public interest immunity. The general thrust is in a similar direction to that taken in Australia with the enactment of a provision in the proposed new evidence code relating to matters of state. This is intended to incorporate the common law balancing of the competing public interests.

In its draft provision the Law Commission identifies matters of state as including communications and information in respect of which disclosure can be resisted for reasons provided for in specific sections of the *Official Information Act* 1982. Since the tendency has been for the courts in New Zealand to regard the *Official Information Act* as providing guidance in the consideration of claims to public interest immunity[96] there is logic in this. However, there seems little practical significance in the express cross-referencing of the relevant provisions rather than the unstated general correlation preferred in Australia. But, it may have the potential for blurring the quite different issue for determination on a public interest immunity claim than is involved on an application for official information under the *Official Information Act*. With the latter it is a matter of whether or not the exemption from disclosure is made out. But on a claim for non-disclosure in court proceedings the issue only arises if there is a reason for non-disclosure and then it must be decided whether that reason is outweighed by the need for disclosure to do justice in the particular proceeding. Further, the broad scope of the specified exemptions in the *Official Information Act* may tend to encourage more claims to public interest immunity.

The New Zealand Law Commission does not favour a statutory definition of the process of decision preferring unfettered flexibility for the courts and anticipating that the courts will draw upon the guides available in the *Official Information* and *Privacy Acts*.[97] The Commission does not reject class claims which are considered to be appropriate occasionally. That the documents are claimed in a class that should not be disclosed is to be considered as a factor in the weighing process.[98]

95. Paper 23, March 1994.
96. *Fletcher Timber Ltd v Attorney-General* [1984] 1 NZLR 290 at 302 per Richardson J, and at 305 per McMullin J.
97. Para 435, p 176.
98. Para 448, p 180. There is provision in the New Zealand *Crown Proceedings Act* 1950 for conclusive certificates of the Prime Minister (as to likely prejudice to security defence or international relations) and the Attorney-General (as to likely prejudice to criminal investigations and prosecutions) enabling protection from disclosure on discovery of the existence of documents—the ultimate in class claims. This seems to have no counterpart in Australian *Crown Proceedings Acts*. The Law Commission recommends the repeal of this provision which appears never to have been used. But it should be noted that similar provisions are to be found in access to information statutes—*Freedom of Information Act* (Cth) s 25, *Official Information Act* (NZ) s 31, *Privacy Act* 1993 (NZ) s 32.

Access to information statutes

Access to information legislation has been enacted in many countries in the form of freedom of information or official information statutes and privacy statutes. They have in common the presumption of availability of official information or documents.[99] Although quite differently drafted, the Australian and New Zealand statutes are very similar in substance. They provide for access to official and personal information held by government agencies and by a wide range of public authorities.

The statutes do not address the availability of documents or information in court proceedings and do not detract from the common law or statutory public interest immunity. However, in their scheme and purpose can be found similar principles to those employed in consideration of claims to withhold from disclosure documents or evidence in litigation. They provide exemptions from the obligations to disclose. Those exemptions represent the grounds on which the legislature has considered it is reasonable to deny citizens access to official information or documents because there is considered to be a greater interest in non-disclosure. Some exemptions are absolute (perhaps subject to review) while, in the case of others of less sensitivity, there is a test of public interest against disclosure or provision for override by a particular public interest demanding disclosure. In this second category there is involved a weighing or balancing of public interest factors for or against disclosure which is generating its own body of case law.[100]

The exemptions have a familiar ring about them. Those in the higher level absolute category generally are where disclosure would be likely to damage security, defence, international relations or law enforcement or would expose high level government decision making or policy formulation. Exemptions of that kind reflect broadly accepted aspects of Executive government for which secrecy, at least for a time, is considered desirable. They correspond with grounds upon which claims to crown privilege in legal proceedings frequently are made. Of course, merely because a citizen is denied access under this legislation does not mean that a claim to withhold the same documents or information in legal proceedings is to be upheld. Indeed, in practice it will commonly be the case that the issue of disclosure in litigation will arise only because access has been denied under access legislation. Then the issue will be whether the reason for which access has been denied reflects a public interest that should be outweighed by the need for disclosure in the particular legal proceedings in the interests of justice. The interests protected by the exemptions and their scope and the experience under the acts in identification and weighting of public interest factors[101] (where applicable) can be expected to be taken into account by the courts in determining public interest immunity claims, although they

99. The *Freedom of Information Act* 1982 (Cth) relates to documents, while the New Zealand *Official Information Act* 1982 relates to information.
100. See Taylor, *Judicial Review* (1991), Ch 9; Australian Law Reform Commission, *Freedom of Information*, Discussion Paper No 59 (May 1995), p 49 et seq.
101. Extensively examined in Eagles, Taggart and Liddell, *Freedom of Information in New Zealand* (1992).

relate to only one side of the courts' balancing task. In this respect the New Zealand courts have shown willingness to recognise such legislative trends. The High Court of Australia has been criticised for not showing similar willingness. [102]

In New Zealand a decision of the Court of Appeal [103] by way of review of a decision of the Ombudsman on access by an accused under the *Official Information Act* to prosecution briefs of evidence now forms the basis of effective discovery by the Crown in criminal prosecutions. [104] As a result, complaints and appeals on the ground of failure to disclose to the accused relevant material, and disputes as to information and documents withheld by the police, are not frequent. In this particular area the determination under the access statute also effectively determined in a broad general way the judicial approach to police claims to withhold documents and information in criminal proceedings.

Freedom of information statutes, resting as they do on the presumption of availability, provide a clear identification of the public interest and that is in contrast to the ethos of secrecy in government against which the common law principles of crown privilege developed. However, beyond that and the general identification of aspects of public interest which are reflected in the statutory exemptions from disclosure, they have little to offer the courts in considering public interest immunity claims.

IS PUBLIC INTEREST IMMUNITY IN EXPANSION PHASE?

The debate over whether the decision to allow government papers or information to be withheld from legal proceedings should be made by the government or by the courts seems to be closed. It is accepted that the balancing of public interests is for the courts. The Executive nevertheless retains the ability to trump by legislation if it considers that the courts are giving insufficient weight to claims for immunity. There are already innumerable specific statutory provisions conferring secrecy in various ways. [105]

There may still be concern as to the ability of judges accurately to measure the true political or economic interest in sensitive documents or evidence, but this should be capable of being met in particular cases by evidence if that is necessary. So long as the role of the judge is adjudicative and he or she is not left to engage in a subjective personal assessment of material out of its context, that independent decision is to be preferred to one by a party interested in suppression.

102. Ibid at 12; and Taggart, "*Osmond* in the High Court of Australia: Opportunity Lost" in Taggart (ed), *Judicial Review of Administrative Action in the 1980s: Problems and Prospects*, p 65 as to the narrow view taken on legislative guidance from neighbouring jurisdictions in *Osmond v Public Service Board of New South Wales* (1985) 159 CLR 656, 669.
103. *Commissioner of Police v Ombudsman* [1988] 1 NZLR 385.
104. A Law Reform Commission proposal for a separately legislated discovery code for criminal cases (Report No 14, June 1990) has not been acted upon thus indicating reasonable satisfaction with the present situation.
105. See the review by Eagles, "Public Interest Immunity and Statutory Privilege" [1983] CLJ 118.

The principal difficulty for the courts over the years has been with class claims. Against modern concepts of open government, assertions of the need for secrecy of documents irrespective of their contents can rarely be justified. Perhaps in highly sensitive security areas, or in cases involving the informer branch of the rule, such claims may be upheld. In cases of doubt the power to inspect documents, if exercised, generally will have the effect of converting class claims into contents claims.

The focus of most modern discussion is as to the scope of the rule. The change of label from crown privilege to public interest immunity has been seen by some[106] as an invitation to characterise the rule as conferring a wide power to exclude documents or evidence on the ground of public interest. This has led to tendencies to associate the rule with the treatment by the courts of claims to protect confidential information and with discretionary powers to exclude evidence, as under statutory provisions relating to communications with religious or medical advisers.[107]

Certainly from England there have been mixed messages. The decision in *D v NSPCC*[108] may be contrasted with judicial emphasis that public interest immunity is a matter of public not private law.[109] In Australia there have been divergent views among judges[110] and commentators.[111] Recent Commonwealth legislation purporting to codify the common law has as the relevant heading "matters of state". The New Zealand proposal employs the same heading but then, by reference to the *Official Information Act*, in effect invites application of the rule to an extensive range of information.

Any broadening of the range of documents or evidence that might qualify for exclusion on public interest grounds will have the corresponding effect of potentially increasing the instances in which litigation is to be conducted without the availability of relevant material. When experience has shown already that the articulated worst fears of those pressing for suppression seldom materialise, the case for wider application of the rule is not strong. Even in relation to Crown agencies the opportunities for invoking the rule have expanded as government activities have extended further and further; though the scope of modern government may now be on the wane.

State commercial and trading organs and agencies emanating from the Crown, at least to the extent that they have public law duties, would seem potential claimants to invoke the rule. But they could hardly justify greater protection for commercial documents and communications than those private enterprises with which they compete. The same considerations that

---

106. Eg, counsel in *D v NSPCC* [1978] AC 133.
107. Eg under s 35, *Evidence Amendment Act No 2* 1980 (NZ) and the rule relating to disclosure of journalists' sources: *McGuinness v Attorney-General of Victoria* (1940) 63 CLR 73.
108. [1978] AC 171.
109. *Science Research Council v Nassé* [1980] AC 1028 at 1081 per Lord Scarman.
110. See eg Woodward J and Toohey J in *Aboriginal Sacred Sites Protection Authority v Maurice* (1986) 67 ALR 247.
111. Compare McNicol, *Law of Privilege*, op cit, p 429 et seq and Aronson, *Review of Administrative Action*, op cit, p 380 et seq as to the extent to which the rule applies beyond Crown agencies.

led to the narrowing of sovereign immunity seem applicable. [112] Public interest immunity should not be available to protect purely commercial information of state trading organisations merely because of public ownership. Any claim based on the confidentiality of information should be carefully scrutinised for true public interest need for secrecy. [113] That of course is to be clearly distinguished from the private law right to restrain breaches of confidence subject to the defence that disclosure is in the public interest (the iniquity defence).

Similarly, the fact that the public interest immunity rule involves a balancing of public interests does not mean that it is a matter of judicial discretion. It is a rule. If the public interest in disclosure is found on analysis to outweigh the public interest in withholding the document or evidence then there remains no discretion under the rule to exclude.

Just where the public interest lies and what weight it is to be accorded can be questions of great difficulty which are not to be answered intuitively or in response to broad assertion. Rather, they must be carefully investigated, analysed and subjected to reasoned judgment of the kind expected of our judges in all of their decisions. Because of the importance of the specific circumstances of each claim, previous decisions, even those relating to the same kind of information or the same type of litigation, will be of only limited assistance.

If state secrets are not to be disclosed unnecessarily and to the real detriment of the community and, if individual litigants are not to be denied relevant information without justification, each claim must be carefully assessed on its particular merits. General arguments of the need to protect candour in communications or the flow of information from designated sources, policy formulation, collective responsibility and the like are not to be taken as resting upon established rules but are merely aspects to be evaluated when raised in particular contexts. There is no need for the rule to be made any more complicated than that.

---

112. *Playa Larga (owners of cargo lately laden on board) v I Congreso del Partido (owners)* [1983] 1 AC 244; *Trendtex Trading Corp Ltd v Central Bank of Nigeria* [1977] 1 All ER 881.
113. *Commonwealth v John Fairfax & Sons Ltd* (1980) 147 CLR 39 at 51 per Mason J.

Chapter 10

Standing and the State

JUSTICE K E LINDGREN*

1. INTRODUCTION

The title of this essay raises fundamental questions touching the legal system. What is the role of the courts vis-a-vis the executive and the legislative organs of government? Is their role limited to that of protector of private rights and interests? Does the courts' role extend to safeguarding public rights and interests and ensuring the accountability of public institutions? Are value judgments necessarily reflected in judicial pronouncements on standing? Is a decision on standing ineluctably a "political" act?

It is not possible, or perhaps desirable, to pursue these and other questions thoroughly within the scope of this essay, but they infuse all discussions of locus standi.[1]

2. STANDING UNDER THE GENERAL LAW

Introduction

"Standing", "locus standi" and the private law notion of "title to sue" signify the same thing. "Title to sue" relates to infringement of private rights; "standing" and "locus standi" terminology is used in relation to infringement of public rights and liberties.

One of the prerogative powers of the Attorney-General is that of litigant-protector of public rights and liberties. A member of the public may assume that role only where the Attorney-General grants consent (the Attorney-General's "fiat") or where the person has "standing" in her or his own right to do so. In the former case, in the absence of statutory provision, the proceedings are brought in the name of the Attorney-General "at the relation of" (ex relatione) the person and are known as "relator actions". In the latter case, the proceedings are brought in the person's own name.

* I acknowledge the assistance of my associate, Mr Michael Bray, my secretary, Mrs Rosemary Hewitt and Ms Rena Sofroniou, barrister, Sydney, in the preparation of this paper, and the comments on a draft of it by Mr Brian J Preston, barrister, Sydney.
1. There is valuable discussion of the questions or of some of them in, for example, the following: Wade and Forsyth, *Administrative Law* (7th ed, 1994), pp 4-5; de Smith, Woolf and Jowell, *Judicial Review of Administrative Action* (5th ed, 1995) at 2-005 and 2-006, pp 101-102; Harden and Lewis, *The Noble Lie* (Hutchinson, 1986), esp at 206-214, 264-265; Dyzenhaus and Taggart, "Judicial Review, Jurisprudence and the Wizard of Oz" (1990) 1 PL 21, esp at 47-50; Galligan, *Discretionary Powers* (Clarendon, Oxford, 1990), esp pp 234-240.

In the Australian Capital Territory, the *Enforcement of Public Interests Act* 1973 (ACT) provides, in s 2(1), that where the Attorney-General gives consent to the institution of proceedings in a court on the relation of a person, the title of the proceedings shall, if the Attorney-General so directs, describe, not the Attorney-General, but the relator as plaintiff, and contain words to the effect that the proceedings are instituted with the Attorney-General's consent. Section 2(2) provides that where, either before or after the commencement of the Act, proceedings are instituted in the name of the Attorney-General as plaintiff on the relation of a person, the Attorney-General may direct that the title be changed so that the relator is named as plaintiff. Section 2(3) provides for effect to be given to such a direction and for the words "with the consent of the Attorney-General" to be added after the name of the plaintiff. Section 3 of the Act provides, however, that where a direction is given, the Attorney-General nonetheless has the same rights in relation to the proceedings as he or she would have had if they had been instituted in her or his name as plaintiff on the relation of the person.

The aim of the Ordinance (it was an ordinance originally) was to remove the awkwardness inherent in a challenge by the Attorney-General to a decision or act of the government of which he or she formed part and in which he or she might have participated. The Ordinance was in fact introduced with the circumstances of *Kent v Cavanagh, Minister of State for Works*[2] in mind. In that case, Kent and other citizens sought an injunction to prevent the erection of a communications tower on Black Mountain, Canberra. The then Attorney-General, Senator the Honourable L K Murphy QC, gave his fiat. The proceedings were commenced by writ filed on Thursday, 5 July 1973 in the name of the Attorney-General as plaintiff at the relation of Kent and others. But, on 4 July 1973, the Ordinance had been made. It was gazetted on 5 July. The Attorney-General gave a direction under s 2(2) of the Ordinance. After that, Kent and others were referred to as the plaintiffs. That the Ordinance should have been thought desirable to camouflage the role of the Attorney-General is relevant to the discussion in the following section.

The granting of the Attorney-General's fiat and relator actions

The practices and policies of Attorneys-General touching the decision whether to grant their fiat to enable relator actions to be instituted no doubt vary. Not much has been written on this subject as distinct from the subject of the conduct of relator actions once instituted.[3] The criticisms have been made that the procedure is secret; that reasons are not given for the Attorney-General's decision; that the Attorney-General is not, or is not seen to be, independent of Cabinet influence; and that there is a potential

2. (1973) 1 ACTR 43 per Fox J.
3. See: Law Reform of British Columbia, *Report on Civil Litigation in the Public Interest* (LRC 46, 1980) Chs I, II, III; de Smith, Woolf and Jowell, *Judicial Review of Administrative Action* (5th ed, 1995) at 2-095 to 2-102, pp 150-154; Law Reform Commission, *Standing in Public Interest Litigation* (ALRC 27, 1985) paras 116, 117, 160-162, 310-318; Wade and Forsyth, *Administrative Law* (7th ed, 1994) at 601-610; Queensland Electoral and Administrative Review Commission, *Report on Review of Independence of the Attorney-General* (July 1993) Ch 4, "Relator Actions".

conflict of interest arising from the fact that the Attorney-General is a member of the government which is responsible for the decision or conduct to be targeted in the proposed litigation. To the extent that these criticisms are valid, they gain force from the fact that the Attorney-General's decision not to grant a fiat is not judicially reviewable.[4]

Two points may be noted here. First, there are well-publicised illustrations of the related criticisms of Cabinet influence and conflict of interest. An example is associated with the flooding of Lake Pedder in Tasmania. Conservationists sought a fiat from the Tasmanian Attorney-General to challenge the flooding of Lake Pedder for hydro-electric purposes and he announced that it would be granted. Cabinet intervened. The Attorney resigned. His portfolio was assumed by the Premier, who refused a fiat. Another example comes from Queensland. Conservationists applied for a fiat to permit them to apply for an injunction against limestone mining in the Mt Etna Recreation Reserve. The reservation of the land as a recreation reserve was revoked by Order in Council. By this means, the basis for the proceedings was removed. The Queensland Attorney-General then refused his fiat without giving reasons.[5]

There are, on the other hand, instances in which an Attorney-General has granted a consent although the proposed litigation might be seen to be unwelcome to Cabinet. An illustration is the fiat granted by Attorney-General Murphy to Canberra residents to permit them to challenge a decision of the Cabinet, of which he was a member, authorising the construction of a telecommunications tower in a national park on Black Mountain in Canberra.[6] As noted earlier, however, an Ordinance was made to enable the citizens rather than the Attorney-General to be named as plaintiffs.

The second point relates to costs. In a relator action, the relator, rather than the Attorney-General, is answerable for costs.[7] So far as one can tell,

---

4. *London County Council v Attorney-General* [1902] AC 165 (HL) at 168-169 per Lord Halsbury; *Attorney-General v Parish* [1913] 2 Ch 444; *Attorney-General v Westminster City Council* [1942] 2 Ch 416; *Gouriet v Union of Post Office Workers* [1978] AC 435 (HL) at 477, 482 per Lord Wilberforce, 524 per Lord Fraser.

5. There was a sub-plot. In fact, an incorporated association sought an injunction against the mining company. The Full Court of the Supreme Court of Queensland held, by majority, that the association lacked any "interest" appropriate to give it standing: *Central Queensland Speleological Society Inc v Central Queensland Cement Pty Ltd (No 1)* [1989] 2 Qd R 512. On 17 March 1989, the High Court granted the association special leave to appeal and, upon its giving the usual undertaking as to damages, restrained the company from mining until further order. I rely on anecdotal evidence for what follows. Subsequently, the company successfully argued before the High Court that prior to the hearing and determination of the appeal, the matter should be remitted to the Supreme Court of Queensland for determination of certain factual matters. Pending that determination, the High Court revoked special leave. It was generally understood that after the determination by the Supreme Court, the High Court would again grant special leave to appeal. But the respondents successfully applied to the Supreme Court of Queensland for an order that the association provide security for costs. The association could not comply and the proceedings were dismissed because of the non-compliance.

6. See *Kent v Cavanagh*, fn (2) above. The final hearing before Smithers J is reported at (1973) 21 FLR 177 and the hearing on appeal, *sub nom Johnson v Kent*, is reported at (1975) 132 CLR 164.

7. *Attorney-General v Logan* [1891] 2 QB 100 at 103 (Wills J), 106 (Vaughan Williams J); *Attorney-General (Queensland) ex rel Duncan v Andrews* (1979) 145 CLR 573 at 582 per

Attorneys-General will grant a fiat only if satisfied that the relator will meet any adverse order for costs.[8] No doubt, the genesis of this practice is the argument that since, if the proceedings were commenced by the Attorney-General ex officio, an adverse order for costs would certainly be complied with, it is not fair to the opposing party that the public (and the government) should have the benefit of an assertion of supposed public rights and liberties by a "litigant of straw". Ex hypothesi the public stands to "gain" from a successful result and the other party should be in no worse position in relation to costs than if public funds were available to satisfy a costs order in that party's favour.[9]

It has been suggested that "screening" of prospective relators on the footing of ability to satisfy adverse costs orders cannot be supported, since it is not a process to which other litigants are subject. But this prompts the threshold question whether the enforcement and protection of public rights and liberties are in the same category as the enforcement of private rights. If there were to be no screening by the Attorney-General by reference to the ability to satisfy an adverse costs order, at least it is arguable that the relator should not enjoy any special concession or immunity in respect of judicial discretions in relation to orders for security for costs, or in relation to the orders for costs ultimately to be made in the proceedings. It is in fact sometimes submitted, and sometimes accepted (in the circumstances of particular cases), that those who litigate not for their own benefit but in the public interest should be treated tenderly on costs by not having to suffer an order for costs if they fail and by being favoured with an order for indemnity costs if they succeed.[10] This view is not always taken and costs problems can prevent or halt litigation by public interest groups.[11]

7 *Continued*
   Gibbs J; *Wentworth v Attorney-General (NSW)* (1984) 154 CLR 518 at 526-527; *Stoke-on-Kent City Council v B & Q (Retail) Ltd* [1984] 2 All ER 332 (HL) at 337 per Lord Templeman; *Gouriet v Attorney-General* [1978] AC 435 (HL) at 477 per Lord Wilberforce.

8. Cf E Campbell, "Award of Costs on Applications for Judicial Review" (1983) 10 Syd L R 20 at 28.

9. It has been accepted, in the context of applications for security for costs, to be unjust that a person who stands to benefit from an assertion of *private* rights should, without exposure as to costs, have those rights asserted in litigation by a company of straw: cf s 1335 of the Corporations Law and its predecessors, and such cases under them as *Pacific Acceptance Corp Ltd v Forsyth (No 2)* [1967] 2 NSWR 402 per Moffitt J at 407; *Buckley v Bennell Design and Constructions Pty Ltd* (1974) 1 ACLR 301 (NSW CA) at 303-304 per Street CJ; *Impex Pty Ltd v Crowner Products Ltd* (1994) 13 ACSR 440 (Qld FC); *Jalpalm Pty Ltd v Hamilton Inland Enterprises Pty Ltd* (1995) 16 ACSR 532 (FCA) per Kiefel J; *Omega Data Furniture Pty Ltd v Email Furniture Ltd* (unreported, FCA, Lindgren J, 22 August 1995 at 13).

10. See, for example, *Kent v Cavanagh* (1973) 1 ACTR 43 per Fox J at 55-56; *Arnold (on behalf of Australians For Animals) v Queensland* (1987) 73 ALR 607 (FCA FC) at 621-622, 635 per Wilcox J and Burchett J respectively, with whom Woodward J agreed; *Australian Federation of Consumer Organisations Inc v Tobacco Institute of Australia Ltd* (1991) 100 ALR 568 (FCA) per Morling J at 570-572; *Re Smith; Ex parte Rundle (No 2)* (1991) 6 WAR 299 (WA FC) at 302-303 per Malcolm CJ with whom Pidgeon J and Rowland J agreed; *Ex parte South West Forests Defence Foundation Inc* (unreported, SC WA, White J, 7 February 1994); *Oshlack v Richmond River Shire Council* (1994) 82 LGERA 236 (L & E Ct, NSW) per Stein J; *Byron Shire Businesses for the Future Inc v Byron Shire Council and Holiday Villages (Byron Bay) Pty Ltd* (1994) 83 LGERA 59 (L & E Ct, NSW) per Pearlman CJ.

11. See n 5, above.

As will be seen below, most recommendations for reform in the area with which this essay is concerned have been directed to a broadening of standing and concomitant diminution in the range of situations in which the Attorney-General's fiat is required. Reform in relation to the role of the Attorney-General and the granting, withholding or revocation of her or his fiat has not attracted much attention. But, in the Queensland Electoral and Administrative Review Commission's *Report on Review of Independence of the Attorney-General*,[12] there are the following recommendations:

> "4.52 The Commission recommends that where an application for a relator action has been refused, or not approved within 60 days, the Attorney-General, within three sitting days of such refusal or expiry of the period allowed for non-approval, table in Parliament a statement which sets out the nature of the application for the grant of the fiat, the alleged breach of public right or liberty and the reasons for the Attorney-General's decision. . . .
>
> 4.53 The Commission further recommends that the Attorney-General provide a reference to the Law Reform Commission to examine the question of standing in public interest litigation."

The Commission included as an appendix to its Report a draft Bill, cl 9 of which was intended to give effect to recommendation 4.52. Clause 9 was as follows:

> "9(1) This section applies if—
>
> (a) an application is made for the Attorney-General to grant a fiat in a proceeding to enforce or protect a public right; and
>
> (b) the application is refused or is not approved within 60 days.
>
> (2) The Attorney-General must prepare a statement that outlines—
>
> (a) the nature of the application; and
>
> (b) the breach of public right alleged; and
>
> (c) the reasons for the Attorney-General's refusal or inaction.
>
> (3) The statement must be laid before the Legislative Assembly within 3 sitting days after—
>
> (a) if the application is refused—the refusal; or
>
> (b) if the application is not approved within 60 days—the end of the 60 days."

The Commission's recommendation has not yet been implemented. Yet it seems to be a good one against which nothing can be said. Informing Parliament as to how the prerogative power is exercised is consistent with the principle of responsible government. As well, the practice would have a tendency to encourage Attorneys-General to develop principles and consistent policies governing the determination of requests for the fiat.

Section 50 of the Australian Securities Commission Act 1989 (the ASC Law) and the relator action

It is interesting to compare s 50 of the ASC Law with the relator action.

12. July 1993.

Section 50 empowers the Australian Securities Commission (the ASC), where it appears to it to be "in the public interest" for a person to begin and carry on proceedings for:

> "(a) the recovery of damages for fraud, negligence, default, breach of duty, or other misconduct, committed in connection with a matter to which the investigation or examination [conducted under Pt 3 of the ASC Law or a corresponding law] related; or
>
> (b) recovery of property of the person"

to cause such proceedings to be begun and carried on in the name of the person. Where the person is anyone other than a company, the person's consent is required. [13]

The cause of action is that of the person, whereas in the relator context it is that of the public. To date, proceedings which the ASC has caused to be begun under the section have named the person in question as plaintiff or applicant without any reference to the role of the ASC. It seems, however, that it would not be inappropriate for the title of the proceedings to disclose that they have been instigated by the ASC and that this might be desirable. [14]

Although s 90 of the ASC Law and the definition of "expenses" in relation to an investigation in s 5(1) of the ASC Law have the effect that the ASC is required to pay "the costs and expenses incurred in relation to a proceeding begun under section 50", there is a question whether this includes costs which an unsuccessful plaintiff or applicant in whose name the ASC has caused proceedings to be commenced and carried on, may be ordered to pay to a successful defendant or respondent.

There are interesting questions in relation to legal professional privilege which can arise while the prospective relator in the one case and the ASC in the other case are carrying out investigations prior to the taking of the decision, in the one case by the Attorney-General to grant her or his fiat permitting the commencement of proceedings in her or his name by the relator, and in the other case by the ASC to cause proceedings to be begun in the name of the wronged person. [15]

Definitions

Standing must be distinguished from justiciability and "ripeness" (see later). Craig says:

> "Locus standi is concerned with whether this particular plaintiff is entitled to invoke the jurisdiction of the court. This question must be distinguished from that of justiciability which asks whether the judicial process is suitable for the resolution of this type of dispute at all,

---

13. For a consideration of this distinction, and of other aspects of s 50, see *Deloitte Touche Tohmatsu v Australian Securities Commission* (1995) 54 FCR 562 and (1996) 136 ALR 453 both per Lindgren J.
14. Cf the words "at the relation of" or "ex relatione" in the title of relator actions.
15. Cf *Somerville v ASC* (1995) 131 ALR 517 (FCA FC).

whoever may bring it to the courts. It is also distinct from the issue
known in the United States as ripeness, under which abstract or
hypothetical questions are not adjudicated upon."[16]

Standing has also been defined as "legal capacity to institute
proceedings"[17] and as "the right of a plaintiff to be considered an
appropriate party to instigate . . . particular proceedings".[18]

Standing without the Attorney-General's fiat

For the purposes of this essay, it would not be a very useful exercise to
analyse the general law requirements of standing associated with the
prerogative remedies of mandamus, prohibition and certiorari. It suffices
to refer to the more commonly sought general law remedies of injunction
and declaration.

In the well-known case of *Boyce v Paddington Borough Council*[19]
(*Boyce*), in which an owner of a block of flats sought an injunction
restraining the Borough Council and the owner of adjoining land from
erecting a screen or hoarding on that land obstructing the light to the flats'
windows, Buckley J said that a plaintiff could sue in respect of an
interference with a public right without joining the Attorney-General in two
cases only: first, where the interference involved an interference with the
plaintiff's private right and, secondly, where the interference caused
"special damage peculiar to" the plaintiff. The first is uncontroversial:
in respect of it, the fact that a public right is also infringed is an
irrelevancy. The second, however, gave rise to dissatisfaction and was to
be expanded.

This was not to happen, however, at the hands of the House of Lords in
Gouriet v Union of Post Office Workers.[20] The "damage" suffered by
Mr Gouriet from the ban on the handling of mail to South Africa as a
protest against its government's racial policies was not "special damage
peculiar to" Mr Gouriet in that it was not damage over and above that
suffered by the public at large. The Attorney-General had refused to grant
his fiat and Mr Gouriet lacked standing otherwise.

The language of "special damage" was not adhered to by the High Court
in *Australian Conservation Foundation v Commonwealth*[21] (*ACF*).
Although it denied standing to the Australian Conservation Foundation
(the ACF), the court introduced the possibility that the existence of a
"special interest", as distinct from the suffering of "special damage",
might give standing. Gibbs J said that Buckley J's expression "special
damage peculiar to" the plaintiff in *Boyce*, "should be regarded as
equivalent in meaning to 'having a special interest in the subject matter of

16. P P Craig, *Administrative Law* (3rd ed, 1994, London), p 479.
17. S M Thio, *Locus Standi and Judicial Review* (Singapore U P, 1971), p 1.
18. Law Reform Commission, *Standing in Public Interest Litigation* (ALRC 27 1985),
    para 20, p 11.
19. [1903] 1 Ch 109 per Buckley J.
20. [1978] AC 435.
21. (1980) 146 CLR 493.

the action' ".[22] His Honour added[23] that "the broad test of special interest" and not the more narrow suffering of special damage was the proper test to apply.

But the ACF's interest in the preservation of the environment did not, according to his Honour, satisfy even this more liberal test:

"I would not deny that a person might have a special interest in the preservation of *a particular environment*. However, an interest, for present purposes, does not mean *a mere intellectual or emotional concern*. A person is not interested within the meaning of the rule, unless he is likely to gain some advantage, other than the satisfaction of righting a wrong, upholding a principle or winning a contest, if his action succeeds or to suffer some disadvantage, other than a sense of grievance or a debt for costs, if his action fails. A belief, however strongly felt, that the law generally, or a particular law, should be observed, or that conduct of the particular kind should be prevented, does not suffice to give its possessor locus standi."[24]

Generally similar views were expressed by Stephen J and Mason J. The possibility of an actio popularis was rejected by Mason J in the following forthright terms:

"In this difficult field there is one proposition which may be stated with certainty. It is that a *mere belief or concern*, however genuine, does not in itself constitute a sufficient locus standi in a case of the kind now under consideration."[25]

Murphy J alone would have allowed the ACF's appeal.

It was not long before the High Court was able to accord standing on the basis of "special interest". In *Onus v Alcoa of Australia Ltd*[26] (*Onus*) two Aboriginal women applied for an injunction restraining Alcoa of Australia Ltd (Alcoa) from carrying out work on land occupied by it which, they claimed, would interfere with Aboriginal relics on that land, in contravention of s 21 of the *Archaeological and Aboriginal Relics Preservation Act* 1972 (Vic) (the *Relics Act*). The Supreme Court of Victoria had denied them standing. The High Court unanimously allowed their appeal.

The plaintiffs contended that the land contained relics of the former Aboriginal occupation by the Gournditch-jmara people and that they, as descendants of that people, were custodians of the relics according to the laws and customs of their people. They had no proprietary interest in the relics.

The High Court held that the *Relics Act* did not create private rights for the benefit of individual Aboriginals but public rights. But, by expressly applying the "special interest" test, six members of the seven-member court were able to hold that, because of the cultural and spiritual significance of

22. Ibid at 527.
23. Ibid at 528.
24. Ibid at 530—emphasis supplied.
25. Ibid at 548—emphasis supplied.
26. (1981) 149 CLR 27.

the relics to the plaintiffs, they had such an interest in the observance of that public right greater than that of the public generally, as to give them standing.

Onus made it clear that a special interest need not be a legal or proprietary interest. *ACF* was distinguished on the basis that the plaintiffs' role in relation to the relics was an interest different *in kind* from that which a group of environmentalists has in protecting the environment. The court emphasised the connection between the plaintiffs and the particular land and relics (compare the reference by Gibbs J to "a particular environment" in *ACF*, quoted above). Indeed, Gibbs CJ and Wilson J suggested that an Aboriginal from a different people would not have had standing.

The liberalisation in *ACF* and *Onus* of the criterion for the granting of standing has influenced cases in which statutory tests of standing (see below) have had to be applied. But the High Court's "special interest" requirement still denies standing to the person who has no connection with the subject matter beyond that of a "mere intellectual or emotional concern" or "mere belief or concern", no matter how strong, and no matter how well-placed that person may be to represent the public interest in relation to the alleged infringement of the public right or liberty in question.

The High Court has not had occasion to consider the issue of standing in relation to public interest litigation in a substantial way since it decided *Onus* on 18 September 1981. There is a brief discussion of standing in *Shop Distributing and Allied Employees Association v Minister for Industrial Affairs*.[27] The court did not hesitate to hold that a union of employees had standing to challenge a decision changing shop trading hours. The court considered that although the change would affect the whole community in various ways, shop assistants who were members of the union and who worked in shops in the area affected by the change, were affected in ways different from the community generally.[28]

As will be noted in the next section, a considerable jurisprudence has developed within the Federal Court of Australia on standing under the *Administrative Decisions (Judicial Review) Act* 1977 (Cth) (the AD(JR) Act) in which it has been necessary to apply the "special interest" criterion.[29]

---

27. (1995) 183 CLR 552 at 557-558.
28. *R v Inspectorate of Pollution; Ex parte Greenpeace Ltd (No 2)* [1994] 4 All ER 329 (Otton J) (*Greenpeace*) is another case in which an organisation was accorded standing, not simply on account of its objectives, but because particular members of it stood to be affected by the decision in question in a way different from the rest of the community. In that case an environmental protection organisation of international repute challenged a decision to authorise the testing of a nuclear power plant. The organisation had 2,500 supporters in the area where the plant was located.
29. Apart from its jurisdiction under the AD(JR) Act, the court has jurisdiction, by reason of s 39B(1) of the *Judiciary Act* 1903 (Cth), "with respect to any matter in which a writ of mandamus or prohibition or an injunction is sought against an officer or officers of the Commonwealth". It is common for applications in the court to invoke both bases of jurisdiction in respect of the same facts.

3. STANDING UNDER STATUTE

Statute may accord standing to any citizen in respect of particular classes of public wrongs; compare the "any person" provisions of s 80 of the *Trade Practices Act* 1974 (Cth) and s 123 of the *Environmental Planning and Assessment Act* 1979 (NSW).

But, more restrictive language is more common. In Australia the best known provision for standing is that in the AD(JR) Act. Sections 5 (relating to relevant "decisions"), 6 (relating to relevant "conduct") and 7 (relating to a relevant "failure to make a decision") accord standing to apply for an "order of review" under the AD(JR) Act in respect of the decision, conduct or failure to decide, to "a person who is aggrieved by" that decision, conduct or failure.[30] Sub-section 3(4) provides that a reference to a "person aggrieved" *includes* a reference to a person whose "interests" are or would be "adversely affected" by the decision, conduct or failure to decide.

Starting from the position that the AD(JR) Act requires something more than that an applicant should sincerely *claim* to be aggrieved or objectively *feel* aggrieved, the Federal Court at first interpreted the statutory criterion as if its terms posed a test indistinguishable from the "special interest" test of the general law. Arguably, it has construed the statutory test of a "person who is aggrieved" more expansively in recent times.[31]

ACF was decided on 13 February 1980. The first reported case on the meaning of "person aggrieved" in the AD(JR) Act was *Tooheys Ltd v Minister for Business and Consumer Affairs*[32] decided on 19 August 1981 by Ellicott J who, as Attorney-General, had introduced the Bill for the Act. His Honour said[33] that "a narrow meaning was not intended" and that although this did not mean that any member of the public was entitled to seek an order of review, the expression at least covered "a person who can show a grievance which will be suffered as a result of the decision complained of beyond that which he or she has as an ordinary member of

---

30. Cf *Administrative Appeals Tribunal Act* 1977 (Cth), ss 27(1), 27A(1) and 31—a person "whose interests are affected" by the decision; *Administrative Law Act* 1978 (Vic), s 2—"person affected, . . . directly or indirectly, to a substantial degree by a decision . . ."; *Administrative Appeals Tribunal Act* 1984 (Vic), s 4(b)—an object of the Act being "to permit a broad range of persons whose interests are affected by a decision to participate in a proceeding"; *Supreme Court Civil Procedure Act* 1932 (Tas), s 75 (12)—standing for certiorari, and s 76(11) standing for prohibition—"any person aggrieved (otherwise than as a member of the public merely)"; *Judicial Review Act* 1991 (Qld), s 20—"a person whose interests are adversely affected by the decision" (see *Friends of Castle Hill Association Inc v Queensland Heritage Council* (1993) 81 LGERA 346, and Nicolee Dixon "The More Things Change, the More They Stay the Same: Standing in the Judicial Review Act 1991 (Qld)" (1994) 15 QL 51); The United States *Administrative Procedure Act*, s 10 (5 USC, para 702)—"adversely affected or aggrieved". And see Kathleen M Mack, "Standing to Sue Under Federal Administrative Law" (1986-1987) 16 FL Rev 319 and M Allars, "Standing: the Role and Evolution of the Test" (1991) 20 FL Rev 83.
31. See M Allars, fn 30, at 101-109.
32. (1981) 54 FLR 421.
33. At 437.

the public". To a similar effect was the Full Court decision in *Ricegrowers Cooperative Mills Ltd v Bannerman*,[34] decided shortly afterwards.

However, it has always been easier to reject limitations as not being required by the expression "a person who is aggrieved" than to describe the expression's boundaries. It has been said that the expression's meaning is "not encased in any technical rules and that much depends upon the nature of the particular decision and the extent to which the interest of the applicant rises above that of an ordinary member of the public".[35] In *United States Tobacco Co v Minister for Consumer Affairs*,[36] the Full Court said in a joint judgment that an applicant must have "an involvement with a case greater than the concern of a person who is a mere intermeddler or busybody", but that the criterion for standing is not restrictive, that "the broadest of technical terms has been selected" and that "the necessary interest need not be a legal, proprietary, financial or other tangible interest" or be peculiar to the particular applicant.

Decisions which have accorded standing have referred to particular factors as supporting that result. Although the nature of an "interest" which may characterise an applicant as a "person aggrieved" cannot be defined, the presence of factors which have contributed to a favourable result for other applicants in past cases are relied on by applicants in later cases, and the absence of particular factors which has defeated applicants in past cases is relied on by respondents in later cases. Although the court has eschewed an approach which would identify certain kinds of interests as qualifying to give standing and others as not doing so, the kinds of interests which have been recognised have covered a wide range. It seems true to say that any kind of interest may qualify, provided it is something more than "a mere intellectual or emotional concern" or "mere belief or concern".

In *Ogle v Strickland*[37] the court accorded standing to two clergymen who wished to apply for an order of review of a decision of the Censorship Board allowing the importation into Australia of a blasphemous film. The respondents conceded that if the clergymen had a "special interest" in the sense in which those words had been used in *ACF* and *Onus*, they qualified as "persons aggrieved". Fisher J attached significance to the fact that "as priests and teachers their interest and their activities are not limited merely to professing the Christian faith" and that their interest "extends beyond that of other members of the Christian community whose limited concern could be fairly described as only 'intellectual or emotional' ".[38]

Lockhart J also founded upon the fact that the applicants were "in holy orders in hierarchical Christian churches" and that "as ministers of religion they are in a special position compared with ordinary members of the public in that it is their duty and vocation to maintain the sanctity of the

---

34. (1981) 56 FLR 443 (FCA FC) at 446-447 per Bowen CJ and Franki J.
35. *Australian Institute of Marine and Power Engineers v Secretary, Department of Transport* (1986) 13 FCR 124 per Gummow J (*AIMPE*) at 133, followed in *Broadbridge v Stammers* (1987) 16 FCR 296 (FC) at 298.
36. (1988) 20 FCR 520 (FC) at 527.
37. (1987) 13 FCR 306 (FC).
38. Both at 308.

Scriptures, to spread the Gospel, to teach and foster Christian beliefs and to repel or oppose blasphemy".[39] His Honour did not find it necessary to decide whether members of the community professing the Christian faith who were not ministers of religion or otherwise part of a hierarchy of a Christian denomination would have had standing.

Wilcox J preferred to allow standing on the basis of the "damage which the [applicants] claim[ed] to sustain as Christians".[40] His Honour referred to the allegation that the film "makes its denials in such a scurrilous and offensive form as to pass the limits of decent controversy and to outrage the feelings of committed Christians".[41] The suggestion is that committed Christians, because of their pre-existing beliefs and consequent sensibilities, are specially susceptible to be detrimentally affected in a way different from the way in which the public generally could be expected to be affected by the same decision. Such a "spiritualised" "special damage" test seems to leave no scope for denying standing to any person who has sufficiently strong beliefs or intellectual or emotional concerns relevant to the subject matter of a decision.

It could be said that in *Ogle v Strickland*, a *vocational* interest was accepted as justifying locus standi. Although the two applicants also shared with Christians generally an "intellectual or emotional concern" with the subject matter of the decision, they were in a special position.

In the last 10 years two factors, in particular, have proved important in establishing standing in cases under the AD(JR) Act. One is that the applicant has had some connection with or involvement in procedures antecedent to the making of the decision impugned, such as that the applicant has been consulted or allowed to make submissions in relation to the decision.[42] Another is that the applicant has been funded or otherwise recognised by government as the representative of a particular public interest involved in the issue to which the impugned decision relates or, more generally, acceptance by the public of the particular interest as one calling for protection and representation and the ability of the particular applicant to represent that interest adequately.[43]

There may be a disconformity between the particular public interest which a statute is designed to serve and the "interest" of the applicant. This was the case in *Alphapharm Pty Ltd v Smithkline Beecham (Australia) Pty Ltd*[44] and *Right to Life Association (NSW) Inc v Secretary, Department of Human Services and Health*.[45] In *Alphapharm* the legislation was

39. Both at 318.
40. At 325.
41. At 324.
42. Cf *AIMPE* at 133; *United States Tobacco Co v Minister for Consumer Affairs* (1988) 20 FCR 520 (FC); *Australian Conservation Foundation v Forestry Commission* (1988) 19 FCR 127 per Burchett J at 131.
43. Cf *Australian Conservation Foundation v Minister for Resources* (1989) 19 ALD 70; 76 LGRA 200 (FCA) per Davies J; *Northcoast Environment Council Inc v Minister for Resources* (1994) 55 FCR 492 per Sackville J; *Tasmanian Conservation Trust Inc v Minister for Resources* (1995) 55 FCR 516 per Sackville J. Cf *Greenpeace*, n 28, at 350-351.
44. (1994) 49 FCR 250 (FC) (*Alphapharm*).
45. (1995) 56 FCR 50 (FC) (*Right to Life*).

concerned with public health and safety, but the applicant's interest was the economic one of a competitor seeking to protect its market share and its profitability by delaying or hindering the introduction of a drug into the market.[46] In *Right to Life*, the interest served by the legislation was again that of public health and safety, but the applicant's interest was the moral and religious one of opposition to abortion.[47]

Several cases have involved decisions which have or may have an indirect impact on a third party's commercial interests or opportunities. It is common that an administrative decision in a commercial context, whether favourable or unfavourable to the commercial entity immediately involved, will have a "ripple effect".[48]

Although not a case under the ADJR Act, *Yates Security Services Pty Ltd v Keating*[49] affords an illustration. The applicant company (Yates), an Australian company, wished to challenge a decision of the Commonwealth Treasurer, the effect of which was that the lease of the Paddy's Market site in Sydney would be able to be assigned by the lessee to a foreign company, notwithstanding the prohibition contained in the *Foreign Acquisitions and Takeovers Act* 1975 (Cth). Yates claimed that if the assignment were prohibited under that Act, Yates and others would be able to negotiate with the existing lessee for the acquisition and development of the site. It was held that Yates did not have the "special interest" in the subject matter of the proceedings required by *ACF* to confer standing. A mere ability to negotiate was not enough.[50] Nor, of course, was a desire that the Paddy's Markets buildings be restored and preserved (the site was listed in the Register of the National Estate kept under the *Australian Heritage Commission Act* 1975 (Cth)). In both respects, Yates was in no different position from other members of the public.

It is important to bear in mind the warning of Gummow J in *AIMPE*, that a person may qualify as a "person aggrieved" by reason of a combination of factors, any one of which alone may not have given that status.[51]

4. REFORM AND PROPOSALS FOR REFORM

In recent years there have been several recommendations by law reform bodies for reform of the law relating to standing.

46. See (1994) 49 FCR at 261 per Davies J, 265 per Burchett J, 280 per Gummow J.
47. See (1995) 56 FCR at 68-69 per Lockhart J and 84-86 per Gummow J; cf *Wall v Livingston* [1982] 1 NZLR 734 (CA) in which a doctor was held not to have standing to seek judicial review of the decision of two specialist consultants to authorise (under a statute) an abortion.
48. The expression derives from Brennan J in *Re McHattan and Collector of Customs (NSW)* (1977) 18 ALR 154 at 157.
49. (1990) 25 FCR 1.
50. Cf *Big Country Developments Pty Ltd v Australian Community Pharmacy Authority* (1995) 60 FCR 85 per Lindgren J.
51. (1986) 13 FCR 124 at 133.

The Law Commission for England and Wales

In March 1976 the Law Commission for England and Wales published its Report on *Remedies in Administrative Law*.[52] While concluding that a liberal test of standing was appropriate, that Commission took the position that any attempt to define in precise terms the nature of the interest required would produce undue rigidity. It therefore recommended a formula which would allow standing requirements to be developed further by the courts having regard to the relief sought. The test was to be a "sufficient interest" in the subject matter of the application.

This recommendation was implemented. An "application for judicial review" was introduced by a new (substituted) Order 53 of the Supreme Court Rules to replace applications for orders of mandamus, prohibition and certiorari, and it was provided that no application for judicial review should be made unless the leave of the court had been obtained. These innovations were accompanied by the express prohibition, now found in Order 53, sub-r 3(7), that "The court shall not grant leave unless it considers that the applicant has a sufficient interest in the matter to which the application relates." Similarly, s 31(3) of the *Supreme Court Act* 1981 (UK) provides as follows:

> "No application for judicial review shall be made unless the leave of the High Court has been obtained in accordance with rules of court; and the court shall not grant leave to make such an application unless it considers that the applicant has a sufficient interest in the matter to which the application relates."

These requirements were judicially considered shortly after the new Order 53 was introduced, in *Inland Revenue Commissioners v National Federation of Self-Employed and Small Businesses Ltd*.[53] As a result of that case and the Court of Appeal decision in *R v Monopolies and Mergers Commission; Ex parte Argyll Group plc*,[54] there has been established a two-stage test of standing which is described in the words of Lord Donaldson MR in the *Monopolies and Mergers Commission* case as follows:

> "The first stage test, which is applied upon the application for leave, will lead to a refusal if the applicant has no interest whatsoever and is, in truth, no more than a meddlesome busybody. If, however, the application appears to be otherwise arguable and there is no other discretionary bar, such as dilatoriness on the part of the applicant, the applicant may expect to get leave to apply, leaving the test of interest or standing to be re-applied as a matter of discretion on the hearing of the substantive application. At this second stage, the strength of the applicant's interest is one of the factors to be weighed in the balance."[55]

52. Law Com No 73, Cmnd 6407, HMSO (1976).
53. [1982] AC 617.
54. [1986] 1 WLR 763 (CA).
55. [1986] 1 WLR at 773H.

Illustrations of the operation of the two-stage test will be found in *R v Department of Transport; Ex parte Presvac Engineering Ltd*,[56] and *Greenpeace*[57] in both of which the second-stage test was described as "discretionary".[58]

The Australian Law Reform Commission

In Australia, on 1 February 1977, the Commonwealth Attorney-General referred to the Law Reform Commission the task of reviewing and reporting upon the adequacy of the existing law relating to, inter alia, the standing of persons to sue in federal and other courts while exercising federal jurisdiction or in courts exercising jurisdiction under the law of any Territory.[59] In 1977, the Law Commission published a working paper and a discussion paper on the subject.[60]

Ultimately, the Commission produced its report in 1985, *Standing in Public Interest Litigation*.[61]

Notwithstanding the liberalisation of standing tests under the general law which had occurred in Australia, the Commission recommended legislative extension of this trend to apply to the following classes of proceedings in courts defined by reference to the constitutional limitations of the Commonwealth Parliament:

"• proceedings in any court for a declaration, an injunction, or a writ of certiorari, prohibition, mandamus, or habeas corpus, or an information of quo warranto in respect of a matter—

— arising under the Constitution, or involving its interpretation;

— arising under Commonwealth or Territory statutes (other than those of Northern Territory and Norfolk Island); or

— against the Commonwealth or Commonwealth officers;

• proceedings in any court other than a court exercising jurisdiction under Northern Territory or Norfolk Island law for—

— an injunction; or

— a declaration,

if the Attorney-General could have commenced the proceeding in his own name; and

• proceedings for relief under certain specified Commonwealth Acts and ACT ordinances."[62]

The Commission did not recommend that standing rules be relaxed to the extent of permitting "any person" to commence proceedings. The

56. TLR 4 April 1989 per Purchas LJ (*Presvac Engineering*).
57. fn 28, above.
58. [1994] 4 All ER at 349g, h.
59. The question of "class actions" was also referred to the ALRC as part of the same reference.
60. *Access to Courts—I Standing: Public Interest Suits* 1977 (ALRC DP4); *Access to Courts—I Standing: Public Interest Suits* 1977 (ALRC WP7).
61. ALRC 27, 1985.
62. Ibid at para 2, p xxvii.

recommendation was that in lieu of the existing general law rules which determine standing, which would be abolished in relation to a proceeding to which the legislation would apply, every person be given standing to commence and maintain such a proceeding unless the court, *on application*, found that the plaintiff was "merely meddling". A copy of cl 8 of the Bill which was annexed to the Commission's report is annexure "A" to this essay. At para 13 of the "summary" of the report, this appears:

"13 *An 'Open Door', but with a 'Pest Screen'*. The laws of standing in public interest litigation should be broadened and unified. Of the range of the suggested tests examined, the conclusion is that any person should have standing to commence public interest litigation within the range outlined above, unless it can be shown that, by doing so, the person is 'merely meddling'. This criterion should be elaborated in the following respects:

- *Personal stake*. A personal stake in the subject-matter or outcome of the proceedings should be a *sufficient*, but not a *necessary*, condition of standing.

- Ability to represent the public interest. Standing should be denied to a plaintiff who has no personal stake in the subject-matter of the litigation *and* who clearly cannot represent the public interest adequately.

- Presumption of standing. There should be a presumption that the plaintiff has standing *unless* the court is satisfied that a person is 'merely meddling'.

- Application generally needed. The court should not deny standing unless one of the parties makes an application to dismiss the case for lack of standing. However, where the plaintiff has no personal stake in the subject-matter of the litigation, such an application should not be necessary if the court finds that the plaintiff clearly cannot conduct the case adequately.

- Standing normally not a preliminary matter. The question of standing should not be determined as a preliminary or interlocutory matter unless the court considers it desirable to do so for special reasons in the particular circumstances of the case. The normal approach should be to reserve standing for determination along with the merits." [63]

In 1994, the Access to Justice Advisory Committee, appointed by the Commonwealth Attorney-General and the Minister for Justice, in its Report *Access to Justice: An Action Plan*, remarked on the fact that the recommendations had not been implemented and added that the Commission's recommendations appeared to the Committee to be "sound, with a sensible balance between protecting the courts from wasting time with baseless actions while allowing individuals and groups with a real interest in a matter to be heard by the courts". [64]

63. Ibid at para 13, pp xxi-xxii.
64. At para 2.103, p 59.

On 17 May 1995, the Attorney-General, the Honourable Michael Lavarch MP, referred to the Commission for inquiry and report, the following matters:

> "(a) what changes, if any, should be made to the recommendations and draft legislation contained in the ALRC 1985 Report on *Standing in Public Interest Litigation* in the light of subsequent developments in law and practice and recent and proposed reforms to court and tribunal rules and procedures;
>
> (b) whether, in the light of developments since 1985, any further general changes are now required to present law and practice in relation to the capacity and right of persons to be heard in courts and tribunals exercising federal jurisdiction; and
>
> (c) any related matters."

The terms of reference require the Commission to make a final report not later than 29 February 1996. In October 1995, the Commission issued Discussion Paper 61 entitled "Who Can Sue? A Review of the Law of Standing". (See Postscript to this chapter.)

The Law Reform Commission of British Columbia

In 1980, the Law Reform Commission of British Columbia published its *Report on Civil Litigation in the Public Interest.*[65] It recommended that any person have standing to seek relief in respect of an actual or apprehended infringement of a public right or liberty subject to two qualifications. The first is that the person must first request the Attorney-General to take action. The second is that, even if the Attorney-General refuses or fails to do so, the person may bring the proceedings in his own name only after obtaining the court's consent. The Commission expressed the view, however, that consent should be given unless it is shown that there is no justiciable issue to be tried. Annexed to this essay and marked "B" is a copy of the Commission's "Principal Recommendation" of its "Suggested Scheme for Reform", including relevant provisions of draft legislation recommended.

The JUSTICE—All Souls Committee in The United Kingdom

In the United Kingdom, the JUSTICE-All Souls Committee dealt with "Standing" in Ch 8 of its report, *Administrative Justice—Some Necessary Reforms*, published in 1988.[66] The Committee was established by JUSTICE and All Souls College, Oxford in 1978 with a distinguished membership of persons having a practical knowledge of administrative law.

Unlike the Australian Law Reform Commission, the JUSTICE-All Souls Committee did not accept that a screening of "mere meddlers" should occur by reference to their ability adequately to present the case. The

---

65. LRC 46, 1980.
66. Oxford; Clarendon Press, 1988.

Committee suggested that the extent of that ability might not be clear at an early stage. It also observed that there are plaintiffs with an undoubted personal stake in litigation who do not adequately present cases. The first two of the four recommendations in Ch 8 of the report (recommendations 3 and 4 were not of such general import) were as follows:

"1. The law in connection with relator actions should be changed. The requirement to obtain the fiat of the Attorney-General in a 'public interest' suit should be dropped. The decision to accord standing should be taken by the court. The judge should have regard to the whole circumstances of the case and ask himself whether the action is justifiable in the public interest in the light of these circumstances.

2. Relevant factors for the court to take into account should be:

(a) the importance of the legal point;

(b) the plaintiff's links with the subject matter of the case;

(c) the chances of the issue being raised in any other proceeding;

(d) the extent to which there is public interest or support for the issue being raised." [67]

These "factors" overlap those which have been taken into account by the Federal Court of Australia in its application of the "person aggrieved" test imposed by the AD(JR) Act.

The Ontario Law Reform Commission

In 1989 the Ontario Law Reform Commission published its *Report on the Law of Standing*. It recommended legislative reform by the introduction of an *Access to Courts Act*. Annexure "C" to this essay is a copy of its "Summary of Recommendations" as taken from the "Executive Summary" of its Report. In the "Executive Summary" which accompanied the Report, the Commission said that under the proposed Act, "the basic rule" would be that "every person should be entitled to commence and maintain a legal proceeding unless a person challenging such a right satisfies the court that the factors against proceeding outweigh the factors in favour of proceeding". [68]

5. GENERAL

Standing, justiciability, ripeness

The notions of standing, justiciability and "ripeness", referred to earlier, are closely interrelated. [69]

67. At 208.
68. At 2.
69. The interrelationship between standing and justiciability has been most recently remarked upon by Gummow J in *Right to Life* at 84, where his Honour notes passages in the judgments in *ACF* and *Onus* which also refer to it.

In a recent case lying outside the public law area, *Scandrett v Dowling*, (the *Ordination of Women* case), [70] the principle that a breach of a consensual arrangement intended to be binding only "in honour" or "in conscience" does not give rise to a cause of action was referred to as a principle that such a breach does not give rise to a "justiciable issue".

An interesting question on the relationship between standing and justiciability arose in *Right to Life*. At first instance the trial judge determined three questions which he had, at the parties' request, ordered to be decided separately from any other question in the proceedings. Those of present interest are firstly, whether the applicant-association (Right to Life), was a "person aggrieved" within the meaning of the AD(JR) Act and, secondly, whether there was a "decision" by the first respondent within the meaning of s 5 of that Act. His Honour answered the first question "No" [71] and, in a separate judgment delivered subsequently, [72] answered the second question "Yes". His Honour so answered the second question after referring to various matters which would suggest a negative answer to it, and said this:

"Notwithstanding the matters to which I have just referred, question two must be approached on the hypothesis that on a final hearing it is established that . . . the applicant is a 'person aggrieved' for the purpose of s 5 of the AD(JR) Act. Once this approach to question two is taken, that question becomes a narrow one and much of the difficulty touching it disappears." [73]

On appeal, [74] Lockhart and Beaumont JJ agreed with the primary judge's answers to the questions. However, Gummow J, while noting that "the substance of the matter is that the appellant has failed to overturn the order of the primary judge that the application be dismissed", [75] approached the questions differently. His Honour said that the two questions were closely intertwined and that he would have dealt with the question of standing only if he had first concluded that there was a justiciable decision. Gummow J would have answered that question in the negative and then found it unnecessary to answer the question as to standing.

The question whether the issue of standing or that of justiciability should be decided first is clearly an important one which does not seem to have been explored.

"Ripeness" is frequently referred to in the United States. [76] *Presbytery of New Jersey of the Orthodox Presbyterian Church v Florio* [77] affords a recent illustration. Because ripeness is not a notion familiar to Australian lawyers, I will give a somewhat detailed account of the case.

70. (1992) 27 NSWLR 483 (CA).
71. (1994) 52 FCR 209.
72. (1994) 35 ALD 264.
73. At 268.
74. (1995) 56 FCR 50.
75. Ibid at 91.
76. The United States cases must be read by reference to the requirement of Art III s 2 of the Constitution which restricts federal jurisdiction to "cases" and "controversies".
77. 40 F 3d 1454 (3rd Cir 1994).

The plaintiffs were the Orthodox Presbyterian Church (OPC), a national denomination with 170 member churches, and one of its pastors. They sought against the Governor of New Jersey and other public office-holders a declaration that amendments to the New Jersey Law Against Discrimination (LAD) violated their First Amendment right to freedom of speech.

The LAD was enacted in 1945. It prohibited discrimination in employment, labour organisation membership, public accommodation, and real estate, financial and business transactions. In 1991 the New Jersey legislature added "affectional or sexual orientation" to the personal characteristics of race, creed, colour, national origin, ancestry, age, sex and marital status previously protected. The Act made it unlawful for an employer "to refuse to hire or employ or to bar or to discharge or require to retire" any individual on the basis of a "protected characteristic". It also prohibited the printing or circulating of any statement expressing, directly or indirectly, that employment opportunities for persons with the protected characteristics would be limited. The LAD also made it illegal "to aid, abet, incite, compel or coerce the doing of any of the acts forbidden under [the Act] or to attempt to do so". It exempted religious organisations from compliance in the selection of their own employees and permitted them to restrict rental or use of their own property to members of their own faith.

The State could enforce the Act's civil penalties against violators. As well, an aggrieved individual might begin the process of civil enforcement by filing a complaint with the State Division on Civil Rights or by proceeding directly in the State court. The Act expressly granted standing to sue to "any individual who has been discriminated against" and "any organisation which represents or acts to further the interests of individuals who have been discriminated against". A successful plaintiff might recover compensatory and punitive damages, fines and attorney fees. The Act provided that it was to be liberally construed to accomplish its purpose of eradicating the kinds of discrimination prohibited.

The OPC taught that homosexuality, bisexuality and heterosexual sex outside of marriage are grievous sins. The plaintiffs alleged that they had always spoken and preached against homosexuality, adultery and fornication and printed and disseminated materials condemning sexual sins, and had continued to do so since the amendments.

On 16 November 1994 the United States Court of Appeals for the Third Circuit decided (unanimously) that the controversy was not "ripe" with respect to the Church since the State had no intention to prosecute the Church but, (by majority) that the controversy was ripe with respect to the pastor himself because the complaint fairly asserted his rights both as a minister *and as a citizen*, and the State refused to offer an assurance that it would not prosecute him if he spoke out against homosexual acts outside his church, that is to say, as a citizen.

The majority opinion contains the following useful discussion of the distinction between "standing" and "ripeness" (references to authorities are generally omitted):

"[6, 7] Federal courts may only resolve actual 'cases' and 'controversies'. *See* US Const art III §2. The existence of a case and controversy is a prerequisite to all federal actions, including those for declaratory or injunctive relief. . . . 'Concerns of justiciability go to the power of the federal courts to entertain disputes, and to the wisdom of their doing so. We presume that federal courts lack jurisdiction "unless 'the contrary appears affirmatively from the record.' " ' . . .

[8, 9] The concepts of standing and ripeness are related. Each is a component of the Constitution's limitation of the judicial power to real cases and controversies. Correct analysis in terms of ripeness tells us when a proper party may bring an action and analysis in terms of standing tells us who may bring the action. . . . ('standing focuses on whether the type of injury alleged is qualitatively sufficient to fulfill the requirements of Article III and whether the plaintiff has personally suffered that harm, whereas ripeness centers on whether that injury has occurred yet'). Because these concepts are so closely related, they can be confused or conflated. 'It is sometimes argued that standing is about *who* can sue while ripeness is about *when* they can sue, though it is of course true that if no injury has occurred, the plaintiff can be told either that *she* cannot sue, or that she cannot sue *yet*.' . . . It is the plaintiff's responsibility to allege facts that invoke the court's jurisdiction. . . .

[10, 11] The district court did not reach the issue of standing but focused on whether any of the plaintiffs presented a ripe controversy. Ripeness prevents courts from 'entangling themselves in abstract disagreements.' . . . '[R]uling on federal constitutional matters in advance of the necessity of deciding them [is to be avoided].' The ripeness determination 'evaluate[s] both the fitness of the issues for judicial decision and the hardship to the parties of withholding court consideration.' Ultimately, the case must involve ' "a real and substantial controversy admitting of specific relief through a decree of a conclusive character, as distinguished from an opinion advising what the law would be upon a hypothetical state of facts." ' . . . 'A federal court's jurisdiction therefore can be invoked only when the plaintiff himself has suffered "some threatened or actual injury resulting from the putatively illegal action. . . ." ' . . .

[12] As Professor Chemerinsky recognises, '[r]ipeness properly should be understood as involving the question of *when may a party seek preenforcement review of a statute or regulation*.' Thus, it is not surprising that the ripeness inquiry often involves declaratory actions which present special problems. . . . ('Basically, the question in each case is whether the facts alleged, under all the circumstances, show that there is a substantial controversy, between parties having adverse legal interests, of sufficient immediacy and reality to warrant the issuance of a declaratory judgment.').''[78]

In Australia the question whether a particular party would be entitled to challenge the constitutional validity of State legislation would, it seems, be resolved in terms of "standing".

---

78. Ibid at 1462-63.

But standing is not superseded by the concepts of justiciability and ripeness in the United States, as the recent decision of the United States Supreme Court in *United States v Hays*[79] (decided on 29 June 1995) shows. The case may, however, mark a new point of departure for the "standing of standing" in the United States.

The respondents (appellees) claimed that Louisiana's congressional redistricting plan was a racial gerrymander which violated the Fourteenth Amendment's Equal Protection Clause. Their claim's primary focus was District Four, but they themselves lived in District Five. The United States District Court for the Western District of Louisiana invalidated the plan but the Supreme Court held that the respondents had lacked standing to challenge it.

The opinion of the court was delivered by Justice O'Connor. It includes the following passage:

"The question of standing is not subject to waiver, however: 'we are required to address the issue even if the courts below have not passed on it, and even if the parties fail to raise the issue before us. The federal courts are under an independent obligation to examine their own jurisdiction, and standing "is perhaps the most important of [the jurisdictional] doctrines." ' *FW/PBS, Inc v Dallas*, 493 US 215, 230-231 (1990) (citations omitted).

It is by now well settled that 'the irreducible constitutional minimum of standing contains three elements. First, the plaintiff must have suffered "an injury in fact"—an invasion of a legally protected interest which is (a) concrete and particularized, and (b) actual or imminent, not conjectural or hypothetical. Second, there must be a causal connection between the injury and the conduct complained of. . . . Third, it must be likely, as opposed to merely speculative, that the injury will be redressed by a favourable decision.' *Lujan v Defenders of Wildlife*, 504 US 555, 560-561 (1992) (footnote, citations and internal quotation marks omitted); see also, for example, *Allen v Wright*, 468 US 737, 751 (1984); *Valley Forge Christian College v Americans United for Separation of Church and State, Inc*, 454 US 464, 472 (1982). In light of these principles, we have repeatedly refused to recognize a generalised grievance against allegedly illegal governmental conduct as sufficient for standing to invoke the federal judicial power. See, eg, *Valley Forge Christian College*, supra; *Schlesinger v Reservists Comm to Stop the War*, 418 US 208 (1974); *United States v Richardson*, 418 US 166 (1974); *Ex parte Levitt*, 302 US 633 (1937) per curiam). We have also made clear that it 'is the burden of the party who seeks the exercise of jurisdiction in his favor,' *McNutt v General Motors Acceptance Corp*, 298 US 178, 189 (1936), 'clearly to allege facts demonstrating that he is a proper party to invoke judicial resolution of the dispute.' *Warth v Seldin*, 422 US 490, 518 (1975). *FW/PBS*, supra, at 231. And when a case has proceeded to final judgment after a trial, as this case has, 'those facts (if controverted) must be 'supported adequately by the evidence adduced

79. (1995) 132 L Ed 2d 635.

at trial' to avoid dismissal on standing grounds. *Lujan*,supra, at 561 (quoting *Gladstone, Realtors v Village of Bellwood*, 441 US 91, 115, n 31 (1979))."[80]

As would be said in Australia, a general interest in seeing that electoral laws are observed does not give standing to persons not part of the particular electorate since those persons are not affected in any way differently from members of the community generally.

In the case of statutory jurisdictions such as that conferred by the AD(JR) Act, the statutory prescription of the circumstances entitling a person to apply for relief supplants, for the purpose of the statute, the general law notion of justiciability. In the case of the AD(JR) Act, a justiciable decision is a "decision of an administrative character . . . under an enactment". This may suggest that such "statutory justiciability" is to be decided simply by a process of statutory construction. But in fact the general law notion of justiciability can influence that process.

Determination of standing as a preliminary question

A court has a procedural discretion as to the stage of proceedings at which an objection to standing will be determined[81] and like any judicial discretion, this one should not be circumscribed. Yet it is often said to be desirable as a general practice that standing be determined, not as a preliminary matter, but as part of the decision at the end of the hearing when all the evidence is in.[82] But this is not necessarily so. The course to be followed must be determined in the context of the facts of each case. If one can be assured that all relevant facts on standing are agreed or found at the preliminary stage, substantial savings in costs and time for both the parties and the court can be achieved if the standing question is decided first.[83] However, a court must be careful not to fall in too readily with a party's request for a preliminary determination of the issue and must ensure that that course is appropriate.

Standing and discretion

Is standing properly characterised as a matter of judicial discretion? The range of matters potentially relevant to a determination of standing may suggest so. If standing is a matter of discretion, the strength or weakness of the substantive case might be relevant. In *Inland Revenue Commissioners v National Federation of Self-Employed and Small Businesses Ltd*[84] Lord Diplock said of the requirement of Order 53 of the

80. Ibid at 642.
81. *Robinson v Western Australian Museum* (1977) 138 CLR 283 at 302-303 (Gibbs J).
82. Cf *Inland Revenue Commissioners v National Federation of Self-Employed and Small Business Ltd* [1982] AC 617 at 630 per Lord Wilberforce; 636 per Lord Diplock; *Onus*, above at 38 per Gibbs CJ; *Central Queensland Speleological Society Inc v Central Queensland Cement Pty Ltd (No 1)* [1989] 2 Qd R 512 (Qld FC) at 523-525 (Thomas J diss); ALRC No 27 at para 13, p xxii and at paras 261, 262 at pp 141-143; and see Allars, op cit, fn 25 at 89-91.
83. *Central Queensland Speleological Society Inc v Central Queensland Cement Pty Ltd* [1989] 2 Qd R 512 (Qld FC at 530-531 per Derrington J, 535 per de Jersey J.
84. [1982] AC 617 (HL).

Supreme Court Rules that leave to apply for judicial review be not granted unless the court was satisfied that the applicant had a "sufficient interest in the matter to which the application relates", that it did not "remove the whole—and vitally important—question of locus standi into the realm of pure discretion". [85]

Standing under the AD(JR) Act has been described as a mixed question of law and fact. [86] On this view, the boundaries of relevant evidence would be more narrow than if standing was discretionary, yet the broadness of the notion of the "interest" required for standing renders many facts and circumstances relevant to it and may render a decision of a first instance judge on the issue difficult to reverse. [87]

A "touchstone" case

Many of the issues referred to above may be usefully considered in the context of the facts of a particular case, *Stanbridge v Minister for Defence*. [88]

Mr Stanbridge applied under s 5(1) of the AD(JR) Act for review of a decision of the Minister for Defence to have a large number of military weapons melted down. He also joined as a respondent, the "board of directors of BHP (Broken Hill Proprietary) for 1994/5". Mr Stanbridge put material, including newspaper reports, before the court that indicated that BHP had been engaged to carry out the melting down task. Drummond J set down for determination as a preliminary question whether Mr Stanbridge was an "aggrieved person" for the purposes of the AD(JR) Act. The factual background is adequately encapsulated in the following passage from his Honour's judgment:

> "His [Mr Stanbridge's] concerns centre on the decision by the Minister to have a large quantity of what he says are perfectly serviceable weapons melted down when the Australian military now has to rely on what he submits is an inferior basic weapon. He fears that this decision will encourage the invasion of this country. He has identified many other concerns he has which he says are associated with these two core considerations. I accept that he has gone to much trouble and effort to inform himself about the decision, the background to it and what he identifies as the consequences of it. He has no doubt taken a much greater interest personally in the matter than most other Australian citizens." [89]

85. Ibid at 631c.
86. *Tooheys Ltd v Minister for Business and Consumer Affairs* (1981) 36 ALR 64 (FCA) per Ellicott J at 79.
87. Cf the discussion of whether a decision that a contract is "unjust" under the *Contracts Review Act* 1980 (NSW) is a discretionary decision in *Antonovic v Volker* (1986) 7 NSWLR 161 (CA) and *Beneficial Finance Corporation Ltd v Karavas* (1991) 23 NSWLR 256 (CA).
88. Unreported, Federal Court of Australia, Drummond J, 18 May 1995.
89. Judgment transcript, at 2.

Drummond J applied the ruling of the Full Court in *Broadbridge v Stammers*[90] in which the Full Court approved and found satisfied[91] Gummow J's criterion in *AIMPE* that before a person can be an "aggrieved person" there must flow from the decision challenged, a clear and imminent rather than remote, indirect or fanciful danger and peril to the person's interests, and further that the person must be able to show that that interest is of an intensity and degree well above that of an ordinary member of the public. Drummond J concluded that although Mr Stanbridge was much more concerned personally about the Minister's decision than were other Australian citizens, he had no "interest" beyond theirs and was therefore not entitled to invoke the court's jurisdiction, adding:

> "His concerns are not matters which the law permits him to raise in the courts. They are concerns that can only be ventilated in the political forums, and in the forum of public discussion provided by the media, to both of which I understand Mr Stanbridge has already had recourse."[92]

Could Mr Stanbridge's application have been dismissed at the preliminary stage on the basis that the Minister's decision was not justiciable, or rather, in the context of the AD(JR) Act, that it was not a "decision of an administrative character under an enactment"? Alternatively, could his application have been dismissed at the preliminary stage on the basis that his case lacked "ripeness" in that there was no immediate threat of harm to anyone? If the answer to either of these questions is "yes", would it have been desirable that it be dealt with on such a basis rather than as a question of standing? Was it desirable that Mr Stanbridge's application be subject to any kind of preliminary "screening" at all rather than be allowed to run its full course?

I suggest that the answer to the last question, at least, is "yes". Drummond J's course of doing so no doubt saved considerable time and cost to both parties.

Standing for all?—the actio popularis ("the citizen's action")[93]

Should every citizen have standing to challenge legislative or administrative action which exceeds the bounds of power accorded to legislative and administrative bodies? This question may be answered differently according to one's concept of the role of courts. If one assumes that the courts exist to constrain the legislature and the executive within their lawful bounds, the answer suggests itself that any citizen should have standing. But the notion that the courts exist primarily to enforce and protect private rights has to date characterised thinking in the public law area.

90. (1987) 16 FCR 296.
91. At 298.
92. Judgment transcript, at 6.
93. On the comparative advantages and disadvantages of an "open system" and a "more closed system" see Sir Konrad Schiemann, "Locus Standi" [1990] PL 342 at 346-349.

In recent years, the recommendations of law reform bodies and judicial requirements for standing have tended in the one direction: liberalisation.[94] Has the requirement of locus standi ceased to perform any purpose which would not be better served by requirements of justiciability and ripeness? If an issue is justiciable and there is an actual or imminent threat of infringement of public rights or liberty, why should any individual or organisation who is sufficiently concerned about the matter be denied the opportunity to vindicate that right or privilege, provided only that the individual or organisation has the capacity to do so adequately? Would an "opening of the gates" prove to be an "opening of the floodgates"?

How many, and what proportion of, cases in which standing is denied might be described as "vexatious" or "frivolous"? Anecdotal evidence is that there are few such cases under the AD(JR) Act, and that *Stanbridge v Minister for Defence*, noted earlier, is exceptional.

It should not be thought that in all cases in which an objection to competency is successful, the commencement of the proceedings was vexatious or frivolous: like substantive issues, a question of standing can be finely balanced. Moreover, at different times and in different factual contexts, applications for judicial review may be perceived differently in terms of their seriousness. The "interests" of environmental protection organisations and other public interest groups are more readily recognised as valid and serious today than they were even 50 years ago. In time of war, even the grievance advanced by Mr Stanbridge might be at least perceived in a different light, even if again without a determination that he had standing.

Constitutional cases

It has been suggested that a more restrictive approach to standing is warranted in the area of constitutional litigation.[95] As Burmester observes:

"Locus standi is closely linked to the role of the courts in our society. Thus, the perceived role for judicial review in interpretation of the constitution will inevitably be reflected in the view taken on the standing required of a party seeking to raise a constitutional issue. As Professor Allan recently said: [T R S Allan, 'Pragmatism and Theory in Public Law' (1988) 104 LQR 422 at 423.];

'Constitutional theory . . . cannot escape from an explicit choice of political values, and in the definition and protection of those values lies the only path to rational and legitimate review.'

An expansive view of the role of the courts will normally be accompanied by a broad view of who has sufficient standing to raise

94. For accounts of the trend see, G D S Taylor, "Individual Standing and the Public Interest: Australian Developments" [1983] Civil Justice Quarterly 353; F G Brennan, "The Purpose and Scope of Judicial Review" (1986) 2 Aust Bar Rev 93 at 100; P D Lane, "Standing to Sue for Declaration and Injunction in the Public Interest" (1988) 18 Q Law Soc J 115; Andrew S Bell, "Trade Rivals: Standing to Sue—A Survey of Some Recent Cases" (1992) 9 Aust Bar Rev 67.
95. Cf Henry Burmester, "Locus Standi in Constitutional Litigation" in H P Lee and George Winterton (eds), *Australian Constitutional Perspectives* (Law Book Co, 1992), Ch 6.

a constitutional issue. By contrast, a restrained view of the judicial role in constitutional interpretation is likely to be content with more restrictive rules of standing."[96]

Whether the tests for standing in public interest litigation which, as noted earlier, have been liberalised in recent years, are appropriate for constitutional cases, is an issue which the High Court has not yet clearly addressed. In *Davis v Commonwealth*,[97] Brennan J seems to have assumed this to be so.[98] In that case the High Court did not take the opportunity of dealing with the standing of taxpayers, although the judgment leaves open the possibility that in future cases a taxpayer will be accorded standing. The High Court has readily recognised that the States have standing to challenge the constitutionality of exercises of Commonwealth power. In the United States, however, the Constitution is seen as granting and limiting the power of government over *the people*, and the States are not seen as occupying a position different from that of individuals and so are subject to the same restrictions on standing.

If emphasis is given to the primacy of the political process and the subsidiary role of the judiciary, one will be more ready to insist upon a more stringent test of standing.

6. CONCLUSION

The following observations of Schwartz, writing in 1991 of the position in the United States of America, are applicable to Australia:

"No aspect of administrative law has been changing more rapidly than the law governing standing. The courts have come to recognise that standing requirements should not be barriers to justice. In consequence, standing barriers have been substantially lowered in recent years. The restricted conception of standing that used to prevail has given way during the past two decades to an ever-broadening concept that has increasingly opened the courts to challenges against administrative action."[99]

It is in the nature of many public rights and liberties that individual members of the public will have no more than a mere "intellectual or emotional concern" or a "mere belief or concern" that they be respected. Environmental protection and conservation organisations, churches and religious denominations, femininist groups, animal protection societies and political parties come to mind. Members of such groups, bound by a sharing of certain beliefs or ideals, can be expected to feel keenly about certain classes of administrative decisions. The very fact that many like minded persons associate themselves together in a structured organisation invites a different perception of them from that which can be expected by an isolated complainant.

96. Ibid 148.
97. (1988) 166 CLR 79.
98. Ibid at 105.
99. Schwartz, *Administrative Law* (3rd ed, 1991) para 8.12, p 496.

It is, however, easy to say that if organised groups of that kind or their individual members are not accorded standing, infringement of public rights and liberties will go unremedied, and that for this reason standing should be accorded, provided only perhaps that the proposed plaintiff or applicant is able satisfactorily to "represent" or safeguard the public interest in question. That line of reasoning assumes that the Attorney-General, either ex officio or ex relatione, will not protect those interests. It is therefore a question of prime importance whether reform is not more appropriately directed *in the first instance* to improving the mechanism of the relator action rather than to widening locus standi independently of the Attorney-General.

POSTSCRIPT

After the foregoing chapter reached the stage of galley proofs, the Australian Law Reform Commission issued its report "Beyond the doorkeeper — Standing to sue for public remedies".[100] The report makes 19 recommendations. Space permits only a summary account of the report's recommendations. The recommended "New test for standing" is stated as follows in Appendix F to the report:

"Recommendation 1 — standing reforms to apply to public law proceedings

Reforms to the law of standing should apply to

- proceedings to obtain a remedy under the *Administrative Decisions (Judicial Review) Act* 1977 (Cth)
- proceedings for an injunction or declaration where
  - the Attorney-General could have commenced the proceedings in his or her own name or
  - rights, duties or powers created by or under an enactment are in dispute
- proceedings for prerogative relief (such as certiorari, prohibition, mandamus, habeas corpus or quo warranto)
- proceedings to obtain a statutory remedy which is similar in function to any of the foregoing remedies

where the proceedings relate to a matter arising under the Constitution (or involving its interpretation) or federal legislation or are against the Commonwealth or a person acting on its behalf.

Recommendation 2—any person should be able to commence public law proceedings

Any person should be able to commence and maintain public law proceedings unless

- the relevant legislation clearly indicates an intention that the decision or conduct sought to be litigated should not be the subject of challenge by a person such as the applicant; or

100. ALRC 78, 1996.

- in all the circumstances it whould not be in the public interest to proceed because to do so would unreasonably interfere with the ability of a person having a private interest in the matter to deal with it differently or not at all.

Recommendation 3—standing to be determined as a preliminary issue

As a general rule, any issue as to standing should be resolved as a preliminary or interlocutory matter."

Other recommendations deal sympathetically with the granting of leave to a person to participate in public law proceedings and favour the implementation of the recommended new rules for standing and for intervention by the enactment of "a Commonwealth standing statute".

ANNEXURE "A"

Standing to bring proceedings

8. (1) In relation to a proceeding to which this Act applies, the principles and rules of the common law and of equity the operation of which determines the standing of the plaintiff to bring the proceeding are abolished.

(2) Subject to the succeeding provisions of this section, every person has standing to commence and maintain a proceeding to which this Act applies unless the court, on application finds that, by commencing and maintaining the proceeding, the plaintiff is merely meddling.

(3) The plaintiff shall not be taken to be so meddling by reason only that—

(a) the plaintiff does not have a proprietary interest, a material interest, a financial interest or a special interest in the subject-matter of the proceeding; or

(b) the interest of the plaintiff in the subject-matter of the proceeding is no different from the interest of any other person in that subject-matter.

(4) In a proceeding concerning the performance or purported performance of duty, or the exercise or purported exercise of a power or function, that is imposed or conferred for the benefit of a person or persons other than the plaintiff, the court shall, in determining whether the plaintiff is so meddling, take into account, to the extent that it is practicable to do so, the wishes and interests of the person or persons in relation to the proceeding.

(5) Without limiting the operation of sub-section (4), where the plaintiff does not have a proprietary interest, a material interest, a financial interest or a special interest in the subject-matter of the proceeding, then, in determining whether the plaintiff is so meddling, the courts shall take into account the question whether the plaintiff is able to conduct the proceeding as plaintiff adequately and, if the court finds that—

(a) the plaintiff is manifestly unable to conduct the proceeding as plaintiff adequately; and

(b) because of that inability, the conduct of the proceeding by the plaintiff would, or could reasonably be expected to, cause or result in harm to a person's interest (of whatever kind) in the subject-matter of the proceeding,

the court shall find that the plaintiff is so meddling, whether or not an application as to the plaintiff's standing has been made.

(6) The question whether the plaintiff has standing to commence and maintain a proceeding shall not be determined as a preliminary or interlocutory matter in the proceeding unless—

(a) a preliminary or interlocutory application as to the plaintiff's standing has been made; and

(b) the court is satisfied, in the circumstances, that it is proper to determine the question of the plaintiff's standing as a preliminary or interlocutory matter.

(7) Where, in relation to a proceeding to which this Act applies, an enactment provides that an act is to be or may be done by a specified person for the purposes of conducting the proceeding as plaintiff, the act may, if the proceeding is commenced under this Act by some other person, be done by that last-mentioned person instead of the person so specified.

(8) The preceding provisions of this section do not limit any discretion that the court has to refuse relief, but the court shall not refuse relief by reason only that—

(a) the plaintiff does not have a proprietary interest, a material interest, a financial interest or a special interest in the subject-matter of the proceeding; or

(b) the interest of the plaintiff in the subject-matter of the proceeding is no different from the interest of any other person in that subject-matter.

ANNEXURE "B"

1. Principal recommendation

We support the general proposition that any member of the public should have the status to bring proceedings in respect of an actual or apprehended violation of a public right, whether it be an infraction of a statute, a public body exceeding its power or a public nuisance. We do not believe that the right to bring such proceedings should remain within the Attorney-General's exclusive jurisdiction. We do not mean to suggest, however, that the Attorney-General is never the appropriate plaintiff in such cases. We believe it desirable that the Attorney-General should continue to have an opportunity to participate and exercise some degree of control over public interest suits. He may wish to participate for a number of reasons. For example, he may have doubts as to the competence of the person to conduct the proceeding, or that the case is one which would benefit from having the full resources of his ministry behind it. At the same time he may not wish, for a variety of reasons, to be involved in the proceeding at all. As a result of our recommendation, his decision not to participate will not give rise to any suggestion that this decision has prevented an otherwise meritorious case being brought before the courts.

We suggest that where a person wishes to maintain an action in respect of an alleged interference with the public right, and such an action is one which at present can only be brought in the name of the Attorney-General, either ex officio or in a relator action, that person should serve an application on the Attorney-General, together with a copy of the proposed originating process. On receipt of this application, the Attorney-General should have the option either to commence and conduct the action himself or consent to the use of his name in a relator action. Thus, up to this stage, we would not be recommending any change to the present practice and procedure.

We take the view, however, that if the Attorney-General should refuse or neglect to take any action within a specified time, the person who served the application upon him should have the right to seek the consent of the court to commence the action in his own name.

We would suggest that to avoid any undue delay, the Attorney-General should be allowed 10 days from service to make a decision as to whether or not he wants to be associated with the action. This would, to our mind, give the Attorney-General and his staff adequate time to reach a decision. At present, for example, only six days notice is required to be given to the Attorney-General where the constitutional validity of a statute is going to be argued in a proceeding.

We recommend that if the Attorney-General does not notify the person who applied of his decision within a period of ten days, that person should be permitted, after obtaining the consent of the court, to commence and conduct the proceedings in his own name.

Furthermore, we believe that such consent should be given automatically unless the court considers there is not a justiciable issue to be tried. To us, a requirement that the consent of the court be obtained is desirable for a number of reasons. For example, notice of any application for such leave should be required to be served upon the Attorney-General and the proposed defendant. They would then have an opportunity to speak against the application and to show that there is not a justiciable issue to be tried. While in any action it is always open to a defendant to make such an attack, our recommendation would ensure that this issue was decided before proceedings commenced, saving both time and expense.

An issue is justiciable if it raises a question that may properly come before a court and which is appropriate for decision. For example, the courts have declined to entertain actions based by hypothetical questions or to give advisory opinions. A recent example of the court questioning the justiciability of an issue is the decision of the House of Lords in *Imperial Tobacco Ltd v Attorney General*, which concerned a claim for a declaration as to the legality of an advertising scheme that offered the purchaser a chance to win prizes. Criminal proceedings had already been instituted against the claimant charging that the scheme was an unlawful lottery. It was held that because criminal proceedings had been instituted, the claim for the declaration was not justiciable in that it would not be a proper exercise of the court's discretion to grant to the defendant in the criminal proceedings a declaration that the facts to be alleged by the prosecution did not in law prove the offence charged.

Another case in which the non-justiciability of an issue precluded the granting of relief is *Re Pim and the Minister of the Environment*. In that case the applicant sought a declaratory order that the Minister failed to recommend certain regulations as required by statute and an order directing that regulations be filed. It was held that the question whether the Lieutenant Governor in Council can be required to file such regulations was not a justiciable one since on the wording of the statute, the power was a prerogative power.

We also recommend that the court should be empowered to give its consent on such conditions it considers appropriate. For example, the court might order that no settlement can be made without the approval of the court.

Finally, we recommend that where consent is given, it should always be open to the Attorney-General to intervene in the proceeding or to be joined as a party of record. He may, for example, want to intervene or be joined as a party so that he can present issues to the court that might not otherwise be drawn to its attention, or present arguments as to why a particular form of relief should or should not be granted.

ANNEXURE "C"

SUMMARY OF RECOMMENDATIONS

The Commission make the following recommendations:

THE LAW OF STANDING:
PROPOSALS FOR REFORM (CHAPTER 4)

1. (1) Subject to the right to commence and maintain a proceeding that is conferred by or under any legislation other than the Act proposed by the Commission in this report (see Recommendation 6), the present provincial law of standing should be abolished, to be superseded by a new *Access to Courts Act*.

   (2) The new *Access to Courts Act* should contain a section expressly articulating the principle that the Act is to be read expansively and liberally, so as to increase access to the courts by granting the right to commence and maintain a proceeding to many persons who now would not have that right.

   (3) The Act should establish a single, more liberal rule respecting the commencement and maintenance of proceedings. In particular, every person should be entitled to commence and maintain a proceeding unless a party challenging such a right satisfies the court that there exist factors against proceeding that outweigh the factors in favour of proceeding. (See, also, Recommendation 4.)

   (4) The proposed rule respecting the commencement and maintenance of proceedings should be applicable to all types of civil proceeding, including proceedings under the *Judicial Review Procedure Act*.

2. The proposed *Access to Courts Act* should provide that no proceeding shall be dismissed and no pleading struck out only on the ground that the person bringing the proceeding

    (a) has no personal, proprietary or pecuniary interest in the proceeding; or

    (b) has suffered or may suffer injury or harm of the same kind or to the same degree as other persons.

3. While the new legislation would, in its effect, preclude the Attorney-General from exercising his or her existing right to block access to the courts and, as a necessary concomitant, would also abolish relator actions, nothing in such legislation should limit or affect in any way the right of the Attorney-General to commence and maintain a proceeding to the extent permissible by law.

4. With respect to the commencement and maintenance of proceedings, in determining whether the factors against proceeding outweigh the factors in favour of proceeding (see Recommendation 1(3)), the court should be required to consider,

    (a) regardless of whether or not the interest of the plaintiff is personal, proprietary or pecuniary,

        (i) whether another proceeding has been instituted against the same defendant in which the issues include those present in the proceeding that is opposed, if the interests of the plaintiff can be met by intervening in the other proceeding and it is reasonable to expect the plaintiff to do so;

        (ii) whether to proceed would be unfair to persons affected, but the fact that the outcome may affect a person whose interest is personal, proprietary or pecuniary shall not necessarily be considered unfair; and

        (iii) whether or not another reasonable and effective method exists to raise the issues that are sought to be litigated; and

    (b) where the interest of the plaintiff is not personal, proprietary or pecuniary,

        (i) whether the issues raised in the proceeding are trivial, and

        (ii) the number of persons affected in any way, whether personally or otherwise;

and the court may consider any other factor that the court considers just.

5. (1) Subject to Recommendations 5(2) and (3), the present law respecting the entitlement of a defendant to bring a motion to challenge the right of a person to commence and maintain a proceeding, and the discretion of the court to defer the issue for consideration until after the hearing of the merits, should be retained.

    (2) On a motion challenging the right of a person to commence and maintain a proceeding, the court should be required to defer the issue for consideration until after the hearing of the merits of the case, unless the court is satisfied that, in the particular circumstances of the case, it is desirable that the issue should be determined at an earlier time.

(3) The decision of the court to adjourn the issue for consideration until after the hearing of the merits should not be appealable.

6. The provisions for the commencement and maintenance of a proceeding in the proposed *Access to Courts Act* should be in addition to, and not in derogation of, any right to commence and maintain a proceeding that is conferred by or under any other Act.

Chapter 11

Reflections on Law and Government

The Hon Sir Anthony Mason AC KBE
Chancellor, University of New South Wales.
National Fellow, Research School of Social Sciences,
Australian National University.

The last decade has seen a notable advance in Australian public law. That
advance has been marked by a greater willingness on the part of the courts,
particularly the High Court, to re-formulate the principles of law and to do
so by reference to matters of substance rather than form. That approach
has involved greater weight being given to policy considerations, to some
values such as procedural fairness and fairness in the criminal process. It
has also involved the recognition and protection of individual rights,
whether these rights be classified as fundamental rights or rights recognised
by the common law, such as the right to procedural fairness and the right
to a fair trial. At the same time, there has been a stronger insistence on
exposing the exercise of public power to judical review, a resistance to
attempts to oust the jurisdiction of the courts by ouster or conclusive
evidence provisions and a recognition, in some respects uneven, that the
rights and obligations of the state (and public authorities) vis-a-vis the
citizen are to be equated as nearly as possible to those of the citizen vis-a-vis
a fellow citizen—a concept referred to in the preceding pages as "the
equality proposition".

What I have just said is not intended to convey an impression of an active
Judiciary and of a torpid Legislature and Executive. Far from it. The
Executive and the Legislature can complain with some justification that the
judges took a long time—virtually one hundred years—to give effect to the
equality proposition enshrined in "the claims against the government"
statutes. And the other arms of government have been at least as energetic
as the courts in expanding the concept of standing and protecting certain
individual rights. What we have seen, to repeat a statement made by the
federal Attorney-General, Mr Lavarch,[1] is a healthy interaction between
the Judiciary and the other arms of government, one which arises out of,
and is affected by, the tensions which necessarily exist in a democracy with
a separation of powers and an independent judiciary. Teoh's case,[2]
referred to in earlier chapters, is a celebrated illustration of that interaction,

1. Address at "The Mason Court and Beyond", 9 September 1995 (to be published).
2. (1995) 183 CLR 273.

though the interaction was not as productive as it was in the case of *Mabo v Queensland (No 2)*.[3]

This evolution in Australian public law has been influenced by a variety of considerations. I shall mention four of them. First, there is the modern conception of democratic government; that conception extends beyond simple majoritarianism to the protection of fundamental rights and respect for the dignity of the individual. Secondly, there is the recognition that public power is to be exercised in the interests of the people—a recognition that is expressed in the statement that sovereignty resides in the people. Thirdly, there is the equality proposition which has led to the abrogation of some—but certainly not all—of the privileges and immunities of the Executive government in its capacity as the Crown. Finally, there is the common law insistence on procedural fairness which is evident in the development of the criminal law and administrative law.

The rule of law, a vital element in the modern conception of democratic government, requires that public power be exercised in conformity with the law. We know that this will only occur if the principles of law and legal procedures offer full scope for judicial determination of the validity and legality of public action and, subject to some qualifications, for legal remedies on the part of individuals who have suffered loss or damage as a result of the wrongful exercise of public power. In this respect, by equating the citizen-state legal relationship to the relationship between subjects, we will expand the availability of remedies against the Executive government.

Professor Campbell's chapter on "The Citizen and the State in the Courts" draws attention to that aspect of the tension between the judiciary and the other arms of government which is exhibited in the legislative attempts to restrict judicial review of administrative action. By way of contrast to *Anisminic v Foreign Compensation Commission*,[4] where the House of Lords sets its face against legislative attempts to preclude judicial review of administrative decisions made in excess of jurisdiction, the High Court has long accepted that legislation may limit the scope of judicial review under s 75(v) of the Constitution, provided that the decision in question is a bona fide attempt to exercise the relevant power, that the decision relates to the subject matter of the legislation and that it is reasonably capable of reference to the power.[5] The recent decision in *DCT (Cth) v Richard Walter*[6] reinforces the High Court approach and indicates that it is not possible to preclude a judicial determination under s 75(v) of invalidity on the ground that the power has not been exercised in conformity with the relevant statute otherwise than by reference to the three conditions stated above. The judgments in that case require close attention.

The Parliament has, in the *Migration Act* 1958 (Cth), restricted the grounds on which review is available, while leaving the High Court's jurisdiction under s 75(v) relevantly untouched. At the same time, the

3. (1992) 175 CLR 1.
4. [1969] 2 AC 147.
5. *R v Hickman; Ex parte Fox* (1945) 70 CLR 598 at 615 per Dixon J; *O'Toole v Charles David Pty Ltd* (1991) 171 CLR 232 at 250 per Mason CJ.
6. (1995) 127 ALR 21.

Parliament has limited the High Court's power to remit relevant matters to the Federal Court otherwise than on the footing that the restrictions apply in the Federal Court to a hearing pursuant to such a remitter. Whether the Parliament can deny to the High Court a power of remitter in circumstances where such a remitter is necessary for the effective exercise of the jurisdiction conferred upon it by and pursuant to the Constitution is perhaps a question for the future. No doubt the Parliament can withdraw an express power that it has conferred but it may perhaps be that a power of remitter is necessarily implied in the Constitution.

The requirements of s 51(xxxi) of the Constitution, which calls for acquisition of property on just terms, present an obstacle to the validation of illegal conduct and to the barring of actions.[7] And, as Professor Campbell suggests, there are strong reasons for denying to Parliament power to limit recovery of compensation for unlawful detention pursuant to a statute held to be invalid for excess of constitutional power.

Generally speaking, Australian public law has achieved a more effective and better balance between the interests of the citizen and the exercise of power by the State and public authorities. In turn, that balance should contribute to the responsible exercise of power so that it conforms more closely to the dictates of the law and the requirements of due process as well as making the exercise of power more responsive to community concerns and the interests of individuals.

It is more than a century since the first Australian colonial statute dealing with claims against the government was introduced. In all that time, as Justice Finn's essay reveals, the courts have been slowly expanding the operation of the relevant statutory provisions, notably s 64 of the *Judiciary Act* 1903 (Cth), without, even now, giving full effect to the intent and purpose of those provisions. Justice Finn points out that the judicial decisions on the provisions have left untouched, or largely so, the common law rules which favour, or confer privileges or immunities on, the Crown. One such rule is the *Auckland Harbour Board*[8] rule which enables the Crown to recover moneys paid out of consolidated revenue without legislative authority in circumstances where defences would be available to a private plaintiff in an action for money had and received. For reasons which are not apparent, lawyers have failed to relate the legislation to the operation of these common law rules. It is an area with promising potential for argument.

On the other hand, it is possible that the courts have travelled too far in treating the words "as nearly as possible" in s 64 as meaning "as completely as possible" and as excluding from consideration "the special position" of the Crown. The comment by the majority in *Commonwealth v Evans Deakin Industries Ltd*[9] that it might be necessary, in some cases at least, to take that into account, may perhaps mark a turning point and pave the way for a recognition of Justice Finn's thesis that "as nearly as possible" requires a consideration of countervailing public policies. There is much to

7. *Georgiadis v AOTC* (1994) 179 CLR 297.
8. *Auckland Harbour Board v The King* [1924] AC 318 at 318-322.
9. (1986) 161 CLR 254 at 264.

commend this view, though, for my part, I doubt that the judgment of Dixon CJ in *South Australia v Commonwealth*[10] provides much support for it.

In the past, the exposition of the statutory provisions was encumbered by too much emphasis on the relationship of the Crown to its subjects and too little emphasis on the relationship between the modern state and its citizens. The emphasis on the former has resulted in a continuing acceptance of common law rules and, perhaps, a failure to perceive that the legislation required the elaboration of principles appropriate to the modern citizen-state relationship. Fortunately, the courts are now alive to the need to interpret statutes in light of the fact that the Crown is the Executive branch of government carrying on many activities through servants and agents who have no immunity from the ordinary law.[11]

The steady relaxation of the strict rules relating to standing has played a significant part in making legislative and Executive exercise of power subject to the rule of law. Here relaxation has come about as a result of legislative initiative and judicial decision, more so the former than the latter. With the benefit of hindsight, it is surprising that *Boyce v Paddington Borough Council*[12] influenced our thinking for so long. In Australia, the second limb of Buckley J's proposition has been relaxed so that the requirement of "special damage peculiar" to the plaintiff has given way to a requirement of a "special interest" in the plaintiff, such an interest being satisfied by something less than a legal or proprietary interest.[13] The High Court has stated that a mere belief or emotional attachment does not constitute a special interest.[14] It might be said that the public interest in the availability of a remedy to a citizen to challenge unlawful acts requires a broader approach to standing. And it may be that judicial concern about the interfering busybody is exaggerated, just as the old "floodgates" arguments have been exaggerated in other areas of the law. However, in England, where a stricter view of standing has prevailed, only the Attorney-General can sue on behalf of the public for the purpose of preventing public wrongs even when individuals might be interested in a larger view of the matter.[15] It is strange that the law should countenance this conflict in the Attorney-General between government interest and duty to enforce the law.

Another aspect of standing which confronts a litigant seeking to mount a challenge on constitutional grounds to the validity of an appropriation statute is the proposition, last recognised in *Logan Downs Pty Ltd v Federal Commissioner of Taxation*,[16] that a citizen has no relevant interest to support such a challenge. The Supreme Court of Canada has decided otherwise.[17]

10. (1962) 108 CLR 130 at 140.
11. *Jacobsen v Rogers* (1995) 127 ALR 159 at 164-165.
12. [1903] 1 Ch 109.
13. *Robinson v Western Australia Museum* (1977) 138 CLR 283 at 292, 302-303, 328-329, 340, 344; *Onus v Alcoa of Aust Ltd* (1981) 149 CLR 27.
14. Ibid.
15. *Gouriet v UPW Union* [1978] AC 435 at 481, 494, 513.
16. (1964) 112 CLR 177.
17. *Thorson v Attorney-General of Canada (No 2)* (1974) 43 DLR (3d) 1.

Perhaps the best example of the erosion of Executive privileges and immunities is the stricter view now taken, particularly in Australia and New Zealand, of public interest immunity, a topic discussed by Justice Gault. Here the movement in favour of greater openness reflects the force of the conviction that a trial should take place, so far as is possible, on the basis of all relevant evidence. Here, again, the erosion of the immunity has gone further in Australia and New Zealand than in England where secrecy rather than freedom of information seems to have been more highly valued, at least in relation to the operations of government.

In Australia, claims for immunity in respect of a class of documents have been scrutinised very carefully. In *Alister v The Queen*[18] and *Sankey v Whitlam*,[19] the claims were rejected but, more recently, a claim for immunity for notes recording deliberations of Cabinet was upheld in a case in which allegations were made of unconscionable conduct on the part of Ministers.[20] In that case, *Commonwealth v Northern Land Council*, the High Court held that documents recording the deliberations of Cabinet are a class in respect of which strong considerations of public policy support non-disclosure, regardless of their contents.[21] Even then, the immunity is not absolute and will give way to exceptional considerations justifying departure from the strong case for confidentiality.[22]

The rule, in England, is that the court should not inspect documents which are the subject of a claim of public interest immunity until satisfied that the documents contain material that gives substantial support to the case of the party seeking disclosure.[23] How that party can discharge the burden without seeing the documents is difficult to understand. Cross-examination on the affidavit claiming immunity is a pointless enterprise. The rule has not been adopted in Australia, New Zealand or Canada, though in Australia, in conformity with *Northern Land Council*, in the case of documents recording the deliberations of Cabinet, the judge will only inspect the documents when exceptional circumstances exist and such circumstances will almost certainly be confined to criminal cases.[24]

Northern Land Council might appear to run counter to the continuing trend towards greater openness in government and to the general run of judicial decisions in that direction. However, in the interests of efficient government it is necessary to recognise the confidentiality of Cabinet deliberations and to protect that confidentiality otherwise than in exceptional circumstances.

Dr Kenny's chapter on statutory interpretation reveals that the High Court eliminated or qualified some old privileges and immunities attaching to the Crown which seem to have little relevance to the citizen-state relationship today. One intriguing element in statutory interpretation is the tension which exists between the courts and the other branches of

18. (1983) 154 CLR 404.
19. (1978) 142 CLR 1.
20. *Commonwealth v Northern Land Council* (1993) 176 CLR 604.
21. Ibid at 616.
22. Ibid at 618.
23. *Air Canada v Secretary of State for Trade* [1983] 2 AC 394 at 395.
24. Ibid at 618-619.

government when the legislature seeks to narrow judicial review of Executive and tribunal decision-making by introducing privative clauses and conclusive evidence provisions. The decision in *Richard Walter*, already mentioned, on the conclusive evidence provision in s 177 of the *Income Tax Assessment Act* 1936 (Cth) as amended, is the latest example of this tension.

The prevailing theme in a number of the recent decisions has been that expressed by Gibbs CJ in *Townsville Hospitals Board v Townsville City Council*:

> "All persons should prima facie be regarded as equal before the law, and no statutory body should be accorded special privileges and immunities unless it clearly appears that it was the intention of the legislature to confer them."[25]

Though monarch and subject were not equal, the relationship of state and citizen nowadays is very different and the activities of the Executive government are all-pervasive. In these circumstances, it was only to be expected that the old rule that a statute does not bind the Crown unless it so appeared expressly or by necessary implication would be qualified. And so it was in *Bropho v Western Australia*[26] where it was decided that, for the future, while a presumption that the Crown is not bound remains, it might be more readily displaced—there is no need for a *manifest* intention to bind the Crown.

Townsville and *Bropho* contribute to the integrity of the legislative process by eliminating and reducing the impact of presumptions in favour of the Crown, thereby requiring those who introduce legislation to spell out privileges, immunities and exemptions that are to be conferred upon government or statutory authorities. *Coco v The Queen*[27] runs in a different, though not a contrary direction, by insisting upon a manifest expression of intention to abrogate or curtail a fundamental right, that is, by the use of unmistakable and unambiguous language. General words are not enough. This requirement will also compel the proponents of a Bill to spell out any such intention and bring home to the legislators what is intended, thereby enhancing the integrity of the legislative process. It is interesting to note that, in *Coco*, the court chose to speak of a fundamental right as well as a common law right. The class of fundamental rights may well be more extensive than the class of common law rights.

Dr Kenny makes the point that, in *Teoh*,[28] the court extended the rule that the courts will construe a statute in a way that accords with a treaty to which Australia is a party if the statute is enacted after, or in contemplation of, entry into, or ratification of, the relevant international instrument. In *Teoh*, the majority of the court went further and said that if the statutory provision is susceptible of more than one construction, the court should adopt the construction which is consistent with Australia's international obligations.[29] That approach seems the obvious and sensible

25. (1982) 149 CLR 282 at 291.
26. (1990) 171 CLR 1.
27. (1994) 179 CLR 427.
28. (1995) 183 CLR 273.
29. Ibid at 287-288 per Mason CJ and Deane J (with whom Gaudron J relevantly agreed).

one and it conforms to the approach advocated by Latham CJ in *Polites v Commonwealth*, [30] in relation to statutory interpretation when a rule of customary international law is relevant to the question of interpretation.

In passing, I should mention that at the seminar we were told that explanatory memoranda are not prepared by the office of Parliamentary Counsel, but by the instructing department. Perhaps that is the reason why they are availed of but rarely.

Mr Keith Mason QC, in his "Money claims by and against the State", points out that the notion of equality before the law and the recognition of the state as a juristic person supports the view that the state should not be deprived of the rights and obligations of the citizen who enters into a corresponding transaction. As money claims by and against the state are largely governed by the general law of contract, restitution and tort, principles which are based on special characteristics which the state is thought to possess are coming under closer scrutiny. Viewed against that background, the *Auckland Harbour Board* principle seems anomalous. The principle rests on historic constitutional foundations and, as the author indicates, there are difficulties in asserting that it allows a place for defences of estoppel and change of position. However, I am not convinced that the law is incapable of developing in such a way as to enable them to apply, even without bringing s 64 of the *Judiciary Act* to the party. As yet, there is no sign of such a development.

We do not yet know whether Australia will embrace *Woolwich Equitable Building Society v Inland Revenue Commissioners*. [31] We have, of course, abandoned the mistake of law limitation on restitutionary recovery. [32] To that extent, we have gone further than *Woolwich*. However, the true basis of *Woolwich* is not altogether clear. It was not a case of causative mistake—the unjust factor was either the ultra vires character of the exaction or the absence of consideration of the payment. The decision stands in contrast with United States authorities which deny recovery in the case of an unconstitutional tax and the view expressed by La Forest J in *Air Canada v British Columbia*. [33] The likelihood, the author suggests, is that *Woolwich* will prevail if only because the burden of government's mistake should not be borne by the individual taxpayer. I agree.

However, the author suggests that the law, while not denying recovery, should take account of the crippling disruption that would flow from an unrestricted right of recovery. One suggested means of achieving this is the device of prospective overruling. The High Court adopted this technique in a very different case, *McKinney v The Queen*, [34] but has not applied it in any case involving the constitutional invalidity of a statute. The discussion of the justification for the use of the technique is provoking.

The passing-on or windfall gain defence has not so far been enthusiastically received by the courts. But, as the author notes, statutes now make provision for it in some Australian jurisdictions.

30. (1945) 70 CLR 60 at 69.
31. [1993] AC 70.
32. *David Securities Pty Ltd v Commonwealth Bank of Australia* (1992) 175 CLR 353.
33. (1989) 59 DLR (4th) 161.
34. (1991) 171 CLR 468.

Professor Allars, in her discussion of tort and equity claims against the state, argues that the equality proposition cannot be accepted without qualification. Much of the discussion centres upon the policy/operational distinction, a distinction introduced by Lord Wilberforce in *Anns v Merton London Borough Council*,[35] though it had earlier origins in the United States. While the distinction can be drawn at the level of the abstract, it is not easy to classify actual administrative decisions in this way. In *Sutherland Shire Council v Heyman*,[36] I endeavoured to formulate the distinction along lines which would deny the existence of a duty of care in relation to decisions which involve or are dictated by financial, economic, social or political factors or constraints. I pointed to budgetary constraints and their impact on resource allocations as examples. Courts are reluctant to review policy decisions of that kind and to hold that they can give rise to a duty of care. The constraints which such policy decisions impose limit the basis for constructing a duty of care on the part of the decision maker.

On the other hand, the equality proposition enshrined in the claims against government legislation invites the courts to disregard these factors and to treat the government as an ordinary litigant would be treated. On this view, the fact that the defendant's freedom of action or choice is limited by budgetary constraints or policy considerations is by no means a bar to the existence of a duty of care.

If financial constraints cannot be relied upon by a private defendant to thwart the existence of a duty of care, why should they be relied upon by a public defendant? If a private railway company is subject to a duty of care, notwithstanding financial constraints, why should the Commissioner for Railways be dealt with differently? Of course if the constraint is based in statute, it will be different. No duty of care will be imposed if it is at variance with a statute. That apart, insistence on the equality proposition leads some to say that only compelling policy considerations should preclude the existence of a duty of care. And it should be noted that the policy/operational distinction does not sit well with a duty of care founded on general reliance, a point well made by Professor Allars.

Although the "no fettering" principle also commands some support in the cases, an argument based on the equality proposition can be mounted against it similar to that directed at the policy/operational distinction. The no-fettering principle seems to provide government with a very broad shield indeed.

The perennial question whether there is an administrative tort is a little closer to solution. *Rowling v Takaro Properties Ltd*,[37] and the judgment of Brennan J in *Northern Territory of Australia v Mengel*[38] are against it. As the joint judgment in *Mengel* rejected the principle in *Beaudesert Shire Council v Smith*,[39] it is difficult to see in *Mengel* support for the existence of an administrative tort. *Mengel* also decided that knowledge of an official that the act causing damage is in excess of power is not enough to establish misfeasance in public office; an intentional element is also required.

35. [1978] AC 728.
36. (1985) 157 CLR 424 at 469.
37. [1988] AC 473.
38. (1995) 129 ALR 1.
39. (1966) 120 CLR 145.

Mr Weinberg QC has given us a chronological account of the recognition of a common law right to a fair trial and the assertion of the jurisdiction to grant a permanent stay on the ground of abuse of process. In retrospect, one wonders why the common law was so slow in recognising the right to a fair trial and why the courts were not more astute to provide an effective remedy for abuse of process. These developments have enhanced the court's capacity to supervise the criminal process.

Mr Weinberg has pointed to some unwanted side effects. One is fragmentation of the criminal process. Although the High Court has set its face against applications which have this tendency, Mr Weinberg points out, correctly, that once a jurisdiction is recognised, parties will invoke it, especially in criminal cases, despite meagre prospects of success—delay may be an end in itself. It is said that the potential for fragmentation of the criminal process plays into the hands of affluent accused persons who can afford to contest every step taken by the prosecution, make interlocutory applications and bring every available appeal.

Another adverse side effect is the difficulty which a trial judge experiences in dealing with an application for a permanent stay for abuse of process in a complex case in advance of the trial. Generally speaking, complex cases are not suited to treatment in this way. An application for a stay is not a preliminary hearing of the trial.

Again, it is said that the decision in *Dietrich v The Queen*,[40] apart from adding to the potential for fragmentation, imposes a considerable cost burden on the state. Whether this is so remains to be seen. At this stage it seems to have resulted in a redirection of legal aid funds, with a higher proportion now going to criminal cases.

There is some force in the concern expressed about fragmentation of the criminal process. On the other side of the ledger, the new developments have unquestionably ensured that the criminal justice system operates more fairly and justly. Criminal proceedings can be oppressive and undue delay in prosecution of them is inexcusable. The recognition of the right to a fair trial and the exercise of the jurisdiction to grant a stay for abuse of process will compel the prosecuting authorities and the Executive government to proceed in criminal cases with due diligence.

In England, the Australian development in staying criminal trials on the abuse of process ground has been evidently viewed with some distaste. Perhaps that is because, in England, the courts have not been confronted with delays in the criminal process similar to the delays experienced in Australia. It seems that there, criminal trials are brought on for hearing within a reasonable timespan, so that the need for the exercise of a jurisdiction on the ground of abuse of process has not been as apparent as it is here.

Procedural fairness, examined by Mr John Griffiths, has been a focal point of Australian administrative law for some time now. The concept of legitimate expectation has become a matter of debate. Although the High Court has accepted and applied the concept, it has encountered criticism,

40. (1992) 177 CLR 292.

particularly from Brennan J, on the ground that it is a vague and amorphous notion. Overall, as Bingham MR has remarked in England, it is a valuable doctrine.[41] So far, in Australia, we have not embraced a doctrine of substantive unfairness. Indeed, *Attorney-General (NSW) v Quin*[42] seems to point in the opposite direction. Yet the doctrine of substantive unfairness has been accepted in England and New Zealand, as Mr Griffiths notes.

He is right in saying that the courts have made themselves more vulnerable to criticism by moving away from rigid formulae such as the existence of a duty to act judicially and the mandatory/directory classification. But as administrative decision-making became more complex and as it moved further away from the judicial model, the old formulae became less appropriate. Now, as the chapter makes clear, it is often a matter of securing effective participation in the decision-making process. Those processes are now so varied that it is not possible to enunciate a series of hard and fast rules.

Minister for Immigration and Ethnic Affairs v Teoh is, of course, the culmination of insistence on procedural fairness. The case is interesting, not only for that reason, but also because it presents a classic illustration of how separation of power problems can arise as a result of the increasing impact of international Conventions on domestic law, particularly in a case like *Teoh* where the Convention, though ratified by Australia, has not been legislatively implemented.

Much has been said and written of *Teoh* and it will be interesting to see how the proposed legislation to counteract the decision turns out. It is said that the object of the legislation is to ensure that a provision in such a Convention does not constitute or generate a legitimate expectation. However, it may be that it is hoped that the decision maker will be free to decide whether regard should be had to such a Convention provision and that, in this respect, the decision will not be reviewable. Whatever happens to the proposed legislation, the tension between the claims of national sovereignty and the internationalisation of domestic law is bound to generate movement in this area of the law.

I have left for last Professor Zines' contribution. That is certainly not on grounds of lack of merit or importance. It is simply because it is convenient to deal with the subject of protection of individual rights separately. Professor Zines exhibits a measure of scepticism about the notion of sovereignty residing in the people and the value that this discovery has for constitutional interpretation. Here he is at loggerheads with Justice Finn. Clearly enough, political sovereignty now resides in the Australian people. That circumstance, along with the proposition that the Australian Constitution provides for a system of representative democracy or government,[43] obviously has some significance for constitutional interpretation. But, as Professor Zines suggests, there are limits to the use

41. *R v IRC; Ex parte MFK Underwriting Agents Ltd* [1990] 1 WLR 1545 at 1569-1570.
42. (1990) 170 CLR 1.
43. *Nationwide News Pty Ltd v Wills* (1992) 177 CLR 1; *Australian Capital Television Pty Ltd v Commonwealth* (1992) 177 CLR 106.

which can be made of these building blocks in distilling fundamental rights out of the Constitution. That the Constitution provides for a system of democratic government was the platform for the "one vote, one value" argument in *McGinty v Western Australia*, in which judgment is awaited. But, putting to one side the possibility of implications, similarly based in favour of freedom of assembly, association and movement for like political purposes, it is not easy to see representative government as a vehicle for other broad-ranging rights.

Apart from *Leeth v Commonwealth*,[44] the other non-federal "rights" which have been implied in the Constitution are either of a "representation-reinforcing" kind, such as freedom of communication, or are implications made from Ch III. Not that implications made from Ch III are unimportant. The more that is read into Ch III, in particular by treating it as providing for what inheres in the common law conception of hearing, trial and determination, the more the common law conception is constitutionalised and rendered immune from legislative change, as Professor Zines points out.

Chapter III is a more likely battleground of constitutional implication than fundamental rights as such. Chapter III provides more opportunity for deployment of argument along the lines favoured by Ronald Dworkin that concepts for which the Constitution provides can be elaborated in terms of principles. Or it may be possible to constitutionalise "doctrines" on which Ch III is based, to use the term employed in one well-known High Court judgment. To guard against possible misinterpretation, I should make it clear that this is not a view which I am advocating.

My own views about the implied right to substantive equality discerned by some Justices in *Leeth* are made plain in the majority joint judgment in that case. Just how far such an implied right would carry the court is by no means clear. And there are unresolved problems, as Professor Zines indicates, with the notion that legislative powers are limited by the "fundamental principles of the common law". Unless the principles are identified, one cannot feel any degree of assurance that they can operate as a limit on legislative power granted by the Constitution. And identification of the principles will not in itself dispel the difficulties facing those who assert the existence of the limitation. Those difficulties are set out by Professor Zines. Constitutionalising the common law, even more so the common law as at 1901, has an air of unreality about it.

Constitutional implication is, of course, a vexed question. Carried too far it raises concerns about the legitimacy of what the court does. On the other hand, the continuous process of constitutional interpretation, spelling out in detail what is not apparent in the terms of the text is in one sense, and a very real sense, implication. The current debate about constitutional interpretation and implication as well as the High Court's role in formulating general principles of law has not only alerted the community to the work of the court and what it does, it has also encouraged Australians to think about their Constitution and their system of government.

44. (1992) 174 CLR 455.

In conclusion, I should record the great pleasure expressed by the participants in the Seminar on Justice Finn's elevation to the Federal Court of Australia. On behalf of the participants, I acknowledge the signal contribution which he has made to the development of the law by organising and participating in these seminars. We look forward to his ongoing contribution to the law in his new role and we are delighted that he intends to continue the Seminar series.

Index